*Conversations
with the Capeman*

Conversations with the Capeman

The Untold Story of Salvador Agron

By Richard Jacoby

*Dear Tom & Shannon,
Thank you for reading my work...*

Introduction by Hubert Selby Jr.
Author of *Last Exit to Brooklyn*

*Love,
Richard Jacoby*

Painted Leaf Press
New York City
www.PaintedLeaf.com

Copyright © 2000 by Richard Jacoby

All rights reserved. Printed in Canada. No part of this book may be used or reproduced in any manner whatsoever without prior written permission from the publisher except in the case of brief quotations embodied in critical articles and reviews. For information, address Painted Leaf Press, P.O. Box 2480, Times Square Station, New York, NY 10108-2480, or E-mail cocadas@bway.net.

All newspaper articles and letters used with permission.
Cover photo used with permission of AP/Wide World Photos.

Cover design by Travis Ward
Typesetting by Brian Brunius

Library of Congress Cataloging-in-Publication Data

Jacoby, Richard, 1945-
    Conversations with the Capeman : an intimate biography of
    Salvador Agron / Richard Jacoby.
       p.cm.
    ISBN 1-891305-50-6
     1. Agron, Salvador. 2. Murderers—New York (State)—
    Biography. 3. Murder—New York (State) I. Title.

HV6248.A275 J33 2000
364.15'23'097471–dc21
                                                    99-086962

*This book is dedicated to my friend,
and brother, Salvador Agron*

Introduction

by Hubert Selby Jr.

This is a much needed book. It is thoughtful, thought provoking, objective, and most important, written with love and respect, not just for the subject of the book but for all people, and the magnificent and ineffable spirit within all of us. In that sense, this book is a celebration of life.

There have been countless studies written on this subject by experts in so many different areas of social science, criminology, etc., all contributing to our knowledge of the subject, but Mr. Jacoby is the only one I am aware of who does not deny his love and respect for the subject of his work, yet remains objective. Let me quickly add that Mr. Jacoby is not a novice; he has studied criminology in Graduate School, and has interviewed many inmates on Death Row in a study to see how their consciousness is affected by the experience. But the main reason this book is valuable, so readable and interesting, is the fact that Mr. Jacoby is an excellent writer.

It is literally impossible to put the book down once you start reading. The facts are interesting, fascinating and of great interest and importance to our lives today, but it is Mr. Jacoby's literary abilities, the lucidity and clarity of the writing that makes it so compelling. He is also uncannily objective, even though the reader is aware that he loves and respects the subject of the book, he never proselytizes, which would be so easy for him to do. I must assume it is his commitment to his vision of the truth that presents him from falling into so many available, and tempting, traps.

As an indication of Mr. Jacoby's writing ability, this is the type of book that can bring out a few of my prejudices, and warp my perception, yet that did not happen. I have never been able to tolerate professional do-gooders, people who ride through a slum, take a few notes, at most, then start organizations and/or petitions to help the poor downtrodden people. Such is not the case with Richard Jacoby. He spent twelve years with Salvador Agron, and his family, here and in Puerto Rico. He knows the roots of Salvador Agron, and shared them as intimately as is humanly possible. He has lived inside Salvador, sharing his heartbeat and heartache to an extent that is absolutely extraordinary. They truly became *brothers*.

Salvador Agron, *The Capeman,* is so easy for me to judge, to dislike, to hold in utter and complete contempt, as did most people who heard of the murders of the two teen-aged boys he killed when he was 16 years old. When arrested he said, "I don't care if I burn, my mother can watch." So easy to detest someone who says that after killing two boys. He later justifies the murders because of the abuse he received all his life. My immediate reaction: Millions of people are abused, but they don't all become murderers. I have always been incensed by the arrogance of ignorance.

All of this is such fertile ground for my prejudices, my judgments, my attitudes, my contempt prior to investigation. Richard Jacoby not only investigated, but wrote a book based on his years of investigation, not only void of my attitudes, but wrote this book with such insight and respect, that I am literally unable to hold on to my attitudes and so they just slip away.

The structure of this book reflects the way we live and perceive. We not only get involved with our own thoughts, we are also wondering how we are being perceived by others. This is reflected beautifully in the structure by changing the voices, the individuals and perceptions. And, as is life, the book is not directly linear, but moves around in space and time just as we all do...one moment it's yesterday, the next it's tomorrow. Yet this book is always and completely coherent.

In a letter dated, 4/16/74, Salvador says: *"Many people don't know me because I made myself invisible to them. Only my friends get to know my goodness."* What an extraordinary statement, and insight, for a man to make after murdering two boys. What happened in those years to bring this about. That question is answered by this book! In that same letter, just a half a dozen lines later, he says, *"I don't like ignorance. I love reality."* What another extraordinary statement for a young man who taught himself to read and write while in prison. Of course I do not know precisely what he meant, but I find it stunning that he separates, *"ignorance,"* and *"reality."*

There was a group at Greenhaven Penitentiary, called the Sunni Muslims, and in a conversation with Richard Jacoby, Salvador said, *"They had a reverence for life, and they emphasized taking personal responsibility for one's actions instead of always pointing a finger at someone else."* Again, a sentiment you would not expect to hear from a murderer, especially one who attempts to hold his abusive past responsible for his actions. Once again, the question arises: "How did he get from there to here?" Mr. Jacoby does not force an answer upon us, nor give us his "opinion," but instead presents Salvador's life as completely and clearly as possible, and thus we can find our own answers to the question from our own life experience. I cannot say too much, or enough, about the quality of Mr. Jacoby's writing, and its simple directness, clarity, and objectivity.

While incarcerated, Mr. Agron created a lot of problems for himself and was transferred from one prison to another, including several stays in the Dannemora Hospital for the Criminally Insane. In time he learned how to channel his rebellious energy into creativity and he agitated and fought for the rights of prisoners and for prison reform.

At sixteen years of age, Salvador Agron was the youngest person ever sentenced to death in the State of New York. A group of influential people, including Eleanor Roosevelt, petitioned to have the death sentence commuted, and Governor Nelson Rockefeller eventually commuted the sentence. After serving more than twenty years in prison, Salvador Agron was paroled from prison, and returned to New York City and to what he thought would be a whole new life.

My initial reaction to this book was this: all of this could have been avoided, the tragedy of two teenagers being killed, and the terrible, interminable grief of their parents. How many times did the birthdays of those come around and the parents thought, *"He would have been......years old today."*

Yet, what may be an even greater tragedy is the simple fact that we have done nothing to prevent this from happening again, nothing to prevent the constant and escalating repetition of this tragedy. How sad and tragic that we, as a society, would rather spend a million dollars to punish someone than spend ten thousand to prevent the need for punishment. So the inevitable and unavoidable question: Who is being punished? This is not a cute attempt at word play, but a deadly serious question we are all confronted with both as individuals and as members of our society.

Senator Orrin Hatch recently proposed to plug a bill

Introduction

that would require states to try juveniles thirteen and older as adults, and eliminate the separation of juveniles and adults in prison, in exchange for Federal grants. Now, if the states want more Federal funds, all they have to do is make the abuse of children a function of the state. This, in spite of the fact that the National Center for Juvenile Justice concluded that "Today's violent youth commits the same number of violent acts as his/her predecessor of fifteen years ago." A 1997 Justice Department report states that violent juvenile offenders, "are not significantly younger than those of ten or fifteen years ago."

I am always, at best, suspicious of statistics. However, there have been such an overwhelming number of statistics indicating that we, the adult population, are not fulfilling our responsibility to our children and, because they are defenseless, we are determined to hold them responsible for our failure.

I hope everyone will read this book. I hope everyone will be affected by the tragedy of the CAPEMAN. We as a society, as a nation, need to be aware of what we are doing. We desperately need to be aware of the problem. Obviously, you cannot recognize the answer until you have identified the problem. And the problem is not the children. We fight over the capital gains tax while millions of children are hungry and malnourished, have no medical care, and die daily of neglect. *Children!*

Let me hasten to say that Mr. Jacoby does not speak of these things in his simple and eloquent book, nor does he judge or agitate. What he does so well and beautifully is to give us Salvador Agron from birth to death, brings him to life not only physically, but his heart, mind, soul...and dreams, as well as his torment and frustrations. Mr. Jacoby also gives us Salvador's family, their everyday struggles with overwhelming and unrelenting poverty, their unwavering dignity, hopes, prayers, and love. It is reliving the events of 1959, and the subsequent years of Salvador Agron's life, that brings these, and other, simple facts to my consciousness. If children are our future, why then are we brutalizing them?

I am 70 years old and have had many hopes and dreams. I have also had 70 years of experiences living in this society. I have no hope we will do anything to correct or ameliorate this situation, *as a nation*. However, there are many, many pockets of people in communities and neighborhoods, who are doing all they can to help our children to not become either a victim or victimizer. Perhaps these people with no vested interests to serve or protect, no obsession to punish, no egos or images to defend, will succeed in preventing our society from giving birth to another CAPEMAN.

In any event, it is *"a consummation devoutly to be wished."*

          Hubert Selby Jr.
          1998

*Conversations
with the Capeman*

I am Salvador Agron, "The Capeman."
I am about struggle.

I was a semi-illiterate kid of sixteen years of age with the mentality of a twelve year old in 1959 when I was in a gang fight in Hell's Kitchen that left two Anglo Saxon American kids of sixteen dead and one severely wounded. I was a member of a teenage gang called the Vampires. I wore a black cape and carried a Mexican dagger. I was young and ignorant, and when I was arrested, I told a reporter "I don't care if I burn, my mother can watch."

My outfit attracted much public attention. The news media had a Roman Holiday with me—calling me "Capeman" and publishing inflammatory articles which demanded my execution in the electric chair. My case quickly become a racial and political issue, even though it involved a street gang that mistakenly attacked non-gang kids. The Yankee press hurled racial epithets at all Puerto Ricans in New York City.

I was tried, convicted, and sentenced to death.

"Convict" and prison inmate" were added to a long list of labels used to describe me during my life: premature infant, late walker and talker, malnourished, epileptic, hyperactive, truant, drop-out, incorrigible, illiterate, juvenile delinquent, gang leader, criminal, murderer, psychotic, schizophrenic, psychopath, sexual deviant, troublemaker, religious fanatic, revolutionary, and drug addict. I have been all these things and yet none of them say much about what my life has been like.

In prison, I began to study, sharpen my mind, my memory, and question myself and the Capeman and Dracula legends that the media built around my personality in order to fabricate a monster.

The only thing left was the will to struggle and tell the story of my life. No one could take that away from me, and that impulse gradually came to shape and form my being. The will to struggle overcame my fear. I struggled to be born, to be socialized, to be educated, to speak out against injustice and oppression, and to be free. I don't know if the struggle will ever end for me, or if anybody even wants to hear my story. I have to tell it anyway.

I've come a long way from my childhood in the poorhouse in Puerto Rico. I've been told my life is an inspiration to others. I don't know if it is or why, only that I lived it, and it was difficult. Lots of people have said I was a murderer, and that I deserved to die. But I say, I dug my own grave, and the State of New York has been trying to bury me in it ever since.

Chapter One

SALVADOR

Salvador Agron
Institution Number: 28298

Date: 11/23/73
Dear Mr. Jacoby:

    We are writing in the interest of the above-named person, who is presently under our care, and who has requested authorization to correspond with you.

    Because Departmental objectives include the re-socialization of offenders and assistance in resolving their problems, it is felt that correspondence and visits could contribute to their morale and rehabilitation, both in the facility and in the community.

    The policies governing the correspondence and visiting programs, require that you submit answers to the following questions for review as basis for authorizing correspondence and visiting. Any false statements will be cause for rejection.

    This form must be completed and returned by mail and approved before correspondence and visits are granted.

Very truly yours,
Harold J. Smith
Superintendent

December 17th, 1973
Attica Correctional Facility

Dear Richard:

I received your first letter a few days ago. Your letter is the first that I have ever received from a college student, and also the first request that I have ever received inquiring about my stay on death row in the Death House.

Please do forward a copy of your intended thesis, "Consciousness Expansion on Death Row." I would be more than glad to help in whichever way I possibly can.

I was planning on doing a thesis myself dealing with the death penalty but because of my subjectivity and biased thoughts on it I gave up. Someday I'll take up the challenge again.

When you write back, send some stamps—I need them.

When I was on death row at Sing Sing Prison I was very young and my impressions of that time are in a sense very "immature," but now my reflections are more valuable, and I will be glad to pass them on to you. Yes, I write poetry, and I wrote this poem for you.

I hope you like it.

Very truly yours,
Salvador Agron
#28298

RICHARD JACOBY

Reaching into the unknown
Into a walled, imprisoned city
Cast in iron, steel and concrete
Having found doors that do not unlock
And having established communication
Research, brother, and deliver
Death Row's thesis to the world

Jail University, where all minds meet
Answering each other's oppression
Carefully search out this ground
Objectively look into this hell
But be forewarned
You will be delving into man's inhumanity to man!

By Salvador Agron   #28298
December 12th, 1973

I met Salvador Agron for the first time in late March of 1974 in the visiting room at Greenhaven Correctional Facility in Stormville, New York, just several months after he had been transferred from Attica Correctional Facility in the western part of the state.

Nearly six feet tall, he would always stand out in a crowd. His hair, long and black, was parted down the middle. Combed straight back, it was tied together with a colored rubber band.

He had the pale and sallow skin of someone who had spent long periods of time in dark places. He had large hands and feet, along with hazel-colored eyes that were gentle and hard at the same time. He reminded me of pictures I'd seen of a Native American warrior, sitting high on a horse, with feathers in his hair, on a mountain top, surveying the endless valleys in front of him. This is all mine, he seemed to be saying, and this is exactly what I thought Salvador Agron was thinking as he stood across the counter from where I was sitting on a wooden chair.

Before the Attica prison riots, convicts were separated from their visitors by floor-to-ceiling screens. Made from woven wire mesh, the screens made contact of any kind virtually impossible. After Attica, the screens had been torn down, and were replaced with wooden counters and benches.

Seated on a wooden chair behind a metal desk at the front of the room, and dressed in his blue blazer with the seal of the State of New York emblazoned across his breast pocket, the guard in charge of the visiting room seemed far more interested in the comic book he was reading than in the goings on around him. As I watched the tiny pink tongue of the woman sitting on my left dart in and out of the mouth of the man sitting across from her, I stood up. Extending my hand across the counter, I embraced the enormous hand of Salvador Agron.

Given the size of his hands, I wasn't surprised at the firmness of his grip, yet nothing he had written in the many letters I had received from him in the months before my visit could have prepared me for the uneven sound of his voice. Deep, but jagged, his first words seemed to tumble out at abrupt right angles in a flowing stream that was anything but smooth.

"You don't look nothing like the way I thought you would," he said.

"Really?"

"Yeah, you know...like I thought you'd look like a college student with a tie and everything...you know what I'm sayin'?"

"Well...but, I'm in graduate school and we don't usually wear ties and stuff."

"Would you get me something to eat?"

"Excuse me?"

"Some food from one of the vending machines, would

you get me something?"

"Oh...sure, yeah...what should I get?"

"Some chips, maybe a soda, and a sandwich...any kind."

Getting up from the bench, I walked down the isle about fifty feet to the four vending machines, lined up side by side like silent soldiers standing at attention. One machine sold coffee, one sold cookies, cakes, and candies, another sold soda, and the last one sold what looked like a wide variety of cold sandwiches. Reaching into my pocket, I took out a dollar bill, and as I slid it into the soda machine, I caught a glimpse of myself in the reflecting glass of the machine. With my curly blond hair rushing past my shoulders, blue jeans, and denim jacket, I had only a passing resemblance to a college student. Later he would tell me that his first impression of me with my long hair and hooked nose was that I looked like a Jewish General Custer, which made me laugh. Later on it was his turn to laugh when I told him that my first impression of him had been that he looked more like an American Indian than a Puerto Rican from New York City.

Attica Correctional Facility
January 1st, 1974

Dear Richard:

First, let me acknowledge your letter of December 20th which I received on December 28th. I also received your December 26th letter with the intended thesis outline on January 1st, 1974.

I will begin work on your thesis questions, starting from the day I was sentenced to die, and will end when my death sentence was commuted two years later. But I will have to forward my answers in parts because I can only send a certain amount of these letterheads stapled together.

Don't worry about big words bothering me—they don't. I'm very wordy, but I would rather stick to simple words when *it comes to my own thing. Simplicity is the mother of art. If you want to send me some magazines and books (which I would appreciate), you will have to manage sending them from the publisher—you know how to do it. Okay? Or you can send them via your college or a bookstore. Send any type of magazines or books. But be selective.*

*Very truly yours
Salvador Agron
#28298*

Before Attica, the screens had made contact so improbable, that even the thought of contact with a loved one in the visiting room was never anything more than a drifting jailhouse dream. It was not uncommon for a convict to go for years, if not the entire length of his sentence, without being allowed to touch his wife, his girlfriend, his daughter, or his mother. Convicts under a sentence of death were exempted from this rule, but only on the night they were scheduled to die. Then they were allowed one last hug and a kiss before being led away to the electric chair.

But now things were different. Convicts and their visitors could touch, hold, kiss, and hug as much as they liked, just as long as they did not cross over whatever line of decency the visiting room guard felt he could arbitrarily impose on any particular day for whatever group of convicts and visitors he had been assigned to supervise.

Placing a peanut butter and jelly sandwich, a Coke, and a bag of potato chips in front of Salvador on the wooden counter, I took a peek at the woman on my left, the one whose tiny tongue had been dancing back and forth with the tongue of the guy who was sitting across from her. Now their tongues were quiet but their hands were all over one another with a vengeance. I was trying hard not to look at them, but it was far more comfortable to be a peeping tom than to watch the way Salvador was shoveling down his sandwich. Not only did he resemble a mountain lion devouring a rabbit, the way he quickly tore the sandwich apart, piece by piece, but he was making such loud sucking noises that I had no choice but to keep my eyes on the girl with the dancing tongue and roving hands. She was probably no more than eighteen, though it was hard to know for sure because she was wearing so much makeup. As I tried to figure out what her story was, like where was she from, and why was she here, Salvador's uneven voice suddenly interrupted my thoughts.

"Think maybe you could get me something more to eat?"

"You want more?"

"Yeah...but like why don't you see if maybe you can't get something different than the peanut butter and jelly."

"Chicken salad be okay?"

"Yeah...yeah, and maybe some coffee...with some cream and lots of extra sugar."

Greenhaven
February 5th, 1974

Dear Richard:
    I'm glad you liked parts one through four about my trial and time in the death house at Sing Sing.
    When I was released from death row, I actually felt cheated by God. It seems as though I had to now earn the right to enter heaven. I was sent to the box (segregation) for a while, and from the box in Sing Sing I was transferred to Auburn Prison. It was Rockefeller who granted commutation—I believe it was more for his political purposes (the Puerto Rican and Black votes) because social and political pressure was being put on him by figures such as Munoz Marin, and Mrs. Eleanor Roosevelt
    Life is not only comical (as you can see from some of what I've already sent you) but it is also very tragic. If one can understand life, he also can understand history and autobi-

ographies. I always thought that I could write an autobiography under an assumed name but after thinking the whole situation through, I found that the facts of life and the hard core reality of my life were too obvious to hide behind an ambiguous title or an assumed name.

My present legal status is this: I have been locked up for fifteen years, since 1959, and while I could apply for a pardon, it's doubtful I could qualify because my "behavior record" is a contradiction of my "educational record."

I have a lawyer who is presently working on my case, but personally, I don't have respect for any lawyer. They are some of the coldest people I have ever come across—most of them are hypocrites. I see the Parole Board in 1979 but I cannot hope on that either unless come changes are brought about in the parole system.

I hope this answers your question about my current situation.

Here's what I'd like you to do: type all the parts I sent you, correct the errors, and send me a copy, okay? Now is the time for you to ask all your questions. I am ready.

When you get your death row thesis together, send me a copy.

Keep on keeping on, and don't give up.

Life is struggle.

Stay together,

Salvador Agron
#16486

Back at the vending machines, I remembered a discussion we'd been having the other night in one of my Sociology classes about how, since Attica, a whole new wave of reforms had been implemented throughout New York's prisons, and how even the vending machines in the visiting rooms were symbolic of this reform movement. One warden, or "superintendent" as they were now called, said the vending machines would allow the convicts and their visitors "to break bread together," and create the illusion that they were eating in a college cafeteria instead of in a prison visiting room. But our professor had also pointed out that there was nothing unusual about this kind of thinking. That in fact it was totally consistent with the new penal philosophy in New York State mandating that prisons now be called "correctional facilities." Inmates would be called "residents," and guards, who would be known as "correctional officers," would be required to wear a state-issued blazer instead of the formal uniform of basic blue. The reasoning was that the less they looked like cops, the more people would be able to relate to them as people who did more than merely close the door and lock the lock.

Greenhaven
February 19th, 1974

Dear Richard:
   I received your February 12th, 1974 letter and I also received the following books: "Wretched of the Earth," "Down These Mean Streets" and "Black Skin, White Masks." I got right into Fanon's "Wretched of the Earth." He describes the sufferings of Third World "Natives" very vividly. Anyone intending to write a thesis on poor natives would do well to read him first. Of course, his voice is an angry description of the despicable conditions that exist within a violent context.
   I guess he put it all down hoping that those who read it would find a cure for the dehumanization he describes.
   We must find our own solutions.

Cordially yours,
Salvador Agron
#16486

Looking at Salvador as he attacked his new tray of food, it was hard for me to believe this was the same man who had appeared on the front page of the New York *Daily News* nearly fifteen years ago.

Back then his hair had been curly and he had looked lithe and wiry. But now the person sitting across from me was bigger, bulky almost, and of course his hair, pulled back the way it was, gave him an entirely different look.

"Back then" was late August, 1959, when Salvador had been given the name the "Capeman" because he wore a red, satin-lined nurse's cape into battle against a group of teen-agers in a Hell's Kitchen playground. Two boys had been killed that night, and another critically wounded. Salvador and another boy (who was dubbed the "Umbrella Man" because he'd carried an umbrella whose tip had been sharpened to a lethal point) were arrested, tried, convicted, and eventually sentenced to death. Later it was learned that the murdered boys had been innocent bystanders with no known gang affiliations.

Salvador was sentenced to death, and he spent nearly two years in Sing Sing's death house before Governor Nelson Rockefeller commuted his sentence to life imprisonment. From there he had gone from prison to prison, with several years in an insane asylum, run by the state in Dannemora, New York, about eight miles south of the Canadian border.

Greenhaven Correctional Facility
February 21st, 1974

Dear Richard:

This letter will acknowledge receipt of your six page letter of January 10th, 1974, which was forwarded from Attica and which I received today, the twenty-first. I also received "The Descent of Woman," and the dictionary. Muchas Gracias. I also received your letter of January 18th. When I receive the books, "Manchild in the Promised Land," and the

"Teachings of Don Juan," I will let you know. Yes, I got the enclosed stamps.

I will try to stay at one prison so that all your letters and books will get to me, but I can only do this if the non-people don't decide to sabotage our efforts by sending me to yet another prison!

As for your six-page letter, I will cover certain things in it for the time being. Okay? Thank you for complimenting me on my acquired style of writing. However, I don't really think I am "a natural born writer." It took hard work and much study to "acquire" this ability, and I have yet to perfect it. It may be a trait I picked up unconsciously from a great-great-great grandfather (who really knows?).

Wow! Your Spanish is awful—but we'll get that together as time goes on. There are many things we could teach each other. However, your English is wonderful. My Spanish is bad, too, my only advantage being the natural ability which I have only lightly cultivated. There are actually only two things which I admire in a person: 1. the measure to which he is capable to accept reality and 2. his truthfulness. By this we can accurately judge a person. You have this, and please do your best to cultivate this to the utmost. I don't know what it is, but your name (from the very first day you wrote) has a very familiar sound.

I am under the impression that we've met before. I could be wrong. However, I just wanted you to know. Yes, I do remember the music of the 1950's. They were wonderful years. I think the most enjoyable of my life.

I really liked your idea of becoming "a psychoanalyst for the people." I am sure you can do this. However, it is a difficult task. Many poor people would love to have a psychoanalyst that could relate to them, free of institutional programming—it would be an opportunity that even Che Guevara would envy. Of course, considering circumstances, he took another road which gave him the same fulfillment in life. He was a wonderful man—a symbol to all the Latin American countries.

Again, thank you for all the nice things you said about my writing. You really made me feel good with what you said.

Your amigo,
Salvador Agron
#16846

Fifteen years, and many prisons later, here he is sitting across from me: Salvador Agron, the infamous Capeman, shoveling food into his mouth like there's no tomorrow. And as I watched the chicken salad dripping from the corner of his mouth to the collar of his shirt, I asked him about the prison food. Not about what I've bought for him to eat from the vending machines, but about the food they serve in the prison.

"Is the food here any good?"

Before he could answer, we both turned our heads at a sound coming from my left. It was the woman with the dancing hands, and the sound was coming from the scratching of her nails moving back and forth. Despite the wooden counter between them, and despite the guard sitting at his desk in front of the room, the woman had somehow managed to make her way across the counter and into the shirt of the man sitting to the right of Salvador. Realizing where the sound was coming from, and not wanting to intrude on their privacy or, worse, attract the attention of the guard, I quickly turned my attention back to Salvador.

I will never forget the look on his face. It was as if a dark and violent wind, ripping and tearing, had suddenly sapped his face of everything save a look of such overwhelming lust that it was all I could do not to look away in embarrassment. Years of exile in a womanless world must have done quite a number to his head. But having never been arrested, stood in front of a judge, or spent a night in jail, I had no idea what it was like to live as a convict in a maximum-security prison. I had taken nearly a dozen graduate level courses in Criminology, along with half as many field trips to all kinds of jails, prisons, and police stations. Yet I still didn't have a clue as to why someone like Salvador Agron did the things he did, much less a clue about his sex life for the fifteen years that he'd been in prison.

"It's pretty lousy."

"Excuse me?"

"You asked me how the food was in here and I said it's pretty lousy...but it's like I've been eating this stuff in here for so long that I don't even look at what it is...like I just put my spoon down and throw it in my mouth."

"Yeah...so I've noticed"

Laughing, with the wide gaps between his teeth more noticeable than ever, it seemed he'd totally removed himself from what he'd seen of the woman with the dancing hands and what she'd been doing with her nails to the guy sitting across from her. He knew I'd seen the same thing, but something stopped him from commenting. It was like what we'd seen had never happened.

"So...did you bring it...I didn't see it when you went to get my food at the machines."

"Bring what?"

"The typewriter, didn't you bring the typewriter?"

"Oh, yeah, no problem. It's out at the front desk, they said I had to leave it with them for inspection before you could get it inside."

"What kind is it," he asked.

"Uh...I think it's a Royal but I could be wrong...I'm not sure."

"You're not sure? How could you be not sure? Where's this thing from anyway?"

"It's from a hock shop...I bought it yesterday...it works, and I know it does because the guy who sold it to me let me try it first...but I don't remember if it was a Royal or a Smith Corona."

"But it's portable, right?"

"Definitely...definitely, a portable," I said.

Whether the typewriter would last a long time was anyone's guess, though probably not, given how much I'd paid for it. A few bucks at a lower Manhattan pawnshop for a typewriter that was not much to look at. But it worked, or at least it would work long enough for me to know whether he was really serious when he'd written a few months back that he would be willing to take me up on my offer to collaborate on a book about his life.

Greenhaven Correctional Facility
February 22nd 1974

Dear Richard:
I received your letter of February 9th, 1974 on January 17th. I must admit it is a very flattering letter, and I want to thank you for expressing such faith about my literacy. However, I must be modest because I believe I am not ready to write the first Puerto Rican classic. But my beliefs do not necessarily mean that I am not capable. I really don't know, it is difficult for one to judge his own self. I've always thought about putting my experiences on paper, and at one time I wrote about 200 pages, nevertheless, I tore all the papers up and burned them and flushed them down the toilet. Life is so vulgar that it is difficult to tell it like it is. I guess I got it all in my brains how it should be told but it would take volumes to explain what is in my head. Then, there is the fear of censorship. Another problem is dates (exact dates) I don't like to guess about this or that—I like to approximate my life to the basic factors of age, time, and place.
One thing I don't like about "Manchild in the Promised Land" is that it is not accurate and it lacks dates, and this makes me think the author should stick more to fiction—in other words he lied about many things and he was afraid to stain his petty-bourgeois student standards which he acquired.
I could not practice such duplicity even if I wanted. I might not say it directly, but I would say it indirectly. You can be reassured that I wrote those parts about my trial, sentence of death, and time in Sing Sing's death house directly from my head—there were things I did not mention, but it is all gospel truth. Now, I would write a book even if it means being exiled. But there are many complications I must overcome.
I must first talk (and not through the mail) this out so you can know what it involves. It is not easy to do it (unless one writes fabrications).

> *I can easily fabricate a story—but, that's not what I want. My objective in life is to speak and live a reality based on truth. These two things are principals with me, and that is one of the conditions I must put forth before I begin my autobiography.*
>
> *Tu Amigo y hermano,*
> *Salvador Agron*
> *#16846*

As part of my study about death row, I was writing to dozens of men who were either on death row, or who had spent time there in the past. The study was designed to find out whether people sentenced to death had ever undergone any kind of emotional transformation while they were waiting to be executed. It was loosely based on some previous research conducted by a poet in New Mexico who had interviewed several men under sentence of death and had concluded that, at least for some, a transformation of some kind or other had taken place. His argument was that the transformation had been so profound that in a sense the state was now faced with the prospect of executing an entirely different person than the one who had originally been sentenced to death.

Given his age, and his notoriety, Salvador was a natural for this kind of study, and he was one of the first people I had written to. Not only did he respond right away with an offer of assistance, but what he wrote over the next several weeks, starting with his sentence to death and ending when the sentence was commuted nearly two years later, was nothing short of extraordinary. He had a voice that was his, and his alone.

Greenhaven
March 7th, 1974

Dear Richard:
    I received your letter of February 28th, 1974 and I can see that you have a good picture of what this book entails—good. As long as we both know the problems, we can better tackle them.
    Now that I am at Greenhaven, it should be easier for you to visit me than when I was at Attica.
    Yes, writing this book is a major project. So get some rest and take a good walk every now and then—this helps stimulate thought. I have been hearing about bio-feedback as a science of learning. Can you find me anything on this subject? I'd like to look into it—it sounds sensible.
    Here is the address and telephone number of a friend of mine who helps me politically. When you visit with my mother someday, she will be a good person to have with you because my mother's knowledge of English is limited. Her name is Genoveva, and she lives on the Lower East Side of Manhattan.
    Well, the visiting hours here at Greenhaven are from 10:00 AM until 3:00 PM everyday, and on Saturdays and Sundays there are visiting hours from 6:00 PM until 9:00 PM. That should answer your question.
    You come up here, I get called to the visiting room, and that's about it.
    I'll be expecting you.

Tu amigo and hermano,
Salvador Agron
#16846

By the time I was processed into the prison, which included making sure I was actually on Salvador's approved "visiting and correspondence" list, it was nearly eleven o'clock. After my hand was marked with a tiny rubber stamp, the door to the visiting room slid open, and I was assigned a seat by the visiting room guard. Nearly an hour later, Salvador finally walked in the door.

More than two hours later, and with just under an hour left before the visit would come to an end, we'd reached an agreement about the book we were going to write. I would ask questions, and he would write back his responses, two pages at a time. Little by little, the book would be written. He said he had already written about me to a political friend of his, a woman named Genoveva, and she had agreed to meet me so that arrangements could be made for me to visit his mother in the Bronx. Salvador said his mother didn't speak much English, and that I would need someone like Genoveva to translate. This was important because if anyone could provide details about his early life, it was certainly his mother. I also agreed to attend as many prison festivals as I could.

"They've got all kinds of festivals going on here at Greenhaven that I can invite you to...and they'll be great for what we're doing because nobody's gonna check you out too carefully when you're leaving to go home...so like you can probably get my stuff out if you're cool about it."

"Yeah?"

"Like we'll set it up so that I'll pass you my writing and you can just walk out the door with it because there's so many people and there's no way they can check them all out...you understand what I'm sayin'?"

"Did you have stuff like this when you were in Attica?"

"Nah...maybe they've got them now, but nothing like this ever happened when I was up there."

"I've never heard anything about this stuff."

"Think maybe you could bring in some women for one of these things?"

"What?"

"Women...you know, girls, muchachas...don't you know any nice college girls you could bring in here?"

"For who?"

"What you mean, for who? For me and the guys in here, that's for who."

"Well...I'll see what I can do."

"You married?" he asked.

"I was...but I'm divorced."

"You got a girlfriend?"

"Nah...but I do okay."

"Playing the field, eh?"

"More or less...but there's nothing serious."

"Well...see what you can do for us."

"And you can invite me?"

"Just as long as you're on the right list, you won't have any hassles getting in...and like there's even buses coming up here from Harlem for some of the Muslim festivals...so you could take a bus with them right from Manhattan somewhere."

"I don't live in Manhattan."

"Since when?"

"Since...I dunno...I lived there once, but that was years ago...and just for a little while."

"So how come all your letters have a return address from East Houston Street...ain't that in Manhattan?"

"Yeah...but that's just a store with lots of mail boxes for people who don't want their mail sent to their homes...I just rent a box there...but didn't I already tell you all this?"

"I thought you was living in Manhattan," Salvador said.

"My faculty advisor at the college said that if I was going to write to prisoners I should set up a postal box...he said it was for my own protection."

"Yeah, well...I can dig where he was coming from...lots of people in here can't be trusted...how long you been living in Brooklyn?"

"About sixteen...or maybe seventeen years...or something like that...and before that I was living with my parents up in the Bronx, around near Bedford Park."

"That's right near where my sister lives...she's near Jerome Avenue....you know where that is?"

"Yeah...I do...I lived near there when I was a little kid, over on Bainbridge Avenue...near Gun Hill Road," I told him.

"I remember that place...I was in a fight over there one time with some people who called themselves the Fordham Baldies, or something like that but this was years ago, so maybe I got the name wrong...your parents still living back there?"

"Nah...they moved away years ago and they're living in Brooklyn now...not too far from where I am...what about you?"

"My mom is in the Bronx, near where my sister lives, and my dad's in Puerto Rico...but I haven't heard from him in years..."

At exactly ten minutes before three, the visiting room guard announced that visiting would be over for the day in ten minutes, but for those people who would be taking the bus back to New York City, they would have to leave five minutes earlier.

"How did you get up here?"

"I took the bus."

The daily bus between the Port Authority Bus Terminal in Manhattan and Greenhaven left Manhattan at exactly seven-thirty in the morning. The first stop was the federal penitentiary in Danbury, Connecticut. Then it continued to Greenhaven, where it would arrive about ten or fifteen minutes before visitors were officially allowed to enter the prison.

But no matter how early the bus arrived at the prison, the doors would not open to visitors until exactly ten-o'clock. There were no exceptions. It could be raining, dark, cold, or a blinding snowfall, but still the doors would not open. Rules were rules, and there were no exceptions for age, health, or the weather.

"Does your moms come up to visit you much?"

"Nah...there's too many hassles."

When the visiting room guard announced the last call for anyone taking the bus back to New York City, we both got up, shook hands, and said our good-byes.

"Don't forget to do those things I asked you to do," Salvador said.

"What?"

"Genoveva...you gotta call her so she can take you to see my moms."

"I'm gonna call her as soon as I get back to the city."

"You got her number?"

"Yeah...I wrote it down when you sent it...but what's your mom's name?"

"Esmeralda...Esmeralda Rodriguez Agron."

Greenhaven
March 31st, 1974

Dear Richard:
　Your visit was very interesting—I enjoyed myself and I hope you did too. One thing I am still trying to place, and which I remember from somewhere, is your name and you also. However, I know that I know you but it seems I cannot place exactly where from. That sounds sort of strange, but it is also the truth.
　Well, let's skip that for now...we'll settle that later.
　I got your letter of March 27th, with the enclosed photo and the map of Puerto Rico. And I'll let you know when I get the other stuff.
　For this book I will need diagrams, photographs, dates, and all sorts of charts—and these are not easy simple things.
　My intention is to start my book with an " introduction by the author," or a foreword, and then from there I will go into the origins of the Rodriguez and Agron families. From there I will write the story of my life, starting from April 24th, 1943, the day I was born. Your suggested method for writing this book—a question and answer process, is an excellent idea.
　Richard, there are many problems in writing a book, many problems that you have been lucky not to encounter—unique problems which belong to a different captive class. In prison, a man can write a book about a horse, a dog, etc. But there

are things he cannot touch upon because of censorship and because this would incur the wrath of those on top of the totem pole. I am more than surprised that what I wrote got to you though the regular channels of correspondence—things are a-changing.

What I am concerned about is can you take the pressure, would you dare read the book, and would it cause you, or anybody, harm, hurt, or guilt feelings?

But we can deal with all of this—where there is a will, there is a way.

I am willing.

*Tu Amigo y hermano,
Salvador Agron
#16846*

Chapter Two

ESMERALDA

April 7th, 1973
Greenhaven Correctional Facility

My beloved mother:
    I received your letter dated April 5th, 1974, along with the money order for fifteen dollars. Thank you.
    You are a very good mother, and I mean this with all my heart and soul.
    I don't have too much to say. Genoveva has returned from California. She sent me four beautiful postcards. She says that California is a very beautiful place, but that there are very few Puerto Ricans there. Maybe someday you and I will go there for a visit. Okay?
    Mrs. Davis came to visit me and she said that Zapata, my lawyer, does not wish to ask the governor for clemency because he believes he will be able to make something happen for me in the courts. I don't care if he goes to the governor, or to the courts, just as long as whatever he does, will allow me to leave this cursed hell!
    I have a new friend. His name is Richard Jacoby, and he came to visit with me recently. He is helping me to write my autobiography.
    I have asked him to meet with Genoveva, and soon they will be visiting with you, so that you can help Jacoby with our family history.
    Until next time, I send you all my love, and my prayers.

Your son,
Salvador Agron
16846

At five feet two, Genoveva was shorter than I was by at least three inches, and in her late forties, she was nearly twice my age. But her skin was smooth, lightly tanned, and free from lines and wrinkles. She wore her black, kinky hair in an afro, and on her coat was a button that said, "Keep Puerto Rico Free."

In his letters, and during my visit, Salvador had given me some of Genoveva's history. Born in Río Piedras, Puerto Rico, she had been a university student and teacher before migrating to New York in 1948.

She had helped to organize Puerto Rican tenants on the Lower East Side about deteriorating housing conditions. Salvador said the word on the street about Genoveva was that she was not only political, but also highly regarded for how aggressive she was whenever she was supporting a particular cause.

In 1964 she had been called before a grand jury investigating the organizers of a protest that followed the shooting of a fourteen-year-old boy in Harlem. Refusing to testify, she was jailed for thirty days and fined two hundred and fifty dollars. Salvador said this time in jail was what had motivated her to become more politically involved, and to actively work to defend the rights of Puerto Ricans imprisoned for their political beliefs.

Maybe she was just nervous about meeting me, or she had something troubling on her mind, but sitting across from her in Ratner's restaurant, before a waiter took our order, there was no mistaking the strong vibe she was sending in my direction. Perhaps I was nervous too, but whatever it was could not have prepared me for the directness of her questioning.

"Are you kosher?"

"Excuse me?"

"Isn't that why you wanted to eat here?"

"I just figured it'd be easier for you since you live so close by...and also because I work just right around the corner..."

"Where's that?"

"At the health food store over on Sixth Street...I usually work there a few nights a week."

"But you do eat kosher, right?"

"No...no, it's not that...it's because I don't eat meat and I figured it'd be easier to eat here than in a place that's just vegetarian...this way we'll both be able to find something we can eat."

"You don't eat any meat?"

"Nope."

"When was the last time you had any?"

"Five, maybe six years. I used to eat it all the time but then my wife turned me on to macrobiotics..."

"You're married?" She asked questions as rapidly as Salvador did.

"Not any more...we separated a few years ago."

Married in the fall of 1968 to someone I'd known since high school, the marriage lasted three years before we'd broken up in 1971, almost to the day of my graduation from Brooklyn College, and just as we were preparing to live with a dozen other people on a commune in New Hampshire. We tried to get back together, and even decided to try living together on the commune. But four months spent shoveling snow and collecting firewood, had been more than enough to send us both back to Brooklyn, where I took an apartment, and returned to Brooklyn College. This time I enrolled in the Graduate Division of the Sociology Department, with a specialization in Deviant Behavior.

"How did you meet up with Salvador?"

Before I could answer, the waiter was at our table. Looking confused as she read the menu, Genoveva took my suggestion and ordered potato latkes, or pancakes, while I ordered a plate of kasha and noodles, along with a pot of tea for the both of us. When the tea was brought to the table, the waiter poured each of us a cup, and I talked at length about my death row thesis. I told her that I was writing to people all over the country in order to determine whether being on death row might lead to some kind of expanded consciousness while they were waiting to be executed.

"What does this have to do with Salvador?"

"What'd you mean, what does it have to do with Salvador, he was in the death house for almost two years, and that's why I wrote to him in the first place."

"And you think this happened to him, this...what did you say, expanded consciousness that you're talking about?"

"Maybe," I told her. "I don't know, but he still writes better than most of the people I've written to so far...and I've written to lots of 'em."

"Like who've you written to?"

"Sirhan Sirhan, Charles Manson..."

"You wrote to Manson?"

"He was one of the first...I wrote to him at Folsom, that's in California...but he wasn't interested."

"Why would you want to write to him? He's a murderer!"

"So was Salvador."

"He's not like them," she said. "He's different."

September 2, 1973
Attica Correctional Facility

Dear Geno:
You and I already know each other. The basis of this knowledge being our politics. As for myself, I am first a revolutionary nationalist in my daily practice, and an independent socialist in my outlook. My lumpen background has been the motivating factor in how my political outlook has evolved over the years. I am not a professor in politics but I do know a little and everyday I learn more and more.

I uphold Boriquen as my first cultural identity, and I have a distaste for Puerto Ricanism.

I have been instrumental in the building of the Cadre for

the Revolutionary Nationalist Party within the prisons, and I have also been instrumental in the teaching of a Yocahu Atarei concept which is similar to the Yin-Yang principal found in Taoist teachings. There are other projects that I have been involved with over the past several years. Some have gotten off the ground for awhile, then were suppressed, again and again, but still have managed to emerge for yet another time, and often even stronger than the first time.

Due to conditions that are beyond my control, I tend to isolate myself in my thoughts and this is due to the people in whose company I often find myself without my having any say as to whether I want them near me or not. However, my humanity always seems to draw me back to the fold. The only genuine leaders I recognize and respect are 1. Alrizu Campos, 2. Karl Marx, 3. Lenin, 4. Mao, and of course Che Guevara. However, they were not perfect, and anybody who says otherwise actually disrespects their memory.

I really enjoy reading your letters. They help me to better define myself politically. Down with Imperialism, Racism, and sexism—and all power to the people!

Hasta La Victoria siempre,
Tu hermano,
Salvador Agron
#16486

P. S. I wrote a poem for you. I hope you like it!

When I started my study, I thought there were only two realities: the way the convicts perceived it, contrasted with either that of the people who ran the prisons, or with the public's perception of criminals and what they deserved, or didn't deserve. But as time went on I saw that there was yet another reality, that of the person who becomes emotionally involved with one or more convicts to the point that the emotional tie in time colors their perceptions for better or for worse. Like the woman in the visiting room. Salvador told me she had met the guy she was visiting from an ad he'd placed in a newspaper. He had been looking for someone to correspond with, and she'd responded. Neither of them had known the other on the outside, and so their history was one of prison, and nothing else.

Genoveva Clemente

Gentle soul of our struggling time
Ever ready when duty calls
No revolutionary song or rhyme
Or words that poets invent in all
Visualize the spirit that she brings
Enveloping our Boricua Nation
Vibrant is her image and all things
Admired she gives us inspiration!

Calling upon our people she comes
Living with them she earns
Everyone's love and not just some
Meeting her one is bound to learn
Examples of how a revolutionary sister should be
New born she fits the ideal Latin soul
Totally committed to our struggle for liberty
Ever keeping in mind humanity and our goal.

"How is he different?" I asked Genoveva. "I really don't understand what you're trying to say here."

"He's political."

"I still don't know what his being political has to do with anything."

"He was just an ignorant kid when that stuff in the playground happened...he could barely even read...and so he was just as much a victim as those kids he killed...so it was definitely political...don't you believe this?"

If I'd heard this once, I'd heard it a thousand times. And if not in those specific terms, than in one variation or another. Some men had written to me that they were "political prisoners," while others had written—and this was the majority—that they were "victims of circumstance." Yet what was interesting was that in the letters I received, the actual victims of their crimes were hardly ever mentioned, and feelings of remorse were rare, if not unknown.

4/16/74
Greenhaven Correctional Facility

Dear Richard:
    I received yours of April 9th, 1974, and was glad to hear that you are doing okay.
    Well, about our book contract—draw it up as you think best. I don't know exactly what to do with money, so draw it up in the manner most fair. I trust your judgment.
    I have already written a "Foreword by the Author" (you can write your own introduction after the book is finished). I've been drawing up rough sketches and things are not that difficult as I sometimes make myself think!
    Yes, please send "Journey to Ixtlan" by Carlos Castaneda. I'm interested in its dealing of the pre-columbian era. I have a theory about all this but it is mostly subjective.
    And, you didn't have to write or expostulate about proceeds from the book, etc. You see I 'know' you very good—even more than I can expound upon, and I know that your sincerity is unquestionable and that all that stuff about money and contracts is only secondary. When I look into a person's eyes and things are clear, I don't worry about things like money and contracts, because the only people I don't trust are those that shut their eyes. You see, "the eye is the light of the body," and the light of the body is the soul, so that the eyes are the gates of the soul—some gates have light while others are obscure.
    Your light is truthful and sincere and I have never mis-

judged people too often—I know what lies in the soul of man, whether bad or good. You have good, so relax. Don't get so tensed up over little things like money and contracts—all this is only a formality.

Let me tell you: when I meet somebody, I look at them and I know them. Many people don't know me because I make myself invisible to them. Only my friends get to know my goodness.

My book should be a revelation. And through it many an eye will be open. I only mentioned the contract and money because it is a formality. I guess you can call it the "American Way of Life."!!

When you come up for your next visit, try to feel more relaxed, although I'm sure this is difficult in a prison visiting room. I used to be a racist (due to my own ignorance) at one time but racism today is more against some elements in the whole human race which are backwards—I don't like ignorance. I love reality. You'll get the whole picture as the book develops.

I will have to put myself in a different state of mind as I tackle this project so if you should ever come to visit me and I sound or look a little peculiar, don't worry—I know how to return.

Your friend,
Salvador Agron
 # 16486

P.S. Please send me a copy of "The Upanishads," and the Hindu, "Celestial Song."

Over and over, my professors and my faculty advisors had said to keep a professional distance from the people I was writing to. Don't get involved to the point where your objectivity will ever be questioned. But after nearly a year of writing back and forth to men on death rows all across the country, I only knew one thing for sure: how difficult it was for me, a researcher, to understand the reality of living in a maximum-security prison, to say nothing of what it was like to spend years on death row, waiting to die. The more I wrote to different people, including wardens, lawyers, and guards, as well as to convicts, the more contradictions I found.

To the wardens and the guards, the convicts were there because they had made a choice, and it was the job of the guards and the wardens to respect this choice by making sure the convicts stayed where they belonged: locked up for as long as the law allowed. The convicts belonged to an entirely different class, and this was especially true in how the prison personnel perceived the men under a sentence of death. They were the ultimate bad guys, the lepers of the prison system, the lowest of the low. In most states, this meant almost complete solitary confinement. The condemned spent their time waiting for death in small isolated cells in "death houses," or "death rows," totally removed from other prisoners, except of course those who shared their fate. Breakfast, lunch, and dinner all were served in their cells. An hour of exercise was permitted each day, and one shower a week. Although this routine varied from one death row to another, in the end it was all the same: extreme isolation for years and years until, ultimately, they were executed, or their sentence was commuted to life in prison and they were given a "second chance."

Salvador had been given this second chance, but whether this was "political," or he was simply a "victim of circumstance," was hard to say.

April 10th, 1974
Greenhaven Correctional Facility

Dear Richard:

I received the letter with the $1.00 in stamps. Muchas Gracias! Please see if you can send me the Book of Tao (I Ching) which deals with the Yin/Yang concept and which is closely related to my way of thinking.

Feel free to improve on what I write, because when I say this I know that you will not change the essence of what is being said.

As for the charts and the organization that you mentioned, I have to side with you, though I don't think it's necessary for you to mention each book you're sending. But, I think that you ideas are very good—after all, you do have more expertise in these matters than I do, especially when it comes to the entire book! Yes, I understand your concept on writing—and let me add that the way a person writes has to do more with the way they think than the way in which he speaks. When I get to the dialogue you will see what I mean.

As the book continues, it would be good if you would hold off asking too many questions. These can be asked when the whole project is finished so that you may also enjoy the project as it goes along—suspense is sometimes a touch of the creative, and one must utilize it as a tool of the trade. If I told it all, by just answering questions, you will be deprived of the laughter, tears, and knowledge that just reading it cannot bring. I'll answer some questions here and there but not too many. Okay?

This is what I wrote about you in the foreword to my book:

"And, for my new-found amigo y hermano, who asked me to take on this great project—to you, Richard Jacoby, I dedicate these words from Alexander Pope: 'To err is human, to forgive, divine.' And, I beg your forgiveness for what you will be subjected to after the final word is uttered. Sí, es mucho trabajo."

Well, by the words I wrote about 'to err is human, to forgive, divine,' that is only to let you know that you will have to bear with me and the things I will speak about for the next couple of years until we finish this work. I will be speaking of suffering and of many things that can cause pain, and perhaps sorrow in your own life, as you read all this stuff. People will wonder how you had the heart to read this stuff! Dante's inferno will be nothing compared to my life—many people will think that Job in the Bible went through hell, well, Job never knew what hell really was. To curse the day that one is born is nothing—this is a regular procedure in the life of the wretched and poor people of the earth! What I wrote was more of a touch of concern for your feelings as you work on this book with me.

I have never had a life that one could call "civilized." You will have to be strong(which I know you are) and to put up with what you will encounter of my life because it is all part of a nightmare of a reality which is almost unbelievable. I have been a victim all my life—if there is justice I have never had my share of it yet in this world. The whole structure of society is wrong, and I condemn almost every institution. So I am dedicating these words to you so that you will be able to forgive the animals who run though this story from every direction—you will know them first so be careful because they are like rabid dogs out to destroy and to kill. In other words, as you read, try to keep your cool.

I read every time I get the chance—and you are correct about being tempered by alternate activities, like reading books, or listening to music, while we are working on this book.

I will take your advice on this.
Take care.

Tu amigo y hermano
 Salvador Agron
#16486

August 3rd, 1973
Office of the Warden
Florida State Penitentiary

To Whom It May Concern:

I am writing to obtain the names of all the men in the Florida Correctional system who have been sentenced to die. I would like these names in order to correspond with them as part of my graduate research in Criminology concerning the effects of long-term confinement on death row.

The title of my dissertation is "Consciousness Expansion Among Death Row Inmates," and my study will seek to determine what happens to people who routinely spend years on death row, under the constant threat of a death sentence, while their case is being appealed to one court or another.

My hypothesis is simply that for many of these people, the forced isolation leads more than a few of them to a new way of thinking about themselves, their crime, and maybe even a hint as to the many variables that led to their being on death row in the first place.

A similar study was conducted recently in North Carolina, in conjunction with the North Carolina Correctional System, and which appeared in the August, 1972 issue of the American Journal of Psychiatry.

At the completion of my study, I will be glad to share my findings with your office.

Very truly yours,
Richard Jacoby

The warden wrote back that he was sorry, but prison policies dictating confidentiality prevented him from releasing their names. What he would do, he said, was Xerox my letter and send it to the men on death row. Then it would be up to each man to decide whether or not he wanted to correspond with me.

Eleven prisoners were on Florida's death row at the time,

and ten of them replied. With one exception, all were young men who had either maimed, slashed, or shot their victims, in a wide variety of ways. Some, like Ted Bundy, had killed even more than one person. And although I made every attempt to be objective, and keep to my initial questioning about consciousness expansion on death row, after awhile my letters to these men began to reflect what they were writing to me. There was too much emotion in the letters I received, too much pathos, for me to stay objective. Gradually, almost unconsciously, I became an unknowing participant in the lives of the people I was trying to write about.

One of my professors questioned whether or not sending a convict a book he had requested wasn't in a sense a violation of my study because by doing so, wasn't I contributing to the very phenomenon I was writing about? And all of this in addition to the book I was writing with Salvador.

Not only was I editing his work, I was also sending him weekly "progress reports," letting him know what I was doing relative to the book. Things like taking certain photographs, or doing research for different sections of the book. We had also agreed that I would send him "charts" every now and then with information that I thought would help him work on the book.

Everything Salvador had written so far pointed to a dramatic transformation that had taken place while he'd been on death row. But how true was this for everyone who had spent time there? And even if a person did not undergo any kind of transformation, wasn't it equally possible that the very awfulness of death row confinement might very well lead to further violence if they had their sentences commuted, and were someday released from prison?

Given that the system generated so many contradictions, wasn't it possible that Salvador's transformation would eventually lead to further violence? Some people called him the "Capeman," while others knew him as "Dracula," while for others, and these seemed to be the majority, he was simply one of the many psychopaths who lived behind the walls of New York State's numerous maximum-security prisons. People the public needed to be protected from as if they were the lowest of the low. People to be pitied, perhaps, or at best, forgotten.

Sitting here in Ratner's with Genoveva, sipping tea, I tried to explain all the reasons I felt compelled to work with Salvador on a book about his life, but the words just weren't there. I was obsessed with his story, yet I had no idea whatsoever as to why I felt this way. But as far as she was concerned, we were merely writing a book together.

"And you want me to help with this book?"

"I'd love it."

"So what's the first thing we've gotta do?"

"We've gotta meet Esmeralda."

April 10th, 1974
Greenhaven Correctional Facility

Dear Geno:

I am happy you and Jacoby will be visiting with my mother. But I should tell you that she is very religious, and that I am very limited in what I can discuss with her. I try not to shake her faith in God because it is actually the only thing that keeps her strong. It would be murderous for me to destroy her beliefs. I love her very much. She has looked out for me since I came out of her womb.

She says she likes you, so I hope you'll be able to take all her talk of Jesus and the salvation of your soul.

One time when she came to visit with me at the bughouse (Dannemora State Hospital for the Criminally Insane), she found me in a straightjacket and she started praying and talking in strange "tongues," and all the while praising God that the doctor's were helping me! I just looked at her and told her to take it easy.

Well, you and Jacoby have her address, and I'm glad you'll both be making the visit together.

Hasta La Victoria siempre,
Tu hermano,
Salvador Agron
#16486

Esmeralda lived in the Bronx, on Davidson Avenue, in a racially mixed neighborhood, several miles north of Yankee Stadium.

Boarding the subway at West Fourth Street in Manhattan, we rode the train for nearly an hour before crossing into the Bronx, and when we got off the train a few stops later we were in the South Bronx. Looking at the gang graffiti lining the walls of the subway stairwell, Genoveva said she thought the gangs of the seventies were different than those of the fifties, when Salvador was living in New York City.

"You really think so?" I asked.

"The kids in the gangs back then didn't go around robbing old ladies."

March 29th, 1974
Greenhaven Correctional Facility

Dear Richard:
I got your letter with the $1.00 in stamps, along with the interesting article from the New York Times *about the youth gangs in Brooklyn.*
They are not exactly more sophisticated than the gangs of the 1950's—yet they do seem to be more violent, but on the other hand, they're very much the same, developing from the same background, but only under different historical conditions. We also did a lot of stealing when we were young. And, in fact, we would steal anything that wasn't nailed down! Of course,

the mentality of the 1970's is more advanced than that of the 1950's but the problems are still the same—nothing to do but to hang around on street corners. Our social order is based on lack of means by which to let energy and creativity be released. It is an oppressive and suppressive condition created by wars upon wars and capitalist greed.

Tu amigo,
Salvador Agron
#16846

Years ago I'd lived not far from here, and as we walked to Esmeralda's house, it was easy for me to remember playing on streets that were probably very much like the ones we were walking on now.

Apartment building after apartment building, and except for a slight variation here and there, all the buildings were the same: five or six stories high, with a series of fire escapes running from the roof to the street. The fire escape on the top floor was connected to the roof by a ladder, while the fire escape on the first floor had a ladder stored in such a way that it could only be released in the event of a fire. This way, people passing on the street were unable to climb a ladder from the sidewalk to any of the apartments above.

I will need, from New York City, photographs of the Tombs, Bellevue Hospital, and the Youth House on 12th Street. I will need a picture of the playground on West 46th Street, and a picture of the 16th Precinct police station.

I will need a picture of La Guardia Airport, and also one of the Wiltwyck School in upstate New York. You can probably get this for me from their office in Harlem. I think it was on 125th Street.

I will need, from Brooklyn, pictures of the Farraget housing projects, the Fort Green housing projects at Hudson and Water Streets. P.S. 5, P.S. 117 (Franklin and Willoughby). The school next to the Farraget Projects (Sands Street). Get a pic-

ture of Coney Island—under the boardwalk and the swimming pool and steam baths, if you can. Get pictures, in Manhattan, of 100th Street and the Triboro Theater on East 125 Street. Also Times Square (42nd street) and the corner of 41st Street, near 8th Avenue.

I will need a map, with streets and avenues, of Manhattan, the Bronx, and Brooklyn.

Esmeralda lived in a building five stories high, and since elevators were reserved for buildings six stories or higher, we climbed what felt like an endless series of stairs until we reached her apartment on the fifth floor.

Some of the buildings had buzzers either in the lobby or on the first floor, so that no one could get in without a key unless they were buzzed in by a resident. For the most part, however, the buildings were old, and this kind of security didn't exist. Instead, the people in these buildings barricaded themselves against the unwanted—the heroin addicts, or junkies, forever roaming the streets in search of whatever they could salvage for easy cash—by installing multiple locks, and metal screens on their windows, and especially on any of the windows leading to a fire escape.

There were five apartments on the fifth floor, but none had a name on the door. A few of the doors were completely free from markings of any kind, while the rest had a letter designating the apartment. And since Esmeralda's name was nowhere on the directory in the lobby, we weren't sure exactly where she lived.

"He didn't say nothing to you about which apartment she lived in?" Genoveva said.

"I thought you said you called her."

"I did, but I don't remember which one," she said.

Someone inside one of the apartments must've heard us talking. Suddenly a door opened, and when a man's face appeared, Geno asked him in Spanish, which apartment belonged to Esmeralda Rodriguez Agron. After pointing to a door several feet away, he slammed his door shut before we had a chance to thank him for his help.

"Maybe," I say to Genoveva, "he thinks we're junkies or something."

"More like he probably thinks we're cops because you're white and everything."

In response to Genoveva's knocking, the door was opened wide, and standing in the doorway was Esmeralda Rodriguez Agron. Her hair was black, with spots of gray, and like her son's, parted down the middle and combed straight back. But unlike her son, her eyes were dark, coal dark, and her gaze penetrating and direct to the point that at first I was unable to meet it head on. She was not a tall woman, smaller than Genoveva by at least an inch, but her presence was so strong that she appeared to be taller than she was.

"Buenas tardes," she said, in a Spanish that was slow and easy, or at least far slower than what I was accustomed to hearing from Salvador and Genoveva. Even though I had already taken three years of Spanish in high school, followed by several semesters in college, I still could barely understand most of the Spanish spoken in New York City. At the beginning of a conversation, I could usually identify several phrases, but within seconds I was lost. The Puerto Ricans spoke too fast, and seemed to be continually dropping vowels so that one word seemed to blend into another, and one phrase sounded like the one immediately preceding it. But Esmeralda's Spanish was different, slower, and surely more refined. So much so that as she opened the door and led us into her apartment, I could actually understand a good deal of what she was saying.

We followed her down a short corridor, or foyer, to a small living room. Directing us to sit, she asked Geno if she could get us anything to drink. While she was in the kitchen getting a juice for Geno, and some coffee for me, I took a look around the apartment. The kitchen was off the foyer, and a few feet from where we were sitting a door opened into what looked to be a bedroom. Just before the bedroom was another door, which I could see led to the bathroom.

As the sun streamed through Esmeralda's living room windows, I couldn't help wondering at the many hours she must have spent keeping such a clean apartment. There was not a speck of dust or dirt from one end of the apartment to the other. Of course maybe she had cleaned just for our visit, but looking at the way she was moving about in the kitchen as she prepared our drinks, I knew that the cleanliness was very much a part of who she was. Not only did she radiate a strong presence, but she moved in a way as deliberate as it was strong, so that she gave an overall impression of effortless grace. Watching her as she moved around the kitchen in her simple dress, it was difficult for me to determine her age.

A large crucifix, and several religious pictures were on the living room wall. A picture of Jesus Christ had eyes that appeared to follow me as I walked around the room. Next to this was a picture of the Virgin Mary, and on the opposite wall a photograph of a sad-eyed Salvador when he was a little boy in Puerto Rico. Several times he had asked me to find this exact picture, and finally here it was, hanging on the wall, framed in black. He was probably not more than six years old, and looking at the picture, I wondered what this innocent little boy with the sad eyes would have said had he known that in ten years he would be in the death house at Sing Sing Prison, waiting to die in the electric chair. When Esmeralda returned from the kitchen with juice and coffee, I asked Genoveva to find out where the picture had been taken and how old Salvador had been. Esmeralda said he was seven years old and the picture had been taken at the poorhouse in Puerto Rico, the city of Salvador's birth, on April 24th, 1944.

As the sun streamed though her living room windows, we sat and listened as Esmeralda slowly walked us through Salvador's young life. How he had lived with her for nearly ten years at the poorhouse in Mayaguez, where she'd worked as a maid for eight dollars a week, and room and board for herself and her children. Her daughter's name was Aurea, and she was a year younger than Salvador.

The poorhouse, or El Asilio de Pobres as it was officially called, was a Catholic refuge for the poor. Administered by the Sisters of Charity, it was a shelter for the infirm, the sick, the insane, and anyone who had nowhere else to go.

Esmeralda had brought her children to the poorhouse because it was the only place she could go after she had left her husband. They had arrived at the poorhouse on a rainy night, just before Thanksgiving in 1944, when Salvador was just six months old.

On and on she talked, and whenever she talked of the nuns, her voice grew louder. The nuns had not gotten along with Salvador, who was very rebellious, she said, and who would not listen to anyone.

Hour after hour, Esmeralda talked about Salvador, and the way she talked was like the way she walked, with a decided presence, or a true authority. After awhile her words seemed like a song, or a series of songs, and I became mesmerized by the sound of her voice. Most of what she was saying passed right over my head, but I was able to understand enough to know that this was a woman who had suffered much over the years. At one point, I heard the words, "Sing Sing," and when I asked Genoveva she said that Esmeralda had been talking about how, when Salvador was sent to the death house, she had taken to wearing a medieval hairshirt as penance for the murders.

> *I will need the time or hour I was born. It seems that whenever I write to my mother, she never answers my questions. So perhaps you will have better luck when you visit with her.*
>
> *Find out the exact age I was when I came to New York for the first time. I think it was seven but I am not too sure.*
>
> *It is very difficult for me to write without knowing about*

certain things. Find out my mother's complete name before she got married to my father. I only know her as Esmeralda Rodriguez. Find out my grandmother's name. Find out my father's father's name. Find out the complete name of the "brother" my mother said I had before I was born. I think she said it was Francisco Rodriguez (that's the only thing my mother tells me. She doesn't seem to realize a person should know everything about their past). Find out the names of some of the nuns that used to live in the poorhouse—especially the one that used to play the tambourine in the church. She was sort of heavy. Find out the name of the storm that occurred when I was in the poorhouse—there is an experience I want to touch upon here. Get the date. All these minor details are what I need in order to keep a sort of order going as I get into the deeper things of life.

Somewhere in the course of Esmeralda's narrative, I excused myself to use the bathroom. While I was washing my hands beneath yet another picture of Jesus—this one hanging in a dark frame above the bathroom sink—I heard someone singing in the other room. At first I thought it was a record, or the radio, but when I returned to the living room, I found it was Esmeralda.

Even though I was unable to understand the Spanish words and phrases, I could still feel a mournfulness about her singing and, though I didn't understand the words, I had little doubt as to the passion behind whatever it was she was actually singing about.

Later Genoveva would tell me that before Esmeralda had started singing, she had been talking about the time years ago, after living in the poorhouse with Salvador and Aurea for many years, when she'd met a man and fallen in love. Genoveva said that as Esmeralda began talking about this new man in her life, her face had grown softer, and that all of a sudden she had started to sing. The song, Genoveva said, was about a woman who had lost her husband.

She had a haunting voice. And when she finished the song, and began speaking again, the passion of her singing remained, as she told us how she'd met her new husband. His name was Carlos and he was very handsome. She and her daughter had left Salvador behind in the poorhouse while they went with Carlos to New York City to start a new life. Later, she sent for Salvador, but he landed at La Guardia Airport hours earlier than expected and he cried and cried when she hadn't been there to meet his plane. As she went on with her story, it felt as if she were singing to me. She had lived in an apartment above the storefront church on Hudson Street in Brooklyn, where her husband was the pastor. Salvador had tried to love his stepfather but it was a love that did not grow and many were the nights, she said, that Salvador had fought with his stepfather and stormed out of the house. He hung around on street corners and ran with the gangs until he was arrested, taken to court, and later sent to a reform school called Wiltwyck in upstate New York. As the sun exploded through the windows of her living room, one song followed another, like the sacred beads on a never-ending rosary.

6/1/74
Greenhaven Correctional Facility

Dear Richard:
I am writing to let you know that I got the two books on Puerto Rico. I hope you got the two other letters I sent.
I loved the music of the 1950's, and here is a list of songs that I would like you to record for me:

I'm not a Juvenile Delinquent (Frankie Lyman)
Johnny B. Good (Chuck Berry)
Just Walking in the Rain (Johnny Ray)
Just A Dream (Jimmy Clanton)
Keep a Knockin' (Little Richard)

Dedicated to the One I Love (Shirelles)
Darling, How Long? (Heartbeats)
Do You Wanna Dance? (Bobby Freeman)
Desiree (Charts)
Don't Let Go (Roy Hamilton)
Goodnight, Sweetheart, Goodnight (Spaniels)
Every Night (Chantels)
Everyone's Laughing (Spaniels)
Gloria (Cadillacs)
Glory of Love (Velvetones)

    There's a few others, but I can't remember the titles right now, so I'll send some more another time. Just send what you think was around then.
    Well, this is all for now.

Hasta luego,
Salvador Agron
16486

    Recording these songs for Salvador would be a labor of love. This was the music I had been listening to since I was thirteen years old.
    Music born in high school bathrooms where the halls were a haven of echoes. Or in the subways, where the acoustics cried out for a three-part harmony. The music was doo-wop, and if ever there was a music of the streets, this was it. Music that spoke clearly of warm summer nights, slow dances, and teen-age longings.
    Sometimes the music came from small radios, and sometimes from phonographs perched on window sills, but mostly it came from jukeboxes. Filled with records made from vinyl, and shaped on the outside like miniature cathedrals, they spoke to us from a sea of corner candy stores.
    All over Brooklyn, the Bronx, and back again.

    P. S. Please send me some songs by the "Platters."

After leaving the reform school, Salvador returned to Puerto Rico, where he lived with his father for a while. Taken to court after getting into a fight with another boy, he was committed to a school for delinquent boys. La Escuela de Correctional was near Mayaguez, and Esmeralda said he'd only been there three months before getting a furlough to visit his father, who was living nearby. He stayed with his father for a short time, but instead of returning to the school, he left, with his father's assistance, for New York City. He stayed with his mother in Brooklyn before moving on to stay with his sister, who was living at the time in Spanish Harlem. It was October of 1958, several months before Salvador's sixteenth birthday.

When Esmeralda stopped talking, Genoveva turned to whisper that Esmeralda said she liked me, and that she thought my writing a book with Salvador was a good idea.

"She thinks you look a little like Jesus Christ, with your long hair and blue eyes."

Then it was dark and time for us to leave. As we were getting our coats together, Genoveva said Esmeralda would call her daughter so that she and I could visit with her in to gather more family history.

"Buenas noches," Esmeralda said, as she walked us to the door.

"Buenas noches," I answered back, as I shook her hand.

6/5/74
Greenhaven Correctional Facility

Dear Richard:

When I called my mother up last Saturday, she told me about you and Geno visiting at her house. She really loves the both of you. And she said that you and Geno are the best friends I ever had that she knew of (I think she is correct—100%!).

Speaking about my mother, she told me a way out story when she called me on Saturday. She said that one time she went to a seance (a spiritualist gathering) and that she took me with her. She said that a woman, who was possessed by the spirit of another woman from a previous existence, grabbed me and began to shout: "He is mine! He is mine! And I will take him or I will destroy him—send him to prison and pursue him until I take him back and if he cannot be mine, I will destroy him, and inflict sickness upon him." This made me think of a woman that I've been exchanging letters with. Her name is Joyce, and she's an American Indian. My mother is so psychic that when Joyce sent her a big necklace she was tempted to put it on, but she said that something held her back. And, let me tell you, Joyce comes from a family of shamans.

Pretty soon you should be receiving an invitation to attend one of our festivals here at Greenhaven. This one is called "San Juan Bautista," and it honors John the Baptist. It's usually held on the 24th of June in Puerto Rico (and everywhere else, for that matter), but since this is a prison, we can't always get what we want! So it will probably be held on another day. There will be mucha musica and people are going to be together. As of right now, we are still in the planning stages, and please don't forget about sending me the name of a college girl. If you send it soon, I will be able to invite her to the festival!

When you come up for your visit next week, please try to bring me a food package. We are allowed to have up to twenty-five pounds of food sent in every month, and I would appreciate whatever you're able to bring.

Did you speak with Geno about the possibility of having Moms go with you to Puerto Rico to help get information and pictures for the book?

This would be good for everyone.

Tu amigo y hermano
Salvador Agron
#16486

P.S. I gave Joyce your address so you should be hearing from her pretty soon.

Back in the visiting room at Greenhaven after my visit with Esmeralda in the Bronx, I watched as Salvador walked across the room to where I was sitting, a few feet from the four vending machines.

"You ever think of doing something different with your hair?"

"Like what?" he said.

"I dunno...but like maybe you could let it straighten itself out or something."

"I do that and I'll have all kinds of hassles with the police in here...because my hair's so curly, they be after me all the time to get it cut...but this way I ain't gotta worry about them trying to harass me."

"How'd you keep it down like that?"

"Grease, man, lots and lots of hair grease."

"And it keeps it down like that?"

"You'd better believe it."

The grease kept his long hair straight, and seemed to darken it as well. And since he parted it straight down the middle, it not only made him look like an American Indian, but it also increased the contrast between the dark hair and the paleness of his skin. A paleness particular to jailhouses everywhere: an off-white, even lighter than the skin of office workers who spent long hours behind desks, void of sunshine and light.

Salvador had spent endless hours in a cage behind high walls, but looking at his skin, I couldn't help noticing that he's not only pale, but that his skin was peeling in several different places, especially around his nose and across his broad forehead.

"It's from the box."

"Excuse me?"

"My skin...you're looking at my skin peeling, right?"

"Yeah...well, I'm sorry, but it's hard not to look."

"It's from when I was in the box at Attica...I was in the box for so long with no sun or nothing...they was supposed to let me out a little bit each day but sometimes it was days before they'd get around to letting me go outside in the yard for like a half hour at a time."

"Where were you before they sent you up there?"

"Greenhaven...I was right here...and I was doing alright for a while but then things got crazy and they shipped me out..."

"And there wasn't anything specific that you think made them do it?"

"They can do whatever they want in these places and no one's gonna say nothing."

Honorable Walter Dunbar
Executive Deputy Commissioner
Department of Correctional Services
Albany, New York
September 29th, 1972

Re: Salvador Agron#16486

Dear Sir:
Enclosed is a communication submitted by one of our Sergeants at Greenhaven Correctional Facility describing the attempt by the above subject to incite and inflame our inmate population. This incident occurred subsequent to the disturbance which occurred here between the People's Party and Elijah Muhammed factions on September 15th, 1972. Salvador Agron, nicknamed "Capeman," was received at Sing Sing Prison October 6, 1960. He was convicted after a jury verdict for the crime of murder 1st degree on two counts and attempted murder 2nd degree 12-25 (consecutively). An execution was scheduled for the week of November 21, 1960, and Governor Rockefeller eventually commuted the sentence to life imprisonment.

It is noted that the instant offense for which Agron was initially sentenced for execution was a sadistic and vicious murder, and that the crime received much publicity within both

New York City newspapers and other prominent publications. Subject was designated as a "sensitive case" by the New York State Division of Parole.

This man has made a rather poor institutional adjustment during the years of his incarceration and has compiled a total of 19 disciplinary reports, including three relatively serious reports which have occurred during the current calendar year.

Inasmuch as Salvador Agron is now attempting to function in a disruptive manner by means of inciting our inmate population, it is felt that he could, at this point, eventually be considered for treatment within a RX facilities. As an interim measure, it is accordingly suggested that he now be transferred to Attica Correctional Facility in order that our inmate population may not be subjected to this man's constant revolutionary invective.

      Very truly yours,

      Leon Vincent
      Warden
      Greenhaven Correctional Facility

October 14th, 1972

Hon. Russell Oswald
Commissioner of Correctional Services
Department of Correctional Services

Sir:

I have been kidnapped from Greenhaven Correctional Facility by some of your pigs and brought chained from hand to feet to Attica Concentration Camp.

I never actually believed there was such a hell hole as Attica dungeon. Of course, being that you are the head pig of the Department of Corruption, I am writing to you.

The shit that goes on in here is for the purpose of dehumanizing prisoners. Attica has a bullshit program and the rules are so idiotic that I will not follow them. I would rather be dead than have to put up with this kind of bullshit.

I am presently in the "box" (HBZ) and being subjected to harassment and pig abuse.
Send me anywhere, but I will not tolerate this bullshit.
I am a human being, and I will not be humiliated.

Very truly yours,
Salvador Agron

The officials at Attica called the box "HBZ," or "Special Housing," while at some of the other maximum-security prisons, they called it "Administrative Segregation," or "Protective Custody," but to all the convicts it was always "the box," and nothing but the box, and all the fancy sounding names in the world could not begin to camouflage what in the end was always the same: many days of endless regularity in a small, six-by-nine windowless cell, that was usually cold in the winter and warm in the summer, with nothing to look forward to but meals and yard time. But as Salvador said, this was not always provided and whether or not it was would often depend on the whim of the guard in charge on a particular day. Even then, it was generally for only half an hour, sometimes less, and it usually took place in an area just like his cell, except that instead of inside, it was outside.

Attica Correctional Facility
Attica, New York
November 22nd, 1972

Russell Oswald
Commissioner of Correctional Services
Dear Commissioner:

I was surprised to receive your letter asking for my comments on T-28298 Salvador Agron's note to you.
I am sure you are aware of the reasons for Agron's transfer here from Greenhaven. Commissioner Quick has been

informed of the agitation and militant actions and writings of this inmate while confined here. Reports have been submitted as to the reason for his confinement in H.B.Z. All necessary actions have been held in his case and as he says, I have no objection to his transfer elsewhere. In fact, I would be very pleased to have someone else accept the responsibility for his confinement.

Very truly yours,
Ernest Montanye
Warden

Radios were not allowed in the box, but you could have reading and writing materials, provided of course that you had someone on the outside willing to send you some books, writing paper, and pens. Otherwise, you went without, and all you had was, as the convicts would say, "three hots and a cot."

"What were you in the box for?"

"All kinds of shit...but mostly for agitating and litigating...political stuff, like I put up a sign in the yard asking that people go out on strike so they could finish up the job they'd started during the riots."

"And you just put this sign up right in front of the guards...I mean, like couldn't you have put it up so no one would've known it was you?"

"What kinda sense would that've made?"

A Challenge to Attica Prisoners
   (read this and pass it on)
   Let us continue to strike for more liberal prison attitudes, for the right to organize; for the right to uncensored outgoing mail, for the right to correspond with anybody we want. For the right to have all incoming mail only inspected but not censored. For the right to travel unescorted from one yard to the

other, to the mess hall and to the auditorium. For earned good time, for a maximum of ten years for lifers—Strike! Strike! Seize the times! Don't let the death of our brothers in D-Yard be a vain death! Stop all work! Sabotage the shops!

Deal with the issues now!

Don't walk in twos. Don't march. Be a man! Don't take any shit from the pigs. Speak up!

Long live the 9th of September, 1971!

We must not rest until we get all 28 demands that we asked for during the Attica rebellion.

If we don't change this, then it will change us into robots! Let's finish what the Attica brothers started in 1972!

Salvador Agron (Minister of Propaganda)
#16846

"Was it clean in the box?"

No sooner were the words out of my mouth than I knew by the expression on his face that he'd been completely taken aback by what I'd said. Cleanliness was the very antithesis of why the box had been built in the first place: to create a group of solitary cells for those who had broken the rules, and then to organize this area by giving it an official designation, like "HBZ" at Attica, or "Administrative Segregation" somewhere else, with no thought or regard for cleanliness or comfort.

This was because meals in the HBZ precluded observance of a very basic axiom: don't shit where you eat. Instead of walking to a common cafeteria, and eating their meals with the rest of the prison population, inmates in the HBZ were served on plastic trays by an inmate pushing a wagon loaded with trays from cell to cell. Each convict was given a tray, which was slid through a slot beneath the door of the cell. And since the cells were so small, the convict would either sit on the toilet with the tray on the bed, or sit on the bed with the tray on the toilet. When he was finished, he'd slide the tray back through the same slot beneath the door. The left-over food would fall from the tray, and the wagon dropped crumbs as it picked up more trays of leftover food from the other cells. After every meal there were bits and pieces of food up and down the tiers of the HBZ. The type and amount of vermin varied from prison to prison, and from box to box.

Every maximum-security prison in New York State has its own personality, along with its own rules, but the older the prison, the less sanitary it is.

Sing Sing prison is one of the oldest in New York State, with some of its buildings dating back to the late 1800's. It also has a large population of rodents. More than one convict has complained of being bitten by rats leaping from the depths of toilet bowls late at night. But at the same time, Sing Sing has dozens of tom cats who freely roam the prison yards day and night. Some are the pets of convicts, and are fed by them, though most belong to the prison proper and are tolerated by the guards because of their ability to keep the rats at bay. Although the vermin is somewhat contained at Sing Sing the plumbing is old and rusting. So much so that waste water frequently backs up in the cells, leaving behind a terrible smell. In the HBZ, it's usually damp, and the heating is poor, and this is especially true during the winter months because of its close proximity to the Hudson River, with its dark waters and violent winds.

Comstock Prison, built in the 1940's, and located in the heart of the Adirondack Mountains, doesn't have any rats. Instead, it has many generations of mice. The convicts say that the way the mice move together down the tiers of the HBZ, in and out of the cells at night sounds like the high piercing wail of a police siren, heard from a faraway distance.

Salvador said he saw rats in the death house, when he was at Sing Sing, but in the HBZ at Attica it wasn't mice, or rats, but roaches. Hundreds and hundreds of roaches. Sometimes they would fall on his face as he was sleeping.

Once he even woke up with a few in his mouth.

"Didn't you complain when that happened?"

"Yeah, but then they'd send around an exterminator and the spray they used was even worse than having the roaches in the cell, it smelled so bad."

Attica, built in the 1930's, had bad ventilation, or so Salvador and the other men in the HBZ were always told whenever they'd complain about the lack of heat. So cold, he said, that he usually slept with all his clothes on.

"And you were transferred back here in January?"

"January the 11th."

"So you were in Attica for over two years, right?"

"And most of it was spent in the box."

December 29, 1972
Russell Oswald
Commissioner of Correctional Services

Sir:

Again, I take pen in hand to express my problem with Attica Prison. I will not write again. I am tired, sick and tired of the administrative abuse on me.

On October 5th, 1972, I was brought here to Attica from Greenhaven Prison without any good reason. While at Attica, I was taken out of my cell, pushed and kicked against a wall, searched, handcuffed, and taken by force to the box (HBZ). I was then placed under protective custody against my objections. I was told that I had subversive literature in my cell and that I presented a danger to the safety of the institution. I was told that I am not wanted in this institution. They took all my writings, poems, political research, and a 300 page document that I had put together abut the "Boricua Nation," meaning the history of Puerto Rico.

I want my writings back. I don't give a hell if you or the institution want to take photostatic copies of it—just return my writings—all of them. I don't care what you know about me or my ideas. I have nothing to hide.

> *Again, I request that you do something about transferring me out of here. My life is in danger. I have been threatened with death by Sergeant Filmore while he was sitting on the Adjustment Committee.. He told me that he had "a good cemetery out in back of Attica for me."*
>
> *I want you to intervene in these threats.*
>
> *Respectfully,*
> *Salvador Agron*
> *# 28298   HBZ*

"So how did you finally get them to send you back here?"
"Agitation and litigation."
"I'm not sure I know what you mean."
"Agitating...you know, like writing letters to newspapers about bad prison conditions, or like all those letters I told you about that I sent to the warden...and then doing some litigating by getting writs against the fuckers whenever I could, like against the warden, maybe, or the Commissioner... so after awhile I think they got so sick of me they would've sent me to another country if I'd of asked them to!"

To: Commissioner Oswald
From: Manuel T. Mureia
Re: Salvador Agron # 28298 Attica Correctional Facility
January 22nd, 1973

In view of this inmate's litigious history, it behooves you to take some action with respect to his complaint. He is setting up the props preliminary to filing a Civil Rights action in the Federal Courts, naming you as a defendant. While a reply to him is not warranted, I certainly urge you to have someone look into these charges in the event that they prove to be true. If such were the case, you have been put on notice of the existence of the inmate's civil rights violation and would be held personally responsible.

This inmate is cute; he is baiting the hook, hoping to catch the big fish.

I recommend that an investigation be made of those allegations and reports submitted to you in writing!

June 1, 1973
Peter Preiser
Commissioner of Corrections
Department of Correctional Services

Dear Mr. Preiser:

If you mean good, welcome to the "Department." But, if you don't mean any good, then you can go to hell. As for former Commissioner Oswald, he was full of shit. As for you, I don't have enough data on you to make any rational judgment. Actions speak louder than words and if you act like you speak (I have read some of your views in the newspaper) then we are in for a progressive penal movement.

My name is Salvador Agron, and my position among inmates is recognized as the Minister of Propaganda for the Borricua Revolutionary Nationalist Party of the Socialist Republic of Borriquen. I also function in the position of Representative of the Latino Cadre (first organized in Greenhaven) for the Latino Revolutionary Party. You may be shocked at my outspoken attitude, but don't let it worry you because I am a sincere young man who operates, educates, agitates, and litigates in the open. This is why I will never be a threat to your prisons.

We do not want to literally destroy your prisons. No! We only want to re-structure them. But, if change does not come, then you can expect to see the Attica rebellion repeat itself, over and over again.

Prisons must change because otherwise they will not be able to contain the revolutionary ideology which grows from oppression and repression.

Very truly yours,
Salvador Agron   #28296
Attica Correctional Facility

"So you were in the box when you first wrote to me?"

"By the time you wrote it was almost a year."

"What'd you do in there all day?"

"I just told you..."

"Yeah, I know...you said you agitated and litigated, but like what else did you do?"

"Lots of jerking off...I never knew I could do it so much until I was in the box."

"Yeah...right..."

"Hey...I'm serious!" he said.

"Okay...I can dig that...but I was wondering if you had any people in there you could trust...so you could maybe talk about some of the stuff."

"About jerking off!?"

"Come on...you know what I'm talking about...like how you were being treated and stuff...wasn't there anyone you could talk to?"

"You mean convicts?" he asked.

"No...I mean I was wondering if there wasn't anyone who was official who you could maybe relate to on some level..."

"Like one of the fucking pigs?"

"No...no...I was thinking like there was maybe a social worker or someone like that..."

"The only one who even came close was Reverend Ed. But he never came to visit me when I was in Attica...we just wrote each other letters."

"Who's he?"

"He's the chaplain here...didn't I tell you about him?"

"Is he the one who does those cadre meetings?"

"That's the guy."

The "Reverend" was Ed Muller, the Protestant minister at Greenhaven. He had been a pastor to community churches in New Jersey for nine years before entering the prison system as a chaplain.

In the beginning, things had not gone well, with all kinds of prohibitions, not the least of which had been the unwritten convict code. A code that seemed to guarantee that whatever Reverend Muller said, preached, or wrote, would not be taken seriously by the convicts who made up his ministry. Was he not an instrument of the state? And didn't his paycheck arrive every two weeks with the seal of New York written across the top?

Years would go by before he was able to earn the trust of his ministry, but as he gained the trust of the inmates, he seemed to lose the respect of the administration, most of whom felt that he was far too progressive, radical even, in terms of how he dealt with a group of people who deserved little in the way of compassion, hope, or trust.

The cadre meetings were a good example of how Ed Muller was able to operate within the system at Greenhaven. In reality, they were more like classes, but were called meetings because meetings meant a group of people who got together to give power to each other by sharing a part of themselves with someone else. Sometimes the cadre meetings would concentrate on just one person, and everyone in the group might examine a piece of that person's life. At other times, the meetings would involve a particular theme, with the evening revolving around a study paper.

September 22nd, 1973
Attica Correctional Facility

Dear Rev. Ed:

I received your letter of September 5th on the 7th. I know you haven't forgotten me just because you did not write in sometime. I have asked to go back to Greenhaven (even if I got to be in a cell all day) but it looks like Warden Vincent thinks I'm a "troublemaker." But it is only because I hold political opinions which he thinks (wrongfully of course) are detrimental to the peace and security of Greenhaven Prison! Please rap to him and see if he is willing to accept me. Up here at

Attica I have been in the box (Segregation Unit) ever since I left Greenhaven. The Warden here is Smith. He just took office after having been the Deputy Superintendent. He thinks that I am a so-called "threat to the security of Attica." It seems that I have become "the stone that the builders rejected"—a flesh and blood stumbling block!!

Please try to get me a transfer back to Greenhaven. I would prefer to be closer to New York City. I have told my family not to come up to Attica because it costs too much money, so I would appreciate a recommendation from you on my behalf. I will not promise you that I will be a good "niggerrican" or that I will become a "houseboy" because that would be contrary to my nature—I have been a "field-boy" too long!! But I will try to follow a more constructive path!

I don't know how you can be around a place where the summer has been so quiet—I think that a little agitation is in store for you at Greenhaven. Well, let's hope so—there I go again! Well, some people are just downright proud to be "social agitators." Don't you think so?

So, the lumpens—or unemployable—are returning on parole violation. We cannot expect any less from a society that has not yet learned to cope with its economical crisis, Watergates, etc When the working people in this country take over the means of production from the Bourgeoisie then you will not see so many returning to the prisons!! All will have the necessities of life: food, clothing, shelter, education and free medical care because everyone will have become a proletariat.

Well, I am still catching hell, but I have an iron fist and I will see this through to the end. Give my greetings to the people.

Hasta La Victoria Siempre!

Salvador Agron
#28298

Before being sent to Attica, Salvador had attended the cadre meetings every Friday night, in a basement room at Greenhaven.

"You think maybe you could come up for some of the cadre meetings?"

"Yeah...maybe...I dunno." I said.

"It'll give us a chance to meet somewhere besides the visiting room and I could pass stuff to you for the book...and you could come up with some of the other people who go to the meetings."

"People from the city?"

"There's one or two, I think, but I can find out from Ed if there's maybe someone you could ride up with. You think you could do this?"

"I'll have to see...but I'm open to it."

"Has Joyce written to you yet?" he asked.

"Just a few letters..."

"She's some hot stuff...lemme tell you...one of the first things I sent her was a picture of my cock..."

"What!?"

"My cock...I mean, I didn't take a picture of it but I did send like an outline...I put it up against a piece of paper and outlined it with a pencil and then I sent it along with a letter."

"And the guards didn't say nothin'?"

"Not to me they didn't," he said, "maybe to each other they did some talkin'...but nothin' to me."

Whether or not she had liked it was anyone's guess. All I knew was what she had told me in her first letter. That she lived with her family on a reservation, or a reserve, in British Columbia, and her Indian name was "Wah-Zi-Nak." She was writing to me because Salvador thought it would be a good idea for her to be corresponding with one of his friends on the outside. This was important, he wrote, because of the book we were writing together.

Salvador said she had written to him in response to a short article he had written for an American Indian newspaper, when he was in the box at Attica.

"Just don't mention nothing to her about the festival...

we'll just keep this between you and me, right?"

"What festival?"

"Didn't you get an invitation?" he asked.

"Was that the one for San Juan Bautista Day?"

"That's the one, and you're gonna come, right?"

"Is it on a weekend? Because if it isn't, I can't go."

"It's on a Sunday..."

"Then I can make it." I told him.

"And you're gonna bring me a college girl?"

"Well...there's someone from one of my classes who says she wants to go."

"What's she look like?"

"Aren't you and Wah-Zi-Nak going together?"

"Yeah...but like what's that go to do with anything?"

"What'd you need more than one woman for?"

"We're just writing to each other, nothing else," he said.

"Yeah, but like she's still your girlfriend, right?"

"I can't fuck her through the mail!"

"And you think you could do this with someone at one of the festivals?"

"Just gimme a chance! Hey...what's this woman's name?"

"Rachel...her name's Rachel."

Chapter Three

SAN JUAN BAUTISTA

Like the relaxed visiting room restrictions, the prison festivals were yet another attempt to make prison life slightly more humane for the convicts, as well as for their visitors. Each ethnic or religious group, and there were many in the prisons, from Puerto Ricans wanting to celebrate San Juan Bautista Day to Sunni Muslims inviting outsiders to visit their prison mosques, would be allowed to have a day set aside in order to celebrate a particular culture, or religious belief, complete with ethnic food, music, and whatever. The Puerto Ricans could have rice, beans, and fried bananas, the Italians could have pasta, sauce, and veal, and the Black convicts could have soul food. As long as the convicts paid for the food, they could, within reason, serve up whatever it was they wanted to eat.

Whether or not the prison people could have foreseen the possible security problems with such events is hard to say, but for many of the convicts and their visitors, the festivals were like nothing they could possibly have imagined. At Greenhaven, the events were held on Fay Field, a vast stretch of grass which, although still on the prison grounds, and surrounded by thirty foot walls and gun towers, was large enough that it could easily accommodate all kinds of nefarious goings on. Beneath the many picnic tables couples could hug, kiss, and even copulate, if they were careful.

And visitors could could leave with all manner of things, including the selected writings of Salvador Agron.

SAN JUAN BAUTISTA DAY LATIN COMMITTEE
GREENHAVEN CORRECTIONAL FACILITY
STORMVILLE, NEW YORK

June 12th, 1974
Dear Friend(s)

The Spanish residents of Greenhaven Correctional Facility would like to cordially invite you to attend our first celebration of San Juan Bautista Day.

This day has been set aside for the Latin population of this facility from the hours of 11:00 A.M. until 3:00 P.M. All visitors will enter through the rear gate, and after being processed will be escorted to Fay Field for the celebration.

We will be honored by your presence at this event, and it will be appreciated by everyone in the community.

Hoping to see you soon.
Sincerely yours,
Salvador Agron   #16846   Inmate Coordinator
San Juan Bautista Day Committee
Greenhaven Correctional Facility

Looking at the ruins of Brooklyn through one of the many windows of a Manhattan-bound "D" train, on an early Sunday morning, I thought about San Juan Bautista, or Saint John the Baptist, and the custom practiced all over Puerto Rico which dictates that virtually everyone will avoid swimming in the ocean during any month that has an ' r' in it. No one knows for sure exactly how or why this superstition came to be, only that for many people, their first visit to the beach at the start of a new year always took place on San Juan Bautista Day. Legend further has it that if you took a dip in the ocean at the very stroke of midnight on the eve of San Juan Bautista it would mean good luck for you in the coming year.

Salvador was not only a member of the San Juan Bautista Day Committee at Greenhaven, he was also one of its principal coordinators. This meant that he was the official liaison between the Latin Community and the prison administration. One of his tasks was to insure that San Juan Bautista Day was on the "approved festival list." This wasn't really a list, but simply what the convicts knew would, or would not, be approved as a day to set aside for a particular festival.

Six hundred people, including convicts, guards, prison administrators, and outside visitors were expected to attend the festival.

Salvador and his committee members were responsible for making sure that arrangements to bring in Puerto Rican musical groups from the Latin community in New York City. They were also responsible for making sure everyone would have enough to eat, but not just any old food. This was a special day, and it demanded special food. Everything from appetizers to main dishes, followed by one or more desserts. If arrangements were made well in advance of an actual festival, then outsiders were allowed to bring in dishes from home. But most people avoided this because of the extra hassles it meant when they had to present the outside food to one of the Correctional Officers. Bad enough having to endure being "processed" into the prison without having to spend additional time waiting to have your food inspected. The alternative was that food would be provided by the convict coordinators, with the money taken either from inmate commissary funds, or from funds sent in ahead of time by friends or relatives.

The convicts would supply the food, and the prison people would supply the cooking and storage space in the convict mess hall for the actual preparation, as well as supplying paper goods, plastic utensils, and table coverings.

But beyond the music, the many muchachas, and the fried bananas, one thing, Salvador said, remained perfectly clear. San Juan Bautista Day was a political event.

> *Greenhaven Correctional Facility*
> *Dear Richard:*
>
> *Well, everything is in place for "La Fiesta," but this is the last time I will ever be the coordinator. Being the head honcho for something like this is just too much work, and I have better things to do with my time than to keep watch over a bunch of malcontents. Because in the end, I always have to do much of the work myself! Convicts are a funny class of people. And take it from me, I know what I'm talking about.*
>
> *Just remember that San Juan Bautista is a political day!*
>
> *On October 12, 1492, man named Admiral Cristobal Colon arrived in the area that today we call the Caribbean. The man was from Spain, and he was on a mission of exploration, or "intrusion." And in honor of the prince Don Juan, son of the Catholic Kings, Colon imposed upon the islands the name of San Juan Bautista (Saint John the Baptist), and thus began the skypilot program that was being planned by the so-called "Christianity" under the Catholic Church or Fascist regime. And even though you won't find this in most history books, it's still the gospel truth!*
>
> *I'll see you on Sunday for the festival.*
>
> *Tu amigo y hermano,*
> *Salvador Agron   #16846*

Rachel said she would see me at the festival but no, she wasn't interested in riding along with me on the Sunni Muslim's bus. Too early in the morning, she said, for her to be riding on a subway to Harlem. Besides, she had already made plans with Maria Gonzalez to ride up with her. Why didn't I ride along with them? Wouldn't it be nicer to ride up in a car instead of a chartered bus? Much nicer, I told her, but the Muslims had already reserved a place for me, and not showing up would be taken as a sign of disrespect. The reality was that the Muslims couldn't have cared less if I showed up in Harlem to ride with them to the prison on their chartered bus. But for me, almost anything would have been preferable to spending a few hours in a locked car with Maria Gonzalez.

She was a friend of Rachel's, and we had been introduced one evening when I was having coffee with Rachel in the college cafeteria. Born and raised in a middle-class home, Maria had become a "movement," or political person in her senior year in high school after taking part in an antiwar demonstration on a cold day in December with several thousand other people in midtown Manhattan. The passion of the parade was so powerful, she said, that it had instilled in her an overwhelming need to raise her voice against oppression, and especially against what she said was the "white society" whom she blamed for most of society's ills. That Rachel and I were part of this white society didn't seem to matter much to Maria. Either she was color-blind or, and this was the most logical explanation, race had nothing to do with why she was a "movement" person in the first place. Maria had a relentless need to distance herself from what she felt was the "comfort" that her Puerto Rican parents had provided her with over the years. She wanted to become, in Salvador's words, a *lumpen,* or working-class person. Rachel told me that she had even overheard Maria telling another friend of ours that she came from a family who lived in a Bronx barrio, instead of from a middle-class enclave in Flatbush.

For a while she had even tried to live the life of a radical by shacking up with several other movement people in a cold-water flat not far from where Genoveva was living on the Lower East Side. Genoveva had met her at a renter's strike, but had quickly dismissed her for being what she said was nothing more than a slumming member of the bourgeoisie.

> June 19th, 1974
> Greenhaven Correctional Facility
>
> Dear Brother Little Richard:
> How are you? I received all your letters, and I'm looking forward to seeing you for San Juan Bautista.
> I don't think too much of the New York Left. I think that most of them are full of shit!! A lot of rhetoric and no positive moves. They will protest for another thousand years, and they will scream and scream, with "Right on," "Power to the People," "Free so and so," and, it all boils down to an old civil rights song of We Shall Overcome!!
> In the meantime, babies are dying, people are crying, roaches are multiplying, and martyrs are expiring amidst a pool of blood. These people will get you killed so that they can get a thrill! I see this shit go on everyday—table revolutionaries discussing how a man should eat, what he should wear, and how he should think. Computerized revolutionaries quoting Marx as though it were a religion, determining how people should live and how people should die!
> Petty-bourgeois motherfuckers that could not even fight themselves out of a one way back alley—tremblers who tremble when a black cat crosses their path on a ghetto street because they believe in some taboo about bad luck. They are less conscious than lumpen prisoners. There are only a few guys in here that are worth doing something for. I treasure these people who are a few and it is due to this that I am able to maintain my dignity and sanity in these prisons!
> Well, this is all for now. Vaya con dios!
>
> Con Mucho carino de amor
> Tu amigo y hermano

Despite all the talking she did, Maria never once mentioned something we had only recently found out about her private life. That for the last year she had been writing to a guy at Greenhaven, who was on the Latin Committee with Salvador for San Juan Bautista Day. He had even invited her to be his guest at the festival. They'd been writing to one another for nearly a year, but had never met. This would be their first time together, under circumstances far more lenient than in the prison visiting room.

It seemed like a remarkable coincidence, but the more contact I had with movement people, the more commonality I was finding between many of the radical groups on the outside and those on the inside.

6/17/74
Greenhaven Correctional Facility

Dear Geno:

> Revolutionary greetings!
> I am a little perplexed with some of the Puerto Ricans in this prison.
> Sometimes helping the people or serving them makes one also angry at them. Sometimes I think there is no hope. I get depressed at the whole struggle and it makes me sick to look around and see how idiotic people act or react at certain things. People out there may think there are conscious brothers in these prisons but that's bullshit. The majority of people in here are more like Nixon and company than people would imagine. There is only a very small section of brothers here that are together for when they get out. I would say that 90% of them are more of a detriment than of helping. That there is hope, I have no doubt, but it seems to me that the bourgeoisie is constantly recruiting from these prisons while the movement people sit on their ass and say "right on." You are the only positive element that I have met in the struggle. Sometimes I think that I am the only one left in the whole struggle! Maybe

it is all the anger and hate in me or perhaps my humanity getting the best of me. Even within the cadre I find negative elements, colonial cowards and docile Puerto Ricans, they sap all the energy out of me at times. There are many hypocrites in this place. People that put up fronts and have no sense of political consciousness whatsoever. Sometimes I think that due to my insight into human nature, I am at times the most miserable man on earth. Perhaps this is why I sound so confused at times in my letters or contradictory, after living around these convicts for fifteen years I should be raving mad or insane. The only thing that has kept me going for so long is my sense of humanity and my sense of brotherhood with all the Puerto Ricans here and my affinity for all the Puerto Ricans throughout the world.

*Hasta La Victoria Siempre
Tu Hermano/companero
Salvador Agron   #16486*

After Attica many convicts were in touch with a wide variety of diverse radical groups. Some groups were purely political, and would support prisoner demonstrations whenever they occurred with financial or moral support. Other groups would support the prisoner movement with pro bono legal assistance, provided by a network of movement lawyers who would not hesitate to bring litigation against the prisons whenever an abuse was alleged. This included the practice of confining people for long periods of time in the box, without formally charging them with anything, while limiting visiting and correspondence. Salvador was in touch with many of these organizations, and he had already told me that without their support, things might have gone much worse for him. Like my death row work, when he was in the box at Attica, the contact he had with these outside resources let the prison people know, that he wasn't, in his terms, "a poor, little spic without a pot to piss in."

June 19th, 1974
Greenhaven Correctional Facility

Dear Geno:

I was thinking about you and wondering if I came down too heavy about things in my last letter because I did not get a prompt answer.

But then your letter arrived. I used to write a Chicana sister before from the United Farm Workers but we could not communicate because she was hung up on a Jesus trip. I wrote her a letter and then when she didn't reply, I took this to mean no more communication and I stopped writing to her. I hope she got her head together. I don't know exactly why I'm running this on you, but I just thought I'll let you know.

There's not much good I have to say about any prison (whether in a Capitalist society or in a "socialist" country). Prisons are but a demonstration that we are not yet fully civilized on a whole. However, it is a hell of a problem. If abolishing completely these prisons were the answer it would be easier to decide what to do. I do not have a complete answer myself about prisons, and I've been in these houses of horror for 15 years straight.

If I should say certain things at times that don't sound very good, please try to understand that I am a bitter man. I have lots of anger, but at the same time, I try to keep my cool. Why should I blow my mind? It makes no sense. I am a victim but I try my best not to victimize other people.

Take it easy, hermana, and we will talk more at San Juan Bautista Day.

Your brother and comrade,
Salvador Agron #16486

Aside from the political groups, Salvador was also in touch with a wide variety of women from all over the United States. Some had written because they remembered his case. Others he had met through friends, like me introducing him to Rachel, or through one of the radical groups he was in touch with. Some women had sent him money, some had sent books, while still others had sent him their hearts.

June 19th, 1974
Greenhaven Correctional Facility

Dear Richard:
　I just wanted to let you know that I received your letter, along with the stamps. Muchas Gracias!
　Along with your letter, I just received a letter from an old "soul relationship" that I had quite some time ago. She has been writing to me over the years. She is about my age now, and it seems that she always finds me, no matter what prison I'm in! She's from Wisconsin. Last time I wrote to her was about three years ago and last year she sent me a Christmas card. Last time we wrote each other she was marrying a dentist. She's okay. One of those middle-class Anglo women who are lonely or want to get fucked by someone they like, but who are afraid to say so! They usually just say, "Oh, Sal, if you need anything just let me know—anything—you know there is nothing I wouldn't do for you." Someday we'll go through my mail together and hit the road, stopping in every state. If Wah-Zi-Nak heard that she'd take my scalp! She is special—she is one. There are certain things she needs to learn and then she would be the ideal female. I think she'll be my best cultivation. Well, "lion-hearted," I got to get me some sleep. So take it easy until next time.

Love always,
Salvador Agron
#16486

　　Maria was writing to a man named Roberto Torres. Salvador thought he was in for an armed robbery, but since convict courtesy precludes one convict not asking another what they were in prison for, Salvador wasn't sure if it was an armed robbery, a murder, a burglary, or even a rape. One convict usually knew how much time another convict was doing, but since prison tended to distort unpleasant memories, the majority of convicts were usually vague about the circumstances that had brought them to prison in the first place.

> June 22nd, 1974
> Greenhaven Correctional Facility
> Dear Richard:
>
> *Well, I will try to fix the typewriter you sent, but I don't know if I can do this or not. If I cannot get it back in working order, I'll leave it for you when you come for your next visit. Maybe you can have it fixed for me.*
> *Wah-Zi-Nak wrote and said that you had phoned. Good. She's alright now. Sometimes she gives me headaches. Women are a pain in the ass at times!*
> *Well, I'll see you this coming Sunday for San Juan Bautista—and try to get permission to bring your camera. You may have to call Albany. Also, tell Genoveva to send the names of the instruments that the Group, Los Hermanos are going to use that permission can be gotten to let them come in, that is, the instruments. Okay?*
> *Well, take it easy, my friend, and this Sunday you will eat food that I have prepared especially with you in mind!*
>
> Your friend,
> Salvador Agron
> #16846

Whatever the season, Maria always dressed the same. She refused to wear, she said, feminine garments designed solely to attract members of the opposite sex.

She wore a long, brown, surplus Army coat, with matching pants, and a pair of high-backed combat boots. Shapeless, boring, and drab, this had the desired effect. Most men never gave her more than just a passing glance.

As the train moved across Brooklyn, I wondered what Rachel would be wearing to the festival, and whether anything I said to her on the telephone the other night would influence her decision. Rachel was about my height, with wavy chestnut-colored hair cascading down her back, and legs, that seemed to go on forever. Salvador had asked if she had a big nose, and yes, her nose was big. So big that it dominated her entire face, but her eyes were blue, her skin was clear, and when you looked at the way she walked, without even a hint of self-consciousness, the length of her nose made no difference whatsoever.

"You're gonna have to be careful about what you wear to these kinds of things."

"Careful about what?" she asked.

"I don't know....I mean, you know, the way you're gonna dress and everything."

"Do I have to wear a dress?"

"No...no, that's not what I meant...it's just that these guys haven't been around women too much and so like maybe you've gotta dress down a bit, you know what I mean?"

"Uh...like not wear too much lipstick?"

"Yeah...that's right...and maybe nothing too tight, okay?"

"I never wear anything that's too tight!"

"I'm not sayin' you do," I told her, "I'm just sayin' it wouldn't be a good idea if you did this for one of these festivals, that's all."

"I'll see what I can do."

Part of me hoped that whatever she "could do" would play down her legs as much as possible. Another part of me hoped she would look as provocative as a call-girl on Times Square. This would make Salvador happy, and in the long run would be very productive in terms of the book we were writing. After all, if his basic needs were met, would he not be inclined to write more prolifically? Salvador had said, "Just gimme a chance," when I'd last seen him in the visiting room, and we'd been talking about my bringing him "a nice college girl" to the festival. So maybe it would be better if she did dress a certain way, and if this in turn were to make him horny enough so that "just gimme a chance" could become a reality. But how would he do this? Greenhaven was a maximum-security prison, with high walls, and men with guns watching every move. Was a festival any different?

Over and over these thoughts went through my mind like a vacuum cleaner in a dirty room. All I really wanted was to write a book with him, yet here I was playing the part of a pimp, or so it felt, and this even though Rachel was more than willing to play her part. Hadn't she written to Salvador of her own free will? And hadn't she accepted his invitation to the festival without my encouragement? I was determined to make sure Salvador continued to work with me on the book. And if this meant supplying him with one or more "nice college girls," then so be it.

6/23/74
Greenhaven Correctional Facility
Dear Richard:

The typewriter is now in perfect health, and it is functioning normally. I have some other very important correspondence to get off, so I will delay working on the book for awhile.

I hope you like the title for the book, "Yesterday, today, and Tomorrow."

I will try to keep copies of whatever I send you. This way we won't have to be too concerned if something gets lost at the post office.

Please send the names and addresses of some more col-

lege girls when you get the chance. This is not only for myself, but also for some good Puerto Rican brothers in here that are in need of female energies.

I will pick out good brothers with good consciousness, and I will set them up with whoever you send. I've already hooked up about five brothers and sisters.

Your question: "Tell me something about Puerto Rican food. Is it healthy?" is an interesting one. Well, our diet is a mixture of many cultures, and it draws very heavily on Spanish, native Caribbean and African influences. Is it healthy? Well, it does emphasize lots of fruits and vegetables, but at the same time it does have lots of beef and pork. The basic dish, however, is rice, and rice in all its many variations: white, yellow, etc., and it's usually cooked with beans. What else can I say except that all our food is cooked with sensuality in mind! And this I can guarantee!

Try to send me a map of the stars. I would like to put it on the ceiling of my cell, so at night I can roam the universe.

Your brother,
Salvador Agron
#16846

In the nearly eight months that he and I had been working on the book, I had already edited all the death row material, and had also finished editing a vast quantity of additional material that he'd written about his early life in Puerto Rico. He had also written a foreword, or introduction, and like all his other writing, it had a quality of clarity that I found astonishing for someone who had not been trained as a writer. But of course, this was the reason he wrote as well as he did. Having never been taught the "proper" way to write, he brought to his work an utter lack of self-consciousness.

When the train pulled into Atlantic Avenue, I thought of how Salvador's story had more or less started just a few blocks from where I was sitting in the subway train. To scores of young people who had grown up with the gangs in the New York of the 1950's, "Atlantic Avenue," was more than simply a designation on a subway line. For the gangbangers, the armed robbers, and other assorted homeboys, "Atlantic Avenue" was the Brooklyn House of Detention for Men on Atlantic Avenue. A holding jail for adolescents. A place to be held pending release on bail, a not guilty verdict, or a transfer to an upstate reform school. A jail for young boys, and Salvador's home away from home for the duration of his trial.

> That morning, I put on my brown suit at the Brooklyn House of Detention on Atlantic Avenue, shook hands, and said goodbye to all my boys: the Mau Mau Chaplains, the Chaplains, the Phantom Lords, and the Heart Kings, gangs from Brooklyn and Manhattan. Since they were people I knew for years, it was a warm departure. Some even had hopes of seeing me again because they thought the judge, who was known as the "Sweetheart of Manhattan," might give me a break. I knew better. I didn't have a chance.
> Chained and shackled to my crime partner, Antonio Hernandez, the "Umbrella Man," we were placed in a paddy wagon for the trip to Court.
> Down Atlantic Avenue, the paddy wagon crossed the bridge into Manhattan.

Crossing the bridge into Manhattan, I looked out the window at the winding Brooklyn waterfront. Long ago, Salvador had lived with his mother, sister, and step-father in an apartment above a church on Hudson Street, just a few miles away. The church was a storefront, Pentecostal affair, and Carlos, Salvador's step-father at the time, was its pastor. This was in the late 1950's, maybe 1957, just two years before the killings in the playground.

Esmeralda told us that she and her daughter had lived

from furnished room to furnished room when they first arrived in New York in 1951 before settling into a fifth floor walk-up apartment in lower Manhattan. She had left Salvador behind with the nuns at the poorhouse, and when they had finally established themselves in this new apartment, she had sent for him. I remembered her telling me that she had forgotten what time his plane was supposed to land at LaGuardia and that Salvador had been all alone, for hours, until she was able to get a ride from a neighbor so that she could pick him up at the airport. But how long he had stayed in this Manhattan apartment before moving to the apartment above the church was unclear.

Suddenly the train was dark, and looking out the window I saw that we'd crossed the bridge into Manhattan. The first stop was Canal Street, just a few blocks from Centre Street, the Manhattan House of Detention for Men, and the Supreme Court of the State of New York.

> It was October 6, 1960 in the Court of General Sessions, on Centre Street, now known as the Supreme Court of the State of New York. Before going to court, I had the privilege of meeting New York City Corrections Commissioner Anna Kross and Fini Rincon, sister of Felisa Rincon, Mayor of San Juan, Puerto Rico. They were shocked at the verdict the jury brought in against me and Antonio Hernandez.
>
> My gang-fighting days were at an end, and Society with a capital "S" was going to make me an example of the jitter-bugging '50s. Perhaps by being severe with me, this would give the people of New York City a new way of dealing with gangs. That was the whole objective in my case and in my sentence. I conspired with the news media in creating the mass hysteria surrounding my case. New York City was screaming for my blood. They wanted revenge. But why me? A Puerto Rican? Why use me as an example? I didn't have an answer. All I saw was hate, prejudice, and racism. They were white and I was a Puerto Rican. A light-skinned mulatto, a regulation spic!

> Many thoughts ran through my mind. My head was spinning. I was high on questions. Mostly I thought about the meaning of justice, and how that applied to me personally. I knew it could not be law and order. It had to be something in the middle. Mercy, I thought to myself. Perhaps there was mercy. But no mercy could be found that day.

Salvador's life was like a tapestry that was slowly beginning to unfold. His history read like a dictionary of sad and lonely scenarios, each becoming progressively more complicated than the one preceding it. Salvador had assured me that little by little his history would be revealed, but that this would take time.

I was already familiar with some of his history from what he had been sending me in the mail for our book. And some I had already learned from Esmeralda. More, he said, would be forthcoming when I made a visit to his sister's house.

> When I entered the courtroom, I looked around for my mother and sister, but my lawyer said although they were both in the building, they weren't allowed in the courtroom while I was sentenced. This was what the judge ordered. Glancing around the courtroom, I noticed all the reporters sitting together in one section, waiting for news to develop. Almost fifteen months had gone by since the night in the playground, and still we were news! When would this stop? It was just like in the beginning. With two white boys dead and a third severely wounded, they wanted revenge. And I was the "exampli gratis" of an indignant society and an infuriated judiciary. They were planning to murder me legally. I saw no differences between their form of justice and my law of the jungle.
>
> Looking around the courtroom, I wondered where my mother and sister were right now, and were they praying for me?

His sister's name was Aurea, and she lived in the Bronx, not far from Esmeralda. We had already spoken on the telephone, and she assured me she'd do whatever she could to help us with the book. She was the keeper, she said, of the family history, and whatever I needed to know about the Agron-Rodriguez family, she would be glad to provide. But first, she said, we would have to meet. When I said "that'll be great," we made tentative arrangements to get together sometime early the next month.

> As I stood waiting to be sentenced, I smiled at my crime partner, Antonio Hernandez. But my laughter, my sense of humor, was the bravado of fear and defeat. It was my utter helplessness disguised by belligerent mirth. Because inside I felt defeated and frightened. I knew the mandatory sentence would be imposed, and that according to the law, this could only be death. It was a death designed to burn deep into my whole physical being. Death by electricity. But it felt like my mind had already been executed, and I was one of the walking dead. Electricity—something I had feared for as long as I could remember. Lightening of the earthly gods. This was what I faced.
> The judge in his black robes looked down at me from his judicial throne as though he were saying, "A boy and yet a man now stands before the law." I was only seventeen years old. I had turned seventeen years old in April when my trial had begun. Most of the big words that had been kicked around in the court room were foreign to my limited vocabulary: "objection," "sustained," "overruled," "I take an exception," "Do you have any legal cause as to why judgment should not be pronounced against you?", "poll the jury," "Let the record so stipulate," on and on the rambling went, and the only thing I could do was to ask myself, "What the fuck are they talking about?"
> The judge said something about "Society must stop the outbreak of youthful gang violence in our cities, but this is not a time for compassion, sympathy, or mercy."
> "It is a time for judgment."

"Be sure to give my love to Sal when you go up there for that festival," Aurea said.

"Yes,"I'll tell him, of course I will.

"And when I get back, I'll call you again, so we can set up a definite time for me to come and visit."

He sentenced me to death by electrocution in the electric chair for each of the two charges of murder, to run consecutively, and to a separate term of twelve to twenty-five years imprisonment for attempted murder in the first degree. I would be taken to the Death House at Sing Sing Prison where I would be executed on November 6, 1960, in a month from right this minute! Incredible! The last movie I had seen just before this whole incident happened in 1959 was "The Last Mile." I think I saw this at the Brooklyn Paramount Theater on DeKalb Avenue, the same place where the rock n' roll shows used to take place, the ones put on by Alan Freed.

Expressionless, so as not to show my inner fear, I listened carefully. And when it was all over, this judicial farce, this premeditated murder by the state, I looked aimlessly into space. I had nothing but contempt for the whole body of law, and at that moment I hated everybody. It was a hate I'd never felt before. It was an intelligent hate, because I knew I was more humane and civilized than they were. Even with my limited education, and in my youthful ignorance, I knew this to be a fact. It made me feel like a king on a throne! The thought of this newfound pearl of wisdom me feel like a sinful saint-the paradox was overwhelming. But I remained expressionless, while I felt the glow in my eyes.

It is almost inexplicable and I have only slightly touched upon this matter.

As the train pulled into Times Square, I checked the time. It was a little bit after eight, and Harlem, or 125th Street, is the next stop. From there it's just a short walk over to Amsterdam Avenue, and the chartered Sunni Muslim bus which would take me to Greenhaven.

All I knew about the Sunni Muslims was what Salvador had told me. People, he said, were always confusing them with other groups, particularly with those who believed in Black nationalism; all the many groups who hated whites, all whites, for what they felt were years of injustice. But the Sunni Muslims, he said, were different. They had a reverence for life, and they emphasized taking personal responsibility for one's actions instead of always pointing a finger at someone else.

The Sunni Muslims were considered to be one of the more peaceful elements at Greenhaven, and because of this high regard, they were accorded a great deal of respect by the prison administration. Salvador said the Sunni Muslims were one of the most supportive groups in the prison. That they had a well-deserved reputation for helping people in need, and this regardless of whether or not a person was a practicing Sunni Muslim.

> *After the sentence, I was immediately escorted out of the court room, and taken back to the bullpen. Here I was carefully watched so that I might not beat the state of its prey—my life.*
>
> *After a short time had elapsed, two or three police officers dressed in civilian clothes came up to the bullpen with chains, belts, feetcuffs, and handcuffs. Telling us they were transportation officers, they opened my cell door and I stepped out. They shackled my feet with heavy cuffs. Then they placed a large, thick belt around my waist, and after running a pair of handcuffs through an iron ring in front of the leather belt, they shackled my hands. This was the first time I was ever shackled in such a brutal and secure manner. Was I a wild animal all this time, or did I suddenly turn into one after my death sentence? I couldn't tell—it was confusing. My partner was shackled in the same manner. They say misery loves company. This was at least comfortable, knowing that I was not alone.*

The transportation officers led us away to the elevator and down to the bottom floor. We were in a long corridor, and as we walked, one transportation officer went ahead of us, locking and unlocking doors. The final door led outside. We were in a high-walled enclosure, with the Tombs and the courthouse on three sides and the street on the fourth side. All we could see was a black transportation station wagon and the sky above our heads. We were put in the back seat and the officers sat in the front, separated by a thick screen. The engine was turned on, and directly in front of the car, a large thick, solid iron door slid open and we moved slowly into the street.
I looked out the window.

I remembered Salvador telling me that the term "sunna," by which the Sunnites refers to themselves meant "middle of the road," which of course would explain, to some extent, their acceptance by the people who ran the prisons. The wardens and the guards wanted things to run smoothly, and what better way than to embrace a group known to always police their own. It was no accident that during the Attica rebellion the Sunni Muslims had been chosen by non-Muslim rebel leaders to guard the hostages from harm while negotiations were taking place.

As the prison bus moved on, we passed old neighborhoods—our jungle—like El Barrio, Harlem, and other ghettos and slums. It was sort of nostalgic and I felt as though I was truly a kidnapping victim.

Leaving the train at 125th Street, I wondered how many mosques, or Muslim houses of worship, there were in Harlem, and whether I'd see any on my way over to Amsterdam Avenue.
Salvador said that a mosque could be found in virtually

every prison in New York State. The mosque at Greenhaven was so clean and well situated that he often sat inside for hours whenever he needed a quiet place to work something out that was bothering him.

Five times a day the Sunni Muslims knelt down in prayer.

> *How I wished for a crash. I think I even prayed for one. I would get lost in the mountains, lost to the world, and to myself. Looking out the window, I noticed the garbage on the streets of Harlem, and I thought about the saying, "Keep America Clean," and "Keep America Beautiful." Wasn't this why I was being taken out from the American society, because I was not clean?*
>
> *As we moved on, I had to urinate. I told the transportation officers I wanted to take a piss. Without turning around, one of them told me to use the can on the floor. It was very uncomfortable, but I managed, and I felt relieved.*
>
> *I thought about my trial. Why did they call my friends, "Puerto Ricans" and "Spanish boys" and call the other group "Americans" and "white boys"? Wasn't I also an "American" or a citizen of the United States? My mind kept asking questions I would otherwise have overlooked.*
>
> *It must have been the sentence of death that made me inquisitive about such things.*
>
> *I tried to enjoy the ride as hundreds of thoughts flooded my head in a very confusing manner. Now I knew what it all meant. Freedom was not a definition from a dictionary, but one defined by experience, and by the reality of losing what I never even thought I had, at least to a limited degree.*
>
> *Freedom was what I lost when those gates closed behind me.*
>
> *As the prison bus moved along, and I looked across the highway at the city streets, I thought about freedom. This was something I had never known anyway, or had never fully appreciated.*

Arriving at the corner of Amsterdam Avenue and 125th Street, I looked for the bus. Sure enough it was right where Salvador had said it would be, parked in front of a luncheonette, and just a few hundred feet from a housing project just like the one Salvador said he'd lived in with his sister years before. But he hadn't stayed too long, running wild, moving back and forth between his sister's house in Manhattan and his mother's apartment in Brooklyn.

As I started to walk up the stairs of the bus, an arm shot out in front of me and blocked my path. The arm belonged to a huge black man, holding a clipboard, and wearing a woolen, Muslim prayer cap, which reminded me of a yarmulke.

"Who the fuck are you?" he said.

"I'm on this bus...I'm supposed to be here!"

"What the fuck you talkin' about? No one here but us Muslims."

"Look on the list...my name's gotta be there."

Looking at his clipboard, he asked me my name, and when he found it, he offered a half-hearted apology before waving me onto the bus.

> As the prison bus continued along the East River Drive, I tried to enjoy the rotten view of the concrete jungle. And as I looked at the streets of Harlem in the distance, I thought to myself, "soon you will be gone forever from the whole hypocrisy of New York City and its stinking life."

On the bus, a sea of black faces, and every last one either a woman or a child. Not only was I the only white person on the bus, but one of only three men. The driver, and the guy with the clipboard and the prayer hat were the other two.

There was nowhere to go except an empty seat by a window, directly behind the driver, but I couldn't sit down because it was filled with books.

The guy with the prayer hat and clipboard touched my shoulder.

"That's the *Koran* you're lookin' at, just move it over with the books and you can have the seat, but be careful how you touch them because those are holy books, just like the Bible, you hear what I'm sayin'?"

Placing the books on an overhead rack, I slid into the seat. When the door of the bus closed, the guy with the prayer hat sat down beside me.

Turning on the ignition, the driver let the engine warm up for a few seconds before slowly pulling away from the curb and into the street.

> *As the prison bus moved on, leaving the city behind me, I became more relaxed. I thought to myself—here I go, from the frying pan into the fire! Perhaps the fire would extinguish the pain that accompanies life. My mind was on death, on electricity, and on the horror of dying helpless, without being able to fight this new monstrous machine—the death penalty. I wanted to cry. My pride and youthful arrogance would not permit such a thing. I came up the rough way, always striving to stay alive, and now death had me in a tight grip.*
>
> *Death was smiling. I was very submissive. No sense in struggling.*

The man sitting next to me was named Ali Muhammad. From Brooklyn, he'd done time at Greenhaven many years ago, and now was a practicing Sunni Muslim. Looking out the window at the Harlem streets, I asked him how long the trip would take to Greenhaven.

"We should be up there by noon at the latest."

"But that's like over three hours...it shouldn't take that long."

"This ain't Greyhound...and like, first we've gotta make

a stop at Sing Sing."

"No one said nothing to me about stopping there first."

"They're also having a festival...nothing like the one at Greenhaven...but they're still having one and so we're gonna be dropping some of the sisters off first before we head up to Greenhaven. You didn't know nothing 'bout this?"

"Nope."

"Ever been to Sing Sing?"

"A couple of months ago I took a tour..."

"Say what?"

"A tour...you know...like someone from the warden's office took us all around, showed us the cellblocks, the mess halls...all over the place...they even took us to the death house."

"Now why would you want to be makin' a tour of Sing Sing?"

"It was for this course I was taking...about penology... prison... and the professor thought it'd be good if we saw the real thing instead of just reading about it in books."

Pushing thoughts of anger and rage aside, I thought about my life. When was the last time I had seen the countryside? Outside the window of the prison bus, there was nothing but buildings, concrete, and hard city streets.

I saw a bridge. Not the George Washington Bridge, but smaller. Muhammad said it was the Willis Avenue Bridge. When we crossed, a sign welcomed us to the Bronx.

Passing Yankee Stadium, we continued down the highway, past the Bronx House of Detention, and on to the Major Degan Expressway toward upstate New York.

> All the way up to Sing Sing, it was mostly trees, scattered houses here and there, grass, rivers, meadows, pigs, cows, horses, and all the other things of country life.
> My mind desperately tried to suck in all the beauty.

The bus moved on. Past Hastings-on-Hudson with the New Jersey Palisades on the other side of the river, past Dobbs Ferry, past Irvington, and then off the highway at the sign for Tarrytown.

As Muhammad moved his lips in silent prayer, the bus rode through the streets of Tarrytown with its gingerbread looking houses and the Washington Irving Elementary School.

Past Scarborough and Briar Cliff Manor, finally the bus went down the main street of Ossining. Down one street, up another, then a left onto Hunter Street. It moved until there was nowhere else to go. A high stone wall stood several yards in front of the bus.

> This was Sing Sing. I had heard so much about the prison and I had seen so many Hollywood versions of it, that now I felt a strange sensation on seeing this famous castle of criminality.
> Looking out the window of the prison bus, all I could see were high walls and men with guns.
> The doors locked behind me.

On our right, and off in the distance, near the Hudson River, the Death House stood. To our left is the Administration Building, the first stop for anyone, guard, visitor, or convict, entering the prison.

Clipboard in hand, Muhammad got up from his seat.

"If you're gettin' off here, just make sure you take all your stuff with you...'cause we can't be responsible if somethin' gets taken."

The prison bus stopped inside the enclosure. It was searched and while this was being done, some guards walked over and looked us over as if we weren't even there, or like we were some kind of circus freaks. I put on a mean and angry face for all to see.

We stepped out of the transportation wagon, and slowly, dragging our chains, we went up the stairs of the Administration Building. Inside, we were taken upstairs to a room and told to sit on a wooden bench. After a couple of minutes, our chains and cuffs were removed, and we were taken to yet another room and told to sit down again while several officers came to the door and just stared in at us, amazed, I think, that two boys so young could come to Sing Sing, let alone to the Death House.

As the women left the bus, it looked like each was carrying at least one shopping bag, and I asked Muhammad how long he thought it would take for them to be processed into the prison.

"Not that long...'cause this is a festival and if they don't get them in soon then there'll be even more hassles cause the guys inside'll be complainin' and stuff...so they try to get them in real fast...know what I'm sayin'?"

I heard the guard telling the women that before they could actually enter the prison for the festival that first they'd have to be processed. This meant that someone would be looking through their shopping bags for contraband.

Muhammed said the festival would be held in a fenced-off area down near the river, and after everyone was processed, and their bags searched, they'd be taken down there in paddy wagons.

"Paddy wagons?"

"Sing Sing's big, man, so like they use the paddy wagons to take the guards, and sometimes even the convicts, from place to place."

When I asked one of the guards what would be happening next, he stared at me for a few seconds before answering me.

"Before we take you to the Death House, you have to be processed into the prison."

After waiting a few more minutes, guards took us to a room, and told us to remove all our clothes because we were going to be examined by a doctor.

Sitting side by side on the bench, both of us are naked when a guard comes into the room. In each hand he carries a brown paper bag. Stepping up close to where we sit, he puts my clothes in one bag and Tony's in the other. He asks us where we want our clothes sent.

"We can send them home to your families, or we can donate them to charity."

I give them my sister Aurea's address in Brooklyn, and Tony just shakes his head and says they could give his clothes to charity or throw them away. Either way, he doesn't care.

Writing something on each bag, the officer gives them to another guard standing by the door. Taking the bags, he leaves the room, and we're left sitting on the bench. Then the guard tells us to follow him into the next room where we are told to hold our arms over our heads, spread our feet apart, and then to spread our cheeks so that a guard can look up our ass to make sure we haven't smuggled anything into the prison by using our rear ends. That is the regular frisk. I feel powerless and dehumanized. Being naked, physically and mentally, is degrading whenever it's imposed.

Then we are given state clothes, a shower, and after we get dressed, we are photographed and fingerprinted again.

I am no longer thinking about freedom.

Riding away from the prison, and down the streets of Ossining to the thruway, I tried to catch a glimpse of the old Death House. But all I could see was the huge tower of the prison power plant.

> *My mind is now on the thought of death. My execution date has been set for the week of November 27, 1960. However, my lawyers, Stand and Steinberg, assured me at the sentencing that the date doesn't mean anything. I will not die on that date because first, I have to go through a direct appeal. Although I do not fully understand, I act like I do understand. I do not show any fear, but I am always afraid.*

The bus traveled north, arriving just before noon at the front gate of Greenhaven Prison. A guard, seeing our bus, waved us to the back of the prison, where we'd be processed, Muhammad said, before they took us out to Fay Field.

Getting off the bus at the rear of the prison, we joined what seemed like dozens of people of every shape, size, and description, waiting to be processed into the prison.

Unlike the usually somber tone maintained by those entering the prison, as well as by those receiving them, the atmosphere at the rear of the prison as we were lining up to be processed was one of joviality. Lots of people smiling and laughing. Many men were waiting on line, but as I looked around, it was obvious that the women far outnumbered the men.

Women alone, and women with small children.

> *While being fingerprinted, a guard, with another officer behind him, comes to the door of the room, looks inside, and after staring at me for a while, he turns around and I hear him tell the other one, "They're just kids." The other officer answers, "No, not kids. They're murderers."*

As I was waiting to be processed, the woman in front of me was reaching in and out of her purse. She looked as if she was reaching in for a tissue to wipe the nose of the small child standing close by, whose hand was held by someone else. I could see that whatever she was taking out of her purse she'd quickly hid in her dress somewhere. Moving so fast that unless someone were watching her closely, it would have been impossible to see what she was doing. A little taller than I, with dark eyes and light brown hair, she was a striking woman. While she reached in and out of her purse, I saw, out of the corner of my eye, another woman doing exactly the same thing. I started to look in her direction, but then I came to a table, with a guard looking directly at me.

"Your name?"

"Richard Jacoby"

"And you're with what group?"

"The Sunni Muslims...I came up with their bus."

As the guard checked my name on his list, I slowly turned around. Right behind me, and not a foot from the gaze of the guard, the second woman was shoving something up her dress. Like before, it was done so fast it was hardly noticeable unless you knew what you were looking for.

"Put out your hand."

Turning around, I looked back at the guard.

"Excuse me...I didn't hear what you just said."

"Your hand...I need your hand so I can stamp it...you can't get in without it."

The stamp is like a fingerprint. When you leave the prison, you place your hand under a special light so that the mark will show, and if it doesn't, then you're in deep shit.

Salvador said the mark they made varied from week to week.

> *After being processed into the prison, we were ready to be taken down the hill to the Death House*
>
> *The paddy wagon drops off officers here and there. Sing Sing Prison seems like a city within a city. The wagon stops in front of what looks like a miniature prison within a prison. We*

step down. Some gates open as the paddy wagon moves away. We are left with five guards surrounding us.

When my hand was marked, and my name checked off, the guard pointed to the list on the table.

"Put your signature next to where you see your name, and then put everything from your pockets into one of these boxes."

Signing my name, I emptied my pockets into the box. When I was done, another guard walked over and picked it up. Quickly sorting through some assorted coins, my wallet, and a set of keys, he told me to follow him over to the metal detector on the other side of the room.

He looked me up and down.

"You got anythin' that's gonna make the buzzer go off?"

"Just my keys, but you already got them in the box."

"How 'bout your belt?"

"Yeah, I'm wearin' one...you want me to take it off?"

"It'd save alotta time if you did cause otherwise it's gonna ring, and while you're at it, you might as well take off your shoes cause that'll also screw things up."

As I took off my belt, the same guard who was just sorting though my stuff in the box was now going through the contents of someone's purse. It was the purse that belonged to the woman standing in front of me, the striking woman with the light brown hair, who just a minute ago had been shoving something up her dress.

She was standing in such a way as to give the guard more than just a peek at her enormous breasts. Each one seemed to rise and fall by its own weight, like a plump child on a seesaw, and as the guard looked back and forth from her breasts to a package of open cigarettes lying next to her purse, she tapped him lightly on the hand.

"You think officer that it'd be okay if I was to bring in those cigarettes?"

"Well...we used to let them in but no more, that's the rule...they gotta be in a new pack and otherwise you're gonna have to keep them out here until you leave....sorry."

"Please..."

>An escort of about five police with nightsticks takes us downstairs. We pass some prisoners, who are locked behind some barred door, and we can hear whispers from them. We leave the reception building and are escorted to a bus-like paddy wagon. Then, suddenly, about ten to fifteen cops come out of the same building. We get on the vehicle and they also get in too. They sit all around us.
>
>No one says anything.

Looking at her breasts, he didn't say a thing. Just picked up the pack of cigarettes, and shoved them quickly into her purse. Then he smiled at her from across the table, and as he talked to her in what seemed like a very seductive voice, I tried to listen. But there was so much noise I couldn't make out very much.

>I notice gun towers on my left and gun towers to my right. It is an eerie looking place. A cold chill sweeps through my body. I know this is the famous death row building.
>
>The Death House at Sing Sing. For as long as I can remember, I have heard stories about this place. And now here I am, Salvador Agron, on his way to the electric chair.
>
>As the wagon rolls down the hill to the lower part of the prison, they stare at us and don't say a word. This makes me very uncomfortable. I become very tense. All of them have sticks and I resent their staring and whispering.
>
>We stepped inside, and while the door that we came through was closed and the gate also closed behind us, another gate opened.
>
>We go up the stairs leading to the door and then to an iron

gate which is flung open from inside.
The guard inside said, "Welcome to the Death House."

When Salvador came to greet us, I threw my arms around him. As we hugged one another, he whispered in my ear.

"Welcome to Greenhaven, brother, I'm glad you're here."

Releasing me, he turned to a man with flaming red hair.

"Richard, this here's John O'Neil...he's a good friend of mine."

We shook hands.

John O'Neil is about six feet tall, and aside from his hair, what's most striking about him are his eyes. Blue like the sky, they remind me of a violent, unrelenting wind. Rock hard, they're the kind of eyes people would describe as being "the coldest eyes I've ever seen."

"How's it goin'" he says, in a voice so rough it sounds as if his mouth is filled with small pieces of gravel, moving back and forth, from cheek to cheek.

"Not bad...could be worse..."

Once inside the building, we went through three more locked doors before finally stopping in a small room where we were again asked to take off all our clothes.

Again, we were thoroughly searched, and then our shoes were taken away and we were given soft slippers.

"These are so you won't hurt yourselves," said the same guard who just a few moments before welcomed us to the Death House.

"Call me Pops," he said.

He had gray hair and watery blue eyes, and looked to be in his sixties. He had a little gold pin attached to the collar of his shirt, and when I asked him what it meant, he said he got it just a few months before in honor of having served The Department for over forty years. Forty years, I thought to myself. That's more than twice my age! How could someone work so long in a place like this?

As if reading my mind, Pops said he hadn't been working at "CC" Building the whole time.

"What does "CC" building mean?" I asked Pops.

"It means Condemned Criminals or Condemned Cells, I don't know which, but either way it means the same thing. Any more questions?"

When I didn't say anything, he motioned us to follow him, and we walked through a door and into a long corridor filled with cells. Passing by the first cell, the first condemned man I saw was Frank Bloeth. He was the first man to say anything.

"At last you made the Big House, kid. Make yourself at home."

I just looked at him and shook my head. The next cell was empty—no one was at the bars. The third cell was occupied by Luis Rosario, who had previously had a joint hearing with me on the exclusion of Puerto Ricans from the Grand Jury panel. He looked at me, smiled, and said " Hi, Sal."

Waving my hand, I answered, "Vaya, man. Cómo está?"

The next cell was mine. I went in and sat on the bed. Antonio came down The Row and he went through the same procedure. Then the barred door was shut, the key turned, and the latch closed over the keyhole.

I was alone in my cell.

From where we were standing at the rear gate of the prison, Fay Field was probably a five-minute walk away, but this was a maximum-security facility, and only the people who ran the prison were allowed to walk, "unsecured," as its officially called, around the institution grounds. All the rest, convicts and visitors alike, had to be escorted to the festival area by truck, prison van, or car.

Sitting on a bench next to Salvador in the back of a truck, I took in my surroundings. Off in the distance, are several groups of buildings. Salvador pointed out the buildings housing the cellblocks, the administration complex, and to our left, the hospital.

"That's where they've got the box, on the top floor, and also where they moved the Death House when they stopped usin' it at Sing Sing," he said.

But here it's not in a separate building, and here they've named it something else.

"Here they call it 'K gallery.'"

"And that's where they put the electric chair?"

"That's the place."

I must have fallen asleep because suddenly Pops was in front of my cell telling me that I should get up because supper would arrive in the Death House in a few minutes.

Supper the first night was meat, potatoes, peas, and some kind of gravy, with bread and butter on the side. There was also a small cup of apple sauce, which I figured was my dessert. Whatever was in the cup was anyone's guess. It was tasteless, and had almost no color. Another guy said it was some kind of powdered punch, but he didn't know exactly what, only that the drink was different each day. Coffee was always available, he said, and milk was served in little cartons at least once a day.

The meal was served on a rubber tray. Aside from the metal plate with the food, there was also a metal cup, with a napkin, fork, and spoon. One guard said knives weren't allowed on The Row and I would just have to do the best I could with the fork and spoon.

After supper the place became lively, and the rest of the evening was spent answering questions as to "how is so and so?" and "is so and so still in the Tombs?" Or "are the police still beating up on people"?—all the usual talk which goes down in prisons. The Death House was no exception.

From the other inmates, I learned I could buy certain items from the commissary. Anytime I wanted coffee, I just had to ask the guard. I was given a bowl of sugar every week, and my toothpaste was kept in a drawer outside the cell at a desk where the police would sit and attend to the requests of the condemned men. Only the bars and the barred door were made of metal. The rest of the large cell was concrete.

Radio transmission was outside the cells, and there were two boxes with a volume button on each. The main radio was in a small hall away from the gallery. The hall leading to what was called the Dance Hall (the hall leading to the execution chamber) was the radio control room and there was also a closet with many religious books which the men could read. Those cells that were next to each other had a wooden stand in front of them, hooked up with a piece of wood to the bars. This was in case anyone wanted to play cards, checkers, or chess.

Sometimes we would listen to a radio station that played rock n' roll music, and sometimes we listened to religious stations.

You could get half an hour of yard time in the morning, and often the same in the afternoon, but this could change and it depended on the guard on duty. You could not go out with other prisoners. A guard would always be with you in the yard. Even if they played handball or basketball too, they never turned their backs, not for a second. I think they thought you could commit suicide anytime, but I never saw anyone make a suicidal gesture of any kind while I was in the death house.

The yard reminded me of a cardboard box with four walls and nothing else. But instead of cardboard, the four walls had bricks that were probably once bright red, but were faded now from being so old and having all kinds of weather, like rain and snow, beating on them over the years.

As the prison truck approached Fay Field, I heard the sounds of people laughing and singing. A group of musicians played what sounded like dancing music, and I could heard the banging of drums and the strumming of guitars. Surrounded by high walls and men with rifles, I thought of all the men at Greenhaven who "walked the walk," and "rapped the rap," back and forth, from wall to wall, and back again. Walking what Salvador called "the walk of the living dead." When everything was done, said, and added up, how many miles would they have walked? Thousands? Millions? And how many years will they have served? Thousands? Millions?

Prison was truly a hell on earth. But beyond the high walls, and the men with the rifles, I could still see the deep blue sky.

> Walking back and forth in the Death House yard, I couldn't help thinking of all the other condemned people who sat like me in this same yard—the people who died in the electric chair. Looking around I wondered about the ghosts and who those people were when they were alive. Maybe they were even here with me right now in the exercise yard.
>
> If you didn't count the tower off in the distance with the guard inside, all I could see from where I sat against one of the brick walls was the sky above my head.
>
> It was early October and already getting cold. But the sky was a deep blue. I closed my eyes for a second, and when I opened them again and looked at the sky, it reminded me of Puerto Rico.

Fourteen other people were sitting with us on the wooden benches in the back of the open prison truck. Seven were convicts, each one wearing identical state-issued, green khaki pants. The rest were visitors, except one of course who was a guard.

With his closely cropped crew cut, blue blazer and light colored pants, the guard could at first glance be taken for a visiting alumnus at a college homecoming. But the emblem over the outside vest pocket of the blazer was the seal of New York State.

He was quiet and gunless, with eyes darting from the convicts and their visitors, to the unseen faces of the guards in the watchtowers. I wondered what his life was like when he wasn't in here being a guard.

> That first night in the Death House, I had a dream I was in India in some kind of temple where I was watching, without a telescope, the planet, Venus. The dream was in beautiful colors, with Venus, all green and close to the Earth. In the dream, I started to fly off to Venus, but a voice says, no, because first you must look carefully behind you.
>
> Looking back from India, I saw myself back on death row where my own body was still sleeping.
>
> Then I woke up.

Salvador sat to my left, and John O'Neil to my right. The woman with the light brown hair, the same one shoving something up her dress a few minutes ago, was sitting to the right of Salvador.

Suddenly, the woman reached over, and took Salvador's face in her hands, quickly kissing his mouth. And then, before it hardly registered, their tongues kissed, danced, and surrendered.

Soon, they were going at it like there was no tomorrow. Mouth to mouth. And tongue to tongue.

> Everyone in the Death House seemed to be obsessed with food, and I was certainly not an exception. Back then I thought it was because it was something to look forward to in the darkness of the Death House.
>
> Something to break up the routine. But later I would realize that the hunger we had was a hunger for life in the face of possible death, and food was just one of the many things we were hungry for.
>
> One night I dreamed I was shopping for food with Esmeralda, my beloved mother. We were in Spanish Harlem, at the "La Marqueta," a huge outdoor market, and I was helping her buy all of the things essential for a Puerto Rican household. She was carrying a huge shopping bag, and we slowly filled it with things like chicory, romain lettuce, long-stemmed eggplant, pomegranates, and red and green pimentos. Then my

mother turned to me, and smiling, she gave me the now-filled shopping bag, and then she said, "Salvi, my son, do not worry, for this is all you will ever need in life."

Closing my eyes for a moment, it was easy to imagine I was slowly drifting across a prairie in a covered wagon instead of in a truck filled with convicts and citizens. As the truck rocked from side to side over ruts in the road, all we needed, I thought, was a white sheet to protect us from the elements.

I half expected to see an Indian wearing a full head-dress peeking into the truck, but instead, as I opened my eyes, I saw the hard and unyielding eyes of John O'Neil as he gazed with obvious longing at Salvador's crotch.

At least twice a week while I was in the Death House, I would hear this whining sound, like a generator being warmed up. At first I ignored it, but then when I asked one of the guards what it was, he told me it was the executioner testing out the electric chair.
I never knew whether to believe him or not.

As the men and women in the truck washed over one another with all kinds of affection and ardor, the bogus covered wagon came to a sudden stop in front of a long, rectangular field of bright green grass.

This was Fay Field, a vast expanse of well-manicured lawn used by the prison for everything from football games to many different special events.

First the guard got off the truck, followed by the rest of us, with Salvador and the striking lady taking the lead. As soon as we were off the truck, Salvador threw one arm around my shoulder.

"Hermano mio, it's so good to see you."

"Yeah...well, you knew I'd be here, right?"

"Fuckin' right I knew...hey...lemme introduce you to my friend here..."

Turning around, he took the hand of the woman with the light brown hair. I noticed that her hair was closer to blond than brown.

"This here's Felicia...and Felicia...this here's Richard Jacoby, my main amigo from Brooklyn!"

In a soft voice, with just the hint of an accent, Felicia said what a pleasure it was for her to meet any friend of Salvador's.

"Felicia's a teacher in the Bronx."

"Really? What do you teach?"

"Second grade."

John O'Neil walked over to us, and Felicia excused herself. Salvador kissed her cheek, and she slowly walked away.

"She's good people," he said.

"Where'd you meet her?"

"She wrote me a letter when I was up in Attica. Then I wrote back, and we started a regular thing, writing back and forth, hey, let's you and me take a walk...yo, John, you think I could talk with my man here in private?...nothing personal, you know...but we ain't seem each other for awhile, you dig what I'm sayin'?"

"I can dig it...so I'll catch the both of youse later on."

John turned and walked away, but not before they touched, fist to fist, in a jailhouse sign of understanding.

Death Row leads some people downward and others upward, and still others, sidewards. But whichever way, one becomes more profound by the experience.

Reaching down the front of his pants, Salvador removed a folder filled with wrinkled papers.

"Take this stuff," he said, "but be cool...it's stuff for the book."

> *From the very moment the judge pronounced the death sentence by electrocution, my mind began functioning in a way it had never functioned at any other time in my life.*

With her khaki pants and combat boots, Maria looked like the perfect revolutionary, Rachel, on the other hand, was almost unrecognizable. With a slash of bright red lipstick across her mouth, along with heavy make-up, she looked like someone I'd never seen before. As she moved toward us, her dress seemed to climb several inches above her knees. When she threw her arms around Salvador's neck, several convicts craned their necks to get a peek between her legs.

> *Many of my nights in the Death House were spent thinking about my trial. Had it been fair? I didn't even know if I had been defended properly. All I knew about my case was that from the very start, there had been many people interested in it, especially after we were sentenced to death.*
>
> *Then the real struggle began: how to keep the State of New York from killing me and my crime partner.*

Listening to Salvador, or reading his work, I was learning all that was native to prison life.

Bits and pieces of jailhouse wisdom.

SAN JUAN BAUTISTA DAY COMMITTEE
GREENHAVEN CORRECTIONAL FACILITY
STORMVILLE, NEW YORK

(official menu) Salvador Agron #16846 Inmate Coordinator

Platanos Amarillos (Sweet Ripe Plantains)

Alcapurrias (Stuffed Green Bananas

Guineitos Niños (Finger bananas)

Arroz Blanco (White Rice)

Arroz con Habichuelas (Rice and Beans)

Papa Al Horno (Baked Potato) Coffee and Soft Drinks

Guineos con Crema de Coco (Bananas with Coconut Creme)

Each bit of wisdom seemed to have a life and a direction all its own, complete with causes, effects, and certain definite consequences. Mixed together, they produced a dark symbiosis that seemed particular to prisons everywhere.

The first bit of wisdom was the need or desire to get intoxicated by any means possible. This meant dope in all its many forms, including virtually every type of inhalant, liquid, or smokable substance known to produce even a hint of intoxication. These along with whatever else the convicts were able to beg, borrow, or steal, either from one another, or from someone on the outside willing to bring it in, shove it in, or send it in.

> Often we would listen from our cells across the empty space which made up the yard. From the connected building, in the Dance Hall, would come noises, as if chains were being dragged across the concrete floor, slowly, chain by chain. We

> would try to figure out what it was, but we never could find out exactly what it was. Sometimes weeks would pass and there would be no noise, but if someone listened real good, they could hear something. The guards, who also heard the noise, would check, but they couldn't find anything to connect it with.

When Rachel finished exchanging tongues with Salvador, she walked over to me.

"You been here long?" she asked.

"Not that long...maybe half an hour...so how come you didn't dress the way I said you should?"

"You're not my boyfriend!"

"Hey! That's not the point..." I said.

"So what is the point?"

"The way you're dressed is gonna make him crazy, that's the point!"

> We wondered if group psychosis had taken over due to our thoughts being all enmeshed with death, or if it were something we couldn't even imagine, or guess, for fear of looking childish or sounding ridiculous. Whatever, it made a deathly sound and many times we unconsciously turned the radio up to drown out the sound. It was there anyway. We heard it, jailer and jailed alike. Sometimes I thought it was the devil playing tricks. It sounded like chains being dragged across the floor.

Sexuality in its many varied manifestations was always a given in a maximum-security institution, where the average sentence was twenty years to life.

Everything went down at one time or another. Everything from what the convicts called "short-heist," or dirty books, to groping and poking in the cellhouse, the showers, or any place that was void of light.

> *The public wanted my blood, but slowly the situation began to change. Political people began to mobilize a campaign for my commutation. People such as Eleanor Roosevelt, Governor Muñoz Marín, El Collegio de Abogados of Puerto Rico, the Nationalist, Socialist, and Democratic Parties.*
>
> *Many people from high and low places opposed my execution.*

Just before the killings in the playground, Salvador had been living from furnished room to furnished room. Sometimes with older men, and they paid for the room so that he would stay with them. Before that he had known boys and men in any one of the many places where he'd been locked up for long periods of time. Then he'd entered the system in New York, and there'd been other boys, and other men. How many was difficult to know, he said. All he knew was that there were boys and men in every prison where he had been locked up for the last fifteen years.

Many times, he said, the touching had begun with nothing more than a scribbled note or a passing glance that was held too long.

Walking with Maria to the festival area, I couldn't help thinking how good Salvador and Rachel looked together as they walked in front of us, hand in hand.

With her high heels, Rachel was only slightly shorter than Salvador, and as they walked, they ground against one another with a rhythm older than time itself. Back and forth. Side to side. Hip to hip. And as the rawness of their sensuality washed over me like a down quilt in the middle of winter, I lost all sense of time and place.

Leaning over, she brushed his cheek, while he guided her hand, locked in his, to a point several inches below her back.

My first experience with somebody who was to be executed was when I waited next door while Ronnie Chapman sat through those last agonizing days, hours, minutes, and seconds. He didn't seem to care and I admired his courage. Without him knowing it, he was making me more aware of myself and the thought of my approaching death. When his day was approaching, he grew very quiet and he withdrew more and more into himself. That night, just before he was to be taken to the Dance Hall, or what was officially called the "pre-execution cells, Ronnie shared, in what was a time-honored tradition, his last meal with all the rest of us on The Row.

When he was taken to the Dance Hall, the next morning, I didn't get out of bed until very late.

Ronnie was twenty years old, very black, and very proud. I think he had some kind of death wish. He wanted to die because he had made up his mind that sooner or later he would have to go. He didn't believe in white justice, and his experience with white society had left him convinced there could be no justice for the Ronnie Chapmans of the world. And while he was on The Row, he became more and more cynical. When his appeal was over, he dismissed his lawyers and decided to face the electric chair without fear. I couldn't see any justice in his execution.

Except for the men in the towers, and the high concrete walls, Salvador and Rachel could've been mistaken for a couple walking on a street in Brooklyn, or strolling down a country road, or flying together in an airplane. But when had Salvador last been in Brooklyn, walked on a country road, or flown in an airplane? Fifteen years ago, if not more. No muchachas, no women, and no airplanes. Nothing but shit on a shingle, he had told me, when I'd asked him once to describe, in just a few words, how he would tell someone from outer space what his life had been like in prison.

Shit on a shingle.

I couldn't sleep that night. My mind kept racing out of control. I kept thinking about Ronnie not wanting to see the priest and wondering if the priest would walk along with Ronnie to the chair anyway. That very night I got on my knees and started praying. I also said an "Our Father" and asked the Lord for his divine protection. It was a simple prayer, but it was meaningful.

From where I sat and watched, it was just legalized murder. That was even more evil and more premeditated than that which we were all accused of having committed against another member of a society which we lived in but which I doubt if we cared about in any shape or form. No doubt that was the result of all the abuse and conditioning we'd undergone while growing up.

The night Ronnie left, the sound of silence on The Row was mind-expanding. Death was everywhere, and everyone could feel it, both mentally and physically. At this point, I fully realized this wasn't a game.

It was war.

We were standing by a card table piled high with paper cups, napkins, and plastic utensils, when a man of medium height, with dark eyes, and black hair, walked over and starts to introduce himself. With his loping mustache, he resembled a Puerto Rican Pancho Villa. Checking out Maria, he extended his hand.

"Hi, I'm Roberto...Roberto Torres...and you're Maria Gonzalez, right?"

"Oh, right! Hi...I didn't know what you'd look like...but how did you know it was me?"

"Somebody said that you'd probably be wearing combat boots...and you're not, but since you're walking with Sal here, I kinda figured that it must be you."

"Well...I'm very pleased to meet you."

He asked her how the trip was.

"It was okay...there wasn't much traffic."

"You came up with one of the buses?"

"No...no...I have a car...and Rachel was with me...oh! I'm sorry, Rachel, this is Roberto, and Roberto this is Rachel... and do you know Richard Jacoby?"

"I've seen him around."

> Almost from the very moment that I entered the Death House, I wanted to learn everything I could about the electric chair.
>
> I even asked one of the guards if there was any chance that I could see it before my actual execution. He said, absolutely not, it was against the rules. But then late one night, when everyone was asleep, he came and walked with me to the execution room.
>
> And there it was. Like a dark throne, sitting all alone in a room with some kind of ventilators set deep in the ceiling. The guard said they were there to clear the air.
>
> "There's lots of smoke, and it don't smell so good in here afterwards."
>
> I wanted to sit down, just to see what it would feel like. But the guard wouldn't let me, and so all I got was a quick look before he took me back to my cell. No one knows for sure who built it. But someone said it was built long ago by a convict in the prison carpentry shop.
>
> It was made of heavy wood, probably oak, and it was bolted to the floor. It was sitting on a rubber mat, and it was supported by three legs: two behind, and a big one in front. There were leather straps running every which way, and the guard said they were used to tie the person down so they couldn't jump around when the current was turned on.
>
> They said Ronnie took two steps back when he saw the electric chair, but then walked up and sat in it without any "assistance" from the guards. After his death he became a symbol of bravery for the men on The Row, and he gave everyone some measure of hope and faith. He was an inspiration for us all.

"Richard, me and Rachel here, we're gonna stroll over there by the stage for a while, but I'll check you out later, okay?"

"Yeah...that's cool...but aren't you supposed to be giving a speech or something?"

"Yeah...yeah...but first we gotta eat!"

I filled our plates with rice and beans.

> The day Ronnie Chapman died in the electric chair, my mind clicked into another level. It was another way of seeing things. I learned a lot I'd neglected in the past—things which previously held little, if any, importance in my life as a jitterbugger or a juvenile delinquent. It's a weird experience to be sentenced to die and then feel more alive than ordinary people. It can easily give you the illusion of being immortal if you aren't careful. On some of the condemned, it takes its toll. Some rejuvenate, while others wither away. For myself, I expected the worst, already knowing the oppressive social system, and then I prayed for the best. Though my lawyers said "they" might not put me in the electric chair because of my age, I suspected it could happen. Youth seldom understand death because it really takes living to deal with death.

Dozens of card and picnic tables were spread across Fay Field. Some belonged to various movement groups from outside the prison, and some to the Sunni Muslims. All the rest were piled high with platters of food, drinks, or paper goods.

> Instead of going out to the yard that day, I asked to go to the closet where there were lots of religious books which were hardly ever read by the men on The Row. The closet was in the hallway which led to the Dance Hall. I looked at the door leading to the Dance Hall and thought for the first time, "That's the door to heaven, if the Lord be willing. I will be more than

proud to travel that road with Jesus." That was my way of conquering death—by embracing it as the ultimate reality of life, the beginning of a higher existence. In the closet I found dusty old books about all the different Christian denominations.

Walking from table to table with the plate of rice and beans in one hand, and a cup of ice water in the other, I watched the guards in their blue blazers, and dark sunglasses. Walking back and forth, and talking to no one except each another, they seemed to be practicing a "pay them no mind" attitude.

My sensitivity (almost feminine) was heightened. It started that day and built. I don't remember exactly when the questions formed, but I know they were there.

Why is man born? What is death? What is fate, destiny, predetermination? Can destiny be changed? And if destiny can be changed, will it cease to be destiny?

What and who is God? Is God a man, a woman, a spirit, an idea? Is an idea real or false? When it's real, when is it false? My mind was about to explode.

I was afraid. I feared the answers, but more than that, I feared the thought that there might not be any answers at all. Even more frightening was that I might find some answers and then be executed.

I used to listen to the news all the time to keep up with what was going on in Cuba, and also keep track of all the things people said and wrote about me. I found out people lived more in myth than in reality, and they wrote what they thought were facts, but which I knew were lies. The world was in deception, corrupted, and cruel. At first, when I arrived on death row, things were confusing. I even went to the extreme of making a miniature statue out of soap and putting two horns on it and dancing in a sensual frenzy in front of it until ejaculating in ritualistic sexuality. I began to associate my sexuality with devil worship

> After this, I turned to the Bible because I felt possessed, but before that happened, I had an experience with Ralph Downs. Ralph did time in Comstock and he taught me the ways of guards and inmates. He was out of his cell one day and the guard on death row had walked off the tier for a few minutes. Ralph told me to stand on the stool and put my cock to the bars. I did this and he began to suck on my seventeen year old cock. He held a book next to his face to cover the view in case the guard came down the tier and he would make believe he was showing me something in the book.
>
> While this high yellow-skinned fellow blew me, I looked down at the book's title, American History. When Ralph finished (it was only a matter of minutes), I said, "Thank you for the lesson." I can still remember what he answered. He said, "That's what American history is all about." I thought later about how American history is a big blow job. Some people call it a "snow job" because of its lily white lies. Ralph told me that American history was founded on the big lie of George Washington never telling a lie, and about the cherry tree which is the biggest lie in history.
>
> Every night after that I would jerk off (upon Ralph's request) and put my youthful sperm in a small washcloth and throw it to his cell or in front of it and he would eat it. Looking back, this may sound perverted and disgusting, but when it happened, it was pleasurable and made me feel good that I helped somebody feel much happier under such circumstances of human deprivation and degeneracy.

On the other side of Fay Field was a make-shift stage where Salvador would be giving his speech in a few minutes. "Listen, amigo, I'm gonna have to make my speech, so like you can sit here with Rachel for a while, right?"

> Ralph was the next person who was executed while I was on death row. He was a mixture of emotions. I never knew how he would react under certain conditions. All of us knew fear, but his fear was tempered with a certain kind of maturity.

Before being taken to the Dance Hall, he tore down all the holy pictures on his wall. Then he shredded them all into little pieces and threw them out on the gallery. He cursed God, man, and all living things. He claimed that life was cruel and that there was no justice in America. The rest of us on The Row listened, answering only when the tortured man asked one of us a direct question. We all tried to give him the necessary courage to face his death willingly.

What he did with his religious pictures, he also did with every page in the Bible. All night long he ripped out pages, and then tore them into little pieces in front of his cell. Then he paced back and forth, from one end of his cell to the other. I kept thinking to myself, "Can he be in his right state of mind knowing that tomorrow night they'll be taking his life?" Premeditated death throws a person off balance. How is it possible to execute a legal sentence within the scope of the law when the very sentence is enough to confuse the mind? All the men and women who have been executed have died illegally, I think, because they were driven insane one way or the other before the actual execution.

That morning I wakened early, compelled to see Ralph for the last time. I wanted to look directly into his face. Maybe, I thought, by looking into his eyes I could see his soul and therefore reassure myself that there is in actuality an immortal soul within each of us. I was curious.

When I heard his door open, I instinctively jumped out of bed and stood by the bars. When he came out of the cell, he stopped by my cell door, and taking my hand in his, he shook it firmly. There was a bright, sparkling look in his eyes that probably only God had ever looked upon, or even knew what it meant. His hand was warm with sweat, and I could feel his heart beating while he held my hand. Cold chills ran down my back. Very softly, I said, "Be strong, be strong." There wasn't anything else to say. He just smiled back at me and then in a broken voice, he said, "And you, man. You take care of yourself."

It was a cruel experience. It's difficult to describe my feelings without sounding totally irrational. Ralph divided his last meal with the men on the Row. He sent us chicken and other foods which only a few of us actually ate. He also sent us ciga-

rettes. They were Lucky Strikes, but Ralph never had any luck. I think he died a changed man. Before he died, the song, "Tonight, Tonight," was on the radio. After that night, every time I heard those words, "Tonight, you give me your heart...," I remember those executions. Ralph once said if there was life beyond, he'd let us know somehow. After Ralph left, all we had left of him was his name. Because he never came back.

That night I couldn't sleep. My mind kept racing out of control and I kept thinking about his denial and then his acceptance of religion when the priest sat beside him before he was taken off to the Dance Hall and execution. When I got up the next morning, I began reading a book about the Bridey Murphy case. It was the first book I ever read with any interest. It was mostly about reincarnation and hypnotism. Out of a fear of death, I was seeking an alternate way of thinking. From that day on, I read everything I could get my hands on—magazines, crossword puzzles, anything and everything. I even started reading the dictionary, and eventually read it from cover to cover, copying down words I didn't know. The style and mystery of reincarnation was what fascinated me.

The Case of Bridey Murphy acquainted me with Ireland. It made me understand better the mysteries of the mind and how to draw the demarcation line between mind and brain. Mind is the literary and unseen force that formulates thought and ideas for the brain. Mind was the key for me. Before that, everything was corazon, or heart. I even thought that heart was the formulator of ideas.

Then I began studying the Bible with another condemned man. His name was Curtis McNeil. We would praise God and sing hymns together. We put Billy Graham on the radio and listened to Oral Roberts and Herbert W. Armstrong on the World Tomorrow program. The other prisoners got angry, but we saw to it that they gave us our share of the radio on the tier.

After Ralph's execution, my life became much more serious. I stopped smoking and I would fast from all foods every Sunday. I also began making carvings out of bars of soap and I also tried writing poetry. My first poems were mostly about Jesus, goodness, faith, and hope. Because of our religious differences, I was moved with McNeil to another wing in the

Death House. On the new wing, the first cell was occupied by a guy named Nobel. I was in the third cell, and McNeil was in the second cell. At first I would play chess with Nobel, but because of my involvement with Bible matters, I gave it up as a game that belonged to the devil. Noble was a Christian Scientist and we always had arguments about our religion. These arguments eventually led me to the discovery that the best Christian is the one who uses the Bible to prove his point.

I put everything aside and dedicated my life to God.

Salvador stood between two flags, one American, and one from Puerto Rico. Conga drums were everywhere, along with a multitude of wires for the many guitars, loudspeakers, and microphones.

Several bands were recruited by the festival committee, but only two actually showed up. One is nameless, and the other one is called, Los Hermanos, or The Brothers. Salvador told me they were well known among the left in New York City, and considered one of the more progressive groups.

One day while reading the Bible I got down on my knees and prayed for almost a whole hour. After I gave my heart and soul to Jesus, accepted my sinful condition, and declared myself a born-again Christian, every little sexual thought was immediately interpreted as a temptation from Jesus.

I prayed about three times a day and always before eating. I took a shower every day and maintained the highest form of cleanliness. I quit smoking and gave myself to seeking out answers to the questions of existence—life, death, sin, love, hate, God and Jesus. I found answers in the idealism of the simple but strict Christian living. I became a Biblical scholar and educated myself in the King's English by putting to memory verses from the King James version of the Bible.

I even took a Bible course from the Church of Christ in Texas and wrote poems, letters, and began to express my feelings. I read books on every conceivable religion and also some parts of Hegel's philosophy. I used to listen to the following preachers: Billy Graham, Oral Roberts, and Herbert W. Armstrong (my favorite) and others. I used to imitate their speaking abilities while listening, look up any unusual word in the dictionary and compare such to my Bible dictionary. Herbert W. Armstrong's "World of Tomorrow" was how I got interested in world events.

I tried to get Tony Hernadez (the Umbrella Man) to turn to God, and I used to preach to him. When Tony was on the third floor with me under mental observation in the Brooklyn House of Detention, I had burned the face of a tattoo of Jesus on the cross which he had on his arm. Now he brought this up.

"Sal, you're a hypocrite! You motherfucker! You told me in Brooklyn that when you burned the face on my tattoo of Jesus that I would be able to call on Satan for help at twelve midnight. Now you want me to become a fucking Christian! You're sick!"

I still tried to get him to repent and assured him that I was crazy then, but at the time, on death row, I was sane.

"Repent and be at peace with the Lord."

This lead to an argument. He insulted me; I lost my temper, broke my stool, threw a stick at him. It was war. Tony cursing me and Jesus ,and I was in tears because he had forced me to throw the stick at him, I began to pray and cry for the Lord to forgive me. I was, then, by my own request, transferred to the other wing, or tier.

Tony would come over by the window and taunt me from the yard.

'Hypocrite, you devil! Faggot, punk, sissy..."

I would look up from my Bible and say, "Bless you brother. God Bless you," and this got him angrier. It took him a long time to accept that I had changed."

They played a fast song followed by one that was slow and sensual. When one couple got up to dance, another quickly followed, and within seconds at least twenty couples were dancing, slowly, in front of the stage.

Rachel excused herself to go to the bathroom, and Salvador attached himself to a woman that I'd never seen before. She was tall, with blue eyes, and they made a colorful sight as they fell into one another's arms before joining the other people dancing in front of the stage.

The dance was slow and sensual, with a hint of tropical wind and palm trees, but also highly erotic, and amplified a thousand times on a prison field filled with starving men.

> *I stopped masturbating, prayed day and night, read my Bible continually, threw other books out of my cell as being "inspirations of worldly and Satanic knowledge" and condemned other writers (except the Bible-quoting writers) as carnal intellectuals of the world philosophies.*
>
> *Jesus was the only answer.*

Watching Salvador climb the stairs to the stage was like watching an Aztec king ascend to his throne.

He seemed to be in perfect control, wearing a brightly colored bandanna and a matching poncho, as he made his way to the podium.

Microphone in hand, he surveyed the crowd. Raising his arm, and clenching his fist, he salutes the many people waiting to hear him speak.

"Ola!"

Arms raised and fists clenched, the crowd responded in kind.

"Ola!"
"Ola!"

They fall silent, as Salvador raised his hand, and began to speak:

"Thank you...thank you...my name is Salvador Agron... and on behalf of the San Juan Bautista Day Committee, the Concerned Puerto Rican Coalition, and the Latino population her at Greenhaven, I'd like to welcome all of our visitors who've come here today in order to celebrate with us.

"I don't have too much to say except that I hope that all of you visiting today will take the time to realize that the reason why so many people are locked up in here is because of the conditions in our society...but that these conditions are just the effects that flow out of our life style in a particular society...and that this is what supports certain patterns of behavior which eventually produces even more social problems.

"And it's because of this that I think it's fitting that when we celebrate San Juan Bautista Day that we also honor Don Pedro Albizu Campos...because he was the father of Puerto Rican nationalism...and we should do this because he was dedicated to the concept of a Puerto Rico that would be a model for future generations.

"And lastly...I'd like to say to all our visitors...that if you're really concerned about the return of our Puerto Rican brothers here at Greenhaven to your society...if you are really concerned...we would appreciate your cooperation, your gifts, your employment, and your social and political involvement...and of course anything positive you can do for us will be welcome.

"Thank you..."

Then Salvador began a chant of, "Freedom."

Again and again, in and out, again and again, he chanted what to him was probably a sacred word.

With raised arms and clenched fists, the crowd responded in kind.

Arms raised and fists clenched, the crowd chanted back.

> *I was hated by some inmates on The Row and also by some guards because I sublimated all my fears and spent my time in a happy state singing hymns and praising God. My dream life became vivid and colorful. I killed the purple snakes in*

> *my dreams, raised the dead, healed the sick, and had vistas into other life existence's though I doubted about reincarnation. I took the oppressive conditions in a very understanding manner. I was sincere. I was innocent—as clean as a newborn baby—and so for a while I forgot about the crime they said I committed.*

When Salvador came down from the stage, he threw his arms around Rachel. Then, together, they threw their arms around me.

Hugging one another, we were close enough for me to smell the sweet bananas on Rachel's breath.

> *I began to question myself and I could not see myself committing the killings in the playground. I could not remember the crime and I realized then, more than ever, how I confessed to something I didn't do. People believed me because of the cape I wore and the knife I had.*
>
> *But I did not worry because Jesus had forgiven me and that's all that mattered. I didn't need to convince the world of my innocence. I left it all in the Lord's hands and to my mother's prayers. Politics and social movements built around my case. It became a political, racial, and ethnic issue. Though I didn't understand it at the time, I observed what was going on and I began to question the motives of these social and political forces.*

Sitting with Salvador and Rachel at a picnic table in a faraway corner of the prison yard, I tried my best to look away as their tongues kissed, danced, and surrendered. Maria was here with Roberto Torres, and unless one knew better, they looked like they'd known one another for years instead of several hours. John O'Neil sat on the other end of the table, and without a hint of self-consciousness, his hard eyes roamed back and forth between Salvador and Rachel's tongues to Salvador's crotch.

Our table was one of four sitting directly beneath a guntower, and when I looked up I clearly saw a man inside holding a rifle.

The other three tables were also filled with people. Some were sitting, others were lying underneath. And from the ones underneath, I heard the sounds of soft whispers, and moaning. Mouth to mouth and breast to breast, they all seemed to be on fire with one another.

"Richard, stand in front of us here for a minute."

This said by Salvador in the lowest and softest of whispers.

Taking a position in front of Salvador and Rachel, I saw them slowly sliding beneath the table, and I laughed, as I became their shield.

> It was a week before my scheduled execution when the news came to me in the Death House yard that I'd been granted a commutation of my sentence from death in the electric chair to one of life imprisonment. It was cold—like a blizzard would be rolling over the prison soon.
>
> I am sitting against a wall when a guard walks over.
>
> "You've been saved," he says.
>
> "Yeah, all thanks to God. I was saved when I started walking with the Lord last year. Do you wanna be saved?"
>
> "That's not the kinda 'saved' I'm talking about. It's the Governor. He gave you a commute."
>
> "You mean I can go home?"
>
> "No, but you won't be here anymore. He made your sentence life in prison, so you'll be moving outta here pretty quick."
>
> "Thanks be to God. All thanks to Him."
>
> "Yeah, well, you can thank whoever you want, because to me it's all the same."
>
> "You got any idea where they'll send me?"
>
> "Probably to Elmira. That's one of the kiddie joints."
>
> "All thanks to God!"

"Yeah, well, let's see what you say after you've been there a while."

Leaning against the wall, I think to myself how I have truly been touched by the hands of the Lord. But why me, and not someone else? Why me, the Capeman? Was it my moms with her prayers and her candles? Was it Papi? Aurea? Or did an angel whisper softly about the light of Heaven to the Governor while he slept through the night in his big house? Why me?

"Why me? why me?" This keeps getting repeated over and over in my mind, like a wild drum beat, until, out of nowhere, a slant of sun, literally a ray, flies through the dark clouds like some winged angel on a mission of mercy.

Sitting with my back to the wall, the sun on my face, and my eyes closed, a voice from deep inside whispers to me how the light from the sun is surely a sign from the Lord. A sign for me to move on with my life. And a sign that My Mission from this very day will be for me to perform the Lord's work while I'm living out my earthly life—with my job being to spread His message, His gospel, and His love so that all can share equally in his blessing.

All of a sudden, the message is clear. Why me? Because the Lord has given me his blessing so I can pass it on to others. Me, the Capeman, Salvador Agron, keeper of the holy word.

Nothing is sadder and more melancholy than saying good-bye to someone you care deeply about who cannot go home with you no matter what. And it's always the same, whether from a hospital bed, a home for the aged, or at Greenhaven at the end of San Juan Bautista Day.

Hundreds of arms around hundreds of waists, shoulders, and necks.

Then back on the bogus covered wagons, with kisses, hugs, and waving good-bye.

2/11/62
Sing Sing Prison
Death House

Gov. Nelson Rockefeller
Executive Mansion, Albany, N.Y.

Dear Gov. Rockefeller:
    I write you this letter, with a heart full of thankfulness, for the mercy you had for me. And I pray that other boys out there will learn that the Laws of God are not to be broken. And that prayer and true repentance are the moral guides to a good and respectable life. I will also like for you to know, that I would never let, what you have done for me, be lost. But I will use it for good, and for good alone.

And from my heart I say, "Thank you."
Yours very truly,

Salvador Agron
126-647

Hon. Paul D. McGinnis
Commissioner of Correction
Albany, New York
February 14, 1962

Dear Commissioner:
    Confirming recommendations made to you over the telephone on February 13, 1962 at the time we were discussing another matter, I called your attention to the fact that Salvador Agron, #126647 who was recently commuted from the death penalty and whose date of release is now scheduled as September 12, 1994, should be transferred out of this institution due to the wide publicity his case received in the newspapers prior to and before Commutation of Sentence and subsequently thereafter.

I do not feel that it would be advisable to place him in the general population at this institution as he is considered by some Puerto Ricans as somewhat of a hero and, in justice to Agron and the Department of Correction, he should not be placed in a position where he would become a gang leader within this institution. It is, therefore, my recommendation that he be transferred without too much delay to another institution of your choosing, as at the present time he is being kept separated from the general population and assigned to the segregation building.

I felt that you might be interested in the attached four (4) envelopes received for him yesterday which contain numerous red hearts with various messages inscribed therein apparently from teachers of various grades in Puerto Rico. These, of course, will not be delivered to him as the messages are unsigned, etc. Therefore, you could, after they have answered your purpose, return them to this institution or keep this material in your files in your office, whichever you may desire to do.

       Very truly yours,
       Wilfred L. Denno
       WARDEN

Chapter Four

AUREA

9/26/74
Greenhaven Correctional Facility

My Dear Genoveva:

Revolutionary greetings! I was looking for a beautiful card to send you, just to let you know how much I appreciated what you have done, are doing, and have in mind to do for me.

I cannot finds words sometimes to tell you what I feel for you. I am sorry for the way I behaved during the San Juan Bautista festival, but these things happen!

Sometimes we feel so much for a person that it is best to keep it to ourselves—and this is the right thing to do. But, again, I am sorry for not paying more attention to you at the festival.

Geno, you are wonderful—but sometimes it is difficult to say such things because it may sound ridiculous. But at the expense of sounding ridiculous—you and Jacoby are members of my family. You are both pure examples of what a sister and brother should be. I love you both very much.

What would I ever do without you and Jacoby? He is the man responsible for helping me to write my book (I would not have thought to write this book if he had not encouraged me to do so), and you are my political comrade, someone I can trust, and someone with whom I can open my heart without any kind of censorship. For a political person, having a comrade like yourself, is very important!

So if I have done anything to offend you or Jacoby in any way, please forgive me because it was done unintentionally. I would not do anything to harm you or Jacoby in any way (mentally or physically)—but still I feel I own you both an apology. I should have stayed closer to you both during the festival. But I am sure you understand the reasons why I wasn't able to do this as much as I might have liked.

What did you think of my speech? My rule is: reality and truth.

When we look upon the world as it is in reality, we can better analyze it and cope with it, and change it. When we speak the truth without shame in our brain we are being real—truth is life and life is truth and no matter how much we run and hide we must first live with ourselves and if we are truthful to ourselves we cannot be false to anyone!! Right?

Please write when you get the chance. Whenever you write, I will answer. I know you are struggling out there, and that the struggle keeps you on the move!

I was glad to hear that you and Jacoby will be going back to the Bronx. This time to meet Aurea, and also some of her children. My moms might also drop by. I really hope my moms will be able to travel with you to Puerto Rico. Have you seen the list of places that I've asked him to photograph? I don't know how many places are on the list but it's a lot, and without you and moms I think it will be difficult for him to get around.

I spoke with Aurea earlier today and she is expecting a call from you with the day and time that you and Jacoby are planning to visit. Jacoby will also be calling you.

Con mucho respecto y arino y en solidaridod me despido con un abrazo muy revolucionario.

Your brother/comrade
Salvador Agron   #16486

When I called Genoveva, she said the following Saturday would be okay for a visit to Aurea's house.

"Wanna meet like we did the last time? " I asked.

"At West Fourth Street?"
"That okay for you?"
"It's fine...so I'll call Aurea to make sure the timing's okay...and then I'll call and let you know...are you going to be bringing a tape recorder...or a camera?"
"Probably both...but at least a camera because afterwards I wanna take some shots of the playground..."
"What'd you talkin' about...what playground?"
"The *playground,* you know...where the killings went down."
"Why would you wanna do that?"
" Because he asked me to, that's why!"
" Salvador asked you for pictures of that?"
"Yeah...and you've seen the list he sent, right?"
"But I don't remember seeing that on the list."
"It was there...and also the police station where they took him after he was arrested"
"Was that the place where the people were screaming at him from outside, and where he said that stuff about wanting to kill the reporter or something...and Gabe Pressman was out in front?"
"That's the place."

June 25th, 1974
Greenhaven Correctional Facility

Dear brother Richard:

You seemed to be really enjoying yourself at the festival. But please let me give you a bit of advice: you must be very careful with prisoners, they will size you up, and if they think you are a nice guy or an easy take, they will smile, talk "right on" and they will try their best to take and use you. You are my brother and I must tell you this because I would not like to see someone use you. Convicts will con as long as the system perpetuates the concept that they are cons!! Be cool with the cats you speak with at these festivals.

I'm beginning to sound like a big brother! But it would be wise for you to let me know the people you talk to (at the festivals) because this way I can give you feedback on anyone—I know all these cats like I know the palm of my hand. Many of them have good fronts but are in reality as phony as a three dollar bill.

Love, power, and understanding,
Salvador Agron#16486

Walking on Mosholu Parkway to Aurea's house, I noticed something carved into the wet cement on a patch of sidewalk. Kneeling down, I read the words: *Fordam Baldies.*

"You remember them?" I asked her.

"No...but they sound familiar...who were they?"

"They were this unbelievable gang that used to hang around over on Fordham Road, near the RKO theater, and the Grand Concourse...and they used to shave their heads...that's why they were known as the 'Baldies.'"

"And you knew them?"

"No...no, I didn't know them, but I used to go to school just a few blocks from here and they were always like this mythical gang that everyone used to talk about..."

"Why'd they shave their heads?"

"I don't really know, but I think it was because they didn't want the hair getting in the way when they were fighting."

"When was all this?"

"1958."

Back then the gangs were everywhere: Negro gangs, Italian gangs, Puerto Rican gangs, and White gangs.

I was involved with approximately four different gangs during the 1950's: the Junior Chaplains in Brooklyn, the Tigers in Puerto Rico, and the Mau-Mau's of the Fort Green

Projects, and the Vampires.
I was not the president of the Vampires, like the newspapers said I was, but rather the war counselor.

Aurea's apartment building was on the corner of Knox Place, just a short walk from Mosholu Parkway, and from the street it looked no different than the rest of the buildings. Built from brick, now faded a deep brown, all of them had fire escapes running from top to bottom. At first glance, Aurea's building looked just like her mother's. But Esmeralda's building was a five story walk-up, and Aurea's had six stories, and an elevator.

Aurea lived on the second floor. After she rang us up from the lobby of her building, we rode the elevator to her apartment.

We used to call the fights we had with other gangs, "rumbles."
Sometimes a rumble would start because someone had invaded our neighborhood. This was our territory, or "turf," as we used to call it, and anyone here who didn't belong on this turf would be taking a chance on getting a beating. At other times, a rumble might start because someone's girlfriend had been insulted, or "sounded," as we used to call it, by someone from another gang. Or it might start because of racial stuff, like an Italian gang going after a Black gang, or a Puerto Rican gang going after a white gang.
This was the 1950's, and New York City belonged to the gangs.
One gang in the Bronx was the "Sportsmen," and I think they used to wear red and black as their colors, and then there were the "Bishops" and the "Chaplains" out in Brooklyn, but with brother clubs in the Bronx. Then there was the "Hobo Lords," the "Heart Kings," the "Mau-Mau Chaplains," the "Imperial Hoodlums," and the "Enchanters."
Gangs were all over New York City, and many of the gang

members had been picked up for one thing or another. Some were actually framed on charges which were false in an effort by the different boroughs of New York to clean up the streets to comply with the public and civic pressure being put on by the city. Repression landed many an innocent kid in the can and there was no one to complain to.

Some of the gangs used garrison belts and some of them used zip guns. These were home-made guns built from toy guns that you could buy in almost any toy store. We used to file them down in such a way that you were able to attach the antenna from a car into the barrel of the toy gun. Then you attached some rubber bands to the barrel, put in a .22 bullet and you were all set. But I didn't like using them because sometimes they would misfire and then you were in big trouble.

Other gangs used baseball bats, sticks, knives, or whatever else was available that could be easily used as a weapon.

The first time I had ever seen Aurea Agron was in a photograph that appeared in the New York *Daily News*.

Taken a day or two after Salvador had been arrested in 1959, it showed a young and beautiful woman with the pale skin and black hair of her brother. But where Salvador's eyes were small and hazel-colored, Aurea's were large, deep, and very brown.

When I attended public schools during the 1950's, I was pushed through grades 6, 7, 8 and finally sat as a semi-illiterate with the mentality of a twelve year old in the back row of the 9th grade.

The New York City schools were a failure before I ever became one. The whole entire system was a farce and I think there was the real fear of educating first generation Puerto Ricans due to the fear of the times. The prejudice against the newcomers and the systematic spite of the system against those who spoke a foreign language.

This was at Junior High School 117 in Brooklyn, without

graduating, and in complete disregard for my education. The public school system did not believe in the education of a "spic" and the records of the schools I attended in the fifties can show this undeniable fact.

Aurea was seventeen in the *Daily News* photograph, and now, nearly fifteen years later, the woman greeting us as we got off the elevator looked pretty much the same. So much so that when she took my hand to shake it, I actually started feeling a little dizzy. Partly because of the uncanny resemblance she had to the photograph, and partly because meeting her meant the circle was finally closing.

First I had met Salvador, then his mother, and now his sister. This plus returning to what for me was a neighborhood of many memories—made me ultra-sensitive to my surroundings.

Shaking my hand, she smiled, and then looking directly into my eyes, she introduced herself.

"I'm Aurea Agron...and you must be Richard Jacoby, right?"

Laughing, I said, "Yes...yes...I am."

Turning around, I introduced her to Genoveva.

After shaking Genoveva's hand, she invited us to follow her into the apartment.

When we weren't going to war against other gangs, we just hung out on street corners, or at a neighborhood candy store. Talking, showing off to the girls, and getting high. We used to drink cheap wines, like "Thunderbird" or "Sneaky Pete." Sweet wines that got us high without a hassle. Then we'd stand around and listen to music, mostly doo-wop music.

The apartment, long and narrow, consisted of a living room, a kitchen, a bathroom, and two bedrooms.

Esmeralda was sitting by the window in the living room, and looking past her through the window I saw the trees along Mosholu Parkway.

"These are two of my daughters, and this is my son, Richie."

The two young women, bore a striking resemblance to Aurea, but instead of looking like her daughters, they appear to be her sisters.

Rosie and Madelyn were their names. Rosie is sixteen and Madelyn, the eldest of Aurea's children, is seventeen. Richie, her son, is just a little boy.

Later I would learn that Aurea had a total of seven children by three different husbands. Some living with her, some in foster homes, and some in Puerto Rico.

"You look just like you did in the photograph from the newspaper."

"I do? Which one was that?"

"The one in the *Daily News*, you look exactly the same."

"Get outta here! That was taken in 1959...I don't look like that no more!"

"You do really...Geno, doesn't she look the same to you?"

"He's right...you really do look the same."

"Well...that's nice for both of you to say that...but I don't think I do."

> *Some of us smoked reefer, but not that often because it wasn't that easy to get. So mostly it was wine and goofballs, or barbituates, the stuff that either put you to sleep or made you feel dopy.*

Although Aurea spoke perfect English, the questions I asked were apparently much more complicated than I intended. Instead of answering a question entirely in English, she suddenly switched over to Spanish.

This sudden transition from English to Spanish kept repeating itself, particularly whenever the questions were about what Salvador's first years in New York had been like.

My sense was that very few people had ever asked her such detailed questions about her life, so that until now all these things had been stored up inside.

At least until a few minutes ago

> *Even though I was just a little boy when I first came to New York City from Puerto Rico, there was still pressure for me to become a gang member. But I did not embrace the "gang concept" right away. This took time.*

"How old was Salvador when he came to New York the first time?"

"The first time? I dunno...maybe ten years old...maybe more..."

"How old are you?"

"Why you wanna know this?" she said, laughing at the question. "You shouldn't be askin' a woman how old she is!"

"I'm sorry...but I've gotta know for the story...when's your birthday?"

"I was born on May 16th, 1942 in Mayaguez, Puerto Rico."

"So you're thirty now, right?"

"You got some kind of calculator with you or somethin'?"

> *What I'll never forget about coming to New York City that first time was the bumpy airplane ride. I don't know what kinds of airplanes they've got going back and forth now but the one I was on was real bumpy, like we was always on the verge of crashing.*
>
> *When we landed there was no one there to meet me.*

"Your mother said that when he came the first time there was some kind of mix-up in the schedules and that no one was around to get Salvador at the airport."

"That's right but I don't remember exactly what happened...but my mother did finally get someone to take her to the airport to pick him up and bring him back to Manhattan."

"And you were where in Manhattan?"

"The Lower East Side...we had this tiny, little place somewhere around 9th or 10th Streets, I don't remember the exact address...we moved around a lot when we first came here, but I know that when Sal first got here we was livin' in a place that was downtown somewheres."

> *From the very first moment that I walked into that apartment, there was trouble between me and my step-father. It was like he didn't want to have nothing to do with me.*

His step-father's name was Carlos Gonzales. He was a Pentecostal minister when Esmeralda had fallen in love with him in Puerto Rico, and together with Aurea they had left the poorhouse to seek a new life in New York City.

Moving from furnished room to furnished room until they rented a small tenement apartment on the Lower East Side.

"Did Salvador get along with your step-father?"

"Are you kidding? Carlos didn't want anything to do with my brother...and he was always givin' him a hard time."

"Hard time" meant constant surveillance by Carlos in order to insure that Salvador would abide by all the rules of the house. No listening to the radio, except for the local Pentecostal station. No singing. No playing in the house. No running. No pictures on the wall. No fun. No love. Nothing but screaming, yelling, and frequent beatings in order to remove what Carlos called, "the demons within Salvador's heart, just waiting to come out."

"Wasn't Salvador going to school or anything?"

"Yeah, he was, but not like on any regular basis or anything..."

"So what'd he do all day?"

"He stayed in the house alotta the time...and I remember him once playin' like he was Superman and he fell outta the window from where we was livin'"

"He fell into the street?"

> *I fell from the fifth story of our apartment into a yard with rocks, sticks, broken bottles, and empty beer cans. I was maybe eleven years old when this happened, and I broke my arm. The fire department took me to Bellevue Hospital where my arm was put in a cast. I was playing Superman on the fire escape when I must have jumped or slipped. People said I jumped. I was too caught up in the fantasy of playing Superman to really know. I was influenced by television easily.*

"How long was he in Bellevue?"

"Not that long...but he got into all kinds of hassles when he was over there...because I remember the doctors were always talkin' to my mother about how wild he was."

> *At Bellevue, I refused to eat my peas and when I was ordered to eat the meal, I threw them on the floor. For this action, a net was put over my bed. It looked like a fishing net. I reached into a drawer on a stand next to the bed where I kept a razor blade and with the blade I cut the net to pieces. The nurses and attendants tried to grab me and I went near a window and threatened to jump out.*

Not long after being released from Bellevue, Salvador was accused of committing a burglary, and after a brief court hearing, was remanded to the Youth House, a private organization financed by the City and State of New York for troubled boys and girls.

The organization sponsored several detention centers. Salvador was sent to one on East 12th Street, not far from the tenement where he lived.

> *I was sent to the Youth House at the age of twelve for breaking into a neighbor's house, stealing cigars, some money, and a flashlight. We stole $7 and a flashlight. When we went inside the bedroom of my neighbor's apartment, he was in a t-shirt, lying on his bed, drunk as a stone. I took a cigar and put it in his mouth and we left out the window. I was caught because I tried to sell the flashlight to my step-father.*

"How long was he in the Youth House?"

"I don't remember but it wasn't that long...but when he got out...lotsa other problems started happenin' to my brother...because there was all kinds of trouble between him and my step-father."

> *I spent about nine months in the Youth House. There I learned how to swim, play pool and basketball. At the Youth House I used to be taken out to the park to play ball, but I did not participate, always searching how to escape from my captors but never succeeding.*

As the afternoon wore on, a pattern slowly emerged. Whenever the questions were about Salvador, Aurea conveyed the twists and turns of his life in perfect English. But when the questions dealt with Carlos, and what impact he'd had on Salvador's life, her eyes turned hard, her voice rose, and she spoke only in Spanish.

At one point in our conversation, one of Aurea's daughters, Madelyn, asked me if it would be okay if she braided my hair. I said okay and she sat behind me. And as her mother alternated from English to Spanish, Madelyn deftly braided my hair.

When Esmeralda, watching and listening from her seat by the window on the other side of the room, said something in Spanish, Aurea burst out laughing.

"My moms said you and Madelyn look very nice together."

> At the Youth House I was once punished for a fight by being put all day in a pitch black room. Being afraid of the dark, I cried like the eleven-year old boy that I was. At the end of the day, I was taken out and sent to my room.
>
> My step-father told the Children's Court judge that I was too much to handle, but I felt the same about him.

Later Genoveva told me it was Carlos who had been responsible for a petition to Children's Court, asking that Salvador be sent away because of his erratic behavior both at home and on the streets. What really convinced the judge that Salvador should be placed in a special training school was Carlos telling him how Salvador had broken into the neighbor's apartment.

"So like when did he start getting involved with the gangs?"

"When he got sent to Wiltwyck...that's when lotsa stuff started happening...and then it really got crazy when he got out."

"When was this?"

"I'm not sure...but I think it was maybe 1956..."

"How long was he in Wiltwyck?"

"Oh, man, like a long time...it was at least two years 'cause I got married about that time."

"How old were you when you got married?"

"The first time? Lemme see..."

Using her fingers, and whispering names and dates to herself, Aurea appears to be calculating the exact amount of time she spent with each husband, as well as when each of her children had been born.

"I was fourteen when I got married...and I know this because I had Madelyn a year later in 1957...and Sal was back from Wiltwyck just before Rosie was born, so that had to be 1956."

> The Wiltwyck School was my next stop. I was sent there in 1955 by the juvenile court. There I went to school, but being a bit retarded I could not learn. I tried but my reading and writing was semi-literate. At Wiltwyck I got punished with straps for unruly behavior and I wound up more of a juvenile delinquent than when I went in. I was miseducated. I learned about crime and gangs. I was not given individual care and treatment for which Wiltwyck was successful and boasted for. It was all a public lie. I ran away from Wiltwyck two times and when we were taken to the circus at Madison Square Garden, I absconded, making my third attempt at escaping from my captors a success.
>
> At Wiltwyck I picked up many bad habits, such as the knowledge of pot and smoking. It was supposed to be a home or institution for retarded and troubled kids, problem children, and I was considered such. I knew how to read Spanish a little and English also, but I had no comprehension of anything that I read. I even had trouble in comprehending the Dick and Jane reading books of the 1950s. "Spot jump. Dick run. Jane cry. This is Spot. This is Dick. He is a boy. Jane is a girl." Well, it was funny talk, but I still couldn't make any sense out of such stupidity and so I was considered a bit retarded.

"Aurea, when your brother was living with you and Carlos, did he ever think of him as his father?"

"Yeah...he did...but my step-father didn't want nothing to do with him. Sal would always try to be getting close to him but Carlos always was tellin' him to go away and leave him alone."

"So your step-father didn't think of him as his son or anything."

"No way...and like when my brother would call him daddy, he would get really mad, and tell my brother, 'Don't you be callin' me daddy, cause your real daddy is in Puerto Rico,' and he didn't even like for me or my moms to show him any kind of attention because he said it was against our religion for us to be touching each other."

"So Salvador didn't get much affection then, right?"

"My step-father didn't let him get nothing!"

> *My always sounding and acting like I was mentally retarded was not due to my mental state but because I did not get the parental affection necessary to develop normally. Also, those who were my judges and social worker, counselor, etc. were much more confused than I in that they could not give me the proper attention and care that I desperately needed. This almost distorted my sense of love in life and later on I had to teach myself what love was for me.*
>
> *I can still remember my first day at Wiltwyck. I came up to Poughkeepsie by train and was picked up by a counselor at the Poughkeepsie train station. Mrs. Weiss, my social worker, handed me over to the counselor and also handed him a folder which today seems to be still following me around. I was taken to a car (a 1950 station wagon) and directed to the front seat by the counselor whose name I forgot.*
>
> *As the car moved, I looked down the Hudson River trying to see if I could spot traces or signs that would lead me back to New York if I should ever decide to run away. The only thing that I could see that led back to New York were the railroad tracks. The counselor looked at me and said, "Don't look so*

sad, son. You'll get used to these parts and Wiltwyck is better than Warwick." But, deep in my heart I felt otherwise. I felt out of place. I felt lonely, rejected, unloved, like I was not worth anything, and the counselor was a big Black dude whom I already felt was a fucking liar and could not keep a straight face when he spoke.

"Don't call me son," I said defiantly. "My father is in Puerto Rico."

"Okay, kid."

"Don't call me kid," I said defensively. "My name is Salvador Agron. A-G-R-O-N."

"Okay, Sal. Now that I know that you can spell your name," he retorted as though trying to humor me. But I was not to be humored, and I just turned my head away and looked out the window. He kept his mouth shut the rest of the way and when he got to the Wiltwyck School property, he spoke.

"Well, Sal, we're already home, but you do not seem to be in a talkative mood."

"This is your home, not mine," I said rebelliously.

"Sal, you better start learning to get used to it because from your attitude I think that this will be a second home to you for quite a while." As he spoke, the car pulled to a stop in front of the cottages and straight ahead was the main office. To my right, the mess hall and to my left, on a hill, the wall and the mountains. It is a stone wall that does not enclose anything but which is just there and appears very much like a prison wall.

I got out of the car and walked towards the main building. I was processed, interviewed, sent upstairs, stripped and put through the regular institutional process. Upstairs I was issued my clothing, winter boots, and a coat with squares of yellow, red, and blue. Regular civilian clothes, yet with the institutional smell on them.

"You think he liked it at Wiltwyck?"

"I dunno...like he never said much about it...but he did seem different when he came outta there."

"Like how?"

"He wasn't the happy-go-lucky kind of guy that he was when he went in there...he used to fool around alot...he was always makin' jokes an' stuff and then when he got back from there he was much quieter..."

"So you're sayin' he was different in some way?"

"Yeah...he was very quiet...and it was like he was hiding lots of stuff inside of his self and not letting no one know what it was he was hiding."

While in Wiltwyck, homosexuality was rampant. Attacks, con games, inducements, and the whole seduction process was there. My first experience came with a counselor. I went to see him one night for something and I had to go all the way to his room. He was sleeping so I knocked on the door. He said, "Come on in, Sal." I stepped inside and he ordered me to lock the door behind me which I did. I was standing right there in front of him in my jockey shorts. I was about 12 or 13 and he was in his twenties somewhere, a calculation. I explained my problem. I think it was a stomach ache that I had. He told me to sit on the bed and so I sat there innocent to what was about to happen. The pervert put his hand on my stomach and began to massage my tummy with his hand.

He told me to lay back on the bed, which I did, and he came from under the sheets and he was nude. His penis was hard but I made like I didn't notice. He rubbed his face against mine and I could feel his rough stumps scrape against my hairless face. Then he slowly went to my chest. Now I could feel his cock rubbing up against my body, hot and hard, while his hand worked on my shorts till he pulled them down and began playing with my now erect penis. He took it into his mouth and then came up and kissed me right on the lips.

I felt disgust, but at the same time the perversion was arousing me. He gently guided my hand to his throbbing cock and placed it around it. I knew what the pig wanted so I played with it and he played with mine. He put them together and mine was sort of small next to his. He removed my hand from his hard penis and face-to-face with me he placed his cock between my legs while pushing his hard penis against mine and his belly. His rod between my legs felt warm and hard and I was sort of enjoying this. Then warm liquid hit me and his ejaculation between my legs ran down my buttocks. I could not come but he drove me into a thrill with his mouth on my cock.

When I walked out the room I was still a virgin child in the sense that he did not insert his penis in my rectum and this he did not do because I was so young. I went back upstairs, got under the covers and cried mutely. Shame was in my conscience and I felt lonely, abused and low for what had just happened. And to think that he worked in this institution for kids. I said the Our Father out of guilt for enjoying such dehumanization at the hands of this counselor and I asked God, in the name of Jesus, to forgive me.

I was left with my guilt though and I doubted my maleness. I hated this counselor after this, but I did not want to show it. He treated me extra good after this and because of fear that I should say something, he would let me get away with anything. But he never did this again because he knew that once was enough of a chance.

I have been the victim too. I thought about becoming the hunter of those who made me what I became.

Wiltwyck is not the place that Claude Brown in his fictitious Manchild in the Promised Land makes it to be. Wiltwyck was a school of corruption, a school where I learned how to play strip poker from a female counselor who enjoyed watching us play while she literally played with her cunt and lustfully watched the kids in the nude. Wiltwyck was a house of lust, crime, and further disorientation of the boys and their sanity.

"Did he go back to the apartment on the Lower East Side when he got out of Wilwyck?"

"No, because we wasn't living there no more."

"Where were you?"

"Me? I was livin' with my husband by the time he got out..and I was already pregnant with Rosie...but sometimes

I stayed with my moms...she was living with Carlos by the waterfront...and they had this apartment over a store...and that's where he had his church."

"He had a church?"

"Yeah...and lemme see if I can remember the name here...oh, it was, Messenger of Christ.' "

"And that's where Salvador went after Wiltwyck?"

"Not there...not in the church...but in the apartment upstairs."

> *After leaving Wiltwyck I went to live in Brooklyn with my mother and step-father. We lived down by the waterfront, between Hudson and Water street. On the first floor of the building was the storefront Pentecostal Church. From down below every night came the loveliest of songs and hymns dedicated by the hallelujahs to the Kingdom of God. In this congregation the rainbow people, from ebony black to rosy pink clapped their hands in union to their god. I attended the services to feel some of the brotherly and sisterly love and look over the Pentecostal virgins as they danced around intoxicated by the Holy Spirit, with their tambourines and their beautiful dresses as though they were Garland virgins of dance and song, as a druid would say. At times I sat outside the church, or across the street, and listened to the strumming of the guitarist and the blessings of the congregation.*

The year was 1956, and the gangs were everywhere.

Some wore distinctive jackets with the names of their gangs sewn with bright letters across the backs. Some wore black leather motorcycle jackets, with studded garrison belts, which doubled as weapons whenever a rumble would go down.

The girls were called "debs," or "beatrices," with gang names like, "Shamrocks," or "Dillinger Girls" and were considered to be the "sister" clubs for the boy gangs.

Some, like Salvador, had adopted a distinctive walk. Half

slouch, half roll, it came off as a decided strut, and was known by insiders as "the diddy-bopper walk." Others called it the "Coxsackie shuffle," in honor of the reformatory with the same name for young delinquent men deep in the Catskill Mountains.

The year was 1956, and the diddy-boppers were everywhere.

> *I was living in Brooklyn on 75 Hudson Street, and my hangout was the Farragut Projects around Sand Street. It was there that I joined a gang, the Junior Chaplains, after being released from Wiltwyck. This was when I met a kid named Jones for the first time, and we became good friends.*
>
> *Jones was Black and also a member of the Junior Chaplains. He was a strange fellow in many ways.. We would steal together, fight together, and eat together. However, he wanted to dominate the friendship we had and I felt the same way. This led to arguments and we would jump on the grass in the housing project and fight like two wild cats. But if anybody from the Junior Chaplains tried to intervene, we would both stop fighting and kick his ass.*

"My moms says she's willing to go with you and Genoveva to Puerto Rico."

"Really?" I said.

"Yeah...you just gotta give me the date so we can let her get ready and everything

"We'll let you know the exact date as soon as we figure out when it is we're gonna go."

"When you think you'll be going?"

"Probably on Labor Day week-end."

> *The Junior Chaplains did not have initiations and one could join the gang just by hanging out. We were all Junior because we were trying to imitate the older kids from the Fort*

> Green projects. There was a president, but he did not care much about the gang and so it was a rather disorganized gang—a sort of mimicking of the Fort Green Chaplains who we looked up to.

"What was the apartment like?"
"Which one?"
"Where your Moms was living with Carlos over the church...the place on Hudson Street."
"It was nice, really nice."

> We were considered to be the "little people" of the Chaplains and we usually fought against the little people from the other gangs, like the Bishops or the Sand Street Angels. The little people were actually most of the time the brothers and sisters of the above fourteen year olds belonging to the older gangs which ranged from age 15 to 21. Usually when a gang member became 18 or 21, he or she would quit the gang and become a "coolie," meaning that he was in no gang or had stopped bopping or gang fighting.

"Nice" meant a five-room cold-water flat for thirty dollars a month on the third floor of a three story brick building. Aurea said it was always clean but that there was never enough furniture. Partly because there wasn't much money back then, and partly, she said, because her step-father didn't think it was right for religious people to have too much in the way of comforts.

"That's the way he always was, and I remember that even at Christmas time he'd make a big deal if me or my brother was to make decorations and stuff."

On the wall of the kitchen in the Hudson Street apartment were two plaques. One said, in English, "Don't smoke here please. Christ is our unseen guest." And the other, in

Spanish, said the equivalent of:

"I am a good pastor. The good pastor gives his life for his congregation."

> Coolies with gang reputations were usually challenged by gangs all over when spotted in their neighborhood. They either walked away or defended themselves or went to their house, put on their colors (jacket with gang insignia) and fought to maintain their reputation. The cycle was always present and some who tried to go straight never made it out of the vicious cycle.

Years later someone would write an article about Salvador in which they compared the way Salvador lived during this part of his life with the life of a roaming wolf with unlimited options.

> We all saw a knife duel one time between two coolies. They cut each other up real bad. It was a tough cat from the Chaplains and one from the Elderly Bops. They were at a party in Fort Green when they started arguing over a girl. Both had retired from gang busting, but that night in the heat of argument, they both went home and stepped out flying their colors.
>
> When a coolie goes to his closet and takes out his outfit and comes out flying his colors, it means that he is ready to kill and die. When these two coolies confronted each other in the park near Fort Green, we all watched. Both had to be taken to the hospital from the knife cuts they inflicted on each other.

"Wasn't he going to school or anything?"

"A little...I think he went for a while to JHS 217...or maybe it was 218, I don't really remember, but he didn't go there much because he'd stay out all night and no one ever knew where he was...and he was always getting into hassles with the cops...they'd pick him up and they'd question him...stuff like that all the time."

"What were they questioning him about?"

"All kinds of stuff...burglaries, robberies...and lots of assaults, like he was always accused of beating people up because of the gangs."

"You think he did?"

"He never said nothin' to me about stuff like that."

> One day, as I remember now, a young guy named Bone came and rounded up the whole of the Junior Chaplains. Bone was one of the leading members. We all went and fought the little people of the Sand Street Angels. That night I stabbed two kids. It was a bloody fight and we were victorious. One white boy came at me with a chain and hit me across my chest. Luckily my leather jacket was closed. It stopped the impact, but I hit the ground and not being able to breathe, gang members were scrambling all over. I was given a knife (an extra) by Tom and when I got up, I looked for the guy with the chain. When I saw him, I screamed, "You guinea motherfucker. I'm still breathing" I ran to wack him with a tin garbage can to prevent him from hitting me with the chain again. The chain hit the garbage can top to prevent me from hitting him with the chain again. The chain hit the can top as my hand came from under it and he held his guts calling me a "dirty low-down tropical monkey spic." I stabbed the other two who tried to hit me. When the police cars came, we all ran in different directions."
>
> The next day the older kids from Sand Street were looking for me to kill me, but when the Chaplains of Fort Green got word of it, they came down from Fort Green and told the Sand Street Angels not to interfere in the rumbles of the little people. Otherwise there would be an all-out gang war. They argued about how dirty I was and the Chaplains told them that their little people were just as vicious.

> After much consultation, the older guys decided that it was better to leave the rumbles of the little people among the little people. I was saved from the vengeance of the kids' brothers—big Italian guys. But I never forgot what they said, "You let that spic punk know that as soon as he becomes fifteen and joins the Chaplains or Mau Mau's, we're going to get him. I was about fourteen then. I got out of Wiltwyck when I had just turned fourteen. It was difficult going to school. I had to carry a stiletto with me all the time and look over my shoulder.

"Is this when he went back to Puerto Rico?"
"Yeah...probably...because I was still pregnant with Rosie... and that's when he left to go down there."
"And what year was this?"
"1957...and it was in January when he went down there."

> Being that I was getting picked up for street rumbles and did not attend school, my mother asked me one day, "Son, why don't you go to Puerto Rico for awhile? I looked at mom and agreed. "Yes," I told her, "I should go and visit my father."
> This gang atmosphere was one of the main reasons that I left for Puerto Rico.
> I left at my family's request.

Salvador left for Puerto Rico, Esmeralda said, in January of 1957 with the clothes on his back, and a small shopping bag with his personal possessions.

He stayed with his father and his new wife, a young woman who was into spiritualism, or *espiritismo*, as it was referred to by the locals in Mayaguez. Considering herself to be an *espiristista*, or one who has the power of the spirit, she conducted seances where people tried to commune with the dead.

Sometimes Salvador worked in the sugarcane fields with

his father, and later, when the harvest was over, he helped him at his other job, working for the city of Mayaguez, sweeping the streets.

Aurea said his life in Puerto Rico was nothing but trouble.

"That's when he got into trouble down there when he was in a fight with some kid and he got sent away."

"Was that the *La Escuela de Correctional?*'

"That's the place...and it was bad."

"Did you ever see it?"

"No, but my father told me about it later on."

"That's one of the places your brother wants us to take pictures of when we go down there to get stuff for the book...didn't your father take him outta there or something?"

"Well like my moms went down there to see if she could somehow get him outta there, but the people said no way, so when my brother got a pass..."

"A pass?"

"Yeah...like a furlough to go home for a while."

"Oh...okay, I see what you're sayin'"

"And when he got one of those my father got some money together and took my brother back to New York."

"So like your father helped him to escape?"

"Yeah...you could say that...because that place was bad, and my father wanted him outta there."

> *My father and I got on the plane leaving San Juan for New York. In order not to be recognized by anyone looking for me from the reformatory, I combed my hair and parted it in the middle like I was taught when I was a kid at the poorhouse. That was when my hair was bleached blond from the sun, and long, almost down to my little ass. I also wore dark sunglasses and turned up my collar in case someone was watching for me at the airport. As soon as we landed in New York, I took off my glasses, went into the men's room and combed my hair again in the Tony Curtis style, but I kept my collar up in the Elvis style.*

Sharing your intimate history during an interview with someone you hardly know is a risky business.

The danger is born when the exchange is either uneven, or decidedly one-sided. In the years of my death row study, I had received, over the years, volumes of information from some of the men and women in my study. Some had welcomed me into their lives with a surprising openness, and had, in time, considered me to be as close to them as their natural families. A bond had been formed. But others felt that I had robbed them of their hearts, their time, and their jailed-up memories.

Given the short amount of time that we had known one another, I still felt a sense of family and trust with Aurea and Esmeralda. But since I'd always felt this way about Salvador, it came as no surprise to have similar feelings for his sister and mother. And as the afternoon continued to weave a pattern of trust and good feeling between us, I shared some of my own history. How I was married for a while, but was now divorced. And, of course, how I had met Salvador in the course of my study about death row, and how he and Genoveva had been very supportive regarding my suggestion that we work on a book about his life.

> When I got back to New York City in 1958, my sister was living in Manhattan on 124th Street on the East Side. My mother was living in Brooklyn on 75 Hudson Street where she would take care of Madelyn, my niece.

Looking from Aurea to Esmeralda, I saw how much they resembled the paintings of beautiful women, especially the ones by the artist, El Greco, at the Metropolitan Museum of Art in Manhattan. Aurea, looking up at me, wanted to know how I was doing.

"Would you like some coffee or something?"

"Uh...yeah, that'd be great...uh...are you okay answering some more questions...because I know it's getting late and everything."

"No...it's okay...how long you think it's gonna take for you and my brother to finish the book?"

"I don't know...it's hard to say."

> *My other niece Rosie was staying with Aurea. I was welcomed when I got to Brooklyn by my stepfather and my mother and the brothers and sisters of the Pentecostal Church. The kids and people in the neighborhood would say, "Hey, Sal is back."*

"So you had two children by the time he got back from Puerto Rico, right?"

"I had Rosie and Madelyn, and I wasn't living with my moms no more because I had my own place up in Harlem... but lotsa times my moms would be takin' care of Madelyn for me."

"So Salvador was staying with you?"

"Sometimes with me, and sometimes with my moms... but it was like hard for him over there cause of Carlos not wanting him around and everything...and also Carlos was having problems with my moms because of the church and stuff."

"What was that about?"

"Mostly it was money...my moms worked all the time... and she worked hard...but Carlos never did."

"So they used to fight?"

"Yeah...and about Sal because he was always hanging out with the gangs and not doin' anything...sometimes he'd sleep all day and not get up until it was like late at night."

> As I walked in the neighborhood with my eyes wide open, I saw that things had changed. There were some new gangs, and the old ones appeared tougher. The first gang I ran into was the Sand Street Angels. Their girls were still pretty as ever. They had matured more and wore the new styles. There was the blonde and the one with black hair, very Italiana, who I would eye all the time, but something separated us. The Sand Street Angels still had their mean look and their black leather jackets. Of course I was afraid of those whiteys because I knew they were vicious with their stillettos.

"Richard, I need to talk with you for a minute."

It was Genoveva, and from the way she asked, I could tell something was bothering her. Getting up, I followed her into the kitchen.

"Nothing's wrong," she said, "but we've already been here most of the day and I'm getting tired."

"How 'bout we let her finish the stuff about the gangs and then we'll split?"

"You wanna have dinner afterwards?"

"Well..I still wanna go down to the playground..."

"The playground! It'll be too dark for you to take any pictures!"

"The camera's got a flash...and besides, that's when it happened, at night."

> I came back from Puerto Rico smarter and tougher, but now I was trying to be cool.
>
> In the Farragut projects there were no more Junior Chaplains. It was now the Fort Green Chaplains and the Farragut Chaplains. You were one or the other. They were now under the leadership of Big John the Bop. I walked by and checked in as a "coolie." They would laugh and say, "Sal is now a coolie." That was their magic word for non-gang members and it was like a passport to walk around the neighborhood. It actually meant you were "cool" and did not come to

fight, that you would not disrespect the gang or the girls.

A coolie had more license to look, talk, and dance with the "debs," but with respect. Otherwise he could get his ass kicked. As I walked over to Fort Green, which was a more vicious place than any other, I saw a gang pass by with their leather jackets with two M's on the back. They stared at me as I looked back and one of them said, "The Mighty Mau Maus!" I immediately identified myself, "A coolie from the turf." They kept walking and I burst out laughing, thinking to myself, "Que los Mowmows! Cono, even the suckers are around... The Mighty Mowmows!... They must be out of their minds."

After being a month back in Brooklyn, I decided to go back to school at P.S. 117. I told my mother that I wanted to start school again in order to get my high school diploma. She thought it was the best thing that could happen. I went to see the people at Wiltwyck. They had their offices on 125th Street. When I went in, I asked to see Mrs. Weiss who was my social worker. She was happy to see me and commented on my change, saying that I looked a little more mature.

I told her that I had just come from Puerto Rico and that I was ready to start school and try to graduate. I told her that I needed help—that they could tell me what I should do. She picked this young black man and told him the problem. He was a social worker. They decided to take me to a place in Brooklyn where I could be assigned a school. We went to Brooklyn together and he got me enrolled in P.S. 117 between Willoughby and Franklin Avenue.

"How long was this before the murders?"

"Not that long...he came back in 1958...and it was cold so that it must've been near the end of the year and that stuff in the playground happened in the summer of 1959."

"So did he ever go back to school?"

"Yeah...but not really because whenever he was there he didn't really learn nothin'...he just went there to hang around and stuff."

"What gang was he with around this time?"

"There was lotsa them..."

"But which was the one he was with when he got run out of Brooklyn?"

"He told you this?"

"Yeah...it's in one of the things he sent me...or maybe he told me.. I'm not sure which...but I don't remember the name of the gang."

"It was the Mau Mau Chaplains."

> Members of other gangs were also going to PS 117.
> One day as I came out of school, a group of Marcy Street Chaplains were waiting for me. I already knew they had something for me. I sensed their vibes. As I stepped to the sidewalk they surrounded me and demanded money. It was a shakedown. I saw a couple of switchblades in the hands of some of the guys. Not being armed myself, I went into my pocket and pulled out the only $3 I had and handed it over to the head of the group. As I gave him the money, I said, "Remember this, my man. I'll be back for my money." They were eager for a fight then since I had given them an excuse to beat me up. In the back of my head I thought, "Wait till I catch them alone! I'm gonna cut some faces and necks." They were about to beat the hell out of me. As this was going on, there were two Mau Maus at the street corner—Tito and someone else. When Tito saw what was happening, he ran over to the group and screamed, "Mau Maus to the heart!" He told them to give me my money back and they did it. One guy said, "Tito, he's a coolie. Why do you stick up for him?" Tito said, "Because he comes from my territory."

"Who was this guy, 'Tito,' did you know him?"

"Tito? He was Counselor of War for the Mau Mau Chaplains."

"I know that...but what I'm askin' is if you knew him, like personally?"

"I seen him around...and I talked to him once or twice..."

"And what was your impression of the guy?"

"Really crazy...he was like someone who's really sick in the head, like he used to beat up on lotsa people all the time."

Tito was war counselor of the Mau Maus and had the power to declare a gang war on the group or any other gang, but the Marcy Chaplains were a brother club. I was amazed at the power he had and the way the group feared his threats. Tito explained that the president of the Mau Maus had a brother who was my friend. The president of the Mau Maus was Carlos and his brother was a church attendant. I took the money back and said to the kid who took my money, "Now, how do you want to fight me? With a knife or with your fists?"

He was a bit nervous and backed up, not knowing what to say. When I turned to Tito, I asked him for a knife. Tito looked at me when he saw that the kid did not want to have it out and said, "Sal, forget about it. They are a brother club. It was a mistake." I listened to him, but at the same time while I held the knife in my hand, I stepped closer to the kid and gave him a back hand across his face which knocked him to the ground.

Tito grabbed me by the arm and pulled me away saying, "You crazy motherfucker. Forget about it!" He helped the other kid up and said to him, "Forget this or face a rumble." The kid said that he already had forgotten this whole incident. We shook hands and I warned him, "If you ever pull this shit on me again, I will have to kill you. And prisons do not scare me!" Tito and I walked home.

When we got there, he told the Mau Maus how I handled myself. Tito said it came close to declaring a gang war. One guy said, "Those punks want trouble. Tomorrow I'm going up there and tell those idiots not to bother anyone from the Fort Green area without first asking the Mau Maus."

Tito began to introduce me to the members of the gang— Gago, Carlos, Israel, Chino, Priest—and to the Mau Mau debs—Delores, Vicky, Bernice, Cookie, Carmen. It was a friendly atmosphere. Israel and Carlos asked me if I wanted to join and I said, "Yes." They explained the rules:

One, if you hurt a Mau Mau, we will hurt you. Two, if you kill a Mau Mau, we will kill two of you. And any Mau Mau that turns stoolie will be hanged in the park by his feet and beaten to death. When one had money, he should give the treasurer a couple of bucks to buy the gang outfit with all the colors, or for any purpose deemed necessary by the President, Vice-President, War Counselor, and Treasurer. Without a full vote, no money could be used. The vote was among the four heads and it had to be a unanimous decision.

They explained to me that I would have to go through the "initiation" to be a Mau Mau.

The initiation was either to stand against a wooden wall and have the most nervous guy throw a knife at you. Blind Man was usually picked for this because he could not see too good when he took off his glasses. Or one could take a beating from the gang without screaming or crying one word. It was decided that I should meet them at the Willoughby Center in the Farragut Projects. After I agreed and picked the beating as the safest initiation, I was told this, "Never, as long as you live forget this: Once a Mau Mau, always a Mau Mau." These were unwritten laws of the concrete jungle.

This process of selecting members for the gang made the Mau Mau's the most dangerous gang in Brooklyn.

"Didn't they make him go through some kind of initiation or something?"

"Yeah...and he got really beaten up."

"Were you home the night the night this happened?"

"I was visiting with my moms...and when he came in the house, I remember sayin' something like, 'Oh, my God, what happened to you?'"

A lot of Mau Mau's were already at the Center when I arrived, and they were touching their knuckles as though they had not initiated someone in a long time. My mind raced back to El Cano de Moca who had gotten a beating by the leaders in La Correctional just like I was about to receive. I looked at them real good. They were happy to initiate another member, but they were expressionless. The president Carlos said, "Big Foot, it looks like you're ready. It won't last long!"

I was told to go into the bathroom and me and the Mau Mau's all crowded in. They were calm. I was nervous as hell. One walked over to me and said, "My name is Terror and I'm going to terrorize you right now." As he said this, he took his fist and hit me right in my stomach with a real hard blow. But having trained in Puerto Rico, I breathed in really hard and tensed my body. I raised my hands, but before making any defense about twenty Mau Mau's fists were all over me. I was hit everywhere. One shot landed on my eyes, another on my nose, and one on my jaw. The rest was foggy.

All through the initiation I did not utter one word. I thought I had woken up in heaven with the angels. I went home, an initiated Mau Mau. When I got home, my sister was a bit puzzled about what had happened. My mother asked me, but I told her I had just had a fight. I went inside my room, opened the window, and leaned out while I lit a "yerbo" and turned on the radio. I smoked my joint, lit an L & M and sat there quietly.

"Was it after the initiation that he went to live with you?"

"It was around that time but he didn't actually come to live with me...just sometimes...like he'd tell my moms he was coming here and then he'd tell me that he was goin' there..."

"But he didn't go to either place?"

"Right...it was just like this thing he'd say so we would be thinkin' he's okay because he was with one of us."

"So where did he stay?"

"In the parks...he'd sleep in there sometimes...or in those abandoned buildings...and even in cars...they'd find an open one and then sleep in the back...and sometimes he'd stay in these rooms that he'd rent for a few dollars a week."

> The Mau Mau's were fighters.
> So one night it was time to "go down" on the Bishops from South Brooklyn. I pulled out my bayoneta from out of its holster which I had inside my pants and said, "Ready any time. Ready to leap tall buildings at a single bound. It's a bird. It's a plane. No, it's the tempered steel!" Everyone laughed and the war counselor said, "Okay, give the girls your weapons and walk cool as though we're going to a party. Try not to stay all together." I had no one to give the knife to. I turned to Barbara and she smiled and said, "Why don't you give it to Vicky?" I replied, "She carries Carlos Apache's knife, not mine." I winked at her as she took the bayonet and hid it under her blouse. However, she seldom went to fights with us. She used to stay home.
> That night there was a fight. I chased a group of white boys with my knife, while beating up others. I always used the bayonet to scare my opponents in the rival gang and seldom stabbed someone. I mostly used to stab people on their shoulders or their thighs, not really wanting to kill someone, but I always wanted to hurt them—hurt them real bad. I had anger and hate in my eyes.
> The gang broke up after the Mau Mau's shot a boy in the Penny Arcade near the Paramount Theater. After that, I was chased out of Brooklyn by the Sand Street Angels who actually wanted to kill me for what happened with their friend Anthony at the hands of the Mau Mau's. But me, Big Foot Machinegun Sal was not going to stay around and get killed. I headed towards the bridge. When they spotted me, I had to run across to Manhattan. When I got to the other side I went up to 125th Street to live with my sister. I began to take walks all over Manhattan. I would come down Broadway at times with a cane like Bat Masterson in tuxedo outfits looking like I was Howard Hughes' own rich son. In my imitations of white middle class Americans, I always used to gravitate towards the English, as though I were Winston Churchill or one of the

knights of the round table. I frequented the 80's and 70's on the West Side and passed my time in the park.

One day Vicky, Cookie, Carlos and myself spent a whole day playing around in the park and rowing a boat. Carlos, having been in the Dragons, used to come from Brooklyn. We would walk all over Spanish Harlem and Black Harlem. Junior used to come also and I would take Junior up to my sister's house and relax up there.

After that I met Tony Ralph from the uptown Diablos. Tony and I got a $7 a week room on 77th Street where I was one night stripped of all my clothing as I slept in a drunken stupor. I was initiated by Tony into a Diablo. This was done by putting Red Devil hot sauce up my nose, in my mouth, my ass, my balls, so that when I woke up I was red all over and burning from the hot sauce all over my body. It was here that Tony found out how wicked I was. I went thought a whole set of kitchen knives in a week's time. Tony came with me to the park and we would hold up people. In the long run, we turned into a gang, known as the Vampires, with aspirations of controlling the west side of Manhattan.

Finally it was five o'clock and dark outside. Geno whispered it was time to leave, and as we were getting our coats together and saying our good-byes, Richie, Aurea's son came into the room. Looking right at Genoveva, he wanted to know when his "Uncle Bird" would be coming home.

Laughing, Aurea told us the story of how Salvador got the name "Uncle Bird" a few years back when she had taken Richie to visit Salvador when he was in Dannemora.

"They had those screens up then and it wasn't like it is now with you being able to touch the person you were visiting...what they had was this little space where if you were careful not to let the guard see what you was doin', you could maybe touch hands with the other person but you hadda be careful because if they caught you doin' this they could stop the visit or something...anyways, I'm sitting there with Richie and moms...and moms she be prayin' and stuff...and Richie all of a sudden says to my brother, 'What are you doing in there?' And like at first my brother got all surprised when Richie said this but then he said something like, 'When I was a little kid I was put in here because I was very bad, but when I grew up I was too big to fit underneath the screen and I couldn't get out.' And when he said this we all laughed and laughed..."

"And this was at Dannemora?"

"Yeah...I think so, but it might've been at Auburn cause we also went there a few times..."

"Did you visit him much at the Brooklyn House of Detention when he got arrested?"

"No cause they wouldn't even let me in...I was like seventeen and you hadda be at least eighteen. That was where he met Stella Davis."

"And she was the social worker...right? The one who held those reading classes where your brother got help with his reading?"

"That's her."

"What about when he was in the Death House...did you get to visit him when he was up there?"

No sooner have the words left my mouth than an expression of confusion crosses her face like a sudden wave on a placid lake.

"Uh..are you okay...you look a little startled."

In a shaky voice, and with tears in her eyes, she said, no, it's nothing, she's okay, it's just that when I said 'Death House,' lots of memories all of a sudden started coming back."

Your question about what the visiting was like when I was in the Death House was a good one, and I will try to answer it as best I can.

Of all the prisons and jails that I've been in over the years,

> the visiting at the Death House was the worst. Whenever someone would come to visit me it would be in this little place and a guard would always be standing right behind me, listening to every word you was saying.

"Like when you went up there to visit?"
"I don't even remember how many times I went up there to visit with my brother except for this one time that I went up there with my father, and that's what I was thinking about when you said, 'Death House.'"

> They had this rule about you not being allowed to touch, and the only time they said you could was when the visit was your last one.
> Then you could touch hello, like hug and kiss the other person, and then when the visit was over you could hug and kiss again, but this time it was forever.
> We always knew when a person was having their last visit because of all the screaming coming from the visiting area.

"You wanna talk about it?"
"I may as well...since I just started thinking about it again.
"It was like very cold, right in the middle of winter, and my father had come up special from Puerto Rico."
"This was the first time he'd seen your brother since when?"
"Since when he'd helped him escape from the reform school in Puerto Rico and took him to New York...so it was already like almost two years. And when Sal got arrested I kept writing him letters telling him to come and then when he got the death sentence I wrote him more letters until finally he said he'd come as soon as he had some money. So I sent him some and a few weeks later he took a plane up

from Puerto Rico and I met him over there at LaGuardia Airport and took him back over to my apartment in Harlem. And when I brought him home I'll never forget the way Rosie and Madelyn were crawling all over him because it was their grandfather and everything.

So we made him this real nice bed from extra blankets we had, and we put this little space together for him in the living room with a blanket tied to the ceiling so he could have some privacy. Then the next morning I remember making him this big breakfast, and it was weird watching him eat because it was like I got the impression that he didn't always eat this big when he was in Mayaguez. He kept asking for more, and by the time we left the apartment it was already pretty late and I was getting worried that we'd be late getting up there and that they wouldn't let us in."

"And this was in the wintertime?"

"Right...and I think it was just before Thanksgiving, and when we left the apartment I remember that it was snowing and that there was already some snow on the ground....and I remember thinking that my father isn't dressed for this kind of weather...he was wearing a nice suit, but it was not for winter."

"And you took the train up there?"

"Yeah...first we took the subway down to Grand Central and then a train from there right to Ossining, where we got off, and that's when we got lost. Maybe it was cause my father was there and I was a little nervous about him coming all this way to see Sal and everything...but I didn't remember from when I'd been there before how we needed to go to get to the prison...so we walked all over the town before I decided that we'd better take a cab. But by the time we got to the prison it was already three-thirty and the guard at the gate said no, you can't come in because it's already past the visiting hour. And when he said this I almost started crying but when I looked at my father in his suit, and how cold he looked, I said to myself that I had to be strong for him and not start crying.

So I asked the guard real nice if he could maybe make an exception to the rule because my father had come all the way up from Puerto Rico to see his son, and please could he give us just a little time with Salvador...and maybe it was the way I said it, or maybe it was because I was a woman, or just that it was already snowing so hard...because he said for us to wait while he made a call to see if he could get us permission. But he wouldn't let us wait inside while he made the call...and it was so cold, and the snow was coming down...but then he said okay but we'd only be allowed in for ten minutes, no more..."

> *The visit I remember most when I was in the Death house was when my father came all the way from Puerto Rico to visit with me, and I know it was because my sister had written to him that if he didn't come soon, he might never be able to see me again.*

"He took us over to the administration building where they checked us in and stuff, and then they took us outside and put us on this little prison bus which took us down the hill by the Hudson River where the Death House was. From there it took us another couple of minutes to get processed and then they put us in this tiny little room with a counter. We sat on one side, and then the door opened on the other side and my brother walked in. They said no touching was allowed but when my father saw my brother there was nothing anyone could do to stop him from running over and hugging him."

> *My father sat across the counter from me and together we both cried.*

"But then the guard said you can't do that in here and made my father sit down, and like he did and everything, but when he tried to talk it was hard because every time he opened his mouth he'd start crying, and then I started crying, but my brother didn't cry and I think it was because he wanted to make like he was being strong for me and my father...and then the guard's telling us we have to leave...so when you said 'Death House,' I thought of my father sitting in that place with the tears rolling down his face."

> That was the last time I saw my father. So when you go to Puerto Rico with my moms I would like for you to try and find him. Sometimes I think maybe he's dead and my family just doesn't want to say anything because they don't want to upset me.
>
> He has written me a few letters over the years, and I have all his addresses, so if he is still alive, it shouldn't be too difficult for you to find him.

Chapter Five

THE PLAYGROUND

A light rain was falling, as we walked back to the subway station, talking about what we've learned from the afternoon. While we agreed it was a productive afternoon, the one question we did not ask was whether Aurea thought he did it.

"So why didn't you ask her that?" Genoveva said.

"Why didn't you?"

"Because you're the one writing the book, not me."

"But you're the translator and it would've been easier coming from you."

"There's nothing wrong with Aurea's English that you couldn't of asked her if you wanted to."

She was right of course, and the truth was that asking Aurea whether or not Salvador had "done it," was much like the convict courtesy of not asking too much about whatever crime brought them to the prison in the first place. Nonetheless, she was right, and what was equally troubling was that in all my conversations with Salvador, in the visiting room, or at the festival, neither of us had ever brought this out into the open. I had never asked, "Listen, did you do it or what?" And of course I had never asked him about the victims. "Do you ever think about them?" And those they had left behind? "Do you ever think about them?"

"I'm gonna ask Salvador next time I visit."

"What are you gonna ask him?" Genoveva wanted to know.

"If he did it or not...I'm gonna look him right in the eye and ask him straight out, 'Did you do it?'"

"But didn't he already say he did?"

"Not to me he didn't."

"What about the newspapers...and didn't you say he wrote to you about what happened?"

Of course he had written to me about what had happened, or hadn't happened, that long ago night in the playground. Volumes, in fact, and then on my own I'd read all the newspaper accounts, as well as legal documents that had been made available to me over the past several months. But whatever I was reading, I invariably came away with the same thought each and every time: the memory of a sleep-away camp when I was a little boy, and of the nights spent sitting in a circle around a camp fire, roasting marshmallows. And how a counselor would whisper something in the ear of the person sitting next to him with instructions to "pass it on." On and on around the circle, until the last person would say out loud whatever had been whispered to him. And of course whatever he would say out loud wouldn't even vaguely resemble whatever had been whispered into the first person's ear.

Salvador had whispered what had happened that night in the playground into the ears of countless detectives, prison officials, and newspaper reporters over the years until *"Did you do it?"* had no doubt become a meaningless litany for all concerned. Several newspapers had reported the events of that evening, and while all were similar in their stating of the facts, the tone of each differed significantly enough that I had always wondered whether any marshmallows had ever been roasted when those reporters had been sitting around their respective campfires.

"Maybe I'll get something when I go down there tonight."

"You're still gonna go down there...aren't you tired from all this already?"

"Yeah...I'm tired...but maybe I'll be able to get something."

"The only thing you're gonna get is soaking wet!"

I will need photographs of the 16th Precinct. I don't remember the exact address, but I do know that it's somewhere on West 47th. Most important: I will need a picture of the playground where the killings took place.

Getting off the subway at Seventy-Second Street, I waved at Genoveva through the window of the train as she continued on to West Fourth Street.

It was August 29th, 1959, and earlier in the day it had been raining.

A light rain is falling as I walk up the subway steps to the corner of 72nd Street and Broadway.

This is it, I thought, this is where it all began nearly fifteen years ago, and maybe even right here where I'm standing now, or at least not that far from here.

Aurea said that for several months before the killings, Salvador had lived in a succession of cheap, furnished rooms all along Broadway, from the Seventies, she said, to somewhere in the Eighties. A well-known poet used to call those furnished rooms, "furnished souls," and I wondered what living in those rooms, from week to week, and day to day, had been like for Salvador in 1959.

I was living back then on 77th Street between Columbus and Amsterdam Avenues. I was living in a seven-dollar a week room with two other friends: Anthony Hernadez (the Umbrella Man) and another boy whose name was Ralphie. From hustling on the streets we were able to pay the rent, eat, and buy our clothing. All of us had left our homes, and Tony was the only one who still maintained any kind of contact with his family.

It's Saturday night and Broadway is filled with people of all sizes, shapes, and descriptions.

In the middle of Broadway, and across the street from where I'm standing is a long sliver of park known to all the junkies as "needle park."

Pills, bottles of wine, and small envelopes filled with dope are passing from hand to hand, and mouth to mouth.

> Saturday night and from Seventieth Street to Eightieth Street the night life was taking its usual course. Young Puerto Ricans on the West Side of the City of New York would congregate earlier in the evening, drink the cheap wine, and share it with the different gangs that were considered "brother clubs." It was a typical night during the 1950's. Gangs, clubs, and social groupings of youths has always been a reality of New York City—a youth would either be a loner or be in a group. Some groups are more violent than others. Some liked to dance. Some liked to smoke Marijuana. And others like to fight. There is not much good to be found in cities such as New York, and even more so during the 1950's.

Neighborhood leaders all along this section of Broadway would forever call the invasion of heroin, with its users and dealers, *The Plague*. And this even though many sociologists would say that heroin was the reason why the gangs had all but vanished from the streets of New York City.

> That night I walked from my room to 76th Street. Once I got there I drank about six beers. Later on I walked over to 72nd Street to see if I could hustle up some more money. And when I did have some money, I found someone willing to sell me some goofballs. I took two of the goofballs, and then I walked over to the park, where I sat for awhile before returning to hang out with some other gang members on the corner of 72nd Street.

Music is everywhere, and here I am, walking the same streets, with many of the same smells and sounds coming from the stores, the open kitchen windows of apartments, or from people walking on the streets, talking, making love, or whispering to one another.

Here I am, trying to feel what he had felt.

> *It was about 9:30 PM when a call was received from one of our brother clubs down in the forties. One of our gang members went over and picked up the telephone that rang on the corner of 73rd Street and after talking with someone, he walked back over to us and said that some people from a gang who called themselves, "The Norsemen," had beaten up some Puerto Ricans, and that someone had tried to sell marijuana to someone's mother. It was a confusing story. Gangs seldom check out thoroughly before acting anyway, so that the phone call had already sparked the desire for a rumble.*
>
> *The fellow who answered the telephone told me to wait a little while before a reply could be given. He came over and after I had asked him what was really happening, I went over and spoke to Frenchie.*
>
> *"Who is this?" the voice on the other side of the line asked.*
>
> *"It's me, Frenchie."*
>
> *"Qué pasa, man?"*
>
> *"We got trouble with the Norsemen, man, and we need some help. Some of those guys beat on some of our guys,"*
>
> *"Hey, no problema, man, I'll call some of our people and we'll meet you down at the playground on 46th Street."*
>
> *Then I called some of our brother clubs, like the Hell Burners, and the Mau Mau Chaplains. Everyone agreed to meet us later at the playground. From the playground we would proceed to fiftieth Street for the rumble of the century.*
>
> *The gang that was down at the Forties was the Heart kings, our gang up in the seventies was the Vampires, and on Eightieth Street were the Buccaneers and further up were the Young Lords.*
>
> *Central Park was our home away from home.*

At Central Park, I stop to look over the concrete wall at the sea of trees and grass that seem to stretch on endlessly. Looking at the tall trees, I remember something the father of one of the victims had said to a newspaper reporter, something about how it was time now to plant more trees all over Manhattan because as far as he was concerned the gangs had turned the city into a jungle.

> The Heart Kings had recently become a brother club of the Vampires and the others. The Vampires had already been in existence for about eight months.
> I started the Vampires in order to fight back those other gangs that would otherwise try to control the section between 60th and 80th Streets. At first we received opposition from the nearby gangs (like the buccaneers and the Young Lords) but it did not take long to establish our boundaries and the fact that we were all predominantly Puerto Ricans created a sort of brotherhood. Fiftieth Street and Ninth Avenue was the territory of the Norsemen and down Fortieth Street were the Heart Kings who had territory from 30th on up but who were constantly in trouble because of the race problem existing between Puerto Ricans, Italians, Irish, and others. As for Black gangs (known at that time as Negro gangs) there were not many around those parts. In the Vampires, there were more Puerto Ricans than in any other group. We did have a few Italians, a few Irish, and a few Blacks, but they mostly stayed with us because they lived around those parts.
> I had an umbrella, which I gave to Tony Hernández, and he gave me his black cape with a red, satin lining. I put it on. Weapons were given out and I choose a Mexican dagger. This had belonged to our President, Manny Ortega, and it was the same dagger used when we took our oath months ago in Central Park. An oath taken underneath a full moon, and so named our gang, the Vampires. The oath was taken by lifting the dagger up to the moon and swearing that we would from that day onward defend one another as brother and fellow Vampires.
> That night we also swore that we were going to kill someone in Central Park in order to confirm the oath with blood.

But now, here it was August the 29th, 1959, and nearly nine months to the day that the oath had been taken.

Walking back to Broadway, I take the subway to the West 47th Street station. Out on the street, I begin walking west to the playground.

Across 46th Street, down Broadway, then Seventh Avenue, and finally, in the middle of the block, surrounded by a tall wire fence, is the playground.

A newspaper report at the time said that when the killings had taken place the park had been so dark that even local policemen had expressed reservations about entering late at night.

Some would walk to the playground on 46th Street, some would take a cab, and some, like myself, would take the subway.

Drenched in light from several tall lampposts placed all around the park like silent, watchful soldiers, I tried to imagine what the playground must have been like when all was dark and midnight.

Wooden benches line either side of the park, and in between is a little house, where the custodians store their supplies. A sandbox is in the middle, and next to this is a slide, along with a row of swings.

Across the street on either side of the playground are rows and rows of tenement buildings. Faded brown or deep red, all are old and dirty.

A light rain is falling.

I remember entering the playground, sitting in a corner with my Mexican dagger. Then a fight broke out (this fight was supposed to occur on 50th Street and not the playground).

I remember running around the playground using the term, "gringo," and trying my best to get out with my knife in front of me.

I remember getting out and while walking fast, wrapping the knife in my cape which I had taken off.

It was dark in the park, there weren't any lights, and when we ran outside the gate everyone took off in a million directions.

But I swear by all that is holy, I do not remember using the knife that was in my hand.

New York Herald Tribune
Monday, August 31, 1959

**2 Dead in New Teen Bloodshed
In City Playground at Midnight**

By Newton Fullbright

Police were hunting last night for members of a youthful gang of Spanish-speaking hoodlums who invaded a West Side playground after Saturday midnight and fell upon five boys who had just come from a movie. The attackers left two dead and a third in critical condition from stab wounds.

There were indications that while the victims of yesterday mornings battle might not have had gang affiliations, their assailants might have had either with the Mau Mau Chaplains or the Buccaneers.

It was known that a prime suspect of the search is a youth who appeared to be the leader in the attack and who was wearing a black cape and conspicuously buckled shoes.

I started running to the subway station but then someone grabbed my arm and said, "Let's take a taxi uptown, it'll be a lot quicker.

The playground splits the block between Ninth and Tenth Avenues running from 45th to 46th Street. It is unlighted, and the gates remain open all night. Neighbors said they had complained repeatedly and in vain to police and the Youth Board asking that the playground be closed at night or that the playground be closed altogether. They said the playground had become a nightly prowling ground for boys and girls from other parts of the city.

A fourteen-year-old girl who was with her brother and the four other youths in the playground was permitted to leave as the fight started. Her brother was hit over the head with a bottle, but escaped, as did one of the other boys. They told police that six or seven Puerto Ricans had attacked them, telling them no "gringos" (a Spanish-American contemptuous term for foreigners) were allowed in the playground, though it is in an area of few Spanish-speaking people.

Then we ran over to Ninth Avenue to where there were lots of cabs, and after we hailed down a cab, six of us got inside.

The dead boys were Anthony Krezinski of 330 West 47th Street, a messenger for a publishing house, and Robert Young, of 313 West 47th Street, also a messenger, but who planned on returning to high school in September. They were both sixteen and close friends.

Critically wounded was Edward Reimer, eighteen, of 518 Ninth Avenue. He was operated on at St. Clare's Hospital for stab wounds on the stomach.

Sandra Luken, the fourteen-year-old girl of 372 West 45th Street said she was returning home from a party when she met her brother, Harold, known in the neighborhood as "Billy," and the other four boys, and they decided to take a short cut through the park.

Someone in the cab told the driver we wanted to go to 72nd Street but when we started getting these funny looks from the driver, we all got off instead at Fifty-second Street.

She said they were met at the 45th Street entrance by a group she described as Puerto Ricans, one of whom demanded to know if "Frenchy" was among them. Although assuring them that they did not know "Frenchy," they were attacked almost immediately. She said the intruders let her go after one of them waved an umbrella handle at her threateningly.

From there we divided up. Some of us took the subway to 72nd Street and some of us walked. We were all hyped up from what had happened in the playground, this I do remember.

The witnesses were Mrs. Lillian Heintz, forty-two, and her husband, Frank, forty-six, a painter, who live in a fourth floor apartment at 335 West 45th Street overlooking the playground.

"I heard something," Mrs. Heintz said, "someone running in the playground—the sound of feet. My husband and I looked out. We saw those two poor boys running across 46th Street where they died in the doorways over there.

"Another boy had fallen just before he reached the 46th Street entrance. We could see about five boys run to him and fall on him. They started beating him. One of them picked him up as we started screaming. They threw him down on the hard pavement and then they started running.

"There were more of them over on the other end of the park, and I would say there were seven or eight. They all ran out the 45th Street entrance and took off toward Tenth Avenue. You could see them in the light then. One of them wore a red shirt."

When we got to 72nd Street we went to someone's apartment and listened to the news of what had happened over the radio.

The Kresinski boy died in the hallway of the tenement at 447 West 47th Street, just across from the park entrance. End Zorovich, who lives it the building told about it.

"I heard something outside our door, " she said. "I

opened it, and there was this boy, his face was deathly white but I recognized him as one of the neighborhood boys. He looked up at me and tried to say something, then fell into my arms. He lay there with his eyes open. He was dead."

The other victim, Robert Young, ran into the house next door, at 449 West 46th Street, and managed to drag himself up a flight of stairs to the apartment of his friend, Tony Wozinmantis. Here, John Rooney, sixty-five, stepfather of the Wozinmanis boy, sat in front of a television set.

"Bobby fell on the floor and died right there," he told police, and added, "He couldn't say anything. He just gasped and died with blood all over him."

As soon as we heard the news about the killings I knew there was no way I could keep hanging around 72nd Street because when they found out it was me down there, the first place they'd be looking would be right in this neighborhood.

One lead on which police were reported working had a cab driver picking up six Puerto Rican youths about the time of the stabbing at Ninth Avenue and 46th Street and driving them to 52nd Street.

From the few disclosures made by the police and from people in the neighborhood, it appeared that the fight erupted as the result of conflicts between Puerto Rican and non-Puerto Rican youths over the use of the playground. The victims had stopped in the park on their way home from the movies, according to witnesses.

I went up to the Bronx with Tony and another guy. We stayed where we could, but mostly we slept in the hallways of apartment buildings, or on the roofs.

And we took food from garbage cans.

New York Herald Tribune
September 2, 1959

"Cape Man" Sought as Boys' Killer
"Umbrella Man" is also hunted

By Newton Fullbright

Two youths, one known as the "Cape Man" or "Dracula," and the other as the "Umbrella Man," were sought yesterday as the leaders of a gang of thirteen Spanish-speaking youths who turned a small West Side playground into a slaughter ground shortly after midnight Sunday.

The two youths, one clad in a nurse's cape and the other carrying an umbrella, are said to have led eleven followers to the playground on a mission of revenge as a favor to a friend.

Police believe the "Cape Man" wielded the knife. It was in the apartment of one of the other material witnesses that police found the cape, a seven-inch dagger with a seven-inch blade and a homemade, brass-studded garrison belt, which the "Cape Man" allegedly left there after the attack in the park.

Police said the "Cape Man" and the "Umbrella Man" had disappeared but said they knew their ages, their names, and nicknames, and were watching air terminals, railroad stations and bus terminals in case the pair tried to leave town.

Then two cops in a patrol car called me over. It was late, I think after midnight, and when they asked me what I was doing out so late, and where did I come from, I told them that I was from Brooklyn, and that my father was a minister and we lived in an apartment over a grocery. I told the cops I was visiting with friends in an apartment nearby and then they took me over to see if this was the truth.

The people we had been with said, "Yeah, he was here a few hours ago, like at seven or so. But when the cop said some-

thing about my being a long way from Brooklyn, the kids said something like it was their understanding that I came from 76th Street in Manhattan and not from Brooklyn.

The cops must have gotten suspicious because right away they took me down to the station house and started questioning me, and that's when I told them, "Well, you're going to find out anyway. I'm the guy you're looking for."

New York Herald Tribune
Thursday, September 3, 1959

**'Cape Man' is Booked
As Knife-Slayer of 2**

**16, He Tells Police: 'I Don't Care
If I Burn; My Mother Can Watch'**

By Judith Crist

A pompadoured sixteen-year-old who glories in the nickname of "Machine Gun Sal," and a seventeen-year-old who was a weight-lifting champion in reform school were booked last night for homicide and conspiracy to commit a crime in the slaying of the two sixteen-year-old boys in a West 45th St. playground early Sunday.

I was the first to be arrested, and then they picked up Tony a few hours later.

They took us from the police station in the Bronx to the 16th Precinct on West 47th Street and that's when they started questioning us about what had happened at the playground.

The younger, Salvador Agron, the Cape Man, who wore a navy blue and red-lined cape and buckled shoes was described by police as the youth who wielded the knife in the two fatal stabbings and the critical wounding of a third youth.

The elder, Tony Hernandez, the 'Umbrella Man' used the umbrella, police said, in the gang attack at 12:30 AM Sunday on the seven boys and two girls in the unlit playground.

"I don't care if I burn, my mother can watch," Agron, a delicate featured effeminate youth described as the leader of the thirteen Spanish-speaking attackers, snarled at detectives.

The two, silent and sullen, were booked at the W. 47th Street station at 6:54 PM.

Although the block in front of the precinct house had been close to through traffic throughout the day because of crowds that had gathered, there were about 500 angry residents of the block gathered on the street as the two youths, handcuffed and sullen, were led out for an overnight stay at the West 30th St. police station. There were shouts of "Murderers" and "Killers" and fists were shaken, but the two remained impassive."

Agron's sister, a tiny, childlike girl, who says she is married and has two children and lives at 350 East 124th Street, staying with her mother yesterday, said that her brother was a "good, quiet kid, very religious."

As the rain continues to fall, I walk over to 47th Street and the 16th Precinct House.

If a police station can be described as a sad old whore with a long memory, then the 16th Precinct on West 47th Street is just like all the other precinct houses in New York City. Fortress-like, with an imposing facade built from brick or stone, it provides an illusion of strength and stability.

Walking through the door, I wonder if this is how they brought Salvador in, or did they maybe try to sneak him in around the back? The newspapers said there were huge crowds of people in front of the police station the morning they brought him in. Angry people chanting hatred, and yelling for blood.

Through the door and directly to my left is a long desk

with a railing in front. A uniformed police officer sits behind the desk. Behind him is a bulletin board filled with wanted posters. From the several stripes on his shirt sleeve, I figure he must be at least a sergeant. His name tag says, "O'Reilly."

"Can I help you with something?"

"Uh..yeah...I'd like to know if I could maybe speak to someone about the Capeman case?"

"The who?'

"Uh...the Capeman case...it happened a long time ago...Salvador Agron...it was a famous case."

"When was this?"

"1959...August to be exact."

"1959? I was barely outta high school...but you say it happened around here somewheres?"

"Yeah...right around the corner...at the playground on 46th...and then they brought him in here later on after he was arrested and everything..."

"Lemme ring upstairs and see if I can find a detective who might've been around...you can just take a seat over there."

Maybe some people like police stations, but I never have.

The 16th Precinct was just like all the rest of them. Nothing but sad places with people in handcuffs going to jail.

"Are you the guy askin' about the Capeman?"

Although the person asking the question is in plainclothes, the gun in his shoulder holster leaves little doubt as to his importance in the stationhouse.

"Yeah...I'm the guy."

Rising from my chair, I take his extended hand, and we shake.

"I'm Detective McNulty...you a reporter or something?"

"No...no, I'm writing a paper about the death penalty and he's one of the guys I've been working with...and I'm tryin' to find someone from here who might've been around back then."

"And you know this 'Capeman' guy?"

"Not exactly...I mean we've met and stuff..."

"Where's this?"

"He's up at Greenhaven...and I've been visiting with him up there."

"And you're writin' a book with him or something?"

"Nah...nothing like that...I'm just tryin' to get some information about the death penalty."

"Cause if you was writin' somethin' I'd have to clear everything first through my commander before I started sayin' anything."

"So you was here when it happened?"

"Me? No..no..I wasn't around then...but I remember the case...it was all over the place...but I was out in Brooklyn...I was just starting out...and to tell you the truth, I don't even know if anyone here would go back that far cause most of them would probably be retired already. But what would you be wantin' to know?"

"Not that much...but I would like to see where he would've been taken for questioning...stuff like that."

"Well...if that's all you want...lemme check it out upstairs and if they say it's okay, then that'll be fine with me, okay?" When the detective comes back down he says that no one upstairs remembers the case. In fact no one even has any idea of where he might've been questioned that night.

"Things have changed around alot since that night. You have any idea where it might've taken place?"

"From what I read in one of the transcripts, it said something about it being a cloak room, or maybe a locker room. Does that make any sense?"

"That's the locker room...okay, I know...you wanna take a look?"

"If that'd be okay...yeah."

"Look...I can give you five minutes but that's it...okay? Anything else you're gonna want, you'll have to ask down-

town cause I'm not authorized to give out too much...okay?"
Up a flight of stairs and down a corridor, I'm right behind
him as he opens a door marked, "No Admittance."

"This is it," he says.

> *Handcuffed to Tony, we're taken upstairs. Reporters and photographers are everywhere.*
>
> *The room smells like someone just died inside. One of the cops tells us to take a seat and when we do he unlocks one of our handcuffs and puts it through one of the wooden bars of the chair. Locking it shut, me and Tony are both tied to our chairs.*

I don't know exactly what I expected to see, but the reality is a medium-sized room, filled with chairs, a long table, and not much else, or at least not much in the way of furniture. Lockers line one of the walls, with a bench in front for people to sit while they change their clothes. A clock on the wall says it's a little after nine o'clock.

"Look, if you wanna sit in here for a few minutes, that'll be okay, but just don't forget to close the door before you leave...and I'll be at the desk downstairs."

"Thanks...I ain't gonna stay too long..."

"There's some coffee over on the shelf there if you want some."

As soon as he shuts the door, I pour myself some coffee, and then I take a seat. Is this the one Salvador was handcuffed to? Is this where he was sitting when his mother was brought in to see him?

> *I don't know how long me and Tony were handcuffed to those chairs before one of the detectives came in to see me.*
>
> *"Sal," he said, "your mother's here, and she wanted you to have this."*
>
> *What he's got is a Bible, and before I can even think about what I'm saying, I'm shaking my head and telling him "No way, I don't want nothing like that."*
>
> *"Are you sure?" he says. "Because your mother really*

wants you to have it."

I don't even answer him, and after waiting a second or two, he turns around and leaves the room.

He takes the Bible with him.

The table in front of me is long, brown, and a mosaic of human misery. Nearly every inch has been used to scribble names, dates, and whatever else might have been important to whoever it was who may have been sitting here, as they waited to be questioned about whatever it was that had brought them here in the first place.

Placing my hand through one of the wooden bars in the chair, I try to imagine that I am Salvador Agron, handcuffed to the chair.

> There were two knives on the desk, one was my Mexican dagger and the other was a bloody white-handled knife which was closed.
>
> I told the cops that I used the knife but that I didn't know anyone had been killed until I heard it on the radio later that night.
>
> "Sal, which is your knife," said the detective behind the desk while the District Attorney and other detectives looked on.
>
> "This one," I said, pointing to the dagger.
>
> "Why" asked one of the detectives, "isn't there any blood on it?"
>
> This was a puzzling question, but since I had already admitted to the stabbing of five people altogether, I just said,
>
> "Well, when you stick it in fast and pull it out fast, it leaves no blood on the blade."
>
> They all stared at me for a while and the detective behind the desk asked,
>
> "Then whose knife is this?" He asked this pointing indignantly to the blood stained knife on the desk.
>
> "I dunno, I dunno, man."
>
> "This knife was found in the park, you must know whose knife it is—you are obviously the leader of these cutthroats," he

said.

"Get the spic punk out of here," ordered the detective behind the desk.

They questioned us for a long time and at one point I remember signing some papers that someone put in front of me, and that's probably when I said that stuff about, "I don't care if I burn, my mother can watch me." There were lots of newspaper reporters around and I guess someone was listening when I said it.

Suddenly the door flies open and O'Reilly walks in, and as I try to quickly pull my hand from between the bars of the chair, it sticks a little, and it takes quite a bit of maneuvering to get it out completely.

"You okay there? Get your arm caught or something?"

"Nah...I'm okay...my arm must've fallen asleep..."

"Lookit, my commander says you gotta go, okay? He says it's against the rules and all that...so I'm gonna have to take you downstairs..."

"That's okay..."

Closing the door behind him, O'Reilly gets this very serious look on his face, and then he looks at me with what he probably thinks is a very earnest and honest expression.

"Listen," he says, "Can I ask you somethin' like completely off the record...like just between you and me...and like it won't leave this room?"

"Yeah...I don't got a problem with that."

"You're Italian, right?"

"Me? No...I'm Jewish...or at least my parents are..."

"Okay...you're Jewish...so like why are you interested in the 'Capeman' guy?"

"Uh...well..."

"'Cause I asked around downstairs about this 'Capeman' guy and I found out he was a fuckin' Puerto Rican kid who killed two white kids for no reason whatsoever so I'm wondering that since you're Jewish, and don't be takin' this wrong, but since you're also a white guy, why you'd be wastin' your time over a guy like this, you know what I'm tryin' to say here?"

"Yeah...but he's a human being...and I like the guy."

"You like the guy? Whadda you mean, 'You like the guy'? I don't mean to be gettin' personal here, but are you like into men or somethin'? Is that what this is all about?"

"No...it's not that...it's..."

"So if it's not a fag thing, then what is it with you and this guy? Come on, I'm listening."

But of course he's not listening, or at least he's not listening to me. Instead, the rage in his eyes speaks of quite a different voice, and just as I'm about to say something, it's like I have this sudden flash of what it must have been like for Salvador in this very room. Nearly fifteen years ago, surrounded by a room full of detectives, all breathing into his face, voice on voice, and all asking the same thing, over and over, again and again, like an errant drum roll from hell: *Did you do it, Sal? Did you do it?*

"Come on...I'm listening...what is it with you and this fuckin' Puerto Rican...I'd really like to know."

"*I didn't do it...*"

"Excuse me...what'd you say?"

"I mean...I don't know..."

"You don't know? So what do you know?"

"Lookit...I just wanna leave."

"You wanna leave? Hey...I'm not stoppin' you...there's the door...youse can leave whenever you feel like it."

He opens the door, and almost as quick, I'm out of my chair, through the door, and halfway down the stairs, when he says, in a loud whisper so just the two of us can hear:

"Fuckin' spic piece of shit!"

> Later on when they took me and Tony outside, there were hundreds of people all over the place. Lots of them were in front of the police station and the rest were up and down the streets, all over the place.

Lots of them were screaming at me and Tony. They was saying stuff like, "Kill the spics! Kill 'em all!" Fists were being waved at us, and some people were yelling, "Murderers!" and "Killers!"

Afterwards, when they took us outside, there were lots of reporters and people with cameras trying to take our pictures.

We were handcuffed and we were waiting for a paddy wagon, and I recognized one of the people who was yelling questions at us. It was Gabe Pressman, and I recognized him from seeing him on television.

"Tell me why you want to be president of the Vampires?"
"I don't wanna be no president."

"How do you feel about killing those two boys?"
"Like I always feel."

"How's that?"
"Like this, like I am right now."

"Do you feel sorry for those two boys?"
"That's for me to know and for you to find out."

"Why do you think kids are in gangs today?"
"That's also for me to know and for you to find out."

"Would you kill more if you could?"
"You're wasting your time."

"You feel like a big man today?"
"I feel like killing you, that's what I feel like."

"How do you feel about your mother and father?"
"That I'm sorry about, but nothing else."

Riding back to Brooklyn, I can barely keep my eyes open.

Too many things have happened today. Too many things to digest all at once, and my head feels heavy from listening to the varied voices particular to Salvador's life. The voice of the Law, the voice of his mother, his sister, and even the police.

Each voice claiming to be the voice of truth, the whole truth, and nothing but...yet, all these many varied voices have spoken with such authority, and in some cases, with such self-righteousness, that it's nearly impossible for me to separate one from the other without all kinds of doubts dancing into play.

Aurea had a voice, as did Esmeralda, and then there were the newspapers, the legal papers, the police, and of course, myself. But what voice should I listen to? Which voice is telling the truth?

But as I ride back to Brooklyn, the only truth that makes any sense is that all of us are dancing in the dark. All of us are sitting around the campfire, whispering into one another's ear.

Side by side, voice to voice, and truth to truth.

July 8th, 1974
Greenhaven Correctional Facility

Dear Richard:

I received yours of July 1st, along with the $1.00 in stamps. Muchas Gracias! You always seem to send stamps just when I am needing them most!
I was glad that you and Geno enjoyed yourselves at my sister's house. She is wonderful, and like my moms, she has always been there for me over the years. I hope she was able to fill you in about some of my history. The rest you will learn as the book progresses, and of course when you go with moms to Puerto Rico, all kinds of things will unfold! Smile!
I am looking forward to your next visit, and if you can,

please bring me some typing paper when you come. And if you have any of the pictures you took, the ones of the playground, the police station, and the other places in New York City that I asked for, please bring them up when you come.
    Take care, amigo.

With love, power, and understanding,
Tu hermano,
Salvador Agron #16846

Sitting in the visiting room, waiting for Salvador to join me, everything was just the way it always was.

The four vending machines are still side by side like four soldiers standing forever at attention. In front of the room, a guard at a desk on a raised platform, wearing a blue blazer with matching tie, and white shirt, looking more like a clerk in a shoe store than a guard at a maximum-security prison.

It was nearly eleven o'clock, and except for the sounds of copulation at various levels of completion, the room was silent.

My hands are stretched out before me on the counter, and I think to myself that even after all the time I've spent in this visiting room, I still hadn't mastered the simple art of "seeing and hearing, but not seeing and hearing," all the music of affection drifting across the visiting room like a warm blanket on a cold night.

And as the beautifully perfumed woman to the left of me reached over to the man sitting directly across the counter from her, Salvador made his way over to where I was sitting. "Could you get me one of those sandwiches over there?"

"Yeah…yeah…what'd you want?"

"Anything with some meat in it…"

"You doin' okay?"

"Yeah..I'm doing alright…and gimme one of those sodas while you're at it…and make it a coke…'cause that other stuff they got over there don't go down that good."

Walking over to the vending machines I feel the same self-consciousness that I always did whenever I was here, but especially whenever I bought something from the machines, or stepped outside into the corridor to use the john. Mostly it's because I had this sense that other people in the visiting room were trying to figure out what our relationship was all about. Could be that I'm his lawyer, but if I were, we'd be visiting in a separate, and private, alcove reserved for lawyers and clients. So if I'm not his lawyer, who am I? Not his brother, cousin, or other family member, that much was certain. At the festival we had hugged like good friends, but here Salvador made it clear this was not acceptable. He never came right out and said this, but his body language surely did the one time I reached out to hug him in the visiting room.

Although Salvador had been involved with many men over the years, and had more than once made this very clear in our conversations, or in the writings he had sent, his direction now was clear: women, women, and more women. So that even a hint of something smoldering between us was unacceptable and out of line. Handshakes or a pat on the shoulder were okay, but nothing more. The problem of course was that his apparently recent homophobia was so intense—at least in the visiting room—that he sometimes went to great lengths to maintain his image of *machismo*.

This included barely even saying hello, and how are you, before asking that I get him some food as soon as possible.

Anything with some meat in it.

Back from the vending machines, I watched as Salvador devoured his food. Be understanding, I told myself. True, he eats like a slob, but how would I eat my food if for fifteen years I had been told I had to finish my meal in, say, fifteen minutes? Would I be any different?

"You bring me any typing paper?"

"Yeah...I left some with the packaging room guy when I came in."

"So you had a good visit with my sister, right?"

"Yeah, and she's something else, lemme tell you, but I got tired after a while. She told us all about the gangs...and I never knew how much you'd been involved until she ran it all down for us."

"And you got me pictures of the playground, and the police station and stuff?"

"Yeah...I got everything...and I even sorta traced your steps from 72nd Street down to the playground. Then I went over to the police station...and it was even raining a little bit."

"No shit..it was raining?"

"Yeah...nothing big, though, more like a misty kind of rain."

"Same as that night...hey, I need something more to eat here."

Anything with some meat in it.

On my second walk to the vending machines, I looked at the woman sitting next to me. Her body has contorted in such a way that one of her hands was almost unnoticeable as it slowly made its way across the counter and into the lap of the man sitting on the other side.

Looking into the mirror of the vending machine, I debated whether or not I should say anything about what had gone down with me and the cop at the precinct house. All the way home to Brooklyn that night I had gone over it and gone over it, so that by the time I arrived at my stop in Coney Island, I had pretty much been able to let it go. The cop was a schmuck, but I would be even more of a schmuck to let it bother me too much. More the reason, I figured, not to mention it to Salvador, who surely was no stranger to asshole cops in police stations.

Besides, since it happened in the very same room where he had been shackled to a chair with dozens of cops asking, over and over, *"Did you do it, Sal, did you do it, or what?"* It might really fuck up his mind if I were to tell him what happened, not to mention where. And then of course, if I did tell him, wouldn't it be dishonest to omit that when I was sitting in the room, I was pretending to be him at one point, handcuffed to the chair, to "see what it was like"? Better to keep quiet, but when would I ask him *Did you do it*? When would be the right time? Something inside was whispering, *Take your time, why rush?* but as I sat down again, and placed a tray of food in front of him, another part from inside my chest spoke out loud in a clear and uncensored voice:

"So did you do it, or what?"

"Do what?"

"Did you do it...you know, the stuff in the playground. Did you do it, or what?"

If the eyes, as the philosophers say, are the "windows to the soul," then what I'd asked had surely lifted the curtain to the inner workings of Salvador's soul. Up until that very moment it had been unspoken, this, *Did you do it?*; not taking into account, of course, that he had already sent me reams and reams of words on this very subject. But now, finally, it had been spoken, out loud, and his soul, it was clear, was wondering why I was even bothering to ask.

"It's like I've always said...I remember using a knife...but not killing nobody...I don't remember nothing about that... so like I don't remember doing it..."

Words formed, and sentences began, but looking into his eyes, I couldn't bring myself to ask him again whether or not he did it. Because it felt like his soul was saying to me that *"Did you do it, Sal,"* has been like an echo bouncing in his head, back and forth, just like the guys "walking the walk" of the living dead in the prison yard, until someone, just like me, would ask him for the ten thousandth time: *"Did you do it, Sal, did you do it, or what?"*

So, I asked him something else.

"You ever hear anything from the families?"

"From the kids in the playground?"

"Yeah...from Kresinski...or from Youngs?"

"Nah...but one of the mothers did say...and I think it was Kresinski's moms who said it...that she'd be waiting for me outside the prison when I got out so she could kill me.."

"She said that?"

"Yeah...but that was like a long time ago...and I haven't heard nothing like that since when she said it the first time."

"You think about them much?"

"Who you talkin' about?"

"The kids...their parents...you ever think 'bout them?"

"All the time...and what I'd like to do is maybe send them some flowers...to Mrs. Kresinski, at least..."

"Are you fucking crazy, or what?"

"Why you sayin' that?" he said.

"Because she's the woman who said she wanted to blow you away and now you're sittin' here sayin' you wanna send her some flowers?"

"I don't think it's such a bad idea."

"Lemme tell you something, man, like you are absolutely the last person she'd wanna be getting flowers from, believe me."

"I'd still like to do it...not now...but later on like when I apply for clemency or something...to show her that I'm sorry."

"Just out of curiosity here, what kind of flowers would you send?"

"A bouquet of roses in the shape of an angel."

Chapter Six

PUERTO RICO

August 25th, 1973
Greenhaven Correctional Facility

My Beloved Mother:

    Jacoby was here for a visit yesterday, and he told me the good news about the trip you will be taking with him to Puerto Rico. Bueno!
    He also told me about the visit he had with you and Aurea. He is a good man, and I feel that he is now part of our family. I also feel this way about Genoveva.
    I know this trip will be difficult for you, but I ask you to be strong for me because you are the only guide I have to my young life in Mayaguez. Without you they would be lost. I gave Jacoby a list of the addresses I have from papi. He has written to me a few times over the years—and I hope that if he is still alive, you will be able to visit and talk with him. I have asked Jacoby to take certain photographs for me of the places that I will want to write about for our book.
    I will need pictures of the poorhouse, La Escuela de Correctional, the Balboa Bridge...well, Jacoby has the list.
    Please give my regards and blessings to Uncle Israel and his family.

Your loving son,
Salvador Agron   #16846

It was just about one hundred miles from one end of Puerto Rico to the other, and during the day, and depending on the traffic, it took about two hours to make the drive from San Juan to Mayaguez. But we planned on stopping to take pictures from the list Salvador sent us, so it would probably take us longer.

Looking at the road map, we decided that the best way to go was to take Route #2 from Bayamon to our first stop, Manati, and then proceed along the same road to Aquadilla. From there this same road would take us directly to the heart of Mayaguez. We were even thinking of taking a side trip to the surfing beach at Rincon for a quick swim before settling in for the evening.

Without air conditioning in the car, it felt like we were in a floating furnace. Rivers of sweat covered every part of my body, but the heat didn't seem to faze anyone else. Geno talked with Veronica, her friend from San Juan who was driving us, in the front seat, and Esmerada, sitting next to me in the back, looked at me as if I could understand every word she said. Though all I could understand was "Salvador," "Jacobo" and "Gracias Dios," or "Thank God."

Before an airplane from New York City lands at the airport in San Juan, it swings around in a wide arc, and for just a few seconds the people in the plane are given a view of endless shanties by the seashore. But no sooner do they see this then the plane makes its landing and all is forgotten. Forgotten at least to the "gringos" who, like me, would take taxis or special buses to the hotels lined up on Ashford Avenue, in the Condado district of San Juan. But here in the car, driving through Bayamon to the highway, there was no escape from the sights, sounds and smells of overwhelming poverty.

Shoeless children ran in streets filled with refuse. Too many people standing on street corners, passing bottles wrapped in brown paper bags, or standing, staring into space. Music, loud and rocking, was everywhere. Through the open windows of the car I smelled, it seemed, a thousand different foods.

At a traffic light, a little boy stuck his hand in the window and offered us a flower. and when I took it, he put out his other hand, and gestured for me to give him something. As I handed him a dollar from my pocket, and he walked away from the car, Geno said I'd made a big mistake.

"Now all his friends are gonna want something!"

Sure enough a group of boys started walking over to our car, but just before they reached us, the light turned green and we were on our way again. Geno said we had to watch out for beggars when we were traveling around certain areas of Puerto Rico.

"This isn't the hotel district."

After an hour of driving, the tropical heat had become so intense, and so overwhelming, that we decided to put off stopping at Manati or Aquadilla until at least tomorrow. Instead, we'd drive until we reached Rincon, where we'd spend some time at the beach before driving on to Mayaguez.

> I will need pictures from my hometown of Mayaguez:
>
> 1. The Balboa Bridge facing towards Balboa and the reverse, and one looking towards the left—from the Bridge downward.
> 2. Paris Athletic Park
> 3. Miramar—get a picture of the huts behind the Sarah Roosevelt Project
> 4. Get a picture of the red dirt hill of La Mineral
> 5. The market in the plaza
> 6. Columbus Landing—facing from the sea, the buildings to the left corner and the corner store
> 7. The municipal hospital—this was where I was born
> 8. Get some pictures of the meadows
> 9. El Malecon Beach
> 10. The Plaza De Colon—get some of the corners across the

street from the school.
11. *Canjo Majagual—across a small bridge, get a picture of the shacks.*
12. *The Escuela Industrial de Menores (this was a reform school that I was in for awhile, and it's outside of town).*
13. *All the theaters and the main churches (Catholic).*
14. *All The schools.*

I will need a picture of the Agron house, or shack, on the road leading out of town, and if you can't find the house, then a picture of a mountainous region will be okay.

I will need a picture of La Escuela de Correctional, a reform school for boys outside of Mayaguez.

Well, that about does it for Puerto Rico—also get some good photos of the San Juan Airport (the one that was being used in 1958). Also try to get some photos of the "Centros Espiritistas," where they hold seances—there are some in Mayaguez. There used to be one near the school not too far from Roosevelt projects. When I get my father's address, I'll send it—he probably could point out the places I want for you. We don't write to each other for some time—I suspect he's dead and my family doesn't want to tell me. Like if I were going to suffer too much—they don't quite understand my stoical attitude or that I'm almost immune at this point in time to my own suffering!

I will need a picture of La Escuela de Correctional, a reform school for boys outside of Mayaguez. Also, see if you can pick up a good astronomy map of the universe.

I will start work as soon as possible, but, I must have this information in order to give things a feeling of reality.

On and on, the highway pulled us along in the tropical heat. And on either side, the men in the sugarcane fields swung their long scythes back and forth in the glare of an unrelenting sun. Back and forth, making a swishing sound like a woman in a long dress, walking across a ballroom floor, and into the arms of her lover. But here in the field there were no lovers, women, or long dresses, only the cane, the cane, and nothing but the cane. As Salvador said, "Cane will be the death of my father, and this I know as if it were a sacred truth."

> *For Puerto Rico to obtain independence it must advocate revolutionary nationalism, and it is only through this process that it can accomplish some degree of socialism within its boundaries. When we establish revolutionary nationalism, we will open the door for socialist development.*
>
> *We can only start the socialist revolution, but to think that we can complete this socialist development within the national boundaries is a dream that no country that is striving to be socialist has accomplished.*

The men in the fields reminded me of pictures I'd seen of prisoners tied together on chain gangs in the deep south. On the road to Mayaguez, there were no chains, and no prisoners, yet the only difference I could see was that one group of men went home at night, while the other slept in prison cells.

> *Therefore, when colonialism is the law, revolutionary nationalism is the order of the day. Socialism is international, and this can be felt as soon as it begins to burst asunder from the national boundaries.*
>
> *We can successfully contain a revolutionary nationalist revolution and then move carefully in the establishment of socialism in the social process of our nation.*
>
> *Puerto Rico is a backward nation, and all you have to do to see the truth of this is to walk swiftly through the sugar cane fields.*
>
> *Sugar cane doesn't lie, and if you listen closely it will whisper that socialism is the future of Puerto Rico.*

Past hundreds of men in the sugar cane fields, past the cities of Arecibo and Aquadilla, until finally we reached Rincon. We parked the car, put on our bathing suits, and quickly ran into the surf.

Even Esmeralda joined us, though not in a bathing suit. Instead, she took off her shoes, rolled up her stockings, and waded into the surf.

> *All national liberation movements should use the political instrument of revolutionary nationalism in their struggle. Not to stop the progressive internationalist movement, but to reach the highest degree of socialist development possible.*
>
> *This is Boricuan Socialism as understood by the Boricuan Revolutionary Nationalist Party here at Greenhaven Correctional Facility. This is a belief in the dialectical and historical materialism of Karl Marx.*

Late in the afternoon, riding south on Route #2, we reached Mayaguez in less than half an hour. From there, we followed Esmeralda's gestures up one road, down another, then up and down several hills until we arrived at the home of her brother.

His name was Israel, his wife was Lillian, and as we got out of the car several little children surrounded us. A young man of uncertain age, who smiled as we made our introductions, stood apart from the group.

The house was made of wood, with light green walls, and a tin roof. The windows had shutters instead of glass, and the house had no indoor plumbing. Clothing wash lines criss crossed the front yard, and on the roof sat a large tv antenna.

Inside, the house was clean and neat, but looking down at the floor I realized it was the first time I had ever been in a house where the floor was made of solid earth.

Israel, a handsome man with broad shoulders, black hair, and the blazing eyes of a Pentecostal preacher, looked at me and laughed. Then he pointed at me while saying something in Spanish to Genoveva.

"He says you should be a Pentecostal preacher because

of the way you look with your long hair...and he wants to know if he can take you to see his church."

"Does he wanna do this right now?"

"That's what he says."

Sitting next to Israel as he drove along the now dark mountain roads of Mayaguez to his Pentecostal church, I wondered if the house where Salvador was born and raised was nearby.

Holding out my camera to Israel, and speaking in a fractured Spanish, I said,

"Es necessita para me tome picturas de la casa de Salvador."

Meaning roughly that I would need some pictures of Salvador's house.

We conversed like this until a few minutes and several miles later, when he pulled over and leaned out the window. He pointed to a ramshackle house sitting all by itself on a small hill.

I walked from the car to where I could get a better view of the house where Salvador had been born over thirty years ago, and where he lived with his mother, sister, and father before leaving for the poorhouse when he was barely five years old.

Lifeless and abandoned, with boards covering the windows, it was indistinguishable from any other house. In fact, except for the boards covering the windows, it looked just like Uncle Israel's house.

Walking over to one of the windows, I pulled back a loose board so that I could take a peek inside.

> We lived behind the Eleanor Roosevelt housing projects, an area of poverty—with dilapidated houses or shacks with tin roofs (some even had roofs of palm tree branches) that stood on four very large logs. The wooden walls had all sorts of cracks, big and wide enough to house extended families of mice and roaches. And in typical fashion common to all the shacks in the

area, the rooms were criss-crossed with lines of rope. Sheets were then hung on the ropes to divide the area into "rooms."

On a typical night a centipede might crawl across the splintered floor, while the howls of wild dogs roaming the streets were intense in the distance. Almost everybody had a chicken coop under their house, including us. They were a poor man's chickens. The seldom laid eggs, and even if they did, some neighbor's kid stole them anyway.

Everyone but Lillian and Genoveva were sleeping when we got back to the house. While Lillian was making up my bed in one of the front rooms, I sat with Genoveva on the front steps.

The air was warm, moist, and sensual. And with few lights from the surrounding houses, the light from the stars shone brightly, As we talked, our words blended in with the sounds of the *coqui*, a small animal resembling a bull frog, known all over Puerto Rico for its distinctive sound.

"What did you think of his church?"

"We never got there."

"How come?"

"By the time I got through taking pictures at the house it was too late to go anywhere else."

"What house are you talking about?"

"Where Salvador lived when he was a kid...the one in Balboa...and it's not far from here."

"You went there? I thought we were gonna go there together with Esmeralda tomorrow."

"Well...I was in the car and I figured like why not do it now and get it over with instead of waiting...because we've got such a big list of places he wants us to photograph."

"What was it like?"

"All broken up...and there were boards on the windows... but I took one off so I could see inside a little bit."

"So no one's living in there?"

"Not a soul."

> *The coqui is an ancient little creature in Puerto Rico with the appearance of a mini-frog but with a loud sound. Some people believe the coqui is a creature left from the legendary Alantis, that it has occult powers and the sound it makes is a code to the stars and other intelligent beings that live among the stars. Some say that if the coqui disappears, so will the island of Puerto Rico. And it has been proven time and again that the coqui cannot live except on the island.*

After an early morning breakfast of rice, beans, and strong coffee, we left for the Municipal Hospital. From there we would try to find Salvador's father.

Salvador had described the Municipal Hospital as "a place of healing for the poorest of the poor," and as we stopped in front of what appeared to be the main entrance, I could understand exactly what he was talking about.

Beige walls, hardened and faded by years of unrelenting sun had given it a look of seediness, much like an unkempt garden, all brown, and waiting for rain.

Sitting in the car next to Genoveva, I said I wanted to take a look inside, and that it shouldn't take me more than a few minutes.

"Why would you want to go inside? Didn't Salvador say he just wanted a picture of the main entrance?"

"Yeah...but.."

"So why don't you just take the picture and let's get going?"

"Because I want to see where he was born, that's why."

The first person Genoveva asked was an elderly nurse of uncertain age who said he was probably born on one of the wards upstairs. She wasn't sure which one because that was a long time ago, yet she thought it would have been the one marked, "Ward Three."

With benches for waiting fathers-to-be on either side of

the entranceway, "Ward Three" turned out to be a sun-drenched alley of a room with women and babies lying on iron beds, all smiles and crying. The smell of talcum powder was everywhere.

I sat on one of the empty beds as Genoveva conversed with one of the nurses, and wondered if it was the bed where Salvador had been born.

> It was a typical spring night in Puerto Rico on April 24th, 1943. Warm and sensual, with thousands of stars in the sky, a bright moon and a clear sky. The sound of the eguirros y quitaras, so common to the nightlife of Mayaguez floated from nearby houses. Mist that fell gently upon the mango and avocado trees swept across the green pastures and mingled with the lakes and rivers.
>
> The story of my birth is an interesting one, and later on in my life, it was told to me by many different people who knew my family well when we were living in Mayaguez.
>
> Just after midnight, the silence of the night was broken by the screams of a pregnant, nineteen year old woman. This was my beloved mother, Esmeralda, who was lying on a bed inside the old broken-down shack that belonged to my father, Gumersindo Agron Valentin in the section of Mayaguez known as Balboa, not far from El Parque de Paris.
>
> "Sindo! Sindo! Por favor, take me to the hospital! This is a tough one. The child is already kicking and pushing forward. The time has come. Ohooo, I can't take this any longer," my mother said. "Hold on for a while," my father said, "I have to go out and get a taxi, "as he moved around in the dark looking for his clothes.
>
> Later someone would tell me that my father stepped out into the night in search of a publico to take Esmeralda or "Mela" to the Municipal Hospital of Mayaguez, the only hospital for poor people. It took him a half hour to locate a publico to drive the short distance between Balboa and the hospital. When it arrived, the neighbors were already up and surrounding our home, commenting and gossiping while my year-old sister tried to figure out what the hysteria and running around was

all about. The car sped away. In less than ten minutes we were all in the emergency room—my father, sister, and mother with me inside of her. The doctor examined Esmeralda and declared her ready for delivery, but it was to be a premature birth. My family has always maintained I wasn't fully developed at birth and I was trying to get out of the maternal womb before my time by kicking hard.

Here in this faraway place, deep in the belly of Mayaguez, and perhaps on this very bed, is where it all began for Salvador Agron at a little past three o'clock in the morning over thirty years ago.

The Capeman: pushed and pulled from Esmeralda's womb, all red, soft, and innocent.

A little baby in the arms of its mother. And as the sun streamed through the hospital windows later that morning, his tears, Esmerada said, had appeared to her as tiny hearts of holy water.

> When the doctors informed my father I was a boy, I'm sure he was overjoyed. My sister Aurea, who had fallen asleep on one of the hospital benches, opened her eyes, looked around and then went back to sleep. Sindo went into the room where my mother lay and held her hand. Looking at her intently, as he always did when he had something in mind, he suggested, "Juan is a good name. It's your father's name. Why don't we call him Juan" Mela, objecting to this, said, "No, you were the one who named Francisco, our first child. When Aurea was born, I gave her the name. Now, my father wants to name this child and he has already chosen the name Salvador—as you well know. That will be his name." Mother seldom ever spoke about Francisco Agron Rodriguez, my brother who died young. Sindo was about to interject something, but he was cut short by the appearance in the room of Esmeralda's father, don Juan.
>
> "Bendicion, papa," said Mela in the customary manner.
> "Dios te bendiga, hija."
> Don Juan then put his hand on Sindo's shoulders and

reminded him, "You know, Sindo, the name Salvador is a beautiful name."

"Si, don Juan, but the padre catolico says he doesn't want to baptize anyone with the name of the Lord." Sindo knew the name Salvador (meaning "savior") was not well accepted by the Catholic priest even though don Juan insisted that if Mela had a boy, he wanted to give the boy that name because the name was revealed to him in a dream.

"Well then, I must have another talk with the padre. It's not actually the name that bothers the padre. It's that you rebels have been running all around Puerto Rico, living here and there, in the common law style without being legally married by the Church. You're both living in sin. That's why the padre objects to the name Salvador. But what the padre seems to forget..." Don Juan said, pausing, "...is that Mary and Joseph weren't married to each other either. I'll talk to the padre again, and he'll get my message."

Moms was aware I would be her last born, for she had consented to become sterilized. During this period in Puerto Rico, many women were sterilized by the new American home planning. The Americans told Puerto Rican women it was necessary to get an operation not to have any more babies than they were capable of maintaining. They said the island was overpopulated already and sterilization was a sure way to keep a small family. All this was part of the scheme of the United States to keep Puerto Ricans from being born, so they could maintain a certain control over our families. My mother, naive and young as she was, became sterilized. Sindo left my mother's room and went to where I was behind the glass, while he got a good look at the attractive nurses standing around my small crib. Pops always appreciated women. He returned to my mother, kissed her, and promised to return after taking Aurea to Aunt Maria's house. Somebody had to watch her while Moms was in the hospital, for Pops had to work. He went home, took a short nap, and went to work without being tired. When he got off from work—cutting sugar cane all day, from five in the morning to six at night—he went directly to the hospital.

Moms didn't stay in the hospital too long after I was born,

but my father went to see her everyday for the first three days. After my mother had been home a week, we had a celebration as a family and things ran smoothly for a while. But these were days destined to disappear as though they had never existed in my life and the life of my family.

Back in the car, Genoveva and Uncle Israel spoke in Spanish for a while
"Israel thinks he knows where Salvador's father is living..it's in a retirement home in Columbus Landing."
"Where's that?"
"It's not that far from here."
Up one street, down another, until finally we arrived at a complex of houses that Israel said was where the old people lived.
Each house was connected to the one next to it. Their walls were painted an off-beige color, and they all looked the same. The only sound on the street was made by aluminum walkers pushed slowly by elderly men and women

My father was born in the rural part of the town of Anasco, which is near Mayaguez. He claims his father (whose name I do not know) was of French descent and that his mother was of Indian descent. He confided in me that he also had brothers of African descent because his mother was once married to an ex-slave and she also had African blood in her veins. Though she appeared to be pure Taino, she was actually mixed. It was the practice of the Spaniards to pair off Indians and Africans in Puerto Rico to produce slaves with lighter complexions.

After about ten minutes or so, Genoveva and Esmeralda came back to the car, and Genoveva said they'd found out where Sindo lived.
"Someone is gonna get him for us."
Salvador had said that if his father were still alive, he

would only be a shadow of his former self. Too many nights drinking rum, and mornings getting up to work all day in the sugar cane fields beneath an unforgiving sun, had probably broken him down.

> *Gumersindo grew up in the mountains of Anasco and lived the life of a jibaro in his youthful days. Among the jibaro class much is expected of a youth.*
>
> *He started working when very young, about seven or eight years old, as was traditional in those days and times. He had his father's French hazel eyes and a yellow sort of complexion which he inherited from his Indian mother.*

The man walking toward our car was about six feet tall, with short-cropped cloud white hair, and strong green eyes, just like his son's.

Though well proportioned, his having lived long hours bent over in the sugarcane fields had turned his skin a decided copper color, and twisted his body. As he got closer, my impression was that he could no longer reach his full height without feeling a great deal of pain.

> *Under the heat of the tropical sun his skin turned into a bronze sort of native tinge. His piercing stare gave the impression of intelligence. Although he was not literate in the scholastic sense and in fact was a very poor reader (probably he'd read a couple of books on spiritualism besides his Bible, in all the days of his life), when it came to matters about life and what it takes to survive, he was very intelligent.*

When he reached us, he quickly looked us over, until his eyes stopped at Emeralda, who in turn, quickly walked away.

Stopping when she got about fifty feet from us, and leaning against a palm tree, Emeralda stared at Sindo as if he were a creature from some faraway world, instead of a native son.

> *My father was very observant, and nothing passed by him without his noticing what is right or wrong about a situation. He didn't speak much and his taciturn manner was sometimes deceptive. You could not pinpoint his thoughts, though you could sense his feeling.*

As Emeralda stared at Sindo, it was obvious that she still had feelings for this man that she had not seen in so many years. Her love for him, though no longer active, had not died, drowned, or been forgotten.

> *When my father was in his late twenties, he met my mother at a festival or dance in Las Marries. They danced and talked and made friends. My mother had just turned thirteen. She was a child and he was a man, but a woman was developing inside her mind and her body was beginning to demand contact and sexual fulfillment. That's what was expected. Because her mother died when she was born, she was enlisted to work for the Rodriguez family. Her life was so unbearable, her search for a man was obvious. She saw escape through my father.*

Later Genoveva would tell me that her conversation with Sindo had mostly been about Salvador, but that she hadn't touched on too much of his early history with Salvador and his mother. Only that they had all lived together in the house at Balboa for about eighteen months before Esmeralda had moved out with Salvador and Aurea. He didn't say why they had moved away, or where they had gone, only that this was the last time they had ever lived together as man, wife, and family.

> *After their meeting, my father visited the Rodriguez family and became like one of the household. Don Juan's brother was the man of the family. He ran the house and lived there with his family. Don Juan was poor and so were his children. They had to work for their living as servants to the older broth-*

> er, do the laundry, and take care of the children. Sindo and Mela grew closer to each other; this closeness developed into sexual attraction and they managed to fall in love during their friendship while Sindo visited the house. Don Juan was suspicious, but Sindo and Mela were careful not to show their affection around the house or in his presence. They had to hide when they wanted to kiss and hold hands. One day they became so impassioned for each other that the only alternative left was to elope, and this they did with mucho gusto as soon as Sindo hit the numbers. After he got one thousand dollars from his winning number, he left with Mela. They went to live in the town of Hormigueros, and from there after Mela reached sixteen years of age, they went to San German where she gave birth to my brother Francisco who died at the age of three.

As I was standing and watching them talk, Sindo started to cry.

I whispered to Genoveva that maybe this was too much, all these questions—and Esmeralda not even wanting to talk to him. We agreed maybe it was time for us to leave.

As I silently patted Sindo on the back in a gesture of comfort, I closed my eyes and hoped that when I opened them again Esmeralda would be by my side to wish him a proper good-bye. But when I opened them up, she was already in the car, waiting to go.

> Father was strong and one could see this in his hands as they were rough from too much work on sugar fields or from the large brooms used on the job he had for awhile, sweeping the dirty streets of Mayaguez.

Shaking Sindo's weathered hand, and looking as deep as I could into his hazel-colored eyes, I whispered, *"Vaya con dios"* before turning and walking away.

> When I was about eighteen months old, they had a big fight. This was building because he'd come home intoxicated after being with other women. After this fight, she picked up

whatever little things she had, and ever since that day, they never lived together again.

After we left my father's house, our next stop was Asilo de Pobres, or the poorhouse, in Mayaguez.

Sitting next to Genoveva in the back seat and looking at Sindo through the rear window as we drove away, I wondered if we'd ever see him again. But Geno was more concerned that Esmeralda hadn't even say one word to him.

"You would think that after all these years she would at least want to say something to him," she said.

"Yeah...but keep your voice down because she can hear us talking."

"I just think you have to forgive people..."

I will need a picture of El Asilo De Los Pobres (the asylum of the poor, or just the poorhouse) I will need photographs of the inside and the outside, but especially of the entrance. This is very important because I spent nearly ten years of my life in this place. Just tell the nuns that the photographs are for me, and also see if you can locate some old photographs taken there when I was about five years old. One picture was taken of me next to the fountain. I will need some photographs of the dormitories and of the old men's side, and also some behind the kitchen.

Whatever information you can get on the place will be good.

This place is important

Silently we rode through the streets of Mayaguez until finally Israel stopped the car.

Leaning over the front seat, he said, in perfect English, "This is it."

A paved pathway led to a small flight of stone steps. Then a gray wall, and in the middle a wooden door with flat pieces of steel running back and forth. Through a tiny peephole those inside could examine anyone on the other side before allowing them to gain entrance. To each side of the door, four stone pillars rose perhaps twenty feet in the air as supports for a small overhanging ledge.

The effect was that of an abandoned 18th-century temple, particularly since the color of the building, once white, had become a dirt-streaked gray from lack of paint for so many years.

Officially, all were welcome at the poorhouse under the guise of compassion as practiced by the *Hermanas de la Cariadad*, or Sisters of Charity, an order from Spain whose stated mission was to provide a house of refuge where people were free to stay and live until they had somewhere else to go: all the poor and tired people of Mayaguez with nowhere else to go, all the children without mothers or fathers; the alcoholics, the wretchedly poor, the epileptics; and of course, the insane.

> *Anyone outside could hear the lunatic screams of those who had gone mad, the suffering cries of the derelicts, the dying whispers of the complaining old folks, and the sobs of the lost, forgotten and orphaned children, while the hypocritical nuns prayed to a half-nude man—god on a wooden cross in the secret chambers of the institution. It was a place reflecting hell on earth, and while they beat their breasts three times, in the endless night, under the moaning sounds of pain and ecstasy and sado-masochism, in the name of the Father, the Son, and the Holy Ghost.*

As Esmeralda knocked on the door of the poorhouse, I heard a loud , piercing cry, which sounded like a cat being run over by a car. But there were no cars, no cats, nothing. The sound came again, and this time, listening closely, I realized it was a woman screaming, coming from behind the wall of the poorhouse.

> *The entrance to the poorhouse brings to mind the saying of Jesus, "For wide is the way that leadeth to destruction, and*

many there be that go in there but, straight and narrow is the way that leadeth to salvation, and few there be that find it."
The wide path leading to the poorhouse was the road to hell.

An elderly nun in full habit opened the door. A chain of keys circled her waist, while a huge crucifix hung from a piece of leather around her neck.

Her name, she said, was Sister Marguerite, and after exchanging some words with Esmeralda and Genoveva, she opened her hand in a wide gesture of welcome.

Walking through the door it felt like I had traveled back into time one hundred years.

> This was the world of my childhood, a house of madness, the castle of the living dead, hell and heaven mixed together, one never knowing which one to embrace or reject
> The poorhouse was built a long, long time ago as a house of refuge for the poor, the hungry, and the lost of Mayaguez. But for me, it was always like Dracula's castle. The house of the living dead.

Following Sister Marguerite, we entered a vast courtyard of flowers, and walkways leading to wooden houses, making it feel like an interior courtyard from a faraway time and place. The buildings, the gardens, and even the nuns, looked old, tired, and worn-out

Another nun was waiting for us, and when she saw Esmeralda, she smiled. She and Esmeralda briefly embraced before they walked off, leaving us alone with Sister Marguerite.

"Her name is Sister Isabela," Sister Marguerite said, "and she was Esmeralda's supervisor when she worked in the kitchen, and Salvador and his sister were living in the dormitories."

> In the poorhouse I slept on a bed next to a large gate facing the recreation yard. It was one of the best spots in the dormi-

tory. Every night before going to bed, a stern-looking nun would walk into the dormitory. It was expected that by this time everyone was to be in their pajamas and sitting on their beds. There were four rows of beds, each row made up of about twenty-five beds. When the nun used to show up at the door facing the dormitory, we were all there sitting like little angels. She took a count and then if nobody was missing, she would say with an authoritarian voice, "It's time to pray now. Everyone kneel down on the side of the bed, and let us pray." She would then lead the evening prayer.

"Holy Father, Holy Son, Holy Ghost, and blessed Immaculate Virgin Mary, Mother of God—see thy children. Bless them and protect them in the hours of the night so that they may arise like the sun in the morning with only goodness in their souls."

Nuns in full habits were everywhere, and Sister Marguerite explained that while the poorhouse was a place of compassion, the people who lived within its walls had to follow the rules.

"Would you like to see one of our dormitories?"

"Uh...that'd be great...and uh...you think you could maybe show us where Salvador would've slept?"

Taking us to one of the buildings, she unlocked a door. She threw it open, and it resembled pictures I'd seen of orphanages in eighteenth century England.

The long and narrow room was filled with four rows of twenty-five little beds, so that there was barely an inch of room between them.

The bathroom was in an adjoining area, but there were no showers, or baths, just toilets and sinks.

"We have one shower for everyone on the other side of the building," she explained.

She would then recite the Our Father and the Ave Maria and we would all join in. After about two or three minutes of silent and individual prayer, we would all stand from our kneeling position and jump into bed like trained children— and, so we were. We usually went to bed at seven or eight in the evening and we would get up about seven or eight in the morning.

But I always hated the night. Because from a very young age I had developed the habit of pissing in my bed.

The dormitory smelled sharply of sweat, disinfectant, and urine. In terms of smell alone, I could just as soon have been sitting on a bed in the reformatory at Wiltwyck, a prison cell at Greenhaven, or on a cot in the insane asylum at Dannemora.

One hundred little boys living in a room that would be crowded were there only twenty-five. And one hundred little boys all trying to use the same shower on the other side of the building.

Sitting on one of the beds, with its clean but ancient blanket, and filled with small holes, I could hardly believe that Salvador had lived in this very room for ten years, off and on. He used to piss here at night. And outside this very door was where the nuns made him hold his mattress to the sun until the piss had dried away.

Then I heard the faint sound of someone screaming from one of the upstairs rooms.

How could they call themselves the Sisters of Charity when every morning, when I would wake up with my sheets and quilt soaked in piss, they would make me put the mattress on my head and then stand out in the yard, shaming me in front of all the other children? Then they would make me stand there until the mattress had dried out from the sun. How was I to believe that these nuns were the daughters of Our Holy Father in Heaven?

This habit of wetting my bed would follow me until my fourteenth birthday, when it suddenly stopped and I thought I had become a man. Years later I walk and stand with a kind of forward thrust in my body, and I think that maybe this was in part caused by my having to carry around that guilt of piss when I was just a little boy with no strength in my arms.

As soon as Sister Marguerite's back was turned, I walked quickly to the back of the dormitory, and out a side door. Following the sound of the scream, now more like a low and deadly moan, I climbed a flight of stairs to the second floor. From there I walked down a corridor and past several locked doors until I found one open. Inside was a semi-dark room with rows of beds, feces on the floor, and several people chained to the beds.

Howling, thrashing, screaming, and laughing. One woman, free of chains, walked over to where I was standing. And before I could get away, in one swift movement she reached between my legs and grabbed my cock. I was so taken aback that I let out a scream of my own, and when she let go of my cock, I ran down the corridor, with the screaming and yelling following me as if in a dream

Downstairs, Genoveva was deep in conversation with Sister Isabela.

"Uh, Genoveva, could I speak with you for a minute please?"

Genoveva came over to me.

"One of the crazy people upstairs just tried to attack me!"

"Really?"

"Yeah...and I swear to God there's people chained to their beds!"

"What!?"

"I'm not kidding! Go up and look for yourself if you don't believe me!"

"I believe you...but do you smell what I smell?"

"The shit?" I asked her.

"Yeah...it's all over the place..."

"And upstairs there's people sleeping in it!"

> Moms also worked in the elderly section of the institution. Her job was to change the wet sheets, wash the dirty clothes, empty the garbage, bathe the elderly, and feed those who were either too old to feed themselves or were handicapped. At times she took some of the elderly people outside the poorhouse for a walk, and she did this even though it wasn't a requirement of the job.
>
> She brought many of the mentally disturbed folks back to some sort of sanity and many an elderly person back to active participation in living. She would have the people make things or put them to work on some type of project, such as taking care of the gardens or helping their fellow elders. The only place where she lacked control was over me. When the nuns would ask her why this was so, she would only say that I inherited my uncle's wildness, my grandfather's individually, and my father's foolish heart.

Sister Isabella told Genoveva that Salvador had been a deeply troubled child who wet his bed almost every night. He needed, she said, to be punished nearly every day for any number of minor offenses. Like unlocking the *locos* from their cells, so they could run naked and free in the courtyard until someone came to lock them up again. Or sneaking over to the girl's bathhouse to watch them while they took showers.

Looking at Sister Isabella's hands, with their long and slender fingers, I imagined those same hands spanking Salvador from one end of the night to the other. Hard and smacking, with no thought of mercy, and not stopping until his little child ass was the color of blood and hurting.

Aside from his sister and mother, she said, the only other person who could control him for any length of time without causing him to have yet another violent tantrum was a young nun whom everyone called *La Rubia*.

> *The nuns to my way of thinking were not representative of anything good or decent. They were evil. I was not only afraid*

> *of them, but I thought them to be disgusting and not at all followers of Jesus. Today, I realize there were good nuns, and as I look back I realize there were those I did like.*
>
> *There was "La Rubia," or "the blond," and I called her this because of her blond hair, or at least the little hair that I could see peeking out from underneath her habit. She had pale blue eyes and long slender fingers.*

Sister Isabella said that *La Rubia* was Sister Angela, and that she'd come from a wealthy family in the city of Ponce. Salvador, she said, had been one of her favorites.

La Rubia had been at the convent for nearly fifteen years, but then had quickly left, no one knew why, when Salvador was ten years old, and shortly after he had gone to live with his mother and sister in New York City.

> *La Rubia grew very fond of me, and I would always run to her when the other nuns wanted to beat me for doing something bad. She would put up a good front, grab me by the ear and take me to a room, locking the door behind, and tell me to holler as though she were punishing me. The other nuns would smile while thinking she was giving me a good spanking. But, once in the room she would just hug and kiss me on my lips, fondle me very affectionately and laugh with me in secret.*
>
> *She saved me many times from the discipline and wrath of the other nuns.*

Sister Isabella was probably about fifty-five, but it was difficult to tell with the blue and white habit covering virtually every inch of her. All that showed to the world was her face.

Salvador said that his mother worked in the kitchen when they were living here, and that she also worked with the insane, or the *locos*, as they were known to all at the poorhouse.

"Ask her if she could show us the dormitory for the handicapped and also maybe the kitchen and dinning room."

> There was a walkway that led to the chapel which was at the center of the institution. There was a garden on the girl's side and one on the boy's side. The girl's side was open to the garden, and the boy's garden had a fence around it in order to keep us out of it. Iron doors and fences, wire fences and wire doors, doors with locks, trees and gardens, are what segregated every section of the poorhouse.

Down one pathway to a large room lined with tables and benches, where with a grand wave of her hand, Sister Isabella said proudly, half in English and half in Spanish, that this is the very same dinning room where Salvador and Aurea used to eat their meals.
"Ask her what kinds of food they ate."

> At the poorhouse, we all ate together in the same room. The boys were on one side and we were separated from the girls by a series of tables.
> Several nuns stood behind the tables, and each of them served up the food. First the boys lined up, one by one, and as we passed by the table, a nun would give each of us a plate of food or juice. Then the girls followed after the boys. But before we could eat, we always had to wait until everyone else was seated first.
> Lunch was usually boiled potatoes, bread, and large servings of "plantano," a large green banana most often baked or fried.
> Dinner was a variation of the same meal. Day after day, the same food, for weeks, months, and years.

I wondered if Sister Isabella had ever gone hungry, or spent long periods of time with few options as to what she was allowed to eat.
Her face was smooth, and said nothing, but her eyes were hard, and I had the feeling she was a person who rarely did without.
Genoveva, seeming to read my mind, said that Sister Isabella and the other nuns, including the Mother Superior,

had their own private dinning room in another section of the poorhouse.

> The nuns employed my mother for 7 dollars a week. Because she worked at the poorhouse, we were not allowed to see her except sometimes on the week-ends when she took us to visit my grandfather or her brother Israel. Mornings my mother worked in the ward with the crazies, and later in the day, she worked in the kitchen.
> Nights were lonely, and many a night I covered myself from head to my feet, completely under the covers. I would cry my heart out because my mother, father and sister were so near, yet at the same time so far out of reach.
> I knew I was alone in the world, and what I received from the priests and nuns associated with the poorhouse was nothing more than hypocritical affection from strange men and women who had the nerve to call themselves mother, fathers, sisters, and brothers of God.
> I was always afraid of the dark.

Sister Isabella led us up a flight of stairs, and then down several dark corridors to a huge wooden door. A chain woven around the door knob was attached to a padlock.

Reaching into her habit, Sister Isabella removed a large ring of keys, looking for the right key, as she talked with Genoveva in Spanish. Genoveva whispered to me that Sister Isabella was trying to reassure her that the people we were about to meet weren't dangerous. They only appeared this way, she said, but we should not be afraid because they would not harm us in any way.

She says for us to think of them as "little children without manners."

> How I feared the poorhouse. If a child knew hate, I was that child. I hated the nuns with a passion. I hated the old people, the Church, the boys, the girls, and almost everything about the place.

When the two wooden doors swung open, the stench was so overwhelming that it felt as if I'd been thrown head first into an overflowing toilet bowl.

The dormitory was similar to the one where Salvador had lived so many years ago. Beds lined up, side by side, against each wall, with a corridor down the middle. Some beds with tiny, adjoining tables had washbasins on top, while others had wheelchairs, walkers, or canes close by. As we walked, we looked at the faces, which by now had come alive simply, it seemed, by virtue of our presence in the room. Tired, half-dead, pale and hungry, faces with drooling mouths and eyes with far too much light.

Sister Isabella, with her hands balled into fists, and her arms outstretched, more closely resembled a driving fullback than a nun in full habit. She pushed away the sea of hands reaching out to us as we walked down the corridor, from bed to bed.

"Water," one cried out, while another said "*Puta*," or "Whore." Still another said, "*Caca de toro, caca de toro,*" or "Bullshit," again and again.

Between the overwhelming stench, and how frightening all this seemed to our untrained eyes, we moved more quickly through the dormitory. We were nearly out the door when an old man, with a ruptured face, sitting in a wheelchair, blocked our path. Pointing at Genoveva, he said, "*Muy bonita, muy bonita.*"

Laughing, I followed Genoveva and Sister Isabella out the door, and then I turned around and looked back. Sitting in his wheelchair, the man with the ruptured face and black curly hair looked like the picture of Jesus Christ on the wall of Esmeralda's apartment in the Bronx. Especially the way his eyes appeared to follow my every move.

"*Que pasa?*" I asked him.

Looking me square in the eye, and with a broad smile across his face, he said to me in clear and perfect English:

"Gimme some pussy! Gimme some pussy!"

His words followed me out of the room like a hiss of flying steam from a dying radiator.

> *I could not hate the mentally ill because their screaming, yelling, and violence was about the only resistance clear to me at the time. So I grew to love the crazy people because, for me, they made lots of sense, and the crazier they were, the better I liked them.*
>
> *The locos of the poorhouse, the real locos, the ones who would hurt themselves or others if they were put in the dormitories with the other people, were put in little cells all by themselves, and away from everyone else.*
>
> *And many, many were the times when I used to hide in their living quarters and then when no one was looking I would unhook the steel bar that kept them in their cells. Then they would run out, each one naked, while I would hide behind one of the stone pillars.*
>
> *This would be a big event, this freeing of the locos. People would be running around screaming that the locos were on the loose! And I would sit on the roof of the dormitory and laugh to myself as the nuns tried to get the locos back to their cells. Sometimes this would take an entire day.*
>
> *I enjoyed letting the locos out of their cages, and I would let them out as often as I could.*
>
> *I felt that crazy people should not be put in cages.*

As we walked away from the dormitory, Genoveva and Sister Isabella were talking to each other in rapid Spanish. "What did she say?" I asked Genoveva, when they were through talking.

"She was telling me stories about how when Esmeralda lived here she had like a gift or something because she was one of the only people who could work with the people in the boxes…"

> *Sometimes moms had to tangle with the insane folks, which she maintained and still to this day says were only "possessed by demons and spirits." A few times she came close to*

being raped or sexually assaulted by some insane person. However, she would always light candles and pray to God, Jesus, and the Virgin Mary for the insane at church every Sunday in hope that the demons would leave them so they could return to a normal life. The old folks, the insane, the boys and girls (all in separate sections) got to know about mother's courage, so that she maintained a sort of motherly control over them.

She was well-respected by the elderly and also by the locos because of her policy which earned her respect from some of the nuns, the old ones, and the insane: she treated everyone with respect and dealt with everyone in a very humane manner.

Moms also used to bathe the mentally ill with a hose. Even when an insane person had to take a bath, she did not care how dangerous that person was made out to be. She would still open the door of the cell where they were to try and communicate with them. She said they were welcome to come out of the cell and bathe by themselves if they wanted to. Whenever this appeal failed, she would then use the water hose on them, but only with the greatest reluctance.

"Did she say anything about him wetting his bed and that stuff about the ants?"

"I asked her but she said she wasn't here when that happened, and that she doesn't know nothing about it."

The nuns tried everything to make me stop wetting the bed: talking about it in front of the other boys as a way of humiliating me; having me piss on hot bricks; spanking me, unmercifully; but nothing they did seemed to have any effect on me whatsoever. So the nuns in their wisdom, thought up a new plan that might work.

One day I was asked to see Mother Superior, who was waiting to talk with me in the courtyard. As I was walking across the courtyard, two nuns stepped out from the kitchen, and on my left two nuns stepped out from the clothing room. And as each set of nuns walked to where I was standing, I sensed something very wrong, but I didn't know what it was, only that I had the strangest feeling something bad was about to happen.

Suddenly, almost as if they'd rehearsed all this beforehand, two nuns appeared as if from nowhere.

"Sisters, por favor, come here. Salvador and I have been talking over a problem, and we would like to have your comments. I had Salvador called here this morning because I wanted to give him some candy, but he tells me he went pee-pee in his bed last night."

Pausing, she looked in my direction with a wicked smile on her face.

"Isn't this true, Salvador?"

"Yes, Mother Superior, it is the truth."

Suddenly, two of the nuns had thrown their arms around me, and as I started screaming and kicking, they tried to lead me away from where we were standing with Mother Superior. Just like that, all my suspicions about the nuns and their trickery was confirmed.

As the nuns pushed and carried me along the path, I tried to kick and hit them, but I wasn't able to land many blows. Partly it was because I was so upset and partly it was because of the way the nuns were dressed, with garment on top of garment. But still I kept struggling until, finally, I was so exhausted I stopped fighting them. Instead, I made like I had fainted. This didn't help. Instead, it helped them to totally subdue me. As they lifted me in the air as if I were light as a feather, I screamed for my mother as loud as I could.

"Mami! Mami! Help! Help! Help!"

But my words faded into nothingness as I felt stinging all over my body, like someone or something was biting me up and down my body. It felt so bad that I prayed to God that He should help. My God, please help me, because it felt like I had been thrown by the nuns into the pit of hell. I thought of all the stories the nuns and priests had told me about the damnation of hell, and I thought, yes, I am here, in hell, that's where I am. When I opened my eyes, all I could see were ants, thousands of ants, all over my body, biting and crawling. That's when I realized the nuns, those bitches from hell, had thrown me on an ant hill and what I was feeling was the wrath of the ants whose home had been invaded. They did their best to eat me alive as punishment. Hell was an ant hill and I had been thrown into hell by six Sisters of Charity as a way of curing me from pissing in my bed. After I understood what had happened, I hollered even louder, and when I tried to get up from the ant hill, one of the nuns pushed me down again.

My screaming must have been very loud because suddenly there was my mother running down the path with a butcher knife in her hand. Seeing my mother, the nuns quickly let go of me.

Lifting me off the ant hill, she wiped away the ants and quickly carried me back to the kitchen where she had been working when she had heard my screams. In the kitchen, she took my clothes off, and then quickly hosed off my body with cold water, all the time cursing the nuns for what they had just done to me. For a moment, the pain from the stings felt better. I still had dozens of red and blue marks all over my body. She wrapped me in a large towel and called to her father, Don Juan, who was also working in the kitchen that day, for help.

When my grandfather came into the kitchen, my mother handed me over to him, and with him carrying me in his arms, they walked to the entrance of the poorhouse. When the nun at the door saw my mother, she opened the door and stepped out of the way. On the way down the stairs, my mother told her father while she took me to the Municipal Hospital, he should go and find my father so he could know what happened.

At the Municipal Hospital, which was the same hospital where I'd been born, my mother told the people I had fallen from a tree and had landed on the ant hill. That was why I was all bitten up. Had it been up to my Moms, I'm sure she would have told the truth about the nuns and what they did to me. But Moms was not only a Catholic, she also worked in a place run by Catholics, and not to mention that most of the doctors and nurses at the hospital were also Catholics. My Moms knew that telling the truth about what had happened would probably have meant even more trouble. No one would have believed her, and even if they did, it could have meant the loss of her job. So she kept her thoughts to herself and didn't say anything about what had really happened. This must have been difficult for her as I knew just how angry she was.

After the incident with the ants, I went to live for awhile with my father.

But after living with him for several months, I had to return to the poorhouse because my father and his woman were having fights and he was about to leave her for another woman. My mother thought it would be better for me to return to the poorhouse where she would at least know where I was. My father did leave the woman he was with and took up with another one.

My fears started at an early age. Much of this I owe to the nuns during the years I lived with them at the poorhouse. As I've grown older, I have learned to control my suspicions, but even today I suspect the sincerity of most people. I only admit a small group of people into my trust.

Salvador went back and forth between the poorhouse and his father's shack. But how long he would stay at each would depend on his father's circumstances: who he was living with, and how much money he had.

Sometimes he would stay with his Aunt Maria, but Esmeralda said this usually didn't last very long because they already had too many mouths to feed.

I was growing up, inch by inch, but at the same time I was becoming a troubled child. My sadness was the sign of the troubles inside my mind and heart. I was very unhappy. My father brought me up the wide concrete steps to the poorhouse, holding my fist very tight lest I might get loose and run from the horror waiting for me inside. As the tears rolled down my face, I walked silently beside my father. His face was streaked with sweat from working in the sugar fields. Every so often he would kneel down, and with his dirty handkerchief, he wiped my face. My father was a strong man. You could see this in his hands which were rough and sunburnt from so many years in the fields. That day he was sad, and I sensed this melancholy as we climbed the stairs together

Father would leave me at the door of the poorhouse to be

put back into the hands of the nuns. And while the nuns hypocritically tried to amuse me, my father would slip away and out of the institution, run down the concrete steps very quickly and disappear into town. When this happened, I would soon discover that my father was not around any longer and I would just start crying, throw a temper tantrum (my specialty with the nuns!), kicking at them and screaming to the highest pitch of my voice like I had seen my crazy friends do who were kept locked up in rooms and who the nuns said were insane or "possessed by evil spirits." The nuns would scuffle for awhile, but their long garments got in the way and made it difficult for them to grab me.

When they caught me, I got an evil spanking.

When Esmeralda joined us, I could sense by the look in her eyes how tired she was after spending the last several hours reliving a large part of her past.

At four o'clock, I reminded Genoveva that it was time to leave. Uncle Israel, I told her, would be waiting outside for us.

"What time," she asked, "did he say he'd be there?"

" I don't know...but I think he said four o'clock."

"Then we'd better get going."

When we were living at the poorhouse, Aurea and I could see our parents only occasionally. The nuns were strict and into lots of discipline. My mother used to sneak around to see me and hug me once in awhile. Mother had better access to the section where Aurea was because the female section of the institution was connected, and was on the same side, even though separate from the mentally ill, elderly folks, and orphan girls. The security set up by the nuns was very efficient. It was easier for mother to move around on the female side due to her job in the kitchen. I could see my mother every now and then through the wire fence that separated us. At times I could see my sister by the same means on the girls side.

My father used to come and visit sometimes on Saturday or Sunday. Then Aurea and I would come from behind the

> *fence that separated us and we would go to the visiting section or room. I was becoming a stranger to my sister. The garden was open to them, and the boys' garden had a fence around it in order to keep us out of it.*
>
> *Iron doors and fences, wire fences, and wire doors, doors with locks, trees and gardens are what segregated every section of the poorhouse.*

Walking in silence across the courtyard with Sister Isabella, Genoveva, and Esmeralda, my eyes roamed among the flower beds, with their rainbow of colors, all smelling of heaven and good health.

> *One thing is certain about my early days at the Poorhouse: when I was very young, I had already experienced separation from familial surroundings. A sense of infantile awareness had hit me like a hammer and I knew that love could never be a continuous process in my life.*
>
> *At this early age the world around me was beginning to confuse me. We were all separated from one another, and I was becoming a loner—seemingly in a constant state of alienation.*
>
> *It was like a prison, and I felt as though I were being caged, restrained from being free to run around. I already knew what it was like to be put away from the world into a nonworld where souls are forgotten.*
>
> *The poorhouse was my first prison.*

At the huge wooden door separating us from the streets of Mayaguez, the world, and the light, Sister Isabella bid us good-bye.

"*Vaya con dios,*" she said, as we passed though the door. Go with God.

Q. Since you left the death house at Sing Sing, have you ever consciously thought of the electric chair?

A. Yes, many times, and sometimes I even have dreams about

> *it. One thing I realized while on death row is that people fear life more than they do death. Most people do not have the heart to embrace life without question. Living is an art, and most people have no knowledge of this art, so they die early. Dying in the electric chair is not the only way of dying. Fear of life is overcome in the face of death.*

Back in the car, sweat-stained and exhausted, we resumed our silence. All except for Esmeralda. Wide awake in the back seat, and with a Bible on her lap, she prayed softly as she looked out the window.

After a mile or so of streets, houses, and passing cars, Uncle Israel turned to me in the back seat.

"Do you still want to see Balboa Bridge?"

"Yeah...why? Is it near here?"

"About a mile up the road."

> *Something very important happened to me underneath the Balboa Bridge, so please make sure that you get some photographs for me. This way I can write to you about what happened.*

Taking pictures beneath the Balboa Bridge, I tried to imagine why this place was so important to Salvador. Twice he'd written to remind me to take some pictures of the bridge, and especially underneath, where there weren't any people around. All he would say was that the bridge had played a significant part in the "development of my young sexuality," as he liked to put it.

> *And don't forget to take all the other pictures I asked for. It is a big task, but very necessary if I am to write about my past with any kind of accuracy.*

Later that evening, lying in a large bed set up special for the visiting "*gringo*" in the living room of Uncle Israel's house, I thought about the poorhouse.

Esmeralda, a true believer in signs from God, said she always knew that it had been a definite sign when Salvador had arrived in New York City and no one had been there to meet him. His crying, she said, should have been seen as a sign from God that this was not the place for Salvador, her beloved *hijo*, here in New York City: in the land of gringos and sinners.

The year was 1957, and upon my arrival in Mayaguez from New York City, I went to live in the Caserios Columbus Landing with my Aunt Maria.

My mother sent me money every week from New York so this made things easier for me at the age of 14. It took a couple of months to track down my father who was living in a shanty house in the rural parts that divide Mayaguez and Anasco. As soon as he found out that I was in Puerto Rico, he came to pick me up. I packed my suitcase and put one cotton suit on with my black pants with pink stripes on the side and left with my father. He was living with an Indian woman who I began to look upon as my stepmother.

Her name was Blanca.

Early the next morning we were all sitting together at the kitchen table, drinking strong coffee, and planning our day. First we'd drive to La Mineral, and the red dirt hill called El Fanquito, where Salvador lived with his father and stepmother after he returned from New York. Then we'd visit La Escuela de Correctional, a prison for kids, where Salvador was locked up for over a year.

After the sugar cane harvest was over, my father and stepmother moved to Mayaguez. We lived there for awhile in a small room and my father went back to working with the sanitation department as a street sweeper.

Father would wake up about four or five in the morning and I would open my eyes from the hammock and watch him while he dressed and washed up. Sometimes his dark lady would wake up and prepare the coffee. The odor of percolat-

ed coffee was like incense to the nostrils. At times I would get up also and leave with my father to give him a hand at his work.

Passing a pot of steaming coffee to Genoveva, I whispered to her that she should ask Esmeralda about Blanca

Even now, Esmeralda didn't want to talk about Blanca. When Geno mentioned her name, the effect on Esmeralda was that of a blind being drawn in a light-filled room, or like the sudden appearance of a dark and gloomy rain cloud. Not only wouldn't she speak about Blanca, but she also pushed her chair back from the table and quickly left the room.

But Salvador had already told us enough. That "Blanca" in Spanish meant "white" and this, he said, was pretty much the color of her skin. Her eyes were light, her hair was dark, and she was deeply into *espiristimo,* or spiritualism.

> Blanca was my step-mother. I liked her right away. Why I liked her I could never really understand, for I seldom said anything to her and she to me. But there was an understanding between us. She was a quiet type of woman. She had a nice figure. Her face was always bright and her dark brown eyes were always sparkling.

Driving with one of Uncle Israel's sons to La Mineral, I asked Geno to tell me what she knew about him. He seemed strange, retarded almost, but not quite. There was just something about him that made me wonder who he was, and why. He walked, talked, and looked as though he'd been in an accident, fallen off a bike and hit his head, or was pushed in the path of an oncoming subway train, and at the last minute, had slid underneath, but was saved, or had fallen off a roof, only to have something, or someone, break his fall.

His name was Papo, and in a soft whisper, so that Papo, in the front seat with Esmeralda, couldn't hear us, Genoveva tells me his story, or what she thinks his story is from what she's been able to piece together from Esmeralda.

Papo was in his twenties, and had been traveling back and forth between the Bronx and Mayaguez for several years. Living for a while in the Bronx, and then returning to Puerto Rico. Then leaving again for the Bronx.

The first time he went to the Bronx was four years ago, and soon after he arrived, another brother tried to force him into selling drugs. And when Papo said, no way, in anger his brother had laced his drink with a psychedelic drug. Papo quickly became psychotic, but not realizing that he was under the influence of a drug, he got even crazier. So crazy that he had to be taken to a psycho ward somewhere in the Bronx. And when he came off the drug, he was never again the same as before. Docile and gentle, even child-like. A new Papo. Always smiling.

"What kind of drug," I ask Geno, "was he given?"

"Nobody knows, but they think it was LSD."

> *The first time I went to live with my father and Blanca, she came over to me and gave me a warm welcoming embrace. It felt strange. Here was a woman not at all related to me by blood treating me as though I was her son. When she embraced me, I tensed up and she took notice that I didn't feel comfortable. This must have turned her off because she never again gave me a hug.*

Finally the car stopped and we were surrounded by a flotilla of wooden shacks with brightly colored peeling paint, barefooted little children running loose in ragged clothing, and an ocean of reddish mud.

Through the window of the car, and maybe fifty yards away, was El Fanquito, or the tall red hill of dirt and mud that I'd heard so much about from Salvador.

> *This is La Mineral, which compared to the more modern part of Mayaguez, looks more like a North American Indian*

reservation, set apart from the mainstream of the life of its more affluent sectors.

We lived half way up a hill of red, muddy dirt called El Fanquito. The hill had houses to the left and to the right, and the center was the reddish dirt road.

On the sides there were irrigation ditches.

Walking with Esmeralda and Geno to El Fanquito it felt like we were walking through an unfiltered dream, filled with browns and grays. Partly because the ground was one part mud, and one part water. And partly because the actual sight of the red hill was nothing short of astonishing. Salvador had described it as a hill, but still I was unprepared for just how steep it was. Rising at least a quarter of a mile, it resembled a giant brown tongue rising nearly straight into the sky. Houses lined either side. The closer we got to its base, the steeper the hill appeared until, when we actually got there, we had to tilt our heads more than slightly back in order to see the uppermost house that was perched like an eagle's nest way at the top.

As the mud of El Fanquito covered our shoes, we slowly walked up the middle to see if we could find the house where Salvador had lived with his father and Blanca.

These dirt trenches were so deep that when it used to rain the water would flow downhill, emptying into a river way down below the public water pump. In the water coming filthy from the hill one could see all the accumulated trash which had piled up during the dry months.

Shoes were a luxury in La Mineral. Many people in this section of Mayaguez did not have this luxury

All water in the neighborhood had to be brought up in cans and buckets. The water pump was public

Despite her age and the early morning heat, Esmeralda was far ahead of us. As she walked, she was either singing softly to herself, or talking to everyone who crossed her path: shoeless children, staring men, and old women carrying pails of water. She talked with all of them.

"What's she saying?"

"She's asking if anyone knows the house where Sindo was living with Salvador and Blanca."

> *No matter how clean things were kept, whenever the water and red dirt would mix, it would still look like filthy water. It was impossible to remain clean for ten minutes.*
> *We were always filthy.*

Drenched in sweat, feeling dirty, and our shoes blind with mud, we still kept climbing. Finally, a woman who seemed to be at least one hundred years old, walked from one of the broken-down shacks. Listening to Esmeralda for a minute, she took her hand, and gestured for all of us to follow.

Down a short alley to a shack that looked like all the rest, with open windows, a thousand flies, and a hot tin roof. But this house was different, or at least it was to me, because this had once been the home of the Capeman.

A small bridge covering part of the irrigation ditch led to the front door of the house. Following the ancient woman, we crossed the bridge and entered the house.

> *The house in which we lived was like a small shack. It had a partition made from cardboard boxes which my father had cut up and put up to separate the living room, the kitchen, and the bedroom. An imitation of a real house, I would sarcastically call it.*
> *It had a wooden floor, wooden sides, and a tin roof. When the sun would hit the roof in the morning, one could tell that it was time to get up because the house would become warmer.*
> *The house stood up on eight pillars of round tree trunks. The front door had in front of it a small bridge that extended over the trench at the rear entrance of the house.*

Sitting at a table was another ancient woman. Brown of skin, with shiny gray hair, she could easily have been Esmeralda's sister.

Newspapers lined the walls, and when I asked Geno why, she said this was not uncommon in houses with little money for wallpaper, let alone for food.

Across the living room and in what appeared to be a bedroom was a hammock. Watching it swing back and forth from a light breeze swirling in from an open window, I wondered if this hammock was the one Salvador used to sleep in when he lived here with Sindo and Blanca. When Geno asked, the woman said, yes, it might have been but then again, she couldn't be sure. She didn't remember much about Sindo. Only that he was very good-looking and that he lived here with many different women over the years.

She didn't remember him having a son named Salvador.

> *My hammock hung from both corners of the house. At night, I could hear my piss falling through the wet hammock on the wooden floor. I used to do this all the time, usually while I was sleeping. But sometimes I would even piss in the hammock when I was awake because I was afraid to get out of bed. Afraid that something was waiting for me in the darkness.*
>
> *My father and Blanca slept in the bedroom. It had a low but large bed, and next to the bed was the altar. By the foot of the bed there was a closet where my father kept his clothes. There was a large wooden bureau where Blanca kept her things. And on top of this there was a huge mirror. I could see the mirror from the hammock where I slept. The candles on the altar cast a stream of light right on the bed which in turn would look very clear in the mirror. The altar near the bed was full of saints, and rum, dice, and old lottery tickets. There was also incense and candles burning. The altar was covered with flowers of all kinds, new and old coins, and many assortments of things like herbs and alcohol. At night, it was a beautiful sight to behold in the night with its upside down saints and all the things that seem to attract the supernatural mind. It looked a*

lot like the altars I have seen in photos or magazines that speak of Hindu gods and goddesses and temples.
  To me, it was holy.

Nailed to the newspapers were pictures of Saints, crucifixes, and a large picture of a woman who appears to be the Virgin Mary, but when I commented on how beautiful the picture was, Geno said it's not the Virgin Mary.

"Then who is it?"

"It's the deity, Yemaya, and she symbolizes the sea but makes believe that she's the Virgin Mary."

"Where's this from? Is that some kind of Greek mythology or something."

"It's from the religion of Santeria."

I lay in the hammock of my father's house in La Mineral, while in the bedroom the candles to the saints burn on my father and step-mother's spiritualist altar, draped with magic formulas and designs. My father is doing something to Blanca that is making her breathe hard and make sexual sounds.

All I knew about Santeria was what Salvador had mentioned a few times. That many of the people who practiced *espirisimo* also practiced one or more forms of Santeria, a religion created several hundred years ago by West Africans held as slaves in Cuba. And like the Sunni Muslims, the followers of Santeria gave special emphasis to the here and now, rather than in an afterlife.

Yemaya was just one of many deities, each one represented a different aspect of nature, like rain, along with a human characteristic, like power.

My father always warned me, "Don't you ever touch anything on that altar, boy. If you do, I will put the belt to your hide!" I respected his altar more out of sheer fear than out of the idea that some supernatural curse might befall me.

But Geno said she didn't think Sindo and Blanca were Santeria devotees, or *santeros and santeras*. Instead, like Esmeralda, and many other Puerto Ricans who were into *espirisimo*, they borrowed a few of its customs and traditions, building make-shift altars, complete with offerings of old coins, flowers, or maybe even pieces of paper with the names of people in need of healing, prayer, or both. Some would even sacrifice animals, usually fowl and goats, as a way of cleansing the soul and giving strength. Still others began their day with the ritual of offering up prayers to deities, or orishas.

Rumor had it that in New York City, there were Puerto Rican policeman who would pray to the deity Obatala, the father of all deities, before slipping on their gunbelts.

> *Father and Blanca gave more care, love, and attention to this holy altar than they ever did to me. The saints were never left hungry in my father's house.*
>
> *But sometimes, when I was very hungry, I would steal the fruit and bread that they had put on the altar as offerings.*

When the ancient woman, whose name was Juanita, offered to make us some coffee, we gladly accepted.

"Un momento," she said, as she disappeared behind a curtain into what was probably a kitchen area.

After several cups of coffee, I asked Genoveva to find out where the bathroom was.

"It's in the back," Geno says, "right near the latrine."

> *There was a back door which would open up at the top or the bottom and it led to the back yard from where you could see the latrine.*
>
> *All the houses in La Mineral had latrines in the back yard. All water in La Mineral had to be brought up in cans and buckets. There was no indoor plumbing in any of the houses, and the water pump was public property.*

Shielded from the elements by several pieces of plywood, the latrine was an open trench with a makeshift toilet bowl.

Standing and urinating into the open hole, I wondered if this was what Salvador meant when he said to me that he liked having contacts with people from outside the prison because he didn't want to be known to the wardens and guards as nothing more than "a poor little spic without a pot to piss in."

Back in the house, I sat and listened as Esmeralda, Juanita, and Genoveva chattered in rapid Spanish.

Hours passed, more coffee was served, and then it was time for us to leave. When it turned out that Juanita was a member of Uncle Israel's Pentecostal church, Esmeralda invited her to join us later on for the evening service.

Walking slowly down the hill to where Popo was waiting to take us to the reform school, we passed several people carrying water hanging from bamboo sticks balanced with precision across their shoulders. While other people were carrying pails of water balanced on their heads, along with one in each hand.

>   *The water pump was located at the bottom of the hill on a street called Broadway. It had this name because those who lived on this main street had better access to the water pump than those on a hill, and the houses down Broadway were a bit better built than those that one would see the higher up one went up the hill.*
>
>   *Over the hill, and moving into the interior of Mayaguez, was strickly Jibaro country where bohios (Indian palm tree huts) were still in use on the island. It was probably given the name Broadway because the people living down by the water pump were of the upper poverty-stricken bracket.*
>
>   *Water was carried up the hill in wooden or metal buckets.*
>
>   *Some people in La Mineral were able to make money by just being water carriers. This task would be like a prep school*

for the sugar cane fields where water carriers used to make good pay.

A man cutting sugar cane needs to have cool water when he is working under the hot tropical sun.

I wondered what the reality of La Escuela de Correctional would be compared to the official literature:

The school stands in a photo-perfect location in the beautiful city of Mayaguez. It is an institution of reform and education for the confinement and the instruction, discipline and industrial training tending to reform delinquent youths. Only those under sixteen years of age are admitted, and inmates are placed at liberty not later than when they reach twenty-one years. Confinement in the Reform School must be upon order of a Juvenile Court or of the Federal Court.

The average number of inmates is 230, who are given academic instruction and agricultural and industrial training on the farm and in the shoemaker, carpenter and tailor shops of the school. Music is also taught. The Reform School Band, composed of 40 inmates, is reputed as the best boys' band on the island, and is much sought after for promenades, parades, etc. in the different towns of the island.

For the recreation and amusement of the inmates the school counts an auditorium for movies, a park and athletic field for military drill and exercise.

While I was living with my father and Blanca, I got myself into a fight one day with this young fellow who worked as a delivery boy. We used to tease him by calling him a girafe because of his big neck. This used to get him real angry. One day he was passing on his bicycle and I called out to him in a teasing manner. He got off his bike and took some empty milk bottles that he had in the basket in front of his bike and began to throw them at me.

I ducked about four bottles that came flying one after another while he called me all kinds of dirty names. I then grabbed the neck of one of the bottles and began chasing him. He ran towards the store. I stood outside and told him, "You punk. When you come out I'm going to cut your fucking neck off!" The woman who ran the store came out and told me to leave him alone and that if I didn't, she would call the police. I dropped the bottle and got away from there, but I told him,

"When I catch your ass, your neck is going to be mine!"

The cops went to see my father and told him that they were out for my arrest. When my father said this to me, I went to the police station and walked in. I identified myself. I was placed in a cell. Then I was taken to court the same day in handcuffs. My father showed up and the judge said that he would have to put me away. My father told the judge that I was a juvenile delinquent and that he was afraid of me.

I said good-bye to my father and was put in handcuffs. Then I was placed in a jeep and taken to the La Escuela De Correctional on the outskirts of Mayaguez.

Years of studying criminology from textbooks, and visiting dozens of reform schools, jails, and prisons had taught me to be wary of the people in charge; the ones who closed the doors, and locked the locks. Not that there weren't sincere wardens and compassionate guards, along with perceptive psychologists and a caring medical staff. But the very act of confining people against their will almost invariably led to an abbreviated sense of reality. Things in prison were rarely what they seemed to be, and what might seem unimportant, trivial even, in the free world, often took on an entirely new meaning in a correctional facility. And this wholesale perversion of everyday reality often transformed otherwise good people into caricatures of evil-doers. Well-intentioned people found themselves playing a daily game of smoke and mirrors in order to present a prison reality to the public that appeared well-run, trouble-free, and sterile.

The brochures, and a brief telephone conversation with

one of the school's administrators, gave the impression of order, education, and a program of progressive penology.

> *I looked around at the gates, doors, and bars as the jeep drove up to the place. Again I was aware that something or someone was taking my freedom from me.*
> *From the moment I got out of the jeep, I knew that this so-called 'school' was nothing more than a prison for children.*

Although the reform school could pass from a distance as a local junior college, as soon as we were at the entrance, the bars on the windows said otherwise.

I pointed out to Geno how the building was shaped in such a way that it formed a natural wall for the group of other buildings right behind this one.

"How do you know this?" Geno asked.

"Because these places are all the same."

> *Handcuffed, I'm being led up the steps of the administration building when the really big guy comes out the front door. Walking over to me, he stands so close to me that I can smell the onions on his breath.*
> *"You'd better not fuck around here, boy, or you'll wish you'd never been born!"*

In the Office of the Superintendent, we were introduced to a man in a blue suit with matching tie and black shoes. His hair was black, and his eyes looked beady behind thick glasses. He could easily have been mistaken for a Wall Street broker instead of what he really was: the warden of a Puerto Rican prison for little boys.

Walking over to where we're standing by the door, he extended his hand to each of us.

"*Buenas tardes,*" he said, as he shook our hands and introduced himself.

"*Me llama, Jose Menedez.*"

> Inside an office marked "Office of the Superintendent," I am introduced to a man whose name I can't remember. Just that he said he was the warden, and that if I obeyed the rules, and didn't cause him or anyone else any trouble, I would be okay. But that if I broke the rules, I would be punished severely.

Jose Menedez told Genoveva he would be happy to show us around but that he only had about fifteen minutes to spare. Esmeralda was not taking the tour with us because of how tired she felt.

"You were right," Geno said, "about the way the building was built...it looks just like Greenhaven in here."

At Greenhaven the inmates all wore identical state-issued green khaki. Moving down the corridor we passed groups of children all dressed exactly alike. But instead of green, the color here was gray.

Some children stopped, stared at us, and then started to follow us as we walked further and further into the institution.

> It took a few hours before I was processed. I was a young kid with a Tony Curtis hair style, black chino pants, loafers, and a brown sparkling shirt with a collar up in the air. I walked in with a bunch of new arrivals who had just been sent here from Mirramar, another institution. Through the whole admission process, even while I was being interviewed, I carried a one edge razor blade in my mouth. After being searched I went to the bathroom and placed the razor blade up on the edge of the shower. But someone must have seen me and took the razor blade because when I went to look for it the blade was gone.
>
> The clothes we wore were of khaki. We woke up every morning, lined up after washing and went to the yard where we marched like soldiers in military style, like the army. Then all the troops would follow the band, and line up in companies and listen to El Himno Nacional. After it was over we all pledged allegiance to the two flags. We would have to listen to the lecture from Mr. Frog Eyes, the director. He would peer at everyone from behind his glasses. I stared at him directly and listened to the do's and dont's

By the time we'd toured the cafeteria, the dormitories, and the workshops, there were nearly fifty little boys behind us.

Surrounded by the little boys in their khaki pants, we sat at a table in the vast courtyard with Jose Menedez, sipping iced-tea that had been brought to us by an inmate waiter in a white coat.

Geno asked about Salvador, and I didn't need much in the way of Spanish to know that Salvador Agron was not one of his favorite subjects.

He wasn't here when Salvador was an inmate. That was years ago, before his time, he said. But he had gone through all the records and it was clear to him that Salvador had been more than just a troubled child. He had been involved in homosexual acts, had gotten into fights, and had even run away several times.

> *Most of the time he would speak very angry, reproaching people as though they were subjects of the state or wayward children. He was paternal in his way of speaking but he also wore that damn blue suit, white shirt, black shoes, blue on blue ties and his Panama hat or gray Capone type hat. On Sundays I would go up to spy on his daughter as she came out of the house, wearing her blue dress, and they would get into their 1958 Oldsmobile. At times I would spy on him with his wife and at times with the American blonde that we all figured was his mistress.*

Finishing our tea, we followed Jose Menedez down yet another corridor. On either side were classrooms, and opening the door to one, he said in broken English, that this was where the boys learned to speak English.

> *I was put in the shoe shop, in the music class, in the barber shop and moved out because either I refused to work, or was considered too dumb to learn. But it was here that I learned that I needed an education. I asked to be put in school*

> but was denied because I was needed in one of the shops (shoe shop)—I refused to work and was punished for it by a curtailment of all my privileges. Finally a psychologist saw me and after giving me tests recommended that I be put in a class or two. I went to the classes and became interested in history, but though I did not read or write, I became a good listener and was able to answer simple questions about Puerto Rican history where the other guys could not. It was a failure but I tried without much individual assistance and care.
>
> The older guys would look at me as though wanting to approach me sexually but I had made up my mind not to do anything I did not want to do, and when it came to sex I would not let anyone impose it upon me. Anyone who tried to rape me, as they did the other kids, would bear the cut of my razor blade. Or if anyone came to my bed at night to try to fuck me forcibly I would crack their head with the piece of pipe I slept with under my pillow.
>
> I would only have sex if this was what I wanted to do.

Inside the classroom, several little boys, all dressed in khaki, said over and over again, "Hello, how are you?" and "What is your name?"

Q. Did you develop a 'philosophy of life' while on death row?

A. Yes, I did develop a "philosophy of life" while on the row—a philosophy that one must constantly search for self and the knowledge that death is waiting to get at us anytime and the knowledge that there is some form of intelligence in the universe which is completely unrelated to the traditional 'God.'

When Geno asked him if we could see where they kept the boys with disciplinary problems, he shakes his head. "There is nothing to see," he says in halting English,

> I escaped from my captors there about three times but was apprehended the first two times. I had one advantage, I could

> speak English and so everyone thought I was intelligent but I still had the mind of a child.
>
> During one of my escapes, when I went to live in Manati, my mother came from New York and took me back to the Industrial School. I was let alone until she failed to obtain my release with a Habeas Corpus to take me back to New York. She left Puerto Rico without me and the same day that she left I was beat up by the counselors and thrown in isolation—a room with bars on the window and a room without a toilet or sink. One had to knock on the door to go to the bathroom and, one had to wear slippers and pajamas, it was called "Disciplinaria," or "Disciplinary Housing."

"Ask him if there's water and toilets in the disciplinary units," I said.

> In that box without a toilet and without water, I cried and became bitter—always asking myself why was I being treated like this. I got very depressed and after seeing some psychiatrists I was put back out in population because I was losing weight and losing contact with reality while in isolation or disciplinary. I then decided to "be cool" and played along with the game. After showing "conformity" and "improvement," I was given a furlough. But I already knew from my father that I would not return.

When Geno asked him about the water and toilets, he gave her a dirty look before answering.
"What'd he say?"
"That it was a stupid question."
Back in the Superintendent's office, we said good-bye. As he shook my hand, Jose Menedez said in broken English that "the pleasure of meeting you was all mine."
Then he turned and spoke softly to Esmeralda in Spanish.

> My father sent me to Aquadilla until he got enough money to buy two plane tickets. He sacrificed and worked hard sweeping the streets of Mayaguez from 4:00 AM to 6:00 PM.

My father saved enough money to live up to his promise to my mother who had left Puerto Rico sad and disenchanted because "they" did not want to give her back her son.

I left Puerto Rico for the last time in 1958 when my father helped me to escape from the reform school. It was winter when I left, and this I know because when I got to New York City there was already snow on the ground.

I was fifteen years old.

In the car where Papo was waiting, Esmeralda said she wanted to visit Uncle Israel's church later on that evening. We were about to pull away when Jose Menendez ran down the steps to our car. He said something to Geno before quickly walking away.

"What'd he say?"

"That he's wants us to send his regards to Salvador."

Q. *What is one spiritual principle that you learned while you were on death row?*

A. *I learned many spiritual principles when I was on death row, but one stands out, and it is something I still believe in to this day. I believe that the poor, ignorant, and uneducated man is able to understand spiritual principles better than the educated man. It seems that he is closer to truth than the educated person is in the spiritual sense because he doesn't carry around so many different ideas in his head at the same time.*

Uncle Israel's Pentecostal church was made of wood. There were candles on the altar, and several pictures of a long-haired Jesus. We could have been in Brooklyn, or in someone's apartment in Spanish Harlem, or the South Bronx.

A young girl on a makeshift stage in front of the room, with hair reaching down to her waist, sat and played a guitar, leading the congregation in a rousing song about Jesus.

When I lived with my father and Blanca in La Mineral they would go to a spiritualist meeting, or seance, about once a week, to consult familiar spirits or to get guidance in their chaotic lives.

He was familiar with seances where the town's espiritistas congregated to hold readings and seek guidance from the spirit world. In Puerto Rican culture this is a modified form of worship left by the original natives of the island. My father claimed he was subjected to familiar spirits and he could hold conversations with the past inhabitants of the island. This may sound primitive, but it's all part of the Puerto Rican cultural structure: vestiges of the past that still hold sway over the soul. One can be materialistic, but there are some things in this world we cannot refute.

But these sessions were very different than the services of the Pentecostal church.

The young girl finished her song, and a tall man with a pocked face stood and addressed the congregation. And as another young girl beat on a tambourine, the tall man with the pocked face began to speak about his life.

In halting English, he gave thanks to God for his good health and for the good Lord protecting him from death in Vietnam. He was grateful, he said, to be here in the home of Christ, his Lord, and Master.

"Muy contento," he said, before returning to his seat. An ancient lady in dressed in black, with long gray hair reaching down her back like an uncontrolled vine, spoke next.

With hands raised to God, she spoke rapidly in Spanish, punctuated frequently saying "Gracias Dios," or thank god. She softly kissed a cross of Jesus from around her neck before saying "Muy contento," and returning to her seat.

The seance began with some prayers which were like opening rites for this type of session. Then people went into a contemplative state of meditation. After some time the silence was broken, then the medium that ran the seance would sud-

> denly go into a state of communication with some strange phenomena present in the spiritualist center (as these places were called) while in a sort of hypnotic trance.
>
> To a child's mind this can be scary, but I was the type of child that though I could scare easily would still always manage to stick things out to the end. Perhaps I did this more out of fear than courage. No one else would ever really know. Here were grown-ups acting like maniacs in front of a young child—turning and twisting in a euphoria of their own making, in a world which I was too young to venture into.
>
> The person most receptive to the spirit, and at that particular time in spiritualistic possession of this departed soul or phenomena, would then burst forth in a loud voice within the congregation in a new and sometimes strange voice at a low or high pitch, as though an expert ventriloquist was talking from the stage.

Then it was Esmeralda's turn to testify. Rising from her seat, she walked to the podium at the front of the room, and began to speak in a loud, firm voice.

> At times I would get scared as hell when someone who was under the power of possession spoke to me or about me during these sessions. Often they did not want me there and would inquire from me what it was I was seeking among them.

Esmeralda called me "Jacobo," and as she spoke I could hear her say my name, over and over, with warmth and affection.

With Genoveva sitting next to me, and whispering a translation, it was almost as if Esmeralda was speaking directly to my heart.

> I could not ask them because this was all over my head. I would just turn and look at my father who was present, telling him with my look to come and bail me out of this jam I had gotten myself into.

"All praise to God," Esmeralda said "for allowing Jacobo to come into my son's life so that he will someday be able to give his own testimony in a book he is writing with my son, Salvador Agron. A book about his life so that others may learn what he has learned..."

I would never go into one of those places by myself, and I was always happy to have my father around during those sessions because he was considered a professional when it comes to handling spirits.

"...and all praise to God as well for bringing Genoveva Clemente into the life of my son, and she is here today in my brother's church because she has come to Puerto Rico with Jacobo to help him with the book he is writing with my son who to this day is still in prison, but who will know freedom someday, and this I know because it came in a dream that soon he will be coming home to me..."

I was lost in this madness. I did not understand what was happening and I did not like the fact that some possessed person would dare ask me what I was doing there. A question which I thought was very silly because any grown-up would know I had come with my father and stepmother. I thought it was the person asking this question directly to me, but my father would explain that it was not the person asking the question, but that it was a spirit speaking through the person. Inwardly, I would laugh because I had never seen a spirit, and I did not believe the shit that they were running down.

"...and all praise to my daughter, Aurea, who has always taken care of me, and all praise to her children and may they always be healthy and have long life..."

When the seance was over I always took notice of how people embraced each other as brothers and sisters and they would shake hands or stand around and talk about different things. My childhood mind could not understand the behavior of older people. They were sort of amusing to see standing there in front of the spiritualist center talking to each other. I have observed this behavior every time a religious service ends and people are standing outside the church, talking. I always have to wonder if in reality they are really happy or are they just living one of their many illusions.

To me, spiritualism was nothing more than a process by which the poor exorcised themselves from their guilt and made up for their poverty by growing rich in the spiritual superstitions of the time.

But my father and Blanca seemed to thrive on espirisimo, and they attended as many of these sessions as they could.

"...and all praise to my brother Israel and his family for having this church and all praise to God that they may always be healthy and have long lives.

"And I am muy contento," she said, before leaving the stage and sitting down with the rest of us.

My stepmother Blanca hanged herself with the rope from my hammock. I remember the day clearly. She had not been well. She would suddenly curse and push her plate away because the spirits used to whisper to her that the food had been poisoned. My father would tell her that she should not curse the spirits, no matter what they told her, because the spirits were merely testing her, trying her soul in order to later on bless her with something great. She paid him no mind. I used to tell my father that what she needed was a good psychologist, like the one I had at Wiltwyck. But he insisted that this was something different, something of the spirit world.

On the day Blanca hanged herself, my father was still at work and I was down the hill at a store, drinking beer and listening to the jukebox as it played "Camino Verde." Someone came running down the hill, breathing hard and into the store. When he saw me, he said, "Dios mio, I found you, your stepmother just hung herself!" I looked at him and said, "So what? I'll be up there as soon as I finish this beer and finish listening to the record." After I said that, he looked at me strange and left running back up the hill.

Frank looked at me and said, "Oye, Salvador, No seas tan malo—no es bueno ser tan main." I stared at Frank and said,"Well, Frank. I'm not bad, but what can I do? When you die, the only thing that can be done is to give you a burial. And I will not mess my day up over death."

After I finished my drink and the record was over, I got up and slowly walked up the hill. When I got to the house after getting through the crowd, I looked at my father, and then pulling a sheet away from the hanging body I saw her wide open eyes. There was a mark on the middle of her forehead. While hanging, she had hurt herself. I stared at the dead body and walked out to the crowd and the fresh air.

My father sent me to tell her family so they could come to the wake, where prayers were said for her soul, where people cry and have coffee all night with crackers while watching the body and praying. There were a lot of people there that night. Her relatives and friends. I could not stay there all night, so I left for awhile to think. My thoughts were about death and the hereafter, which I believed in at that time. I looked at the night stars and said a prayer for her soul, hoping that she would wake up in the arms of Jesus or God's house in the heavens.

"Bless her soul, Lord. Even though she killed herself. Give her heaven for she was crazy and did not mean to take her life. The spirits did that to her. Protect her soul. Ave Maria in the name of the Father, Son, and Holy Spirit. Amen."

But, as always, the heavens were silent. I saw no sign of life except the stars and the full moon. I went back to the house and had some coffee and crackers. I walked over to the casket and gave her a kiss on her forehead, while the people looked at me. A relative advised me that one should not kiss the dead. I just laughed and walked away.

The next day she was buried and things went back to normal. I ate in restaurants with my father who always ordered a mista (rice, beans and meat) and drank a good glass of cold water after finishing.

Early Sunday morning, Uncle Israel drove us to a *publico* stand in downtown Mayaguez, not far from the poorhouse.

Similar to a New York City taxicab, but without restrictions as to fare, or passengers, *publicos* were used by virtually everyone as a preferred method of transportation throughout all of Puerto Rico. Some of the *publicos* sit and wait for passengers at designated stands, while others roam the streets in search of fares, and still others, like the one we would be using, could be solicited by calling a day or two ahead of time.

Insisting that it was only '"proper" we agreed to accompany Esmeralda once again to the poorhouse so she could say good-bye to Sister Isabella.

September 10th, 1974
Greenhaven Correctional Facility

Dear Little Richard:

My mother calls you "Jacobo." Let me first say that what you and Geno have done for my mother by taking her on the trip to Puerto Rico is beyond appreciation. I love you both very much. You both have done her as I had in mind—she came back happy and healthy, and it seems that her spirit has grown stronger from the trip. And I think you were right when you said that by taking this trip moms might be able to work out some of the bad feelings she has about some of the things that happened when we were living in Puerto Rico years ago. She looks so uplifted in the photos you and Geno took that it almost makes me cry for her happiness. Thank you, my dear friend.

You have been more than just a brother to me, and Geno more than just a sister.

I really mean this.

With love from your friend and brother, forever
Salvador Agron#16846

As we left the poorhouse for the second time, Sister Isabella, holding Esmeralda's hand as we walked together to the front gate, said something in Spanish about the "religiosas," or nuns, to Esmeralda and Genoveva.

"What's she saying about the nuns?"

"That they were only doing," Geno says, "what they thought was right."

> *I was in the shower room at the poorhouse when La Rubia called me over to where she was standing, and with a washcloth and soap she began washing my small body. She washed me slowly and very gently, placing the soap on the washcloth and then rubbing me down with it. And while I stood there in the nude, with no one else in sight, she kneeled down in front of me and washed my feet. Then she passed the washcloth over my little penis, washing my balls and pressing them softly. I remember that I had all kinds of sexual thoughts while she did this, and that these thoughts made me feel very uncomfortable and very excited both at the same time. She told me to get under the water and she rinsed the soap from my body, all this with a smile on her face.*
>
> *La Rubia used a big towel to dry me off, and when I was completely dry, she kneeled down again and very gently she started kissing me on my private parts. Then she embraced me and with her hands touching my ass, she took my childhood penis in her mouth and started to suck on it while she whispered to me that I was a good kid and she would send blessings to me forever. I stood there while she was doing all this and then suddenly she put one of her hands under her holy vestment and did something to herself. I didn't know at the time what that was, only that it had made her very happy.*
>
> *She was young and beautiful. And I will never forget her.*

Chapter Seven

MEN AND WOMEN

It is difficult to write the truth, but this is what is demanded of an honest down to earth man. I was young, of a very tender age, and probably about five years old. I was living in Mayaguez away from the poorhouse, and it was one of those times when my father had released me from the grip of the nuns by letting me live with him and the woman he was with at the time.

From the photographs you took in Puerto Rico, I can see that the Balboa Theater is nearby, and that there is a house on the right as one faces the Balboa Bridge from the same side where the theater is located. To the left there is a pharmacy, and it looks just like the one that I remember. On the left side of the bridge, I can see the same house that my father and his woman were visiting at the time

Jennifer was an actress who worked as a waitress in a health food restaurant on East Sixth Street in Manhattan, just a few blocks from the Fillmore East on Second Avenue. Blond and blue-eyed, she was one of many women I had known since my wife had fallen in love with another woman, and had left me several years before,

My mother must have given her consent that I should go and live with my father. He was living with another woman somewhere in the slum section of Balboa. But my mind is hazy

whenever I try to remember the people who were around me at the time. But this particular incident, which was my first real sexual encounter with another man, is very clear in my mind. And I can recall it as if it were yesterday instead of over twenty-five years ago.

It was about nine thirty in the evening, or perhaps a little earlier. And while my father visited, I took a walk outside and starting walking towards the Balboa Bridge. I was only five years old, and even so it was not unusual for me to be taking little walks on my own for short distances.

Jennifer had a five-room apartment on the top floor of a six-story tenement on the Lower East Side of Manhattan.

I do not exactly know or remember how it happened, but I went with some man under the wooden bridge and together we walked down near the water. The man was talking to me about the fish and the crabs that one could fish for at night. I wore short, khaki pants and a short-sleeved polo shirt, which was typical of what little boys were usually wearing at the time.

As we spoke, I realized that I was with a total stranger. Yet I was not afraid because as a child I was never afraid. What I mostly feared as a child was being alone at a dark place or house. Here, under the Balboa Bridge, I was not alone. But there was something about the stranger that kept me on edge but without my becoming afraid.

Without a word the man reached for me and grabbed me by my right arm. His whole hand went around my upper part of my arm but he did not grip me tightly or quickly.

It was a perfect arrangement. I could come and go as I pleased, just as long as I agreed never to show up unannounced. We could sleep together, have dinner, maybe even take in a movie. A quick hug and a kiss good-bye the next morning, and we went our separate ways. An emotional hit and run, but without the blood, the trauma, or the tears.

It was a gentle touch, the kind that would not intimidate me in any way. And being but a child in supreme innocence, I did not resist his approach. He sat in front of me and faced me, but I did not look at his face. With his left hand he unbuttoned my pants in front of me and pulled them down. I did not wear any undershorts. He then began to play with my little prick, but I was tensed from surprise more than from feeling afraid. He kept moving his hand over my small baby body until I started getting an erection, perhaps the first manually caused erection in my life.

It felt very good. I even looked at it myself with surprise.

Where my wife had come to applaud her needs with nurturing and kindness, for Salvador, it had been a different story entirely.

Denied the intimacy of a female as he waded through a steady stream of reform schools, asylums, and prisons, he had taken touch and loving over the years wherever and whenever the need had chosen to speak to him.

The man laughed and placed me higher up on the hill, with his back towards the water. He brought his head down and took my little prick in his mouth and began to suck and lick the head with his tongue. I watched the river flow and the moon shine in the sky while the mouth of a stranger played with me. It was exciting and I was not afraid. While he was doing this, he reached down, letting me go from his grip, and opening his pants zipper, he pulled out his cock and began jerking off while blowing me.

There were never less than three or four women in his life. All at the same time, and each of them oblivious to the existence of the others.

When I saw that big throbbing thing in his hand, I was amazed and began to compare sizes with mine, but in my eyes

> what he had in his hand seemed like a baseball bat. I did not say one word when his left hand felt my little buttocks while he sucked on my little penis and jerked off with his right.

With some of his women, the relationship was limited to correspondence. Letters of passion flowing back and forth, like two wild birds with no place to land.

> Suddenly, he trembled all over, withdrew his lips, and splashed me all over with sperm. The warm liquid shot all over my prick and my small belly and streamed down my body while I looked on with disbelief. After he shot his load, he proceeded to lick his own cum from my body with his tongue. I no longer felt anything except a warm tongue licking me like a dog licks its puppies. It was a thrill and it was soothing. I did not utter a word. He washed me with a wet handkerchief and pulled my pants up and walked me back up to the bridge. I stared at him as he crossed the bridge and disappeared into Balboa.

With other women, the relationships had slowly evolved into more intimate situations. Fleeting liaisons in the visiting room, and sometimes a few minutes together at one of the prison events or festivals that were open to invited guests.

While the morality of having more than one woman at a time never seemed to bother him, I knew he resented having to ask me to help him coordinate his calendar in order to avoid ever having two women waiting to visit with him at the same time. And if this wasn't complicated enough, he would make things even more so by getting involved every now and then in a relationship with one of the men who lived with him in the cellhouse.

> I do not know whether I told my father or mother about this experience but it really doesn't bother me. I can talk about it with the same innocence that I had when I was but a tender child without fear.

> *It was good that this was all he did because if he would have tried putting such a big cock in me, he would have killed me or I would have run away or screamed or brought the whole neighborhood down on him. I must have gone home with my father that night and heard him make love to his woman as I usually did at night. What psychological effect did this have on me? It's hard to say, but somehow it must have affected me.*

It was the summer of 1957. I was eleven years old and living in the Bronx, just a few blocks from where Aurea was living now with her family on Knox Place.

Nearly every high school in New York City seemed to have at least one doo-wop group, and during the months of summer it was not unusual to hear groups of amateur doo-wop singers on street corners, in apartment lobbies, or in school yards everywhere.

All pervasive when I was growing up in the Bronx, and later on in Brooklyn, the music had become an emotional appendage of such nostalgic force that no sooner had I heard the first few words of the song, then I was back in the place where the music was born.

> *While at the poorhouse, among the orphans and poor kids I saw lots of homosexual acts taking place. From age one to seven, sexuality surrounded my world. But I was only able to come to terms with the Balboa Bridge experience, and the experience with the nun. It took me a long time to realize that I could not push those experiences aside and I also never spoke to any psychologist or psychiatrist about them because I did not think they could help me by soothing my conscience into guilt or into having innocent feelings about it.*
>
> *When I was a kid, I remember the other kids would go under the neighborhood houses and fuck chickens for the hell of it. Kids have no knowledge of what is right or wrong. Children get their concepts of guilt and what is right or wrong, from either religion or their parents.*

Married women used the rhythm method of contraception, and sexual intercourse outside of marriage was considered both a moral and social sin.

Bars and churches seemed to predominate, and on Sundays nearly everyone went to any one of several Catholic Masses. Beginning at six o'clock in the morning, there seemed to be one every half hour or so throughout the day until dusk.

Sex back then was an unspoken wish, and carnal wisdom was hard to come by. Rarely acknowledged, except in whispers and innuendoes, it was often misguided in its application. Parents knew nothing about sexual matters; teachers never taught it, and nuns never did it.

> *My father told me that he started working when he was seven years old and that he could not remember when he started fucking. Sexuality was a natural thing to him. To fuck was not a sin, and this was clear from what he used to tell Blanca, his woman at the time, when she would tell my father that the saints would cry from what he was doing to her. This used to inflame my imagination because he used to reply that love was natural and not a sin at all.*

What effect this had on me is hard to say. At the very least, it reinforced the dark images of sexuality that pervaded my entire Bronx neighborhood in the 1950's like a violent wind that would not die.

'"Gay" was an unknown word, or at least not a word used to describe homosexuality. If you were homosexual, you were either a "queer" or simply a "cocksucker." And since being a homosexual back then was one of the worst things imaginable, few would ever openly admit to this preference. Homophobia was everywhere.

10/18/74
Greenhaven Correctional Facility

Dear Little Richard:

    Well, let me acknowledge your letter of the 16th, plus the stamps. Many thanks!
    I am enclosing an article I wrote for an American Indian newsletter. Please let me know what you think.
    Listen, at my sister's house, in her closet, is a large amount of material. It's in a suitcase. I have many poems I have written. Many are about sex and love in prison—they are the cries and passionate feelings which were felt at one time or another. They are the kinds of fantasies prisoners are subjected to after long periods of incarceration without the opposite sex. My sister has lots of my stuff in the closet. There are also lots of writings I did over the years about certain sexual matters. Just tell her to hand over all the things I have sent her so that you can hold these for me. It would be better if you held on to the stuff. This way I will have comments and I can speak on certain things. She has it all in a suitcase, just tell her I said you can look through all that shit I got in the closet. Okay?
    Please do this for me. It's important.

    Your devoted friend, and brother,
    Salvador Agron   #16486

    Sex was yearned for, even prayed for, but to actually do it was something else entirely. Sex was a dark and evil thing, unless of course you were married, and wanted children. Otherwise, the pleasure derived from sex was unclean, not talked about, and above all, shameful.

9/4/73
Greenhaven Correctional Facility
Dear Editor:

    When the white man came, he brought the vice of colonialism, and subjugated your people and my people, and then he handed us over to imperialism. So now we live under two vices. This is why we must come together from the four directions of the earth, back into the inner circle, and fight for what is our true political identity.
    Before 1493, there existed this island which was called "Boriquen" and on this island lived a highly cultured people. They were known as the Tainos. Brother, do you know what this island is called today? It is called Puerto Rico.
    Brother, the Spaniards and the Americanos have always taught that the Indians of Boriquen were completely exterminated—but this is another white lie. We are still around, and still striving to liberate Puerto Rico so it can truly reflect a more perfected form of primitive communalism, which is the heritage that we have received from the first people of Boriquen.
    I hope this will help to explain things, and will help in the search for truth. We are all searching for truth, because only truth can guide the arrow of the warrior to the real target.
    I remain yours truly, your qualtaiao (blood brother) in struggle. Que viva Wounded knee! Que viva Puerto Rico Libre y Socialista! Hasta la victoria siempre.

Yours truly
Salvador Agron   #16846

    One of many people who responded to the article had been a young woman named Joyce.
    Born and raised in British Columbia, her Indian name was Wah-Zi-Nak. A Native American, she had been corresponding with Salvador for nearly a year in response to a letter he had written for an American Indian newsletter about the Puerto Rican struggle.

She lived with her mother on a reservation, or a "reserve" as they were known in Canada, and she had two small children from a previous marriage. She worked in a daycare facility, and was in her early twenties.

More letters followed, and the relationship quickly evolved into something more than merely platonic, with Salvador and Wah-Zi-Nak making plans to marry as soon as he was released from prison.

2/5/74
Greenhaven Correctional Facility
Dear Little Richard:

I wrote the Indian girl and I told her about you, and I asked her if it would be all right to send you her address. So if you don't hear from her soon, then please drop her a line.

She and I are very close, and we intend to make a life for ourselves together someday.

Writing to her will give you another side of me.

Stay strong

Love and understanding,

Salvador Agron
#16486

Salvador wrote that Wah-Zi-Nak came from a long line of shamans. People with magic in their hearts, and hands that healed.

From the photographs she'd sent, she looked to be the female side of Salvador. Long, brown hair reaching softly past her shoulders with high cheekbones, and a full, sensual mouth. Where Salvador's eyes were hazel, Wah-Zi-Nak's eyes were brown. Deep brown, and very direct. And where Salvador was relatively tall, she was short, about five feet one. Or so she said, but it was hard to know this from her photographs.

No sooner did Genoveva learn that Wah-Zi-Nak would be staying with me at my apartment instead of with her in Manhattan, than she warned me in no uncertain terms that Wah-Zi-Nak was off-limits.

"Just remember," Geno said, "that she's Salvador Agron's girlfriend!"

As with anything else at Greenhaven that even hinted at something sexual, whether or not a convict was a faggot, a heterosexual, or a cross-dresser was an endless source of debate back in the cellhouse, along with all the talk about who was fucking who, where, and why.

With an absence of women in their daily lives, their attention naturally turned to one another. And it hadn't taken me very long to figure out that male to male sexuality in prison had little to do with whether or not a particular convict was "heterosexual." or "homosexual." Instead, and with rare exceptions, active sexuality was always a matter of power and control.

11/2/74
Greenhaven Correctional Facility
My Brother Jacoby:

I received your letter dated October 24th, 1974 with the enclosed .50 cents in stamps and the sixteen photographs of Puerto Rico. Muchas Gracias! I am looking forward to your visit on November 6th, and of course to Wah-Zi-Nak's visit on the 8th. Just make sure that you come alone on the 6th because we have lots of things to talk about before Wah-Zi-Nak gets here!

Good, bring her here on the 8th—if she brings a tomahawk with her I will just hit her with the club! I really love her very much, but she makes me nervous every time she mentions marriage to me. But if we do get married, I would be honored if you would be the best man, and Geno can be the best woman. Well, let me not think of these things—it makes me sort of shaky

of loosing my independence.
    Take care of yourself, and I'll see you in a few days.

Your brother,
Salvador Agron
#16846

Whenever prisoners were denied the wherewithal to satisfy their basic sexual needs, then this in itself would quickly define the very nature of their captivity. Prisons bred a sexual subculture, one of my professors had said, complete with its own mores, traditions, and values. And not only did this subculture sanction and approve homosexual behavior, but it provided validation to the convict who claimed that since he was always the "pitcher" in the relationship, and not the "catcher," then there was no way anyone could ever call him a faggot.

> *When I was at Wiltwyck, I had lots of sexual experiences, but one stands out in my mind more than the others.*
>   *This was a sexual experience I had with John Robinson, and I remember his name because we met up again in the Tombs, or the Manhattan House of Detention.*

Unlike the Sunni Muslims' bus, which had taken a direct route from Manhattan to Greenhaven for San Juan Bautista Day, the public bus meandered in and out of New York and New Jersey until it usually arrived in front of the prison no later than ten forty-five, every morning, except Sundays.

First it stopped briefly in Connecticut, leaving off passengers who took yet another bus for a short ride to the federal penitentiary at Danbury, Connecticut.

Four women, each with one or more small children, and carrying shopping bags filled with groceries, left the bus at Danbury for the penitentiary. As I watched them climbing down the stairs of the bus, I made a mental note to call

Rachel as soon as I got back to the city. I wanted to be sure she knew not to make any unexpected visits to see Salvador for a while, or at least not on November 8th. I'd also call Jennifer just in case she was planning to make one of her unannounced visits to my apartment in Brooklyn. She loved walking on the beach, even swimming in the cold ocean during the winter, and it was not unusual for me to get a call from her in the middle of the night, letting me know that she was on her way. After a while, the visits became frequent enough that I gave her a key of her own.

> *The first time I saw John at Wiltwyck was in the dormitory. He was sleeping and his sheet fell off his body. He slept about two beds away from mine.*

As I got off the bus I could feel how cold it was. The sky was as gray as the high stone wall surrounding the prison, and from dozens of past visits I could already predict what the mood would be like once we got inside the prison. When the sun was out, at least there was the illusion of light, and you could almost imagine that you were visiting someone in a hospital, instead of a maximum-security prison. But when the sun was hidden, and it was raining or snowing, the starkness of the prison surroundings, with its high walls, gun towers, and steel bars, left little doubt that you were in a place that had no soul.

> *I must have been about eleven years old. I looked at his naked ass up in the air and I got an erection. I just got up and walked over and after looking a while I covered his body with the sheet. He woke up and looked at me and then the bulge in my shorts.*

Standing in line outside the entrance to the prison, I glanced at the other people waiting outside with us for the door to open. Women alone, or women with small children, and all of them either Latino or Black.

Even if you drove up in your own car, visiting a convict at Greenhaven was still an all-day affair, but even more so when you had to depend on the public bus. First you had to get the bus at the Port Authority Bus Terminal in Manhattan. Meaning a trip by subway from somewhere else in New York City before your trip could even begin. You had to miss a day of work, arrange to take your children out of school, and then carry bags of food, clothing, or whatever, all through the city, on the bus, and into the prison.

> *"What do you want, Sal?" he asked.*
>
> *"Nothing, John," I said with a smile. "Your sheet fell off and I covered you back up."*
>
> *"Thank you, Sal," he said modestly.*
>
> *"Well, it looks so good and nice," I said nervously. "That I had to cover it before someone else enjoys it."*
>
> *"What looks good and nice?"*
>
> *"Your ass. You have a woman's body," I said.*
>
> *"I thought you had seen my cock," he said defensively while pulling the sheet back and showing it to me.*
>
> *"Not bad," I said, while exposing my erection also. "But take a look at this!"*
>
> *We were talking very quietly, almost in whispers.*
>
> *"You wanna trade, Sal?" He boldly asked me while looking at my cock which was now as stiff as a log.*
>
> *"Okay, but not here. Someone might wake up and catch us."*
>
> *"Where can we go?" I asked, but already scheming how to fuck him without him fucking me.*
>
> *"Let's go up on the roof,"*

During the week there were not many people in the visiting room. Aside from everything else which seemed to conspire against the official policy of the Department of Correctional Services which clearly encouraged visits and correspondence, the unofficial rule of thumb was the further away a prison was from the city, the less people would come to visit. Convict lore had it that the people who originally had chosen the locations for the prisons knew what they were doing when they had picked the most remote, and out of the way places to put up the walls and lock the locks: Dannemora, Auburn, Attica, and Greenhaven. Each of these maximum-security prisons was so many miles from New York City that they might as well have been on the moon for all the visitors they received.

> *As he said this, he put on his shorts and got up. "I'll wait for you there. Go out on the fire escape."*
>
> *He picked his blanket up and headed for the door, I followed him and within a few minutes we were on the roof. It was a hot summer night and the stars were visible. I had never inserted my penis in another man before. He was twelve, and I was thirteen and we were both hot and sexually hungry.*
>
> *"I go first," I said.*
>
> *"Okay," he said, while lying on his belly with his legs wide open. I grabbed the Vaseline and put some on his ass and some on my hard cock and slowly drove my prick into his ass.*

Aside from full visiting rooms on Saturdays and Sundays, when people were off from work, and the bus fare was a little cheaper than on weekdays, the only other exception was whenever sentiment came into play.

Thanksgiving and Christmas were always busy times, and this included the weeks leading up to both holidays.

> *He began to moan and he enjoyed what I was doing to him. I turned him on his side and began to thrust into his ass as I brought my hand to his cock and began to play with it so as to make him come while I fucked him. He could not really come and neither could I, but we got a tremendous thrill out of it.*
>
> *After I finished, he told me to do it to him again, and so I did it again. I satisfied him that when it was over, I knew that*

I would still remain a virgin. He would not fuck me and neither did he dare ask me because when I finished I said, "Punk! You think that I'm gonna give you some ass? Hell, no. I already jacked you off. This is my share of this."

"That's okay, Sal. I feel good. Thank you. But remember—you'll never get any more pussy from me!"

I looked up at the sky with a smile and said, "Well, that's too bad. I got what I wanted."

Once inside the prison, it didn't take long for me to get processed. I had no shopping bags filled with food needing to be sent to the package room, and a receipt made out. I had no children, and in my pockets all I had was a set of keys, a roll of quarters, and a few dollar bills.

The quarters were for the vending machines, and after I showed one of the guards, my picture ID from Brooklyn College, he said for me to put all my metal in a little box next to the metal detector, and then walk on through to the other side.

Walking through, the machine was quiet.

"You can go on ahead," he said.

"Is it okay if I use the bathroom first?"

"It's right over there," he said, pointing in the direction of a door marked, "MEN," just by the entrance to the visiting room.

I felt a bit guilty after sodomizing poor John and a bit selfish, but I was soon beginning to learn that guilt and sex do not mix. The next day John wanted to fight with me but I managed to talk myself out of a precarious situation by telling him that I would keep it a secret between ourselves and not talk about it. This relaxed him and he reiterated the fact that I would "never get any pussy" from him again. Later we would become friends. But even though I tried again to make him give me some of his ass, I never succeeded.

He felt cheated but I could not get myself to give up some ass while at Wiltwyck, though at times I did fantasize with the idea of getting a cock and sitting on it, but I was more aggres-

sive than passive. I was not a homosexual, I said to myself, I was just horny.

Like the rest of the prison, or at least all that was visible to an outside visitor, the bathroom was clean enough that a person would have no qualms eating a meal right off the floor. Not a spot of dirt, grease, or dust. Did a guard with a white glove inspect the bathroom everyday? Or did the convict who used the mop, and wiped the floor, stand silently by while the guard ran his white-gloved hand along the floor, looking for anything in the way of dirt? How else to explain the utter spotlessness of the floors, the sinks, and the toilets? But Salvador said, when I asked him, that it was simply a matter of jailhouse boredom.

Dozens of convicts with little to do were always available to clean, dust, mop, or whatever.

"If you're not in a program," Salvador said, "then swinging a mop starts lookin' pretty good after a while."

> *While at Wiltwyck, we would have contests on jerking off. We would all get naked and hold the race to see who would be the first kid to ejaculate.*
>
> *Masturbation became a normal outlet for anger and frustration. The fact that we had nothing more thrilling to play with than ourselves was a pleasurable experience.*

Opening the bathroom window just a little bit to let out the strong smell of disinfectant, I could see a range of mountains through the bars behind the window, the same ones I could see in the distance through the windows of the visiting room whenever I made a purchase at the vending machines, or whenever I came in here to use the bathroom.

Were those the Catskill Mountains?

Combing my hair in front of the mirror, I took deep breaths as I tried to make myself relax a bit before leaving for the visiting room.

Washing my hands, I thought about what Salvador said was "jailhouse boredom," and whether or not there might be some deeper reason for the cleanliness, especially the strong smell of disinfectant.

> *One day we held a contest with the understanding that the last boy to come would have to perform a strip tease in the back room for all of us. We had stolen a pair of panties and we suggested that the last boy to jerk off would have to put them on under his clothes and then do a sensual dance for all the rest of us.*
>
> *We all went inside the shower and we began, one by one, to come. The last boy left became so frustrated by his attempt to come that finally he was unable. 'Okay, I lost," the boy said. "But man, only the guys in the contest can see the show.'*
>
> *'Don't worry, man. We will make sure enough of that," someone told him.*
>
> *We all sat down and waited for the kid who lost the contest to show up but it seemed he was scared because some of the guys wanted to sodomize him after the show. But he was okay after the rest of us assured him that no one was out to fuck his ass, and that all we wanted was to see him dance.*
>
> *The kid put the panties on, and then covered them up with his regular pants. Then we took him to the dayroom, and put on some music. It was "Blue Suede Shoes," by Elvis Presley. The boy got on top of the table and started to dance, stripping slowly while dancing until he was almost nude except for the panties he had on.*
>
> *Everyone was excited. Some of the guys began touching him, dancing with him, and laughing with him. One boy started grinding on the dancing boy's ass, and everyone laughed. The dancing boy lost all his inhibitions. I got up on the stage and placed my hand on his vibrating ass. Another guy got up and wanted to fuck his ass.*
>
> *One by one we all jerked off.*

Giving my call-out slip to the guard at the desk, he assigned me to a chair on the other side of the room,

For all of New York's many correctional facilities, there were enough rules to fill a book the size of a small telephone directory. Regulations governed virtually every aspect of prison life, from the kind of pants a convict was required to wear (state-issued, dark green khaki) to how many times a convict was strip-searched whenever they had a visitor (once, before the actual visit, and then again before returning to the cellblock). But unless a rule was a definite breach of institutional security, as interpreted by the people who controlled the day-to-day functioning of the prison, there was always some room for latitude.

> The last exposure I had at Wiltwyck was when one day this other kid and I took an innocent boy to the forest and we attacked him.
> We sexually assaulted this poor kid as he cried for help. I smacked him across his mouth and made him submit to our attack. Later on I cried at my shameful behavior and I apologized to him. But I was even more shocked to hear from his very mouth that he enjoyed the rape and was looking forward to us doing the same thing to him again.
> I met lots of boys like this at the Wiltwyck School for Boys.

One rule stated that visitors must be assigned seating in the visiting room by the guard in charge. Usually I didn't care if I was assigned a seat or not, because unless the visiting room was crowded, all the seats were pretty much the same. Whenever I was given the choice, my only concern was always how close we would be to the vending machines. As if he were a starving child, Salvador always ate enough to fill the bellies of a small family. It made up, he said, for all the days when he'd gone to bed hungry.

From where I was sitting I could barely see the top of the distant mountain range through the window on the opposite side of the visiting room. When I asked Salvador if he was ever bothered by the close proximity of the mountains, he replied that he had learned never to give them even a passing thought. Dwelling on them could drive a man crazy. Besides, he said, they weren't a part of his reality.

> *There was one boy who was really sick. He would not let anyone fuck him unless they would first take a wet towel and use it as a whip on him by snapping it on his tender flesh. But I did not do this for him, I did it more for myself. Whenever I got horny, I would merely go off into the woods and jerk off. Masturbation was my outlet and I believe I became more proficient in it as my life became more and more institutionalized.*

Waiting for Salvador, I made a count of the people in the visiting room. Aside from myself, there were nine women and five children. More than usual, but again, the closer it got to the holidays, the more people there were.

Giving the mountains behind the windows barely a passing glance, and nodding to the man sitting next to me as he passed him by, Salvador was barely in his seat when he asked me to buy him a roast beef sandwich and a can of Coke.

> *After the reform school at Wiltwyck, my next sexual experience was with a boy in Brooklyn. His name was Leroy. He was black, and like me, a member of a gang called the Junior Chaplains. Leroy lived in one of the housing projects, and one day when we were in his apartment, listening to a new record by the "Platters," he pulled out a large manila envelope from the bottom drawer of a dresser that was in the bedroom where we were sitting.*
>
> *'Sal, wait till you see this!" he said, a bit nervous. When he pulled out some magazines, I was shocked. They were magazines with many men and women performing cunnilingus, fellatio, and so on.*
>
> *I started going through them.*

I was standing by one of the vending machines as Jose Soto made his way across the visiting room. Catching my eye for the briefest of moments, he sat down across from the man sitting next to me, but not before giving my crotch a quick onceover.

Jose Soto was a convict Salvador had introduced me to at the festival. A thin man with short, dark hair and blazing eyes, he was the lover of Juan Gomez, the guy sitting next to me. Juan, equally thin, and equally intense, had done time at Greenhaven, and that's where he'd met up with Jose.

Back with Salvador and his roast beef sandwich, he wanted to know if I'd enjoyed myself this morning with Juan.

"Why you asking me that?"

"Because Juan said you and him rode up together on the bus and I was thinking that maybe you and him got it on together," he said, with a broad smile on his face.

"You should fucking talk! You're probably the biggest cocksucker in here!"

Tilting his head back, Salvador roared with laughter.

> Leroy sat next to me on the bed as I looked through the pornographic magazines. He was sort of relaxed and looking okay but then I noticed he wasn't paying attention any longer. He was staring at the bulge that had suddenly built at my crotch from my swollen penis. I tried to brush the idea aside that he was queer, but I couldn't because I had always suspected it. My mind started working, and I opened my pants zipper and brought my cock out and began playing with it.

After bringing him yet another sandwich, this one a ham and cheese on rye, we got into the specifics of Wah-Zi-Nak's visit, where I'd be meeting her, how long she'd be staying, and how important it was that no one else came to visit at the same time.

"It won't look too hot if someone else was to come in while she's visiting with me in here."

"No one's gonna be here except you and Wah-Zi-Nak, so you don't have to worry about it too much."

"You called Rachel to let her know?"

"Yeah, the other day. But what about me? What am I supposed to do?" I wanted to know.

"Whaddaya mean 'what about me,'—you'll be visiting right along with her."

"I thought you said you wanted some privacy, so how you gonna have this if I'm sitting right there next to you?"

"I've made arrangements for you to visit with John O'Neil, or maybe someone else, if he don't wanna. So all you gotta do is put their name on the visiting list instead of mine when you come up, and they'll call them out instead of me."

On my way to the vending machines for the second time, it was all I could do to avert my eyes from Juan and Jose. Arms locked together across the counter, their heads nearly touching, they traded breath and quick kisses.

> He immediately took my hand away from my hard-on and placed his hand around my cock. Then he started jerking it up and down and I set down the magazine I had in my other hand.
> "Sal," he said, "don't tell nobody about this. "Promise me."
> "I promise," I told him and humorously added, "Scouts honor."
> He laughed and pushed me back on the bed and took my cock in his mouth. I would be a liar to say that it didn't feel good because it felt like heaven. He sucked on it, and then he got up.
> "Sal, I want you to fuck me. But I want you to keep it a secret."

Looking around as I put my quarters in the vending machine, I wondered what the other people might have been thinking when they looked at Juan and Jose. But given the way everyone else seemed to be in various stages of lovemaking, probably nothing.

There was little in the way of censorship from the guard in charge of the visiting room. Little in the way of reproach for secret hand jobs, stolen kisses, or lingering hugs that lasted too long.

> *He took his pants off and then slipped out of his jockey shorts and walked over to the dresser next to the bed and took a jar of Vaseline and put some in his ass. When he walked back, he rubbed some on my erect penis. After this, he lay on the edge of the bed with feet on the floor and his ass in the air.*
> *"Sal, go slow, okay?"*
> *"Don't worry," I told him " I'll do it nice and easy."*

As for the convicts and their visitors, their lack of self-consciousness wasn't difficult to understand, especially if you understood the simple dynamic particular to the prison visiting room. Greenhaven was classified as a maximum-security correctional facility, and most of the men were serving long sentences, with one or more decades the norm rather than the exception. Aside from using their hands, or '"hitting the wood," as some convicts liked to call it, the only other sexual outlet was either shacking up with someone in the cellhouse, or getting what you could in the visiting room. When you were locked up for years, hugless and kissless, wives and girlfriends suddenly took on a whole new dimension.

> *I began to fuck him until I had my cock completely in him. He began to moan and breath hard.*
> *"Now call me a Negro bitch," he said. "Call me a Negro bitch, you bastard. Fuck me Sal, fuck me good."*

The dynamic was simple: if the only place to make any kind of love was in the visiting room, or at an occasional prison festival, then the time must be used wisely. There wasn't enough time to allow morals or ethics to come into play. No time to allow for passing thoughts about what was proper, or what was nice.

Born and nurtured from deep need, the visiting room was hardly the place for anyone who was even the least bit self-conscious about how they looked when they were making love in a public place.

I was too shocked to say anything, and then in an angry voice I repeated what he had asked me to say. I was about to come and in the process of the thrill and sensation, I heard myself saying, over and over again: "You Negro bitch."

"There's nothing you could get me?"

"Well, there's potato chips and cookies from the other machine, but I thought you just wanted a sandwich?"

"Yeah, but it'd be nice to have something for afterwards." Back at the table, less than a minute later, with a bag of potato chips and a chocolate bar, the tuna fish sandwich is already history.

"Whaddaya gonna do," I asked, "when Wah-Zi-Nak comes up? You think you're gonna be eating like this?"

"That's 'cause we'll be too busy making love!"

Many sandwiches later, the guard at the desk announced that in a few minutes it would be time to leave for those visitors taking the bus back to New York City.

"So I'll see you on Friday with Wah-Zi-Nak, right?" Salvador wanted to know.

"I'm picking her up at the airport on Thursday night and we'll be up here on Friday. Is there anything you want me to bring?"

"Just bring my little Wahzi and I'll take care of all the rest!"

When the guard at the desk announced that visiting was over for the people taking the New York City bus, I rose, and shook Salvador's hand. And then as I was walking away, Salvador whispered that it would be nice if I took care of Juan Gomez on the way back to the city. Telling him to go fuck himself, I could hear him laughing at my retreating back, as I quickly walked out of the visiting room,

I shot my load, and took my cock out of his ass. Then I went to the bathroom and cleaned myself out with soap and water.

One street over from the ocean, my apartment in Brooklyn consisted of a living room, a kitchen, and a bedroom. The bedroom had a roll-top desk, a typewriter, and a double-sized brass bed. Lining the living room walls were shelves of books, and running the width of the room was a many-colored hammock from Guatemala. A leather couch doubled as a bed whenever someone spent the night, and I had indoor plants of every size, shape, and description.

The neighborhood was Brighton Beach, and from where I was living it was just a short walk to the beginning of the boardwalk, and a little less than two miles from the amusement park known as Coney Island.

My family had moved here from the Bronx in the fall of 1958 when the population had been overwhelmingly Jewish. Years later, when I moved back to the neighborhood from where I'd been living with my wife on a commune in New Hampshire, it had already begun to change. Puerto Rican families had taken over many of the large apartments vacated by families who had fled to the suburbs of Long Island or Westchester. A few Russians had already moved in, and eventually more and more would move in until the area would be known as Little Odessa.

A friend of my father's had told him there was a vacant apartment available in the neighborhood, and when it seemed certain that my wife and I would not be getting back together, I signed a lease, bought some furniture, and moved in. Graduate school was at Brooklyn College, about twenty minutes away on the subway, or a little longer if I took the bus.

The living room was large enough that I could let Wah-Zi-Nak use it as her bedroom, or she could use my bedroom, and I would sleep in the living room. Whichever was more comfortable for her, would be fine for me.

> When I came back from the bathroom, Leroy was sitting on the bed. He was fully dressed, and he was crying.
> "What's the matter now," I asked.

> "I really don't like to do that, Sal, it's just that I can't help myself."
> "Listen, man, I can understand you liking to fuck, but why must you ask me to call you those names?"
> "So I'm queer, huh?"
> "Don't worry," I told him, "The world is full of homos."

She was due to arrive at nine o'clock Thursday evening, and since I didn't want to use my car, I'd arranged with a local car service to drive me to the airport. The driver would wait for me until she arrived on the flight from British Columbia.

It was a little after nine when I got to the airport, and her flight had just arrived. People were walking down the corridor and into the waiting area. Dozens passed, and when I saw her, our eyes locked in place, as she continued walking to where I was standing with the driver.

"Hi," I said, when she was just a few inches from where we were standing. Dropping her purse, she silently embraced me.

"Do you have alotta luggage?"

"Just two small bags, that's all."

At slightly over five feet tall, she was still several inches shorter than I was, and as I helped her with her luggage from the revolving carousel, I couldn't help noticing how much of a resemblance there was between seeing her like this in person, and the photographs she'd sent me some time ago. Most people are merely shadows of the way they photograph, but Wah-Zi-Nak was surely an exception.

Full-figured, with soft brown hair falling around her shoulders, and dark eyes, she was strikingly sensual. Yet despite all the letters she'd exchanged with Salvador and I during the many months preceding her visit, she was remarkably quiet as we made our way through the streets of Brooklyn to my apartment in Brighton Beach. No doubt the driver's presence in the front seat had something to do with this, but as we made our way up the five flights of stairs to my apartment on the top floor, I could sense that it was a bit more complicated. It could've been simple shyness but more likely she was feeling overwhelmed. Here she was, a long way from home, in a strange city , and with a man she hardly even knew. She would be spending the night in his apartment, and then in the morning she would travel to a distant place to finally meet the man of her dreams.

10/8/74
Greenhaven Correctional Facility

Dear Richard:
I just got your letter along with the stamps. Thank you!
As for Wah-Zi-Nak, I am looking forward to my visit !! I have already told some of my other women friends to stay away while she's here. I do not enjoy telling lies to people. But she is very jealous, so it is not a good idea to mention any of this to her. She is beautiful, and I love her, but she is very unrealistic when it comes to having a relationship with a man. Her first marriage should have taught her a lesson. Women! They create lots of problems!
Well, hermano, take it easy

Love, power, and understanding,
Salvador Agron
#16486

Placing her valises in the foyer outside the kitchen, I showed her around the apartment.
"You can stay wherever you like. Would you prefer the bedroom? You'll have more privacy in there."
"That's okay, really... I'll be fine in the living room."
"Are you nervous about meeting Salvador?"
"Not really...well, maybe just a little."

Fixing a place for her on the living room couch, we went to bed soon after finishing a pizza we'd had sent in from a local pizzeria. I was about to undress in the bedroom when I remembered that Salvador had asked me to take some photographs of Wah-Zi-Nak without any clothes on.

When she had written several months ago that she was coming to New York to visit him, he had asked me to take the pictures. He had asked her first but she had said there was no one on the reservation she knew who would be willing to take them. So he had asked me, his friend, he said, and brother, to do this very important thing for him.

"Come on, you can do it," he said. "I don't got no one else I can ask."

"I don't wanna...it don't feel right, me taking pictures like that. She's your girlfriend, not mine."

"What's that got to do with anything?"

When I tried to explain that this had everything to do with it, and that besides, I'd also feel embarrassed, his reaction to my objections was little more than a blank stare.

In the world where Salvador made his home, such a request was perfectly normal, even encouraged, and as the months passed, and Salvador kept persisting, I finally gave in and said okay, I'd take the pictures. And without telling me anything about it, he had apparently made some arrangement with Wah-Zi-Nak, because no sooner had she entered my apartment and put away her bags, then she handed me a small camera with a flash attachment.

"These are for the pictures," she said.

10/18/74
Greenhaven Correctional Facility
Dear Little Richard:

Genoveva is of the opinion that I should not rush into marriage with Wah-Zi-Nak, but I don't think I'm rushing. Well, now that we know that she is coming, please concentrate on Rachel. I would not want their paths to cross, because women will say what they are not supposed to say. How I got myself into this mess, I really don't know. But it is not my fault. After fifteen years in these dungeons, one is bound to fall into any number of traps! Please be sure that Wah-Zi-Nak gets to meet with my sister, my mother, and Genoveva.

Salvador Agron
#16846

It was still dark outside when we got up the next morning, and while Wah-Zi-Nak was using the bathroom, I prepared a light breakfast of toast and strong coffee.

It was Friday morning and outside my window I could see bits of the sea in the distance as it rolled across the beach. People were on the street, walking quickly to the subway for the ride to Manhattan.

When she came out of the bathroom, she was wearing a long, slinky dress of a soft material that rustled as she walked. A deep black, it reflected her coloring in a very flattering way.

"You look like a dream," I told her.

Since it was rush hour, and there were plenty of express trains, it took us less than an hour to ride from Brighton Beach to Times Square. Then we walked down 42nd Street to Eighth Avenue, and from there it was just a block to the Port Authority Bus Terminal.

Sitting next to me in an isle seat was a Puerto Rican woman who looked to be no more than fifteen, but looking at the two children sitting close by, I knew she was at least five years older.

As the bus made its way through the dark morning, and the heating throughout the bus became more uniform, the woman took off her large overcoat. Underneath, she was wearing a shiny dress of so many different colors that when it caught the light from one of the overhead reading lamps, it almost looked as if instead of a dress, she was wearing a living rainbow.

Offering to help her store the coat directly under her seat, she smiled at me, "Gracias, gracias," she whispered softly before passing a bottle of milk across the isle to the smallest of her two children.

Like most of the other women on the bus, Wah-Zi-Nak had drenched herself in strong perfume. Mixed with the heat from the window vents, the effect was not unlike the smell of a nightclub, long after the dancing has stopped: sweat-filled, sweet, and warm.

"Did you sleep okay last night?" I asked her.

"Not too bad, but I did wake up a few times."

"You were probably nervous about meeting Salvador."

"What if he doesn't like me or something?"

"Listen, that's one thing you don't gotta worry about because he's gonna love you!"

When we'd left Brooklyn earlier that morning, it had been partly sunny. A light wind had been drifting in from the ocean, and the temperature had been in the high forties. But as we neared the prison, the sky was dark, and looking out the window, Wah-Zi-Nak commented on how cold it would be outside.

"How can you tell?" I asked.

"Because back on my reservation we're very sensitive to changes in the weather."

Wah-Zi-Nak was a quiet person, and like many quiet people, her silence had little to do with her depth of soul: how deep it was, what it knew, or what it wanted. Her letters were nothing if not passionate, and if now, in person, she was wordless about her sensual desires, this was not reflected in the way she'd looked at men on our way to the bus terminal. Long, deep, lingering gazes, lacking even the slightest hint of censure. What she did not say in words, her movements could not hide.

Not only was it cold when we left the bus, but the sky was gray, and a light snow was falling all across the parking lot, Carrying Wah-Zi-Nak's shopping bag up the stairway to the prison door, I told her that, yes, she was right about the weather, but that the snow and the cold would probably work in our favor.

"I don't understand," she said.

"Because if it's snowing, then they'll probably have to let us in a little early."

"You think so?"

"Absolutely! Because there's no way they're gonna make us wait out here in the cold and the snow."

10/20/74
Greenhaven Correctional Facility

Dear Little Richard:

This will acknowledge your letter of October 16th, 1974.
As for your suggestions about my case, and the suggestion that I apply for clemency, well, this will take time. My whole concern right now is to just finish the book we've started on. I must continue with this while you and the rest of the people out there work on my clemency. When you come up for a visit, we can discuss strategy.

Tu Hermano y amigo,
Salvador Agron # 16846

As the snow continued to fall, and the wind whirled and whined, the white powder glazing the faces of the waiting women and children looked all the more like dark tears dripping slowly down their faces. These were the weeping women, I thought to myself, the women who waited outside of prisons everywhere. The women who cried, and the women who waited. The women with the shopping bags and small children, who wept and cried in all kinds of weather. Years of tears from the weeping women. But who were these women, and why were they here? Some were visiting husbands, and boyfriends, but others, like Wah-Zi-Nak, had met up with their men through letters. She had responded to an article Salvador had written for a newspaper, while other women had responded to personal ads in magazines specifically designed to bring convicts and lonely outsiders together.

One of my professors had lectured us one night about this kind of prison romance. Forged from deep need, many of the relationships were particular to prisons, and had few if any counterparts in free society. It was one thing, he explained, for the wives and girlfriends of prisoners to visit with their men. At least a mutual history united them, along with children, sometimes, and long nights together, with hands and hearts touching like there was no tomorrow. But it was another thing entirely, he said, when women who'd met men through mutual acquaintances, or through personal ads, became intimately involved with convicts. Then there were no children to share, no memories, and no long nights together. Nothing but volumes of letters, prison visiting rooms, and faulted carnal knowledge. None of which, he said, was ever strong enough to transcend their not having known the man when he was on the streets.

Needy women were drawn to men in prison because it was one of the few places on earth where everything was controlled, rigid, and well-defined. Where else but in a prison would she find a man who would always be there when she came to visit, no matter what? A man who would always be thankful for whatever she brought to the prison in the way of food, cigarettes, magazines, or money? A man who would always be glad to see her when she came, and who would always be sorry to see her go?

The more insightful among these women made every effort to choose convict partners who were serving an eternity of time. The more the better, they secretly told themselves, so as to preclude any chance of the men ever getting out, and the two of them having to "make a life together." These women knew, perhaps from bitter experience, that unless you knew the man from having spent time with him together on the outside, that there was little chance that things would ever work out for the two of you in the long run.

The snow fell, the women wept, and the temperature dropped. Finally, the door of the prison was opened by a bored guard; and the warm heat from inside the prison hit us like a drifting cloud from heaven.

11/2/74
Greenhaven Correctional Facility
Mi Hermano, Ricardo:

I received your letter dated October 24th, 1974 with the books. Muchas Gracias. Yes, bring my Indian up here on the eight.
I really love Wah-Zi-Nak, but she makes me nervous every time she mentions marriage to me—but if I do get married, you will be the Best Man, and Genoveva will be the Best Woman. The idea of Genoveva coming up at the same time as Joyce is not a good idea. I would not want to leave Genoveva all by herself. She might think that I am more interested in holding Joyce than in what she might have to say. So let's just say that you will come up with her as planned on the eight, and we'll leave it at that, okay?
The whole idea of knowing women is not to know them— I just accept women for what they are individually and I do not think that I should bother myself with understanding them. If they want me to understand them the only thing they got to do is explain themselves, and I will preserve my right to say YES or to say NO! It's all very simple. I do not put any restrictions on women—let them do as they please. The only thing I want is that she speak the truth and be realistic and free.

When you come up for the next festival, please try to bring some girls with you for the fellows. Convicts must have something to look forward to if they are to be motivated to try to get out of these joints!

I love to see love develop between people.

> Your brother, forever
> Salvador Agron   #16846

"Who you here to visit?"

"Salvador Agron," Wah-Zi-Nak tells the guard, followed by his prison number with such speed as if it were stored forever inside her soul.

"And you?" he said, pointing to me.

"John O'Neil."

Identification was shown, purses were emptied, pockets turned inside out, and it didn't take long before we were all seated together in the visiting room.

Maybe it was because they made us wait outside in the cold a little longer than usual, or maybe it was because it was near Thanksgiving, because instead of assigning us seats, the visiting room guard simply waved us into the room.

Sitting two seats away from Wah-Zi-Nak, as she waits for Salvador, and I wait for John O'Neil, we're able to talk without raising our voices too much.

"This isn't bad," Wah-Zi-Nak says, "at least they've got vending machines and it's pretty clean."

"So you work with little kids at a daycare center?" I asked her.

"I do, but when I say my work, I mean my political stuff."

Before I had a chance to answer, Wah-Zi-Nak's mouth seemed to drop, and she suddenly became very pale.

"Are you okay? Do you need to use the restroom?"

"No, no, I'm fine..." she said, not looking directly at me. And when I turned around to see who or what she was looking at, everything became very clear. Pass in hand, and standing on the other side of the visiting room, was Salvador Agron. Standing very tall, and with his hair combed straight back, his eyes were locked on Wah-Zi-Nak's, with the same intensity as hers on his.

When the guard said it was okay, Salvador walked to where we were standing together. Quickly hugging me, he walked a few feet further to Wah-Zi-Nak. They kissed, hugged, and with their eyes undressed one another with such an intensity that I had to turn away. Within minutes they were seated across from one another, and by the way they touched, kissed, and spoke, you would've thought their intimacy was one of years instead of minutes. Watching them as I waited for John O'Neil, I had to wonder about the nature of intimacy. Was this simply lust, or was there something even deeper here? Both of them claimed to love the other, and who was to say that whatever it was between them wasn't the real thing? If love was known to be a redeeming force, then how could it be that Wah-Zi-Nak's love was somehow, as my professor had implied, bogus, because of the circumstances?

Trading tongues with Wah-Zi-Nak without a hint of self-consciousness, Salvador could have been lying on a beach in Mayaguez instead of in a jailhouse visiting room. He devoured Wah-Zi-Nak as he devoured his food. Quickly, with hunger, and with passion. Never seeming to get enough from the vending machines, he was always asking for more. "Anything with some meat in it," was his favorite expression, and as I watched him slide his enormous hand underneath her winter overcoat to reach the black silkiness of her dress, I thought to myself that he had finally arrived at a place where the meat was unlimited.

"Richard," he said, "I'm gonna go with Wah-Zi-Nak to take some Polaroids."

"That sounds good...maybe when O'Neil gets here we'll join you."

Along with many of the reforms put in place after the Attica riots, the taking of Polaroid photographs between convicts and visitors was yet another way of defusing tensions. A small area was set aside in a corner of the visiting room for taking the Polaroids. A Polaroid camera was set on a tripod, and for a small fee a convict could have one or more photographs taken. He could keep the photographs or give them to his visitors. The choice was his.

Depending on the prison, the background against which the photograph was taken varied from a tropical setting, complete with a palm tree, to a city scene. Or you could just take the photograph against a blank wall. The photographer was a convict, and was usually very accommodating when someone would ask for a pose that was slightly different than what he might arrange for a family portrait, with sitting on laps being a universal favorite.

Everyone loved taking photographs. Not only could they take something home or to the cellhouse, but it was a chance to come together, however briefly, without barriers of any kind. Salvador and Wah-Zi-Nak seemed to melt into one another, and the photographer, looking as if he was sympathetic, took his time setting the camera up so that they could share some stolen intimacy.

After an hour and a half of waiting for John O'Neil to join me in the visiting room, a guard came over to where I was sitting.

"You're waiting for John O'Neil, right?"

"Yeah..."

"Well, he ain't coming down because he's keep-locked, so unless you got someone else you can visit, you're gonna have to leave."

Keep-locked meant you were confined to your cell for a specified period of time. A few days, sometimes more, for something like not following this rule, or that, and when you were keep-locked you were not allowed to have any visitors. Had I wanted I could have gone outside and signed in as another one of Salvador's visitors, but since this would've meant that I would be required to stay in close proximity to Salvador and Wah-Zi-Nak, I decided to wait outside until their visit was over.

Sitting on a wooden bench in the prison lobby, I spent the remaining hours watching several different convicts sweep and mop the floor, over and over, until it shone as if a light was buried underneath.

Exhausted from her hours of passion, Wah-Zi-Nak fell asleep on the bus back to the city. Her head was on my shoulder, and her hair smelled of perfume and perspiration, her juices mixing with Salvador's.

Aurea was waiting for us when we got back to New York, and she took Wah-Zi-Nak back to the Bronx to stay with her on Knox Place. When I called her apartment later on that week, Wah-Zi-Nak had already met Esmeralda, as well as several of Aurea's children.

"It really feels like they're my family," she said, and she wanted to know if it was okay with me if she stayed with them for the rest of her trip. Then I told her about the letter I'd received from Salvador a few hours before.

11/8/74
Greenhaven Correctional Facility
Dear Hermano:

Please have Wah-Zi-Nak call my friend, Elisa Lopez. She would like to invite Wah-Zi-Nak to a class she conducts up here at the prison. It's about Puerto Rican History, and I think Wah-Zi-Nak would enjoy herself.

She has a car, and she can take Wah-Zi-Nak when she drives up for the class, and then they can drive back to the city together after the class.

Love, peace, and understanding,
Salvador Agron   #16846

All I knew of Elisa Lopez was that she was teaching a class in Puerto Rican history at Greenhaven, and that she was having an affair with a convict friend of Salvador's, who was also a student in the class. I also knew that she lived on the Lower East Side, and worked for some kind of social service agency.

Later on that evening, Wah-Zi-Nak called Elisa, and they made plans to ride up to Greenhaven later on that week when Elisa would be teaching her class. Except for the night before she left for Canada, Wah-Zi-Nak stayed with Aurea for the rest of her time in New York, but we talked on the telephone as much as we could.

"I really love his family," she said, "especially Aurea. She's like my sister...and his family calls me, *La India*."

"What does Salvador call you?"

"Wahzi or mi corazon, but mostly Wahzi."

As we rode together late at night to the airport, Wah-Zi-Nak was silent. Dark circles surrounded her eyes, and her skin looked faded, tired. She must be exhausted, I thought, from all the riding back and forth to the prison. This plus meeting so many new people, including Salvador's family, had probably done her in both emotionally and physically.

"Are you looking forward to going home?" I asked her.

"I really miss my family, but I feel like I should be staying here with Salvador."

"When do you think you'll be coming back again?"

"Whenever I can get the money together."

"Come back soon," I told her. But when I asked her about what had happened when she'd gone to the prison with Elisa, she looked at me a long time before answering.

"I'll write to you about it as soon as I get home."

Filled with passion, and highly descriptive, her letter left little to the imagination. Shortly after Elisa had introduced her as a visitor from British Columbia, Salvador motioned with his eyes for her to follow him into the corridor. With not a correctional officer in sight, they walked about fifty yards until they found themselves in a tiny room with sunlight running in waves through a window crossed with bars. Surrounded by metal folding chairs stacked one on top the other, they kissed and touched until he entered her. Later she would always remember, she wrote, his strong and gentle rhythm. Later that night, and back in his cell, Salvador would write to her that he had been completely taken by the experience.

One week later, and back in the visiting room, I had already received two more letters from Wah-Zi-Nak. Thanking me for my hospitality, she wrote that she was already making plans for another trip, though it was hard to say just when this would be. She also wanted to know whether or not I had developed the nude photographs I had taken of her in my apartment just before I had driven her to the airport, and also what she could do to help with his clemency campaign.

"Hermano, what you doin'? You daydreaming or something?"

Standing directly in front of me, and with a broad smile on his face, Salvador shook his head from side to side.

"You wanna sleep," he said, "then you oughta stay the fuck home!"

When I told him to eat shit, he said no, he wouldn't do that, but would I please get him a turkey sandwich from the vending machine?

Between bites of his turkey sandwich, he wanted to know if I had taken the photographs of Wah-Zi-Nak.

12/7/74
Greenhaven Correctional Facility
Dear Little Richard:

    Now that Joyce has returned to Canada, you and I can get on with the business of writing the book, and applying for

Executive Clemency. I will write a letter of introduction for you to Mrs. Davis. This will make it much easier when you actually go to her house.

As for the marriage to Wah-Zi-Nak, it will go on as planned when I get the permission from the warden. Wah-Zi-Nak already wrote. I guess that Rachel and myself will maintain a platonic sort of relationship (at least for now). She should understand how important this is to me. I like Rachel, but it is not in the sense that I like Wah-Zi-Nak. I think that if you get Rachel one of your friends out there that she will find some sexual release. And, this will mellow our relationship and equalize things. I love Wah-Zi-Nak and I intend to marry her and go up to Canada and live with her when my clemency goes through. Wah-Zi-Nak gives me a sense of responsibility and there is a commitment in her voice. I really love her.

Well, that is all for now. I am enclosing Ms. Davis's address and telephone number.

Vaya Con Dios.
With much love, from your friend and brother
Salvador Agron   #16846

With a built-in flash, Wah-Zi-Nak's camera could take up to a dozen photographs, and I had suggested that just to be on the safe side, we should take an entire roll.

"This way," I told her, "you won't have to take the photos a second time if they don't come out the way you want them to."

Since it was colder than usual outside, and there wasn't that much heat in my apartment, I had installed a small space heater near the couch where Wah-Zi-Nak would be posing for the photographs.

Agreeing that I would just take photographs from her waist up, I asked her to remove her blouse. She was shy at first, but when I averted my eyes for a moment, it seemed to help, because when I turned back, she had already removed her blouse, and was standing with her arms across her breasts as if she were protecting them.

"Take your arms away, and I'll start taking the pictures," I said.

Asking her to turn in several different directions so I could have a perfect angle, I wondered what was going through her mind as I took the photographs. Was she proud of what she was doing, or was it simply that she didn't want to disappoint Salvador? Or had she removed her blouse with the secret thought that perhaps the sight of her breasts would have made me want to make a pass at her, the Capeman's girlfriend?

As I took the rest of the pictures, the thought kept crossing my mind that this was a golden opportunity. I could start out by simply reaching across and grabbing one of her breasts. If she responded, great, we would go on from there. If not, well, nothing was lost, except that she'd probably tell Salvador, and this could mean all kinds of problems. Better to take the pictures, I thought, and just leave well enough alone.

Several pictures later, her face already flushed from revealing her breasts, Wah-Zi-Nak had lost all her inhibitions. Posing provocatively, there was little doubt as to what she was thinking, but instead of turning me on, it had the opposite effect.

Looking at her breasts as they rocked from side to side, I tried to imagine what kind of love it was that allowed her to pose naked in the cold apartment of a virtual stranger for yet another man who, just like me was also a stranger.

As Wah-Zi-Nak buttoned up her blouse, I thought of all the women who lined up every day in front of Greenhaven.

A sea of breasts, waiting to be touched, felt, and held.

12/15/74
Greenhaven Correctional Facility
Dear Richard:

I received all your letters, plus the stamps, and the article from the New York Times.

As far as women are concerned, they are usually so imaginative that they invent and play so many games that when they meet a real man they inevitably wind up doing stupid things and playing more games. Third World women are even more fucked up due to their triple oppression: imperialism, sexism, and racism. As for the woman who is aware, she is a walking contradiction. If you are real with her she does not quite understand it or just refuses to believe that some men are real human beings and so she dislikes it, and if you are deceptive with them, then they will in turn deceive you too and try to win or play on your feelings, and so they inevitably do something dumb and wind up receiving their own selves! If you give them "freedom," they abuse it and do their best to impress you with it, and if you make them submit or protectively subjugate them with your aggressiveness, they wind up accusing you of being a male chauvinist pig, machismo, etc., and thus rebel and try to liberate themselves and in so doing she winds up giving it to the milkman or the delivery boy in the name of female liberation!

The answer to all problems lies within the self. This is why all philosophers have said "Know Thyself." I think that sums it up about women.

Wah-Zi-Nak is special. She is close to being the ideal female. She sent me the photographs you took of her when she was with you in Brooklyn. They were put in my property upfront somewhere. But I'll get them. They let all kinds of magazines in here—Penthouse, Playboy, Playgirl, OUI and many others on sex related matters, but not my girl's photographs. If they don't give them up, I'll have them send them back to her.

I will write the commissioner for them! No one stops a good struggler. I like a mental fight every now and then!!

With love and understanding,
Salvador Agron   #16846

The next sandwich was white meat chicken on rye bread, and in between bites, he told me that the piece we'd put together for the *New York Times* had been accepted.

"No shit!" I said.

"That's right..and they said it'll be out sometime in January."

"Good...because we can use it to start the clemency rolling."

"I'm gonna leave all that stuff up to you, so this way I can keep writing the book without too many distractions," he said.

"Who's this guy, 'RR,' that you're dedicating the book to?"

Salvador had sent me page after page of poetry that he'd written over the years to one person or another. Some were to women, but the vast majority were to someone with the initials '"RR." Long, lingering love poems leaving little doubt in the reader's mind as to what the intentions were of the poet who wrote them. Up to now, I knew very little about the guy except that Salvador had mentioned in a letter his wish for him to be included in the dedication to his book.

"We were together when I was in Dannemora."

"When was this?" I said.

"1968, and it was cold out, just like it is right now."

"And you never heard from him again?"

"Nada, man. Not a word."

December 4th, 1968
Dannemora Prison

My Dear Raphael

The motive for this letter is love. I want to be sincere with you. The minute I saw you, my heart began to beat. Raphael, I want you, and I am well aware that you will want and need me also. And as a matter of faith, you do need me as much as I need you.

I know that you are doing eight years, and I know that you must be aware that I am doing two natural life sentences, as well as a sentence of twelve to twenty-five years.

Now, let me be truthful to you. I want you to live with me. I really like you very much. If you are not really gay, please let me know. I do not want to hurt your feelings.

We are both going to be here for quite some time. And I think we could be very happy together. Will you stay with me, baby? You are very lovely and beautiful and so you are bound to get into trouble. I do not want this to happen.

Of course, we are going to work on our cases, and if this thing between us works out, we can get an apartment together when we get out. I'm serious about this.

Do not get angry at me for telling you this, but already some people in the yard have asked about you, and I told them I knew you from 50th Street in Manhattan. So you see, I have already protected your honor. And I want you to know that if anyone tries to harm you, I will have no choice but to hurt them in return.

Raphael, do not deny me. I am in love with you. I want you and need you as much as you need me. You were meant for me, and of course we are meant for each other. If you look at me closely, you will notice that I am very sincere, and that I only seek to help and assist you in any way I can.

I just want our destinies to cross, and that we should be lovers. Tell me your secrets and I will tell you mine. I will close this letter now, but I will not close my heart. So what will you be?

My friend or my lover?

Respectfully yours,
Salvador Agron
#39640

Chapter Eight

FREEDOM

Meeting with Aurea and Esmeralda in March of that year was the first step in trying to secure Salvador's clemency. Petitions asking for support were already being circulated, and letters would have to be written to the Governor, and the Clemency Board.

Where Esmeralda's apartment was a solitary place, with everything neatly arranged, Aurea's apartment was filled with children running back and forth, radios playing, and neighbors knocking on the door. Several of her windows looked across Mosholu Parkway, and as Esmeralda moved about the living room, serving coffee, and whispering to Aurea, I could see from the trees along the parkway that spring was not far away.

2/10/75
Greenhaven Correctional Facility

Dear Little Richard:

I received your letter dated 2/3/74 with the stamps and the newspaper articles from the New York Daily News. Thank you!
I was going to leave the book for a while, but I felt like getting down to it and I like to remain true to my feelings so I went on with it, and I am enclosing a few pages for your editing. Once I start writing, I don't know when to stop. It has become

a pleasure to write, and I will continue to do so. There is one piece of information that I will need for the piece I am working on. Find out when I got that photo with the hat taken. I think it was right before I came to New York that first time, maybe like a few months before. How old am I in the photo? Have you made copies of it? I am talking about the one in which I was a small child. The one my moms gave you last year when you were visiting at her house. Please send me a copy.

As for Mrs. Davis, my old social worker, (yes—she is the same one listed in my book dedications), she wrote and told me that she would be contacting the lawyer, Zapata, so that he can withdraw any legal action around my case. This will allow us to proceed with the clemency business without anything getting in the way

I find it very difficult to be my true self with that lady. Her notions on rehabilitation and all that other social stuff are unrealistic. It is a shame. However, she has lots of my poetry in her possession, and someday it would be good if you could get it back for me!

I have written many people and informed them of my intention to apply for clemency, and asked them to write letters to the Governor. This way he will begin receiving letters from concerned citizens. So we must move on this as soon as possible!

Your flesh and blood brother,
Salvador Agron   #16846

Thousands and thousands of words would have to be written attesting to Salvador's character, his many accomplishments while in prison, and what if any contributions he might make to society when he was released from prison. The bottom line was simple: would Salvador's release cause any kind of uproar , and would the Governor, by releasing him, be made to appear as being soft on crime? Would Salvador kill again? And if he did kill again, who would be responsible?

When Salvador had been released from the death house

in 1962, his death sentence had been commuted by Governor Rockefeller to one of life imprisonment, with the earliest possible date of release in the spring of 1993. Unless he successfully applied for executive clemency from the Governor, and they in turn recommended him for parole, he would have to walk in the shadow of the walls for at least another twenty years before being eligible to meet with the Parole Board.

"You think my brother's really gonna get out?"

"I think he's got a chance, but you never can really tell about stuff like this," I said to Aurea.

"I really hope so because it would be nice havin' him around and everything...and it would make my moms really happy."

As if on cue, and as soon as she sensed we were talking about her, Esmeralda turned around from where she was sitting in an overstuffed chair by the living room window, and said very softly, "How are you, Jacobo?"

2/11/75
Greenhaven Correctional Facility

Dear Richard:

I spoke to someone about the clemency procedure that he took to go for clemency and he ran it down for me. Last year (1974) inmates began to see the Clemency Board, whenever they submitted papers for pardons. The Clemency Board is presided over by a guy named Oliver Tweedy. It is similar to the Parole Board, They come up here next September and they interview all the people applying for clemency. Then if they recommend someone for clemency, they tell the Parole Board, and they either approve it or they don't. I know it sounds a little complicated, but basically it all comes down to me asking for a pardon because otherwise the earliest I can see the Parole Board is in 1993!!

> *You will need to get all the newspaper articles about my case from Zapata. He also has a film about my arrest that was shown on television at the time.*
>
> *With love and understanding,*
> *Salvador Agron   #16846*

Genoveva agreed to be the political connection for Salvador, and she would start, she said, by writing letters to various political groups in order to network for their support. Everyone from those seeking independence for Puerto Rico to those groups dedicated to working against the death penalty, or in liberalizing the decorum for visitors in New York State's many prisons and jails. It would mean speaking to as many different people as possible, and maybe even galvanizing support from various politicians who might be sympathetic to Salvador's situation.

"You think Herman Badillo might be interested?" I asked Genoveva.

"He could be...he's Puerto Rican, and he's got lotsa pull as a Congressman, so that might help later on. Have you said anything to Salvador about him?"

"Yeah, but Salvador thinks he's bad news because he's a liberal."

"No, I'm talking about Salvador...I can't believe he said that to you...I mean, who cares what his politics are, because as long as he can help him get out of prison, then that should be the most important thing."

The New York Times
OP-ED
January 29th, 1975
Echo of a Rumble
By Salvador Agron # 16486

On a summer night in 1959, 16-year-old Salvador Agron the "Cape Man," went to a gang rumble in a Hell's Kitchen playground. While gang members held two teen-aged boys down, he stabbed them to death. Now 31, he is an inmate at Greenhaven Prison in Stormville. He will not be eligible for parole until 1993. Following are excerpts of a letter he sent to the *New York Times*.

In the 1950's the wave of teen-age gang violence was rampant in New York City. It was very difficult to remain passive under such an atmosphere. One either fought or one either became the punching bag of a rival gang. Violence only engenders more violence, and this was the case in 1959 when the culmination of gang violence took its toll and youth was not properly directed by the civic and social agencies in the New York City area.

The family structure was falling apart, The public schools were slowly deteriorating, and the generation gap was becoming wider.

The 50's brought in the Bohemian concept, which later gave way to the Beatnik generation. I was made a victim of those changes, quantitative changes which had no moral values to them—it was all quantity and no quality. In becoming a victim of my social conditions it made me act in a way as to make victims of others.

For a boy, as I was then, with the mentality of a twelve-year old child, during a time of social transition, without the proper guidance, there was not much I could have done to prevent what occurred.

Both my mother and my stepfather had to work in order to survive in the concrete jungle—I was, therefore, left without parental guidance.

Prison has been a hard life for me, but in spite of the system that it is, I have managed to use it to my advantage and betterment. Perhaps this is due to something that I learned while I was in the Sing Sing Prison death row, at the age of seventeen.

During one of my highest spiritual moments, a time in which the soul is able to see the complete past of one's exis-

tence, or life, while facing the shadows of death, it occurred to me that one must do his best to take evil and turn it into good.

It is due to this acknowledgment of life and reality that I have been able to maintain the little humanity that was left within me, and working at it in the face of backward surrounding, I have been able to increase the value and respect for all human beings.

I have learned how to write poetry, received my high school equivalency, and put legal petitions together in block letters. This is but a small part of my rehabilitation. I have also received my regents diploma, and at the present time, under the direction of the South Forty Program, I have received college credits. It has done a great deal for me in that it has helped me to see the many errors that I have accumulated in my learning process. Today I am better because of it. Therefore, I now come to the end of my prison road.

All those who came to prison for youthful gang participation during the 50's are all out on the street. It seems that I am the exampli gratis of this society. I think that I have suffered enough. And, it is my sincere opinion that even one more year in prison will only have ill effects on me.

I will continue to make this into a positive experience. However, how much is enough? How long does it take to correct or rehabilitate a first-time offender? Surely, five years of this is enough for any person. If the state cannot rehabilitate a person in five years, then something is wrong with our penal system, something is wrong with our professionals, and something is wrong with us as a people.

As Aurea washed a sink full of dishes in the kitchen, she told me she would talk to friends and relatives to see if they would be willing to write letters to the Governor. She would also distribute a general letter that I would write, with the history of Salvador's case, and what we needed in the way of support.

Helping her dry the dishes, and sipping hot coffee at the same time, I was standing close enough that I couldn't help noticing how tired she looked. Working long hours in the laundry room of a local hospital left her little energy, I figured, for much of anything else. In addition to addressing the needs of a house full of children, she was also taking care of her mother. It wasn't that Esmeralda needed taking care of, it was just that living alone the way she did, Aurea wanted to make sure that she was never in need of anything.

"All my moms ever does is worry about my brother."

2/20/75
Greenhaven Correctional Facility

Dear Richard:

I always work on the book whenever I have a chance, which lately hasn't been too often because I've also been working on my clemency application. My daily educational schedule keeps me so busy that sometimes I wonder myself how I manage all this!!

My educational schedule runs something like this: I take classes from Hostos Community College as well as Dutchess Community College

Days	Classes	Time
Monday:	Dutchess:salesmanship	9:00 A.M.
	Free Time	
	Hostos Sociology class	6:00 P.M.
Tuesday:	Dutchess: American Literature	9:00 A.M.
	Free Time	
	Hostos: Puerto Rican History	6:00 P.M.
Wednesday:	Dutches: Salemanship	9:00 A.M.
	Free Time	
	Hostos Sociology Class	6:00 P.M.

Thursday	Dutchess: American Literature	9:00 A.M.
	Free Time	
	Hostos: Puerto Rican History	6:00 P.M.
Friday	Free Time	
	Boricua Cadre Class	1:00 P.M.
	South 40 Cadre Meeting (Rev. Muller)	6:00 P.M.

I work on the book in my free time, and I also do my homework, exercise, and answer my mail! When the summer semester is over, I will have accumulated a total of 45 credits toward my A.A. degree.

Have you heard anything from Mrs. Davis yet? This is important because we will need her help with the clemency. She knows lots of people, and her support will be useful. I also want her to give you all my writings.

Well, this is all for now

Hasta Luego, pana,
Salvador Agron #16846

When the last dish had been dried, and everything had been put away in a cabinet above the sink, Aurea turned around so that we were standing face to face.

"You know," she said, "what worries me more than anything is that my brother's been in so much trouble in prison that they're not gonna want to let him out."

"I don't know...it's hard to say." I said.

"I remember one time when me and my moms went up to see him when he was in Dannemora ... we took the bus up there but when we got to the prison they wouldn't let us in or nothing..."

"And they wouldn't let you in to see him?"

"That's right...because they said he'd been bad and he couldn't have no visitors or nothing."

"So what'd you do?"

"We had to go leave without them letting us in to see him, and it was bad because we was way upstate and we didn't know nobody and since we didn't have no money to stay anywhere, it was hard even going into the stores up there for something to eat because of the dirty looks people were giving me and my moms, and then we had to ride the bus all night back to New York without getting no sleep or nothing."

3/1/75
Greenhaven Correctional Facility
Dear Richard the Lion-Hearted!

    I did receive a letter from Mrs. Davis, and she said that she would be writing you a letter soon so that you could get together. When you meet her, I wonder what your impressions will be? Yes, it will be very wise of you to keep politics out of the meeting you will have with her. You are just a concerned Jewish boy trying to fulfill the laws of the Torah! (smile) in opposing injustice wherever it may be found!
    I think it would be a good idea if you and Genoveva was to let Mrs. Davis do her own thing with the clemency, and just to stay out of her way. The woman has two faces, and I know how to deal with people like that. I have been around those types all of my fucking life, and how I have ever managed to keep my humanity is spite of all the hypocrisy that surrounds me I will never know! Much of this I think I owe to the inner strength that I built up while I was on death row where people that knew you were marked for death came around every day with a hypocritical smile on their face, knowing that they would be the ones to take one to the electric chair and if one should ever put up a fight that they would be the ones who would grab you and tie you down! Leave such people to me, and I will give them heart attacks!
    I have tolerance and perseverance in this life, thanks to death row! I came away from there much stronger than when I went in.

> Okay, Lion-hearted, I got to get me some sleep. So you take it easy, okay?
>
> Love always,
> Salvador Agron   #16846

If Salvador's prison record had ever been used as a reliable yardstick of where he was at politically or emotionally, the people who ran the prisons would have thrown away the key a long time ago. Entry after entry indicated a recalcitrant prisoner unwilling to follow the rules, as well as someone who saw himself as a cross between Che Guevara and Jesse James. A revolutionary, Salvador said, whose sole purpose on earth was to "serve the people."

> 3/1/75
> *Greenhaven Correctional Facility*
>
> *Dear Ricardo:*
>
> *I have a feeling that my lawyer was very relieved when he heard that he was no longer obligated to work on my case. The fault really lies with Mrs. Davis. She pesters these lawyers so much that she gets them to consent when are really not interested!*
>
> *Take care, brother.*
> *Love and understanding,*
> *Salvador Agron #16846*

When I asked a corrections counselor at Greenhaven what if any impact Salvador's prison record might have on his chances of getting out, he said he didn't know, but would get back to me after looking at the record.

The next time I saw him he said Salvador's record, while extensive in terms of disciplinary write-ups, time spent in the box, and harsh progress reports was not that bad, especially for someone like Salvador who had been in the system for such a long time. The positive thing, he said, was that his record seemed to have gotten progressively better over the years, with fewer and fewer write-ups. It was a change, the counselor pointed out which seemed to have begun at the same time as his participation in the South Forty school programs. A good sign, he said, because if nothing else the keepers of the lock would surely see his academic progress in a positive light.

Programs which diverted the energies of men with violent hearts were always welcomed behind the high walls and gun towers of a maximum-security prison.

The real impediment, he said, wouldn't be his prison record, his politics, or his Native American girlfriend, but simply that their might be more than a little reluctance to be known as the people who were responsible for having released "The Capeman."

Greenhaven Correctional Facility
Quarterly Evaluation Report

Name: Salvador Agron   # 16846

Mr. Agron has been incarcerated at the Auburn, Attica, Clinton, and Greenhaven Correctional facilities as well as the Dannemora State Hospital for the Insane Criminal, during which time he incurred numerous infractions and misbehavior reports. It is believed that his maladjustment may be attributed to his youth and lack of sufficient emotional stability to deal effectively with incarceration.

It is noted, however, that he was able to acquire a High School Equivalency diploma at Clinton Correctional Facility in 1967, and a Regents diploma at this facility in 1972.

Salvador Agron's program involvement here at this facility includes the South Forty Cadre with the Reverend Ed Muller, participation in a course in Social and Civic responsibility in the Puerto Rican community, the Creative Workshop, which is designed to enhance poetic expression. He has also functioned as a resident instructor for a class on Puerto Rican culture and history. In addition, he has acquired forty-five credits as a full-time student in the Dutchess Community College Programs under the auspices of the South Forty Corporation. His performance in this program merited his being named to the Dean's list.

His present institutional assignment is as a member of the Open Gate staff, (which is the institutional newspaper) where he serves as a translator of English articles into Spanish.

Mr. Agron is described as an excellent worker who completes his assigned duties without the need for constant supervision.

Back in the living room, with the Saturday afternoon light slowly beginning to fade, I sat next to Genoveva on an overstuffed couch as Aurea guided us through a family album of photographs that was stretched across our laps like a colorful accordion.

Page after page of family photographs, along with school diplomas, church certificates, and whatever other milestones were important in the life of the Agron family.

With each photograph came a story, but except for the photograph of Salvador wearing the hat, when he was five years old, the only other pictures of him were the Polaroid ones taken at Greenhaven, including the one he and I had taken together when we had met for the first time. There were other pictures of me, including several I had taken with Esmeralda and Genoveva when we had been together in Puerto Rico.

Looking back and forth from the photographs to Aurea as she unfolded each page, I thought to myself for the first time how difficult it must've been for her to have been in Salvador's shadow all these years. From the moment she'd received the call that Salvador had been arrested for murder, her life was changed forever. No longer was she just another unwed mother barely out of her teens from Puerto Rico, living with her children in a housing project in Spanish Harlem. Suddenly, and without warning, she was the sister of the notorious "Capeman" killer, and I had the feeling that being Salvador's brother had taken a hefty toll.

Years of visiting him in faraway places in prisons with strange names, and in strange towns, to say nothing of visiting him in the death house when it seemed like his execution was inevitable, had probably made her weary of what the future would hold if and when he was ever released from prison.

3/5/75
Greenhaven Correctional Facility
Dear Brother Richard:

I just received a letter from Assemblyman Arthur Eve of Buffalo, and he is sending a letter to the Governor on my behalf. I also got a letter of inquiry from Congressman Herman Badillo about my case!

I am enclosing a letter I received from someone calling themselves "a citizen" the other day. It's one of the responses I got from the article in the Times, and I wanted you to see the other side of my mail, the side that isn't very supportive. I am also enclosing a letter I wrote in response, and which I would like you to send to the New York Times *for me.*

Take it easy, but take it.
Tu Hermano Y Amigo
Salvador Agron   #16846

> "Dear Brave Cape Man:
>
> Nice to read about you again. You must have felt very brave stabbing two boys to death, who couldn't fight back! I'll never forget the "wise-guy" smirk on your face, as I saw it on television.
>
> You felt like a hero didn't you?! Why didn't you fight with your HANDS?
>
> You came back to KILL those 2 boys with a knife! You dirty, rotten rat! Your helpers are as guilty as you are and they should be there with you, too.
>
> I hope the ghosts of the two boys you murdered will haunt you in your sleep.
>
> Their families should tear you to pieces, you scum. I hope you rot there until 1993!!
>
> A Citizen!

Salvador's case still bought knowing recognition to virtually anyone who had been alive in New York City in 1959, and so letters like this came as no surprise. Passing a petition around, I would often get blank stares if I mentioned the name, Salvador Agron.

"Who's that?" people would ask. But when I would say, "Capeman," "Dracula," or even the "Hell's Kitchen killings at the playground in 1959," the recognition was almost always immediate.

"Yeah! Yeah!" they would say, "I remember...but is this who you're tryin' to get out? Why would you wanna do that?"

At first we advised Salvador to play down the fact that he had ever been the "Capeman," or "Dracula," but in time we saw this was a label that would not die. Salvador Agron was the "Capeman," and no matter what would take this to his grave. Better we said to let it all hang out. Don't hide a thing, and maybe then it would lose some of its importance.

Whether or not I would help Salvador gain his release by working with him on his clemency campaign had never been an issue. Although I regretted the time it would take from writing his book, not to mention how it would complicate my own life, the reasons he gave for deserving clemency went right to the very heart of my death row dissertation. That the few people who had undergone what I had described as "consciousness expansion" in the face of death in the electric chair or the gas chamber were in essence not the same people who had murdered their victims years before, and were—at least by this logic—worthy of compassion when it came time to consider them for some kind of parole. And if Salvador was one of these people then it was my obligation to, as Salvador had said in one of our many discussions on why he was worthy of clemency "either shit or get off the pot."

3/5/75
Greenhaven Correctional Facility
Dear Citizen:

Your letter did not shock me at all. From all my years of being abused on this earth by people just like you, I have built up a sort of shock resistance. It is a shame that people like you are free while true human beings such as myself languish behind bars in maximum-security prisons. Personally, I do not think you should be incarcerated because this would not help you one bit. I had to let out some tears when I read your letter. No, the cries were not because I felt that you had insulted me, or that you tried your best to make me feel like an animal. I am beyond insults, And there is not that much a person could say that would get me angry. I understand human nature too well to react to things of that sort. My tears were not for me, brave citizen, but instead they were for you. I feel sorry for you. You need help. It would be wise if you were to see a psychiatrist or a therapist.

It would be very nice if I could bring you in here and show you the wretched of the earth. Perhaps then you would gain a better understanding of life and people. You are a victim just *like I have been a victim, and just like the two boys in the playground were victims. My dear Citizen, don't you know by now that we are all victims? And have you ever asked yourself why this is so? You seem to have a good education, at least academically, but in the process it seems you have lost something that I have regained, and that is dignity and humanness for my fellow man. I hope it is not too late for you. What I have for you is a message of love, a message of human understanding. No one is born a criminal. Criminal behavior arises from the conditions that citizens perpetuate without being conscious of it because it stems from a system that in its forward movement steps on everything that is even remotely good.*

It seems that technological advancement in the American society has made us forget the meaning of forgiveness, mercy, love, or compassion. We no longer look upon the "why" of crime. Instead, we just look upon the guilt or innocence of the person, as though by doing so we are going to solve the problem. For every action that occurs there is a motivating factor. Crime is not something that happens for the hell of it, If we can correct the error of our social ways then we can begin to eradicate crime and violence from our society.

I hope this reply to your letter will give you the wisdom to see the error of your ways, and will provide you with the help that your soul seems to be pleading for.

With love, peace, and understanding,
Salvador Agron   #16846
Greenhaven Correctional Facility

Leaving Aurea's house later that evening, I thought of how much time I'd spent in the past year or so with her family, and how well we had all gotten to know one another. I had written to her brother, met him at Greenhaven, and we had agreed to write a book together. I had traveled to Puerto Rico with her mother, and spent innumerable evenings with Aurea and her family in the Bronx, breaking bread, and keeping the faith.

That I was now beginning to work on getting her bother out of prison was as inevitable as my photograph in the family album.

> April 8th, 1975
> Greenhaven Correctional Facility
> Dear Ricardo:
>
> I was glad to hear you liked the article. Your opinions are always important to me. The people at the New York Times were going to send me a check, but I did not have a Social Security number! But I will soon have one. Can you imagine? After 31 years, now I have to get a Social Security card? I am slowly but surely being turned into a proletariat!
> As soon as I finish writing my clemency petition, I will send you the original and you can make copies for me. One you can send to the Clemency Board, and one to the Governor. You should also make additional copies because we will probably need these to show to other people as well.
> After receiving the information from the Times that they were going to pay me for the article, it started me thinking about the many articles Mrs. Davis wrote, and I wonder if she ever got any money for them! Well. that is water under the bridge, I guess.
> And don't forget to make extra copies of the Times article. We will need them to send to people as part of the clemency process.
> Take care.
>
> Tu Hermano/Amigo
> Salvador Agron   #16846

Riding back to Brooklyn later on that evening, I thought to myself that we'd already made a good start in securing Salvador's clemency. Salvador had been writing to people about his plans, and this along with the piece he had written for the Op-Ed section of the *New York Times*, was generating lots of support from interested outsiders.

We would meet again at Aurea's house in a month or so, and in the coming weeks I would keep in touch with her by telephone.

In the meantime, Genoveva would be organizing her political contacts in order to insure that Salvador had a broad base of support from lots of different groups. I was also planning to visit with Stella Davis.

For years her name had been interwoven with his, or at least this was the way it seemed whenever an article about him had appeared in the newspapers. He had mentioned her in the dedication to his book, yet whenever he'd mentioned her to me in his letters, what'd he said had been anything but positive.

All I really knew about her was that she had met Salvador shortly after he'd been arrested, and was being held for trial at the Brooklyn House of Detention. She was doing some kind of social work, and had set up a bi-lingual class designed to teach English and American culture to the Puerto Rican inmates. Salvador had joined the class, and gradually a relationship had grown. But this relationship, he said, had not been without its problems. Hers was a strong personality, and whenever he went counter to her wishes, there was conflict. Sometimes, he said, it felt like all she wanted to do was to run his life.

My gut instinct was that Stella Davis had been one of Salvador's earliest mentors, helping him to read, and then sending him letters of comfort in the death house, and later on when he was in the insane asylum at Dannemora. Everything had gone according to plan, or at least it had until he'd begun making decisions for himself.

She had recently written to both him and Ed Muller, the Protestant Chaplain at Greenhaven, and one of Salvador's other mentors, that the article in the *Times*, had been "aggressive and self-serving." Her letter to Salvador had ended with a reminder for him to "think back on the fifteen years and recall the many occasions when I was there for you...."

Now he wanted her support for his clemency, and also the return of all his writings. Early poems, death house correspondence, and letters from the bughouse; all of it, and he figured that if anyone could wean it away from her, it was me.

April 10th, 1975
Greenhaven Correctional Facility

Dear Richard:

Thank you for the comments about the petition. I will send this one to the Governor, and I will make a separate copy for Mrs. Davis. She would only try to discourage what I wrote in the original copy, so I will write up something more to her liking so that I can count on her support!

I received a dozen letters of support this morning, and later on today I'll send you their names and addresses, so you can send them each a card in my name, and will answer them as soon as I get the chance. I will need their support!

Today I got to see the photographs that I was not allowed to have, the ones you took of Wah-Zi-Nak in your apartment. Wow! Is she well put together! How you could take such photographs and keep your cool is very difficult for me to understand! If you did not get a hard on taking those photographs then you must be a fag! Poor little Richard, I bet you are blushing right this minute!

Have you heard from Wah-Zi-Nak? When you do, let her know how much I love her. I plan to marry her as soon as possible!

With love and understanding,

Salvador Agron   #16846

By the time we met again at Aurea's house in the early part of May to plan additional strategy, more and more people had joined our campaign.

As the result of the article in the *New York Times,* along with our petitions and Genoveva's speeches, hundreds of letters had been received. Some had been sent directly to Salvador at Greenhaven, some to the Governor and the Clemency board, and some to me at my postal box in Manhattan.

The letters from the politicians and other people of influence all seemed to sound the same. Carefully calibrated to show support, while maintaining a safe distance, they were professional and to the point. Predictable, and mostly void of emotion, they were worlds away from the letters sent by the everyday kinds of people from Manhattan to California, and back again.

"Dear Governor," wrote a single mother from a little town in Texas, "I ask you to release this man who has paid his debt to society so many times over and because you know deep down in your heart of hearts that this man has served his time. So please set this man free. You are the Governor, and you can do this. May god bless you and bring you health for just as long as you shall live."

A letter written by a woman in Manhattan, on what looked like a piece of wrapping paper, wrote of her connection to that faraway time in the playground.

> "Dear Governor," she wrote,"I was living with my five children in the Amsterdam housing projects when all that stuff went down in the playground, and I can still hear all the police sirens and the people yelling from that night. But I was thinking, Governor, that seeing as how all that stuff happened so long ago that maybe now it's time for everyone to just forgive and forget. So what about it, Governor, can you find it in your heart to let this guy go who has probably suffered enough already? Because if his mother is sill alive, think about what a smile she will have when you finally set him free."

Another letter, from a Catholic nun in Wisconsin, asked the Governor for his mercy, "I ask you in the name of Our Father to release this man, Salvador Agron, who has suffered enough, and I join with all my sisters in sending you our prayers in the hope that you will show him mercy."

Still another, and one which had somehow made its way to Aurea's house, had me laughing so hard when I read it that a piece of home-baked cookie she had prepared for our visit, had fallen out of my mouth.

> *"Dear Governor,"* it read, *"I can appreciate the fact that this letter will be read by one of your assistants, and in all probability your lawyer, and since I realize that he is probably as busy as a one-armed paper hanger, I will make this very brief.*
>
> *"Just remember one thing, Governor, one of your kids could have been with Salvador Agron in the playground that night! I mean, You never know, right? You said recently in the press that prisons don't correct! Governor, allow me to borrow a line here from a famous poem where the poet says, 'tis true, tis true.'*
>
> *"Well, Governor, as an Irishman, and an ex-policeman from New York City, I am convinced beyond any doubt that Sal Agron will be a useful member of society, so why don't you do the right thing here, and just let him go."*

Although Aurea still looked a bit tired, she was her usual gracious self when Genoveva and I came to visit. Offering us coffee, soda, and more of her home-baked cookies, she said there was something else she wanted us to see.

Reaching into a suitcase filled with Salvador's writing, Aurea took out a newspaper article that she had pasted to a piece of cardboard.

"Take a look at this," she said.

Written in 1969, it was a full-page article from the *New York Post* with the title, "The Capeman: from punk to poet via the death house," and had been written almost ten years to the day of Salvador's arrest for the killings in the playground. Aside from the text, there were two pictures, one of Salvador and one of Stella Davis. The one of Salvador was one I'd seen many times before. Originally taken on the night of his arrest by a photographer for the Associated Press, it was a stunning portrait of a handsome young man with curly brown hair gently sweeping his forehead, and eyes that expressed both innocence and world-weariness at the same time. The photograph of Stella Davis showed an older women with a very determined look on her face, and with her gray hair and double chin, she might have been someone's grandmother.

> 4/2/75
> Greenhaven Correctional Facility
> Dear Richard:
>
> My mail is piling up! Everyday there's more and more people writing to me!
> You should be hearing from Mrs. Davis pretty soon because I have already written to her several times about you. I wonder what you will think about her when you do finally get together. I gave her Rev. Muller's address and I told her that maybe the South 40 Corporation would pay for her trip. Who knows, right? Let's see what happens. By the way, please don't ever mention Wah-Zi-Nak to Mrs. Davis at no time, okay? This would only distract her from her real mission: clemency for me by utilizing her "respectable community support" from people in important places. She has connections all over the place, and her support is important. Also, a petition coming from her will be important because of how long she's known me. So let's bear with her, okay. And when you go there, remember to see if you can get my writings back!
> Take care, good brother.
>
> With love and understanding,
> Salvador Agron   #16846

Reading the text, I was impressed with how supportive the article was about Salvador's efforts to rehabilitate himself. Void of even the slightest hint of sensationalism, and with a definite feeling of compassion, the writer detailed Salvador's journey through New York's penal system from the time of his arrest. How he had learned to read and write while in prison, and how Stella Davis—who at the time was a youth worker with the Department of Corrections—had befriended him in 1959, when he was at the Brooklyn House of Detention.

"You think she's gonna do something to help my brother?"

"Well, from the article here it looks like she and him go way back."

"Yeah, but what I never liked about her was that she was always trying to control my brother...like she always knew what was best for him and me and my moms, we didn't know nothing."

The article went on to say that Stella Davis had founded a group called the Puerto Rican Board of Guardians, and was now its acting Executive Director.

Salvador had mentioned her group, the Puerto Rican Board of Guardians, a few months ago. Thinking they would be an obvious source of support, I'd tried contacting them, but no one had known who they were. They didn't have a listing in the telephone book, and no one could even tell us whether or not they had even existed. Genoveva said there had been a similar group, but it was more like a kind of traveller's aid association designed to assist people from Puerto Rico who were stranded in New York City without any money.

"You know anything about them?" I asked Aurea.

"I don't remember, but like what was they supposed to be doing?"

"Salvador said maybe they were set up to help Puerto Ricans or something, but when I tried to find out about them, there was nothing."

"And Stella Davis was supposed to be the leader or something?" Aurea said.

"That's what it says in the article here."

"I don't know nothing about that, but I do know that lotsa times she used to ask me and my moms for money because she said she needed it to help my brother."

"What did she say she wanted it for?" Genoveva said.

"I don't know, but like for trips to Puerto Rico to get support for my brother or to travel up to one of the prisons for some hearing about my brother...all kinds of stuff...and she used to ask me lotsa times but after a while it started bothering me because I didn't have no money and when my moms used to give it to her it was from the money she made from washing people's floors..."

"Washing people's floors?"

"Yeah... my moms does all kinds of cleaning and washing for other people...and she works really hard for the money."

To Mrs. Stella Davis
115 Henry Street
Brooklyn, New York

Dear Mrs. Davis:

Enclosed herewith you will find a form letter which I have sent to many people so that they may write on my behalf. The results have been beautiful! Mr. Oliver Tweedy already has made it known to people who have written to him and the governor that he "will be more than glad to have Mr. Agron put in for clemency this year." Even Governor Hugh Carey himself has already seen the petition (and I have not actually submitted it yet), so that everything is working out wonderful.

Now the enclosed petition is what I will be submitting in the month of May 1st, 1975. One copy will go before Governor Carey and the other will go before Mr. Oliver Tweedy.

My friend, Jacoby, should have contacted you about getting together to discuss my case. He is a good man, and has done much for me in many areas.

I am sending this to you so you can get an idea of what I have done for myself so far. If you should put anything before the governor, which I hope you do, I would like a copy of such a petition. You know much of what I have been though all these years, and you have stuck with me through thick and thin and have helped me greatly—to you—I owe my life and my positive thinking that I have acquired in my pursuit of a higher education. In guidance you have done your best considering the circumstances in which I always strove like a man and in which I will continue to strive in order to perfect my humanism for all people, and with non-violence to struggle for the dignity of all human beings.

My rehabilitation is complete, in the sense that it may be possible under the penal system. However, I have gone beyond mere rehabilitation. I have gone through a process of dehumanization, which is a concept that has helped me counteract the surrounding dehumanization of every day life.

I am sincere in my endeavor to help myself and to respect democratic rights. Today I have a profound reverence for life in all human beings, and to you sweet lady, I owe much of my positive outlook on life.

Thank you from the very center of my humane heart

Salvador Agron   #16846

As Salvador had predicted, about two weeks after my visit with Aurea, a letter arrived from Stella Davis.

Written on a piece of stationery with the logo of a group calling themselves the "Youth Guidance Bilingual Center," and which listed her name as being the "Executive Director," it was a rambling letter, and I knew right away that my involvement with Salvador had apparently struck a raw nerve.

She wrote of her trips to Puerto Rico in Salvador's behalf, and the many hearings throughout New York's penal system she had attended over the years to show her support for

Salvador. She wrote of the positive effect this had on the officials who, she wrote, would have abused Salvador had she not been there as a visible presence on his behalf.

Yet despite her continued support, she wrote, and despite all the miles she had traveled on his behalf, Salvador apparently thought nothing of undermining her efforts with a steady barrage of letters and articles to various newspapers and magazines throughout the country. He thought nothing, she wrote, of writing to radical groups, without ever giving even a passing thought to the effect this might have later on when he applied for clemency.

Many of the groups he wrote to were radical groups who advocated the violent overthrow of America. Was I sympathetic to this philosophy? Where had I met Salvador, and what did I want from him?

Salvador's letter to the *New York Times* was a disappointment, she wrote, and given the damage it had done, she was at a loss as to how she would support him in the future. The letter ended with an invitation for me to call her at my earliest convenience in order to discuss strategy.

When I called Aurea to ask her about the name of the group on the stationery, she said she'd never heard of it, but that maybe it was something Mrs. Davis didn't want her to know nothing about.

"She's always been very secretive whenever she calls us about my brother...like she don't want us to know too much or something."

> *While in the Brooklyn House of Detention, in 1959, awaiting trial, I started reading an old law book that I found in one of the cells. I used to read it very poorly and I carried it under my arm everywhere I went, but I could not comprehend one word of it.*
>
> *The book was a strange English language, but I wanted desperately to appear rational and intelligent and this was my shield or protection. When I tried to give advice from it the*

guards would see me talking with the other inmates about their cases and they would get angry at me.

I began to understand the power of books by the reaction I was receiving from the correctional officers and I began to understand that they were afraid of knowledge in inmates and would try their best to suppress whatever learning they came across.

Many times I was forced to leave the book in my cell by the guards who thought that I was trying to give free legal advice. However, they did not know that I could not read this book that they were so angry about.

While in the Brooklyn House of Detention, there was this old lady. Her name was Mrs. Stella Davis. She was a social worker, who was teaching classes to the Spanish-speaking inmates. She was using something she called, "A New Approach to Youth Guidance," and she called the class a "bi-lingual course in positive thinking." She used to teach in the dayroom from 1:00 P.M. to 3:00 P.M. while the other inmates were in their cells.

This was a golden opportunity for me because it allowed me to be out of my cell from 1:00 P.M. to 3:00 P.M. while the other inmates had to stay in their cells until lockout time. Inmates ate from 11:00 A.M. to 12:00 P.M., and by 1:00 they were all locked in their cells. However, this little group on the fifth floor had managed to get together in a class under Mrs. Davis for studies. Other inmates (both Black and White) were jealous of this fact and thought of Mrs. Davis as a "little jew bastard" who they said treated Latinos better than blacks and whites. They thought of her as racist and that she was giving preferential treatment to Puerto Ricans. I understood the situation but since I was Puerto Rican, and I knew that the other Puerto Ricans in the jail respected her, I always took her side as well.

There was some talk from the blacks of disrupting her classes, but fear of the Puerto Ricans kept them from carrying out those plans. The Brooklyn House of Detention held many people waiting for trial, and there were many leaders of teen-aged gangs from all over New York City:,

We had all kinds of inmates, but it was mostly Puerto

Ricans who took classes with Mrs. Davis. Some of the guards liked her classes, but most of them didn't because they said we weren't worthy of an education. and that it was a waste of time to be teaching spics how to read and write. I finally decided to join the class with the idea that maybe I could finally learn how to read.

When I walked into the classroom with my law book under my hand, Mrs. Davis made a comment about "The Philadelphia lawyer" having "joined us." I did not know what a "philadelphia lawyer" was so I took it as a compliment.

When I was in the class, I began to study. She would put a word on the board, and I would copy it down. Most of the time they were words like, "good/bad," "ugly," or "beautiful," then we would discuss each word. After awhile I lost the need to disrupt the class because I liked learning about things from her. Mrs. Davis would really praise us Puerto Ricans as being different from "Blacks" in that we had a cultural background that went back to the values of Spain but that the Blacks were unruly and did not have any culture. I detected a racist overtone in her manner of teaching but I kept my mouth shut.

One day when Mrs. Davis was making what I felt were racist statements about blacks, I stopped her by saying, "Mrs. Davis, from what I've read, it seems that Spanish culture is as black as Africa—I read that the Moors built Spain."

Evading my statement, she turned to the other students. "You see," she said, "Salvador reads one book which is full of negative information and thinks he knows all the answers!"

She wanted us to think of ourselves as being better than the blacks. I smiled at her racism but could not oppose it because in that classroom she was the supreme authority and the Puerto Ricans were happy about her praises.

Later on in life, and during my many years of prison, I met many ex-classmates who still believed that as Puerto Ricans they were better than blacks, and they told me so.

It was at about this time that I started to take an interest in learning about things. I began to study the dictionary and very slowly, I learned how to read other books. I was learning on my own, and also by listening to what Mrs. Davis had to teach, but I was trying my best to stay free of her influence.

However, with her positive approach to life she was able to influence me. One book that I can distinctly remember reading while under her influence at the Brooklyn House of Detention was: "Houdini," and I remember this because not long before I had seen the movie with Tony Curtis at the Brooklyn Paramount Theater on DeKalb Avenue in downtown Brooklyn.

One day a black guard opened the cells a little earlier than usual and let all the inmates into the dayroom while our class was going on, and we knew he was doing this in order to disrupt our class. The Puerto Ricans in the class became angry and a fight was about to break out between the blacks and the Puerto Ricans. The black kids that came into our class started making remarks about "Now we can get some jewish pussy," and "Let's fuck this old hag," She likes "PuertoRican cock," and other such remarks. Being that a situation was beginning to build up, I got up and told the Puerto Ricans to "be cool" and draw a circle around Mrs. Davis. I also told them to take a defensive stance in this situation and not to fight unless it became a necessity.

I also spoke to the blacks and tried to tell them to "cool it" and they listened to me because I had been brought up with many of them on the streets. Some I even knew from the gangs, and I had a reputation from my past experiences. The situation was tense, but I was able to avoid an open fight between the groups while Mrs. Davis was present. After awhile the officer on duty opened the door to let Mrs. Davis out without her getting hurt.

Mrs. Davis was very passionate back then, and really believed in what she was doing. When this happened, she stomped out of the room, and got into a big argument with the Black guard who she knew had been responsible for what had just happened.

When I did show up again in her class, I was praised for handling the tense situation with "cool" and in a positive manner. I modestly told the class that I did it more out of self-preservation than out of a positive outlook. But, Mrs. Davis insisted that it was done due to her programs and positive influences to students in the course.

Despite what I always thought was her racism, I learned

alot from Mrs. Davis. I must admit she did help me get an interest in learning,
  This experience with the guards and Mrs. Davis would follow me through all my years of incarceration.

6/7/75
Greenhaven Correctional Facility

Dear Ricardo:

  It was very interesting to get your views on Mrs. Davis. I knew that she would readily reveal herself to you in ways she might not do with other people. And I think that you are correct when you say it is good to have some compassion for her because of how much she did for me over the years. Still, I would like to get my writings back from her as soon as possible. In the meantime, she can help with the clemency!
  It makes me feel good to have such an alliance with you and your true brotherhood—to me this is a great experience. You are lovely people. My main amigo, my best friend.
  Your letter was good, I liked it very much.

   Your flesh and blood brother,

   Salvador Agron
   #16846

Through the summer, and into early fall, we worked on Salvador's clemency.

We spoke to people, wrote letters, and sent in reams of signatures to the Clemency Bureau from concerned citizens seeking Salvador's release. Slowly, everything seemed to be falling into place, and by mid-November, we knew that a decision wasn't far away.

11/6/75
Greenhaven Correctional Facility

Dear Little Richard:

Well, everything seems to be set for the clemency.
My typewriter finally gave out! Please let me know when you will be up here with another one, and I'll have this one ready for you to take home.
Did you go through the papers I had at Aurea's house? Well, with those papers you will find some poems, along with an earlier version of my autobiography. Maybe I can use some of the stuff I hooked up with back then. Make sure you keep all that stuff for me in a safe place.
I'm looking forward to seeing you at one of the cadre meetings. I think you'll really dig Rev. Muller. He is a real person, and not like most of the people you will find who work in these places.
I didn't know you had a jeep? When did you get it? What color is it?

Well, amigo and hermano,
Take care,
Salvador Agron   #16846

Before leaving Brooklyn in September of 1971 to live on a commune in New Hampshire, my ex-wife and I used some of our savings to buy a medium-sized jeep. Red, with plenty of room inside for everything from baggage to firewood, the jeep had come with oversized tires and a four-wheel drive.

Christened "Frederick" by my wife, it had taken us up and down the snowy roads of New Hampshire right up until a few days before Thanksgiving when my wife had left the commune for a life of her own in Manhattan. Following her a month later, I had rented my apartment in Brooklyn. We had divided up our few possessions, and a year later our divorce was finalized.

11/5/75
Greenhaven Correctional Facility
Dear Richard:

    Well, I guess I already told you that Congressman Herman Badillo wrote on my behalf to the Clemency Board. I also had a nice conversation with Wah-Zi-Nak the other night.
    I haven't heard from Mrs. Davis for awhile, but I did write her a letter just this evening. I told her to give my writings either to my sister Aurea or to you. So let's see what happens.
    When you asked me for my feelings about Mrs. Davis, I found myself wanting to understand her in the same way you do, with some kind of compassion (and I think I have this, too) but I also know that the medium by which she would want to see me free would be only for her benefit. People such as her I cannot trust because they do things with too many ulterior motives. I will just have to forget her and let her go her own way. She wants to be a mother to me and she doesn't even know about it! These are lost souls. She was lost in the past and she will be lost in the future!
    Take care of yourself, amigo.

    Tu Hermano,
    Salvador Agron   #16846

    A classically-trained pianist, my wife had kept our Steinway piano, and I had kept the jeep. But except for special occasions, I rarely moved it from its parking spot in a friend's garage, not far from my apartment in Brighton Beach.
    It was a little past four-thirty as I crossed the George Washington Bridge, and I figured that by the time I reached the prison it would be completely dark. Just as long as it didn't snow, I thought to myself, everything would be fine. The cadre meeting started at six o'clock and ended at nine. Ed said he would meet me in the lobby of the prison at about five-thirty. This way we could have a few minutes to talk before the meeting started.

11/7/75
Greenhaven Correctional Facility

Dear Richard:

In case you're wondering what I'm planning to do when I leave this dungeon, I thought I should run it down for you.

I have already been offered a sort of support when I get out, a job in Maryland, dealing with community and prisoners. However, I will not take that. I have other plans which I do not like to talk about. I have to start correcting things where the problems in my life began a long time ago.

In Puerto Rico, I want to set up a program similar to the cadre meetings here at Greenhaven at the poorhouse in Mayaguez, and also one at the reform school that I was in down there, La Escuela de Correctional. Then I will come back to the United States and do something here.

Senator Garcia has promised to write on my behalf. I sent him a copy of the Times article plus one of the leaflets you and Genoveva wrote for me. Jose Torres is another person who might be helping me out, but I haven't heard back from him yet.

Another thing I will do when I get out of here is to marry Wah-Zi-Nak!!

Your amigo/hermano in all good and profane things,
Salvador Agron   #16846

Riding through the darkening night of late November, I thought about Salvador's clemency. If his petition were denied, it would not be from a lack of effort. All of us had done as much as we could, and now it was simply a matter of waiting until the decision was handed down.

After my visit with Stella Davis in early June, I'd spent the last several months working with Genoveva and Aurea putting together the final touches of what we felt was a convincing campaign to secure Salvador's release. Soon, I thought, Salvador would be walking the streets of New York City as a free man.

My only reservation was something I'd detected in Salvador's attitude about the families of the victims. Even after all this time he still seemed unable to fully grasp the loss they had suffered, and that under no circumstances should he ever contact them with the intention of saying he was sorry for what had happened to their sons. Coming from him, he said, it would not only be ill-received, but if the newspapers were ever to get wind of it, the repercussions could easily prove disastrous in terms of whether or not he would be granted his clemency

Although I knew little about the mechanics of clemency, or even what the Clemency Board would consider to be a "good risk" as opposed to a "bad risk," my intuition kept whispering to me that to unlock the lock, Salvador would have to appear as contrite.

Nothing would disturb the keepers of the lock more than a lapse in memory, and an arrogant attitude.

On the one hand, a convict up for parole or clemency could be forgiven should he forget the date of his crime, what the weather had been like, or even the specifics of a well-rehearsed speech made over and over again to his homeboys back in the cellhouse about what he would, or would not do, should he be released again to the streets. But what he could not forget, and what would not be forgiven, was a forgetfulness about the victims: who they were, why they had been attacked, and how terrible a loss this was to their families.

This kind of attitude would have been applauded as much as a bag of kittens thrown in the sea.

State of New York-Department of Correctional Services
Executive Clemency Applicant
Greenhaven Correctional Facility

Salvador Agron   **#16846**

Agron states that the victims in the playground in 1959 were not gang members and the instant offense was therefore more of a spontaneous explosion of emotions and feelings which prevailed at the time and not a planned attack. It appears that the instant offense was a manifestation of the frustration which they harbored since the opposing gang apparently did not show.

The instant offense in this writer's opinion appears to be similar to a pack of starving dogs attacking innocent children.

As I got further away from New York City, and the night got darker, I thought about Salvador, and the journey we'd been on together for the past several years.

Given the awfulness of what he had already written to me about his life, his ability to hold on to his humanity was nothing short of astonishing. Not only did his sensitivity seem to be intact, but he had a way of expressing himself which allowed the reader to feel whatever it was he was feeling. Clear and precise, his language was what another professor of mine had described as "coming from beyond the grave." Writing as if he didn't care what anyone thought of what he was saying, his work was lean and unpretentious. He wrote, he said, what he felt was the truth, and did this even though his words would often reveal much more than what he might have intended in the first place.

His soul was intact, or at least this is what I felt whenever I read his writing. But this same professor said that all of this was bullshit. That convicts like Salvador only appeared to be strong because years of living in a dehumanized environment had taught them certain survival skills, but that these skills could only be used within that environment. Salvador, he said, had been "state-raised." More than anywhere else, prison was the only home he had ever known. Without its relatively safe structure of rules and monotony, Salvador would fall apart. The very mechanics of prison that had conspired to slowly break his spirit would, my professor said, be the oxygen without which he could not live.

"Just wait" my professor said, "until he's back on the streets and you'll see what I'm talking about."

> Agron states that if he is granted parole he intends to move back to Puerto Rico with his mother. Agron states that he hopes to marry an Indian, whose name is Joyce (her Indian name is Wah-Zi-Nak Qualt). According to Agron, she lives in British Columbia, Canada, is a divorcee with two children and her parents as well as his are aware of their decision to get married and allegedly do not oppose a marriage. Agron states that he wanted to be married here at Greenhaven. However, his request was denied by the Superintendent with the statement that "under Section 79-A of the New York Civil Rights Law, a person serving a life sentence is ineligible to marry while in prison."

Whether or not this was true was hard to say. On the one hand, given his years of confinement, the chances were great that he would find it nearly impossible to make the transition from prison to street, and would in time make his way back through the revolving door known as recidivism. On the other hand, not only had he taken advantage of virtually every educational program that the prison could offer, but he also had a vast network of mentors and friends who would supply whatever support was needed.

From the poorhouse to the death house, Salvador had known many mentors.

Some had given him books to read, while others had taught him the words of Jesus, but no one, he said, had given him more than the Reverend Ed Muller.

He was a Protestant minister who had given up what had probably been a comfortable life ministering to a group of community churches in New Jersey before finally deciding that his true calling was to address the needs of New York State's large prison population. An internship on Riker's Island, or "the rock" as it was called by the convicts, was what, Salvador said, had convinced Reverend Ed that this was his chosen work.

By the time I reached the small village of Stormville, several miles from Greenhaven, it was just a little after five, and a light snow had begun to fall. A few minutes later and off in the distance were the high walls of Greenhaven. In the darkness, the prison appeared as a gothic castle, and the closer I got the more foreboding it looked.

Visiting the prison during the day was one thing, but at night it was something else entirely. Daytime visits meant people coming and going. A bus from New York City filled with women and small children. Shopping bags filled with food, warmth, and love implied. Perfumed women, holding hands, kisses, and hugs. Wives, girlfriends, and children. But at night: nothing. Salvador said there would be others joining me at the cadre meeting. Interested outsiders, he said, from various religious and social groups whose mission it was to reach out to prisoners. But when I got out of my car in the parking lot, I was all alone, and the only sound was that of the snow from past storms crunching beneath my feet.

> During the interview Agron was cooperative, He stated that he was looking forward to be released from prison. Agron states that if he is granted Executive Clemency he prefers to be released to Puerto Rico since he does not want any publicity because of the notoriety of his case. He states that his mother would move to Puerto Rico with him and that she would also give him a home and help him to find a job. He states that a social worker, Mrs. Davis, who has been with him for many years would also help him in this area. He states that there are also some politicians who would like to help him, but that he prefers to set up his own program since he again does not wish to have any publicity.

Just as I was about to open the door of the prison, the silence was broken by a booming voice from behind me.

"Richard, is that you?"

Turning around I could just about make out a large man standing maybe forty feet from where I was, and as he came closer, I could see that he was wearing a full beard.

"Yeah, and are you Reverend Muller?"

"That's right, and I'm glad to meet you," he said, with a broad smile, "Salvador's told me lots about you."

"How'd you know it was me?" I wanted to know.

"Because the other people who were going to come up canceled out when they heard it was gonna be snowing, so it hadda be you."

"So no one else'll be coming tonight?"

"Not unless they show up later on, but I kinda doubt it because I would've heard something by now."

After the dark night of the parking lot, the relatively bright interior of the prison made the illusion of entering a forbidding castle all the more real.

"More like a tomb," Ed said, as we walked together down a long and dimly lit corridor to where the cadre meeting would be taking place.

"Ever been in here before?" he asked.

"Just in the visiting room upstairs..."

Our escort was a youngish looking guard, who with his surly look, seemed anything but happy with his assignment, and I wondered if he was one of those guards who Salvador said had nothing but hatred for Ed because of all the innovations he had been slowly introducing over the years. Ed was the Executive Director of the South Forty Corporation, a non-profit organization founded in 1967 to sponsor projects offering opportunities to convicts seeking to improve themselves.

In the beginning, it had directed its efforts primarily to those already incarcerated, but gradually it had evolved into something larger, and far more ambitious: to provide a network of programs in and out of the prison, all designed to reduce the high rate of recidivism among felony offenders.

Instead of being caught in the revolving door of street to prison, and back again, Ed was trying to empower the inmates with the tools they would need to keep them from ever having to return to prison. Funded by the South Forty Corporation, the Greenhaven College Program provided inmates like Salvador with access to college courses.

"Lottsa these guards hate Ed," Salvador said, "because he's the guy responsible for niggers and spics getting college degrees."

With his broad shoulders, full beard, and booming voice, Ed reminded me of a cross between a fullback with the Green Bay Packers and a biblical prophet. When Salvador told me about Ed, I had been skeptical. How could a man of the cloth be, as Salvador had put it, "a man of vision"? Aside from receiving his check from the State of New York for his official duties as the Protestant chaplain, wasn't his the very religion that Salvador had abandoned not long after leaving the death house at Sing Sing? So how was it that he could embrace this man?

Walking down the corridor, passing several checkpoints manned by still other guards, we stopped suddenly in front of a door with "D Block" written beneath a small rectangular window,

"Ever seen a cellblock?" he said.

"No...in the movies, but not up close or anything."

"Then take a look."

Looking at the guard, and seeing that he could care less if I looked or not, I moved up close to the window and looked inside. But in the dim light of the cellhouse, I couldn't see very much. Just rows and rows of cells on one side, and large opaque windows on the other side. Radiators lined the walls beneath the windows, and Salvador said that in the wintertime things could get really bad because if the heat was turned up too much, and you were on the top tier, you'd feel like you were suffocating because of how warm it could get with all the heat rising and everything. If the windows were open, and you were on the bottom tier, you could freeze to death. In the box, he said, there sometimes wasn't any heat at all.

Joining Ed, we continued walking together down the long corridor.

"When did you meet Salvador?" I asked him.

"About three years ago...that's when he came down from Dannemora."

"And he got involved with South Forty right away?"

"No...that took awhile...first he had to trust me...and that didn't really start happening until he started coming to the Cadre meetings."

"And the first time you met him was in here?"

"He'd just come in on a draft..."

"What's a draft?"

"That's when prisoners are transferred from one prison to another, they call it a draft, but I think Salvador was a one-man draft when he came here...he was all by himself...and when he sat down in my office he started asking me about the cadre meetings but I could tell he was checking me out..."

"Because you were a minister?"

"That too, but more because I was part of the system and I think he was trying to figure out which side I was on."

When I asked Ed what his first impression had been, he said that at first he hadn't realized Salvador was the Capeman because he'd been too distracted by the two shopping bags Salvador had carried with him into Ed's office.

"At first I thought they were filled with his clothes from whatever prison he'd come from, but when I asked him what was in the bags, he said his whole life was in the bags."

His whole life, Ed said, turned out to be every bit and piece of writing that he'd written since he'd entered the system when he was sixteen in 1959. Ed said he remembered thinking how extraordinarily painful Salvador's life must have been for him to have felt such a compulsion to "get it all down." But what was even more astonishing was that despite the ragged route he had been forced to take from prison to prison, he nonetheless had somehow managed to hold on to all the material.

Two shopping bags overflowing with bits and pieces of yellowed paper. Some still rain- or snow-stained from one or more prison yards, or speckled with dirt from months and years under one of many prison cots. Some he had given to Aurea, and she had stored them away in a suitcase in her closet. And some he had been sending to me in large envelopes over the last several months, until my roll-top desk was covered with so many bits and pieces of yellowed paper that it looked as if it had been dragged though a parade of confetti.

> Interviewed in the home on 11/75, the inmate's mother, Esmeralda Rodriguez Agron, stated that she would be most happy to provide a home for the inmate. The thought that there is a possibility that the inmate could be coming home after 15 years of incarceration has left her in a rather excitable state of ecstasy. She was therefore warned by this writer that there could be disappointment. She said she understood this.

"This is it," Ed said, as he opened the door of a room near the end of the corridor.

Inside was a windowless room, brightly lit, with a large table, and a blackboard right in front. Eight men, all convicts, and all wearing identical state-issued green pants, were sitting around the table. Some had notebooks in front of them, some had loose-leaf paper, and some had nothing. Seeing a few snowflakes on my coat, one of the men, a large black man with a scar running from the corner of his right eye all the way down to his mouth, wanted to know if it was snowing outside.

"It wasn't snowing too hard when I left New York but when I got up here it really started coming down." I told the guy in a loud enough voice so that everyone in the room could hear.

"You from New York?"

"Yeah...I'm from Brooklyn."

"Like what part you from?"

"Coney Island...you know it?"

"Shit, yes, I know it, but I'm from the other side...like over near Prospect Park, near Bed-Sty... but we're close enough that we could be neighbors."

His name was Robert Harrison, and no sooner had we shaken hands, when someone else came up and introduced himself. One by one, I met all the men in the room, and except for Salvador, and one very young looking white guy, all the men were black.

Looking at the faces as I took a seat next to Salvador, I wondered what had brought each of them to prison. Salvador said that all the cadre members were men serving long sentences. Several had even been on Greenhaven's death row just a few years ago, before a moratorium had been placed on the death penalty in New York State, and their sentences had been commuted to life. What a challenge this must be for Ed Muller. Aside from the antipathy most convicts had about organized religion, the fact that he was a white man leading a group consisting primarily of Black and Hispanic men surely hadn't make his journey any easier. Salvador had already told me that there were several guards who resented Ed's efforts to provide murderers and rapists with college degrees.

> The home of Esmeralda Rodriguez Agron is in the Bronx. It is an adequate three (3) room apartment that was neat and clean. The inmate's mother is the only occupant of the home.
>
> The inmate will utilize either the bedroom or, in the living room, there is a Castro Convertible, which she said he is free to sleep on.

When Ed closed the door, the room became quiet. I thought the guard would be sitting in the room with us, but instead he had stayed outside. Later Ed would tell me that the guard usually used this time to have coffee with some of the other correctional officers in a nearby messhall.

Each week Ed brought a different topic to discuss with the group. This week it was a piece he had written called, "Bondage and the Wilderness."

Each meeting began with an Opening Rite, and later, at the end of the meeting, a Closing Rite. As the leader, Ed began, and the men, who composed the cadre group, followed in unionism.

Leader: "Let us come to terms with life."
Group: "Our life is in the human struggle. The struggle is painful and deep. The struggle holds death and life."
Leader: "Out of the struggle of the now, we will create the human world of the future."
Group: "The past is approved. The present is received. The future is open."

When the group finished the words of the Opening Rite, Ed passed around the evening's study paper.

I could see right away that the paper was a strong attempt to use the lessons of scripture in such a way as to make them relevant to the men in the cadre group. Using the concept of the "wilderness" as an analogy to the environment of the prison, Ed led the men in a wide-ranging discussion designed to encourage them to a closer look at the tools they were using to navigate from the wilderness to the promised land. As the discussion weaved through the remaining hours of the meeting, it became more and more clear to me the enormous amount of work involved when you tried to change another person's consciousness, and how terribly important it was for the men of the cadre to have a man like Ed Muller as their collective mentor.

Of the dozens of men and women who had taken part in my study of expanded consciousness, there were only two or three that I could safely say had transcended the experience of being near death for a considerable length of time, and then had come away with a strong enough vision of self that it could sustain them if and when the threat of death was ever removed.

Salvador had been one of them, and as I sat with him in that brightly-lit prison room in the middle of deep winter, I knew what they all shared in common. Just like Salvador, each had known one or more teachers who had guided them through the wilderness. Some had come, stayed awhile, shared their wisdom, and then were gone. Others, like Ed, were still in his life, and what made this all the more remarkable was that Ed was not only Salvador's mentor, but was also mentor to scores of others who were also trying to navigate through the wilderness.

Ed was offering hope to a group of people long considered hopeless by the rest of society, but by doing so he was working against a philosophy that offered but a slim chance for redemption. After Attica, there had been a renewed interest in rehabilitation, but as more and more of the same convicts kept passing back and forth thorough the revolving door of prison to the street, and back again, this new interest had begun to wane. Sensing this change from having witnessed similar movements in the past, Ed could see that unless the men in the cadre group were honestly willing to change their behavior patterns, they were doomed to return to prison almost as soon as they were released.

Listening to their stories as the night moved on, I realized that for the majority of these men, the "promised land" meant being released from prison, or what Ed referred to as their "wilderness," to what they considered to be their own promised land: their neighborhoods, their barrios, their streets.

Looking around the table, what I saw was a thousand years waiting to be served. An eternity of time with nowhere to go but back to one of the cellblocks that I had seen on my way to the meeting earlier in the evening.

Salvador was one of these men, and as they discussed their wanderings, I suddenly had this picture in my mind of all them later on that night, back in their tiny cells, walking, praying, sleeping, or whatever, without a clue as to the immensity of life beyond the wall of the prison. They had forgotten so many things: from opening a can of peas to knowing how to order food in a restaurant.

If Salvador shared one common thread with all the men in the cadre, it was a basic truth I had learned about men who'd lived for too many years in cages. All shared a naive and child-like expectation that everything they had done in the past was dead and gone, and that as soon as the prison door opened, they could just bury it all behind them and become brand new people.

Bondage and the Wilderness

By Edwin Muller

To live in a state of bondage is to live in captivity in a way that one's personal freedom is severely limited. To stay in such a state a person has no freedom at all would be to deny the freedom of the human spirit itself. However, in a state of bondage the spirit is devastated and subjected to severe pain. In bondage, the major concern is with the oppressor, or, whatever else which sets the limits to our existence.

To live in the wilderness is different. Here there may be no oppressor, gun, or whip. The crisis of existence in the wilderness is that one finds life without apparent direction or meaning. Meaning is not to be found in the wilderness itself, rather, in the decisions one makes while there. In this sense, we need to understand that the wilderness is not geographical or physical, rather, a matter of the spirit. In this context then, one becomes a wanderer or a person on an intentional journey. The person who adopts a lifestyle of intention will probably not stay long in the wilderness. His or her sense of purpose or meaning will carry them through to new possibilities.

The wanderer may wander out by accident, or, may even wish after a period of time, to return to some form of well-defined bondage which from the wilderness can sometimes appear attractive.

For most people, the wilderness is the place of greatest danger. This is true because it is usually the place where most of us end up in our fight from pain and struggle. In our escape from what we think might put us in bondage, we are ready to face the great demands that confront us in the wilderness. The demand is for invention and not reaction or rebellion. There are no familiar roads in the wilderness; therefore, new paths must be created and a new sense of authenticity must be established. This is the challenge we face today and the one to which we must respond.

At a few minutes before nine, the youngish looking guard stuck his head in the door. Nodding to Ed before leaving the room again, we all knew this meant that the meeting was about to end. Thanking everyone for a good discussion, Ed led us in the Closing Rite.

Leader: "We stand before the up-againstness in life."
Group: "We stand before the possibility and hope in life."
Leader: "Our hope is in our decision to embrace all that is, as that out of which our life will come."
Group: "We decide if death is life, and if life is death. We will create a human world, by deciding to live the life we have, for the sake of humanity."

Having managed to somehow finagle a pass to walk with us, Salvador was on my right as we followed the guard down the long, dark corridor to the front gate.

Salvador said he could walk with us to the last gate, but then he'd have to go back to his cell on D-Block. On and on we walked, making small talk, and laughing, until just as we were about to say our good-byes at the last gate, Salvador pointed to a small open window set high on the wall. Although the glass was opaque, the window was opened enough to let in a small peek of the world.

"What's that stuff coming in there," Salvador said, as he pointed to something floating through the window to the floor of the jailhouse corridor.

Looking closely at what he was pointing to, I asked him what he thought it was.

"I don't know...is it dust? It looks like some kinda white dust from somewheres."

"That's snow, man...lotsa snow."

"You're fucking with me, right? That's really snow?"

When the last door closed behind us, and Ed and I were less then fifty feet down the corridor, Ed pulled gently on my sleeve. Whispering so close to my face that I could easily smell his breath, he said for me to stop and turn around. Turning around, and looking back through the sea of bars, there was Salvador, oblivious to everything except the snow that was rushing through the widow from the wilderness of the world outside.

The snow was thick and white, and Salvador was laughing as it swept across his face, his hair, and his heart.

Excellency Hugh Carey
Governor of the State of New York
Executive Chamber
Capitol Building
Albany, New York

Excellency, sir:

Enclosed here with you will find my petition for Executive Clemency, and attached to this letter you will find an article or letter which I had published in the New York Times. *The letter is to introduce you to my efforts in my pursuit to better understand myself and my rehabilitation.*

I implore you to please give this your careful attention and that you give me some of your precious time by reading my petition so that you may derive the best understanding of my incarceration, my youth, and my case.

A copy of my petition has been sent to Mr. Oliver Tweedy of the Executive Clemency Bureau, and all concerned people have also been informed.

I think that my experience can be a worthwhile contribution to society, and my intention is to become involved with youth problems if I am granted my clemency appeal. I want to help our youths before they fall into the same trial and tribulation that I have gone through. But I need my freedom in order to do this. I am aware that you understand youth problems better than any previous governor, and you are aware that with proper guidance and direction many youngsters can be helped long before it is too late. I wish to be part of that force that will go into helping our upcoming generation.

My father is getting old and so is my mother, and it would be my wish to look out for them in their elderly days and provide for them what they may need during the last days of their lives. Though they live separately, life is very difficult for them, and I would like to be around to make sure that they do not suffer any more than is necessary. I have made them both suffer enough as it is, and I am sure that I also have suffered enough and deserve some consideration.

If you should want any further information please let me know and I will be more than glad to provide you with whatever you want. I believe I have learned a great lesson and today I am a better man for it.

I hope you can share my belief.

I remain at your service,
Salvador Agron
Greenhaven Correctional Facility
#16846
Drawer B
Stormville, New York

Although everyone had agreed to meet at Aurea's house on Christmas Eve to hear from Albany if Salvador would be coming home after the new year, there was no way I could do this without hurting Jennifer's feelings.

Trying to balance a part-time job with my graduate work had already led to considerable strains in our relationship. Not only had we spent little time with one another during the past year, but when we actually did get together, I was usually too stressed out to give what she said was an "honest contribution" to the relationship. Salvador's clemency campaign had brought increasing strains. Meetings and letter writing meant that my own freedom was limited, and it was a rare night when I found myself with some free time, let alone enough for an evening to spend with my girlfriend.

My relationship with Wah-Zi-Nak had complicated matters even further. No matter how many times I tried to explain that she and I were nothing more than close friends she still believed that Wah-Zi-Nak had been my lover when she'd stayed with me in New York. Reassurances that absolutely nothing happened after I'd taken nude photographs of her in my apartment, had fallen on deaf ears.

Before Aurea had asked me to join the family on Christmas Eve, I'd already made plans to spend the evening with Jennifer at my house in Brooklyn. We were going to cook together, watch some television, and if it wasn't too cold, take a walk on the beach in the moonlight. Christmas morning would find us sipping strong coffee as we opened our presents.

A compromise had been reached when I'd agreed to spend the night with Jennifer after she'd agreed to let me spend the earlier part of the evening with the Agrons in the Bronx so that we could be together when a decision about Salvador was announced.

"Just as long as you're back so that we can wake up together tomorrow morning, that's all I care about," Jennifer said.

> *The petitioner is now before your excellency, Hugh Carey, the Governor of the State of New York.*
>
> *I will humbly give a view into my life, past and present, to demonstrate that I am one of the unfortunate victims of this wretched earth, but on which there is still some form of light as a form of hope.*

Convicts at Greenhaven were allowed one telephone call a month to a pre-approved recipient, and of course the call had to be collect. Most of the time it was limited to ten minutes, but like so many other rules, this was often ignored by the person or persons in charge of monitoring the calls. Monitoring the calls meant that whatever you said on the telephone was far from private, and rumor had it that many of the calls were recorded if there was even the slightest suspicion that the conversation was about an impending escape or, more likely, how so and so was planning to smuggle in some drugs. The truth was far less interesting, with the promise of pussy and the smacking sounds of transferred kisses being what was heard most often

One call a month meant one call a month, no exceptions, so that it might take months, or even years, to get around to all the people you were approved to call. Salvador had put me on his telephone list a long time ago, but it wasn't until the night before Christmas Eve that he had finally gotten around to calling me.

"Sir, this is the operator, I have a collect call for you from Salvador Agron in a correctional facility, will you accept the charges?"

"Yes, operator, I will."

"Thank you, sir, you may go ahead."

"Salvador!"

"Little Richard, how you doin' down there?"

Several minutes followed with both of us trying to say as much as we could in the little time allowed. Back and forth about Wah-Zi-Nak, how was she, and when had I talked with her last. Was his moms okay? Did we think his clemency would go through?

Several times we wished one another a Merry Christmas before all of a sudden, without any warning whatsoever, the line went dead, and he was gone.

No warning of any kind, no beeper, or a soothing operator's voice terminating the call; nothing. Salvador just wasn't there anymore. So much, I thought to myself, for allowing maximum-security convicts to converse with their loved ones as a way of "boosting morale." A familiar refrain that the Department of Corrections was so fond of saying in their lectures to visiting students of criminology.

> *Governor, the crime of which I am accused and convicted, is ugly and shameful on the very face, and it is also a crime brought about by many factors beyond my power of control. It is not my purpose here to bring an indictment against the social duties of society or to blame society in order to exculpate myself from any responsibility; my purpose in this petition is to put forth a short and precise outline of my life of tumult and deprivation, the unfortunate occurrence of this crime as a result of my very life; and what I have done, under our limited penal programs to correct my ways and understand my behavior.*

Given that so many men and women were applying for Executive Clemency, it came as no surprise that there was a protocol regarding the proper dissemination of information. Careful ties had to be sewn with the media to insure that decisions were announced at exactly the right time, and to the right people. This was even more important in the environment of the penitentiary where rumors were more the norm than the exception.

The game had to be played a certain way, and what better time, I thought, than to announce the decision on the evening before the birthday of the very man whose reputation for compassion and forgiveness was universally unquestioned. If Salvador's clemency were approved, then wouldn't it be natural for people to equate this with the man whose birthday would be celebrated later on that evening with a Midnight Mass?

> *Governor, I do not come from a rich or middle class family. I come from the bottom of the social ladder, the poverty stricken arrabales of Mayaguez Puerto Rico, and from the poverty stricken slums and ghetto infested streets and the old broken down tenement buildings of New York City.*

When I had started my death row study years before, this kind of speculating would have been out of the question. Along with a predictable set of behaviors and rules just like the ones in a free society, my professors, with their textbooks, and their countless studies, had offered up the world of prison as an orderly place. One, they said, that we could study, visit, and write about in dissertations. Yet the more I was involved, the more I'd come to see this world as one of unlimited contradictions, where the rule of thumb was simply that things were never what they seemed to be.

If you had a question about prison protocol, or how a specific prison rule was applied, it wasn't unusual to receive five different answers from five different people, and more often then not, you wound up making a dozen telephone calls before you finally got the answer you were looking for. This was certainly true for the protocol surrounding clemency; how the decision was arrived at, who made the decision, and when it would be announced.

> *On April 23rd, 1943, I was born into a world of pain, tears, poverty, and sorrow; a time of social and political transition for the Puerto Rican people on the island.*
>
> *My life was lived in mud, without shoes, dirty and torn pants—surrounded by vice, corruption, spiritualism, superstition, drunkenness, insults, marital fights, and the whole assortment of plagues that thrive in lower class families.*

My intuition was that a decision about Salvador had been made a long time ago, but when I'd asked someone at the Clemency Bureau as to exactly when they'd be letting us know, I'd received several answers. Most said Christmas Eve, but one said that should the decision be favorable, the prison superintendent would probably let Salvador know a day or two ahead of time.

A denial of clemency would be painful, but not nearly as much should the decision be announced on any other night.

Christmas Eve was a time unlike any other holiday in the penitentiary. Some convicts prayed, cried, and sought forgiveness, no matter how fleeting. Others sought to ease the pain of being locked away from loved ones by drinking illicit hooch, or making merry with men they would not have been caught dead with on any other night but this one. On Christmas Eve, sentiment pervaded the penitentiary like a sweet sorrow that would not die. And no matter how false it might have been, the prison people knew that Christmas Eve was the emotional equivalent of an ongoing confessional where freedom was the common prayer.

> At the time of the incident in the playground, I did not know how to read or write, and I had the mentality of a twelve year old boy. I had no parental guidance and no social worker to ask for guidance. I was alone in the world.
>
> In order to fight this loneliness, I had to act violently many times, This was the rule that I knew in the 1950's, and it was to be expected from a child or boy who lived in the streets.

Christmas was evident all over the Bronx as I walked to Esmeralda's apartment on Davidson Avenue. Colored lights hung from fire escapes, and perfect strangers nodded an unfamiliar hello and Merry Christmas as I made my way through a light dusting of snow that had fallen on my way in from Brooklyn.

Passing an imposing Catholic church, with its aura of Gothic rock, and its wooden doors spread open like an invitation on a greeting card, I wondered if this was the church where Esmeralda usually went for Midnight Mass on Christmas Eve,

Rosie, one of Aurea's daughters, said that Esmeralda was a Pentecostal. And that she had changed churches several times over the past few years until she found one where the pastor was more in tune with Esmeralda's particular religious needs. Like many people from Puerto Rico with an extensive grounding in the ways of the Catholic church, Esmeralda was more comfortable in an atmosphere allowing her to "pick and choose." Instead of demanding that she follow a strict catechism, the storefront church of the Pentecostals allowed Esmeralda to praise God in close communion with others of the same persuasion.

Greeting me with a wrap-around hug when I entered Esmeralda's apartment, Aurea handed me a glass of what looked like egg-nog, and wished me a Merry Christmas. Handing me a brightly wrapped box, with a little card that said, "To Jacoby, from the Agron family," she said she hoped I liked what they had bought for me.

"This is for you," I said, handing her a smaller box, "and this other one is for your moms."

Rich and brown, the sweater they had bought for me was a perfect fit.

"Thank you," I told Aurea, "that was really thoughtful."

> *I have been incarcerated most of my life. When I was but one years old, I was put behind the walls of the poorhouse. When I was around eleven (11) years of age I was put behind the walls of Wylwick School for Boys. When I was about fourteen I was put behind the bars in a reform school in Mayaguez. When I was only sixteen, I was put in prison and sent to the death house at Sing Sing for a crime alledgedly committed while I was under the influence of beer and pills, intoxicants that I could not buy unless an adult bought them for me.*

Taking the two boxes I had given her to a Christmas tree in the middle of the living room, she said she wouldn't open hers until the morning, but the one for her moms, well, her moms could open that one right away.

As Esmeralda unwrapped her package, I thought all over again how beautiful she was, and how she and Aurea reminded me of paintings I'd seen in museums. There was an unmistakable aura surrounding each of them, but when I tried to put this into words, I was always at a loss. Maybe, I thought, it was because of the way they carried themselves. Completely lacking in pretense of any kind, Aurea and her mother moved with such a quiet dignity that unless I asked, not a single word of their dark history was ever revealed to me.

> *I haven't had the best behavior record in prison, and to tell your excellency anything of that sort would be very misleading. However, I have use of every educational program that has been made available to men in prison.*

My Christmas gift to Esmeralda was a religious track. A piece of mental mounted on a slab of wood, it was the Lord's Prayer.

"Thank you, Jacobo," She said, as she picked it up. Squinting from what Aurea said was a slight nearsightedness, Esmeralda slowly whispered each and every word as all the rest of us stood and watched.

When nothing was on the ten o'clock news about his clemency, and when no one would tell us anything when we called the Clemency people in Albany, we all figured that nothing was going to happen. So by the time Salvador finally called to tell us that he had been officially denied his clemency, it was already close to eleven o'clock, and no one was very surprised.

"My brother's been through so much that something like this ain't gonna bother him too much," Aurea said, after getting off the telephone with Salvador.

"What else did he say," Madelyn, one of Aurea's other daughters, wanted to know.

"That I should tell everyone that he loved them…"

With the decision no longer on our minds, the tension flew away like a wild bird gone off to roost. Drinks were passed around, gifts exchanged, and promises made to one another not to stop until Salvador was finally free.

> *What I am saying is this: to keep me in prison any longer cannot be of a benefit to me or anybody else. I am now a man, with a realization that when I was young and foolish I made many mistakes, and that I have now come to understand my errors and have done my best to correct myself in spite of the existing prison conditions which tend to alienate more than it does to rehabilitate or correct. I am presently taking college courses, and have accumulated 45 credits in the Dutchess Community College under the auspices of the South Forty Corporation. I also attend Revered Ed Muller's cadre meetings here at Greenhaven, and in my opinion the programs offered by South Forty have made me what I am today.*

"Jacobo," Esmeralda said as she stood standing just a few feet from the entrance to her kitchen, "please come here."

Whether or not she was fluent in English was hard to say, though Aurea said, "Lookit, if my moms wants to make herself understood, she'll know just how it is she has to say it."

Following Esmeralda into the kitchen, I noticed how clean it was. Just like when we'd been here for the first time.

Not a speck of dust anywhere, with all the pots lined up on the walls just like they were in kitchens that I'd seen in Puerto Rico. The stove and the sink were luminescent, and the linoleum floor was clean enough to spread a meal across its length.

> *I have learned more in the last year than in all my previous years. I have corrected some of my thinking, and have*

found out that I was wrong about certain things. And all of this is due to the quality of programs offered by South Forty.

I believe that every life is here for a purpose. Suffering tempers the soul, but when it is unbearable, or in excess, it can also destroy that very soul.

With her back turned to me, she was doing something at the table. Across her shoulders, I could see through the kitchen window a sea of clothing lines across the backyard with laundry blowing back and forth like errant flags in the snow-filled winter wind.

Well, Governor, I think that no useful purpose will be served by keeping me in prison any longer, and I therefore pray that an order of Clemency or Pardon be made by Your Excellency, allowing me, Salvador Agron, to proceed to the conclusion of clemency, as I desire to return to my homeland, being that I sincerely believe that I am prepared, after fifteen (15) years of incarceration from a very tender age, to make my appearance in society and to take on the responsibilities of a citizen of good standing among the people of the United States, the State of New York, and the Commonwealth of Puerto Rico, and as a member of the human race of this world.

Turning around, and with a broad smile across her high-cheekboned face, she was holding two large candles. One was in a glass with Jesus Christ painted on the side, and on the other glass it looked like the Virgin Mary. Handing me the one with Jesus Christ, and keeping the other for herself, she said these were for me and Salvador.

"I pray for you," she said, pointing to my candle, "and I pray for Salvador," she said, pointing to the Virgin Mary. Closing her eyes, she took my hand. Rocking back and forth, I closed my eyes, and as we rocked, and held one another's hand, I could hear the whispered words of Spanish to this man she called Jacobo.

1/3/76
Greenhaven Correctional Facility

Dear Richard:

Happy New Year!

I have already written to Governor Hugh Carey about my wanting to be considered for next year's clemency, and I will keep bugging him for my clemency until he lets me go or puts me against the wall and shoots me!
I do not give up the ship so quickly, and you already know this.
Someday the State of New York will realize that Salvador Agron is rehabilitated one hundred per-cent, and that I am not a robot but a real human being wishing to live in love and be with life!
I hope to see you soon, my good friend, and beloved brother. Take care.

Tu conciencia,
Salvador Agron   #16846

Organizing Salvador's first clemency campaign had been difficult. Aside from soliciting support from hundreds of people, asking them to write letters to the Governor, we had spoken with countless political groups all over New York City.

Whether or not all the other letters, like the ones Genoveva and our committee were constantly soliciting in Salvador's behalf, went unread, or even if those letters were merely perused for a name and address in order for a nameless secretary to send back an acknowledgment, was hard to say. All we knew was that it was important for us to continue the struggle, and so shortly after the new year began, we started his campaign all over again.

The second time was easier. Using the mailing list we'd compiled from the first campaign, Genoveva and I carefully went down the list of names. Taking turns, we either wrote or called everyone on the list. Letting everyone know that Salvador's clemency had been denied, we asked each person to send a new letter to the Governor as soon as possible. Aurea talked with her family and friends, Wah-Zi-Nak wrote to new groups, asking for their support, and by July of that year, we speculated that the Clemency Board had received thousands of new letters in support of Salvador's bid for clemency in 1976.

Using the same petition that he'd written for his first clemency application, Salvador again pleaded his case to the Governor. This time he added a postscript: *"Nothing more will be gained by keeping me in prison for even one more day."*

Enough was enough.

Back and forth to Greenhaven, I attended several prison festivals, including another one for San Juan Bautista Day. Every few weeks I went to the cadre meetings, and whenever I could, I visited with Salvador in the visiting room.

No matter where we were, at a basement cadre meeting with Ed Muller, or out on Fay Field for a prison festival, our conversations never strayed far from the efforts we were making to get him out of jail. Endless talk about why a certain convict had received clemency a few years back but who had done far less time than Salvador. Why had another convict been released, Salvador wanted to know, after serving a paltry fourteen years for cutting off his mother's head? Or why had a convict who'd killed his bookie in broad daylight on the corner of 42nd Street and Sixth Avenue in front of thousands of witnesses, been granted clemency after serving just a few months less than seven years?

Greenhaven Correctional Facility
Tri-Annual Evaluation

Agron recently applied for Executive Clemency but the institution recommended against it at the time.

It is this counselor's opinion that Agron should be allowed to continue at Greenhaven until he has received therapy for a prolonged period and since he doesn't appear to desire any therapy he should be kept at this level of security.

Aside from obsessing about his next clemency application, Salvador had other concerns on his mind. Almost from the very first day that the article had appeared in the Op-Ed section of the *New York Times*, the volume of mail he'd received had increased dramatically. Some were from men, but most were from women. Supportive women who sensed in Salvador a need waiting to be fulfilled. Sometimes it was his need, and sometimes it was theirs, but it wasn't long before their correspondence went far beyond their initial offer of assistance to help set him free from jail.

Some of the women were like the weeping women I had met so many times before in the visiting room at Greenhaven, at the prison festivals, or wherever there were needy convicts looking for needy women. Other women wrote to him because they had a thing about violent men, with their aura of heat, darkness, and fermenting rage.

Overwhelmed by all the attention, and feeling he needed their money, their gifts, and their support, he suddenly found himself writing to nearly three times as many women as he had been writing to before the article had come out. Now not only was I working with Genoveva on his next clemency petition, but I was fielding more and more replies from women anxious to meet him as fast as I was able to make the arrangements.

Complicated as this was, he was also becoming more and more anxious about Wah-Zi-Nak's next visit to New York. She was planning to visit in September, and Salvador said that the tone in her letters suggested more and more often her wish that they get married as soon as possible.

> Agron is not presently attending school. He has received his Associates of Arts degree in Humanities through Dutchess County Community College. Agron is presently editor of the institution newspaper and has served in that function for about two years. The paper, The Open Gate, has received write-ups in Newsday, Claridad, and The *New York Times*. He is also a co-founder of the Communications Workshop and Poetry Workshop which is about to publish an anthology of poetry. He has also taught classes in Puerto Rican history and Pre-Columbian culture. He is also a member of the NAACP and the Think Tank, and he also attends a wide variety of religious services.

When an actor friend of Jennifer's was offered a job with a touring Shakespeare company, and she'd asked us if we'd be interested in subletting her house in California while she was gone, we said yes without giving it even a moment's thought.

The timing was perfect. She would be leaving in late September, and would expect us to begin the lease by early October. Plenty of time for us to put our affairs in order, and then make arrangements to ship what few possessions we had to California.

It would be an easy move. Neither of us had a steady job, or a strong attachment to New York City, so the move could be made, we thought, with a minimum of emotional hassle. My dissertation work could be put aside for a while, and my apartment was desirable enough that the lease could be passed on to someone else. I was even thinking of entering a training institute in California to study psychotherapy, but this would have to wait until I was better settled.

I would miss my family, but when I told them I was leaving, they weren't surprised. Sensing my restlessness, and seeing how tired I'd become from working on Salvador's clemency, they had gladly given me their blessing.

My only concern was Salvador. We had touched one another on some very deep levels, and were now close friends. We had come a long way together, and in making my decision to move across the country, I'd fought hard against the voice inside that whispered about abandonment. All his life Salvador had been pushed from one place to another, and in all that time, he said, he had never had a friend like me. Didn't even know, he said, how to treat a fiend, because every time he'd had one, it had never lasted very long. Prison, he said, was hard on people, hard on friends, and hard on love.

The closer it came for me to leave for California, the more I told myself, over and over, that we could work on the book longdistance, with trips to New York whenever the necessity arose, and when he did get released, maybe we could spend some time together in Puerto Rico. As for his clemency, enough of a framework had been built so as to insure a steady flow of support. Even more important, a new woman had entered his life. Her name was Gail, and she was a movement person who fought strong and hard for a wide variety of left-wing causes. Gail was a person of passion, Salvador said, and if anyone could find the key, she was the one.

After closing down my apartment, storing my books, and saying good-by to friends and family, all that remained was Salvador.

Residence and Employment Report

Reverend Muller said he had known the subject, Salvador Agron, for some time through the subject's par-

ticipation in the South Forty Program at Greenhaven Correctional Facility. He said the subject had completed two years of college and was interested in completing his college education back in the community.

He wished to emphasize that he was personally committed to helping the subject despite the fact that he was unsure as to just where the subject would live. Reverend Muller said that he was personally inclined to assisting him enter Marist College, but that it was somewhat dependent on what the subject wanted.

Should the subject decide to locate in the Poughkeepsie area, he is guaranteed the assistance of the South Forty Corporation. A release program that appears satisfactory.

When the people who designed Greenhaven Correctional Facility had omitted air conditioning in the visiting room, I wondered if they'd ever thought about all the guards who would be forced to suffer in the heat right along with the convicts.

Given the heat of the visiting room, probably not a thought, and I wondered if the heat had ever stirred emotions to the point where fights had broken out in the visiting room over some trivial nonsense.

"Fucking right they have," Salvador said, as he wiped his broad forehead free of sweat.

Looking across the counter at Salvador's pale and sweaty face, I wondered how even in the late September heat, he could still eat like there was no tomorrow. A little after one, and already he had eaten three sandwiches, and a box of donuts.

"Think you could get me one of those tuna fish sandwiches?"

Staring at several small piece of leftover lettuce stuck between his two front teeth, I was about to say something, but thought better of it. Why say something on my last visit?

Walking to the other side of the room to one of the vending machines, my eyes locked with the visiting room guard. His name was O'Leary, and we had a kind of semi-friendship, the hello, how ya doing kind of friendship, from when we'd met several times before at one of the cadre meetings. He had been our escort. We'd made small talk, and had learned one another's names. Passing by his desk, he whispered out of the side of his mouth.

"So what does fatso wannna eat this time?"

Smiling, but not replying, I continued on to the vending machine. At least this guard had a sense of humor, I thought to myself. Better than some of the other ones who seemed to take everything so seriously. The ones, Salvador said, who'd think nothing of strapping someone into the electric chair if that's what they were asked to do.

Back with Salvador, I watched him eat. We discussed his clemency status, and Wah-Zi-Nak's next visit, until finally I said what I had come to say.

"Hey, listen, I'm leaving..."

"Whaddaya mean you're leaving? It's only a little after two...you got like almost another hour.."

"No...I mean I'm really leaving...I'm going to California with my girlfriend."

"You're shitting me! When'd you decide all this?"

"When we were there...last month...it's really what we wanna do..."

"What about me!"

Suddenly the grown man with the ravaged face had gone away, and sitting across from me was the five year old boy with the broad-rimmed hat, and the innocent eyes. That vulnerable little boy from long-ago Puerto Rico.

It only lasted a minute, and then he was gone. Back inside to who knew where, that innocent little boy with the broad-rimmed hat and the innocent eyes, leaving instead this macho man of many complicated parts.

We spent our last hour together making small talk, drink-

ing sodas, and laughing at whatever we thought was funny.
   When the visiting room guard finally announced that all visiting was over for the day, we each stood up. We looked at each other for a second before embracing one another all around, and when we pulled apart, Salvador whispered, "I love you, Jacoby," and I whispered back, "Me too."

Statement From Salvador Agron

   Today, December 24th, 1976, at about 10:30 A.M.. Mr. Walter Fogg, Superintendent of Greenhaven Correctional Facility, informed me that the Governor of the State of New York, Hugh Carey, granted my clemency petition.
   I was granted clemency but with a year deferral. In other words, I will be seeing the Parole Board on January of 1978. The sort of clemency the Governor gave me is one that will make me eligible for educational release. I will go to college during the day, and then return in the evenings to a minimum security institution. I would also be eligible for a furlough, so that I can spend seven days with my family and friends and be part of the mainstream of society again.
   This statement is for the purpose of thanking all the working class people who have supported me in my campaign to obtain clemency. I would particularly like to thank Genoveva Clemente and Richard Jacoby, who served on the committee that helped in getting the people's support in my case. I would also like to thank my family, as well as all the other individuals and groups who were instrumental in helping me to obtain my freedom.
   The faith that my supporters have placed on me will not be violated.

Thank you.
Salvador Agron
#16846

Chapter Nine

ARIZONA

Later, Reverend Ed would say it had been unusually warm that day. Salvador seemed to have enjoyed walking around the huge campus, and it felt to Ed that he was excited about the prospect of becoming a college student.

The only disturbing thing was when they'd heard the news that Gary Gilmore had been executed in Utah. Driving to the college earlier that morning, they'd heard over the radio that he'd been given a stay, but then the stay had been lifted, and the execution had gone on as scheduled. Ed said the news had thrown Salvador into a kind of slump for the rest of the day, and from the way Salvador was talking, Ed guessed the news of Gilmore's death must've reminded him of his own time in the death house at Sing Sing Prison when he was seventeen years old and waiting to die in the electric chair.

January 17th, 1977
Fishkill Correctional Facility
Dear Brother Richard:

Today was my first day at the college. What a trip!
Reverend Ed took me to register, and I will be taking a total of twelve credits for the Spring semester of 1977: Logic, European Philosophy, Introduction to Sociology, and a history

course called "The Ages of Man." Since I registered late, I don't have any textbooks yet, but my parole officer promised that I should have them soon.

Tu hermano,
Salvador Agron   WR# 627

The stipulation was that he would attend classes at Marist College in Poughkeepsie during the day, and return in the evening to the Fishkill Correctional Facility, a minimum-security institution where he'd spend the night before returning to the college the next day.

But when his application could not be processed in time for him to start classes at Marist, an alternate plan was put together, allowing him to attend classes at the State University of New York, at New Paltz, or SUNY as it was known to both students and faculty alike.

February 3rd, 1977
Fishkill Correctional Facility

Dear brother Richard:

My big complaint right now is that I have to go back to the prison every night! Out of all the clemencies granted in 1976, it seems I was the only one with the stipulation that I would have to go to school during the day and return to the prison at night. Everywhere there is petty harassment, especially from the guards at the prison. I thought this would be a minimum-security prison, but this is not the case. Fishkill looks like a mental hospital because at one time it used to house the criminally insane women prisoners!

Another problem is that someone must have leaked it to the press that I was taking classes here, and this has not been good for me. But I have been up against this kind of thing before, and I will struggle against what I know isn't right

Take care, my friend, and keep good thoughts for me!

Tu amigo y hermano,
Salvador Agron #WR 267
Fishkill Correctional Facility

After three months of living together in her friend's tiny bungalow in Southern California, Jennifer had decided to return to New York City. She missed her family, she said, and besides, she wanted to be an actress, and here she was working all over again in a sidewalk cafe as an waitress. At least in New York, she had a circle of supportive friends and family, but in California, all we had was one another.

In the beginning, this had been enough, but when I hadn't been able to find a job right away, the tensions between us had become unbearable, and we'd decided to go our separate ways. I would continue with the sub-lease until I found a place of my own, and Jennifer would return to New York to pursue her acting career.

Wah-Zi-Nak had written several times, but from the tone of her letters, I could sense that she and Salvador were going through their own changes, and I wondered how much longer their relationship would last. She demanded a good deal of attention, and as the weeks went on, and Salvador's life became more and more complicated, there was much less time for correspondence of any kind.

When word leaked out that Salvador was attending classes on the campus, the reaction was mixed. Although he was liked by many of his fellow students, as well as several members of the faculty, the newspapers had chosen to sensationalize the story in a way that could only create more anxiety about his presence on the campus.

Article after article appeared, complete with detailed sketches of Salvador's background. Some got the facts right, and others did not. Several articles made mention of the time Salvador had been confined at the Dannemora Hospital for the Criminally Insane. One article said he'd been there three times, another four, and still another said he was still there as an out-patient. But what was most upsetting, and especially to Reverend Ed, was the continuing reminder that Salvador's sponsor at the college was none other than Ed's group, the South Forty Corporation, the very same group that had sponsored Jack Duane Lewis, who in 1973, while living near New Paltz, had committed a rape murder.

When I asked Genoveva what the story was with Salvador, she'd written back that in her opinion he was having adjustment problems. A friend of hers had seen him on the campus, and said he'd looked tired, with dark circles under his eyes, and she could tell something was bothering him. But when he called Genoveva several days later, and she'd asked him how things were going, all he'd said was, "Everything's just fine."

Salvador Agron   WR # 627
Weekly Parole Report
2/18/77

All the reports that this writer has had from Mr. Agron, and he has been seen in the last two weeks, six times, have been positive. He states that he is doing well on campus, has learned the buildings, talks with the people, and feels that he is well liked by the student body and his professors.

This writer does not get such a glowing report from either the other students or the administration on campus. A quick look at the enclosed newspaper clippings indicate that there is a great deal of community concern for Mr. Agron's presence on campus. There is a movement to limit the number of offenders on campus, and to be very selective in admission of ex-offenders and ex-offenders.

The other inmates on campus also expressed to this writer a great concern over the atmosphere in the community and on the campus. Two inmates have expressed great concern to this writer that the continued publicity and interviews that Mr. Agron grants are doing more harm than good to their situation on campus. They have both stated to this writer that they wish that Mr. Agron would "keep his mouth shut," and let the situation die so that they could go on with their programs.

This writer's understanding is that a member of the Fishkill Correctional Facility has also questioned Mr. Agron's presence on campus and has stated to other members of the Work Release staff that the community is up in arms.

If ever there was one thing Salvador could not do, it was "keep his mouth shut."
Reverend Ed said Salvador had kept his sanity and sense of creativity during his many years in prison by constantly protesting oppressive conditions. That it was not simply something he believed in, but something which his very survival depended on. This was consistent with what one of my professors had said once before was a basic law of prison life: you did whatever was necessary to insure your survival. For Salvador, this meant never letting up for even a minute.

2/13/77
Commissioner Benjamin Ward
Department of Correctional Services

Dear Commissioner Benjamin Ward:

I am compelled to write this letter because I am very unhappy with the way things are going for me in the work-release program. I know you are a progressive thinker, and that is why I am writing about the present conditions that exist at the Fishkill Work and Educational Release Program.

This is supposed to be a "minimum security" institution, but with the bars on the windows and the huge fence surrounding the building where I live, it looks more like a "Koncentration Kamp"!

There are four or five corrections officers here who should be substituted by competent and educated employees. The mentality of your officers is very low, and this tends to undermine the concepts of education and work release. We are treated like little children, and emasculated by the lack of education and civility on the part of the officials who run this place. Why must we be so thoroughly searched whenever we get back from the college? Doesn't anyone here have any trust in us? Why can't we carry our own money around with us instead of having to check this in a locker whenever we return from the college? I would rather hold it on my own person so that I may be able to feel as people in society feel, like functioning human beings ready to meet the world.

During the day I attend college classes, but then at night I have to come back here to a place where whatever I have learned is insulted! I am educated at the college, and then uneducated when I am put through the process of entering back into Fishkill at night. I try to find common sense in the rule here, but this quality is lacking, and the rules and regulations(dumb as they are) are an insult to the very concept of rehabilitation!

All of this might sound shocking, but it is the gospel truth! I hate to see human life being wasted and this is why I am writing this letter to you.

I would appreciate if this letter could be published in the Correction Newsletter, and I hope that I will continue getting your protection from harassment.

Sincerely yours,
Salvador Agron WR #627
Fishkill Correctional Facility

If nothing else, Salvador's limited freedom had quickly introduced a whole new dimension to his relationships. Instead of relying entirely on letters and jailhouse visits, now he could talk on the telephone as often as two or three times a week.

At Greenhaven, his calls had been limited to a pre-approved list, and how much time he could spend was severely restricted. In addition, he was only allowed one or two calls a month, so that if he missed his call to me one month, it took a long time before he could get back to me again. Besides, he said, since there was the strong possibility that our calls were being monitored, if not recorded for official records, it wasn't wise to discuss anything but trivial information.

Now things were different. Walking to class, coming back from class, or wherever and whenever, he could simply pick up the telephone, dial someone collect, and that was that. Sometimes we'd talk for just a few minutes, sometimes longer, but every time we talked, I always came away feeling that something bad was going to happen if he continued much longer in the work-release program.

Salvador Agron   WR # 627
Weekly Parole Report
3/22/77

Salvador Agron continues in his school at New Paltz College in New Paltz, New York. He is still taking twelve credits, but is having difficulty with his logic course. The information that I am receiving is that he will be advised to drop the course even though he is doing better since he has started receiving tutoring.

Mr. Agron is very upset and feels that many of his rights, privileges, etc. etc. have been violated because he was not allowed to lecture at a class recently, or participate in a seminar at the university. Mr. Agron feels that these are part of his studies, and his rehabilitation, and that the prison system is doing its usual oppressive job of dehumanizing the inmates and putting undue restrictions upon them. If a listener is willing, Mr. Agron can go on for hours on this subject.

Another of Mr. Agron's upsets in his furlough status. He definitely wishes to be allowed out of the facility for Easter to visit with his mother and friends in New York City

Aside from the conversations we'd had on the telephone about the oppressive conditions at Fishkill, what we'd talked about the most was his wish for a furlough to see his family and friends back in the Bronx.

Although his relationship with Gail was strictly platonic, she was still an important part of his life, he said, and he was figuring that while he was in New York, they'd be able to spend some time together. The rest of the time he'd either spend with his family, or maybe just take a few long walks around the city.

The only thing which troubled me about his wanting a furlough was his desire to find Mrs. Kresinksi. He wanted to tell her he was sorry for what had happened to her son in the playground, and nothing I said seemed to convince him that he was the last person on earth she would ever want to hear this from.

Work Release Program

2/22/77
To: Institutional Parole Office
From: Temporary Release Committee

Please initiate a Field Investigation of Mr. Agron's proposed furlough residence.

Of special interest is community reaction to Mr. Agron's proposed furlough. In particular, it is requested that the area Parole Office contact Mrs. Francis Kresinski, mother of one of Mr. Agron's victims to elicit her feelings as she expressed animosity towards Mr. Agron in a recent television interview.

As Salvador waited for word on whether or not he would be granted a furlough, his problems at Fishkill continued unabated. How many other people he was in contact with was difficult for me to determine, although I had the feeling that there weren't that many people he felt comfortable enough with that he could call them to discuss his problems.

Back and forth everyday from the prison to the university was apparently taking its toll, and what seemed to bother him more and more was his relationship with the guards. Most of them he didn't talk to, but he said he could easily detect the contempt they had for him because he was going to college at state expense, These were the same guards whose fingers explored his body cavities in search of contraband, whenever he would return from a day of lectures, classes, and college cafeterias.

Sometimes, he said, it felt like all the guards were whispering to him what a guard had told him on his first day back from college:

"You kill us, and we send you to college."

State of New York-Department of Correctional Services
Agron, Salvador   # WR-627
3/18/77   Furlough Investigation

Contact is to be made with inmate's mother, Esmeralda Rodriguez, to determine whether she will welcome the inmate in her home for a furlough visit.

Additionally, the Deputy Commissioner has directed that no contact be made with Mrs. Kresinski, who is the mother of the deceased person that was killed by the inmate many years ago. It was also directed that the address of Mrs. Kresinski be explored as to the relative distance between her residence and the inmate's mother's residence.

Salvador's calls came to me in a little house I was renting near the beach in Santa Monica. Smaller than the bungalow that I'd lived in with Jennifer, it was also less expensive. Within walking distance of a chic Italian restaurant, where I was working part-time as a waiter, it was a perfect living arrangement while I tried to figure out what my next move was going to be.

One large room, with a bay window climbing from the floor to the ceiling, it had a sweet and pungent smell from the serenade of plants and flowers that I kept on shelves all around the room. A futon bed was laid out for sleeping, and my hammock from Brooklyn was neatly stretched from wall to wall. A cast-off desk from a local elementary school served as a telephone table, and whenever I talked with Salvador, I watched the palm trees swaying back and forth through the bay window.

Listening to his deep and familiar voice as he talked of Fishkill, strip searches, and furloughs, the trees reminded me of how far away he really was.

> After Mr. Agron's commutation of sentence by Governor Carey, and transfer to the Fishkill Correctional Facility, a television interview was conducted with Mrs. Francis Kresinksi, and during the interview she purportedly threatened the life of Agron. It has therefore been requested, that Mrs. Kresinski be contacted and her feelings elicited relative to Agron and her alleged threats directed against him.
> Under no circumstances is the inmate to contact the victim's mother.

Early in April, his four-day furlough was approved, and his excitement came through the receiver like an alien from a distant star about to descend to earth for several days of exploration. As I listened, I wished that I could be there with him, walking the streets, visiting with Genoveva, and having dinner with Aurea and Esmeralda. Mostly, though, I wished I could be there to make sure that he made no attempt to find Mrs. Kresinski.

Like his aggressive approach to so many other struggles in his life, I had the sense that he thought his good intentions would outweigh whatever feelings Mrs. Kresinski might have had about what she would do when she opened the door, and there was Salvador Agron, standing in front of her, big as life.

Salvador Agron, I kept telling him whenever we talked on the telephone, was the nightmare of her life, and I guess I must've said it enough times because when we spoke the night before his furlough was about to begin, he had finally agreed to let it alone.

> The night before my furlough I wasn't able to sleep for more than a few minutes before waking up all over again. My mind kept racing out of control with all kinds of thoughts. Everything from whether or not people would recognize me on the subway, even after all this time. Was the Capeman really dead in New York, I kept thinking, or were they simply waiting for my return?

Furlough papers signed, Salvador took the Greyhound bus from Newburg to New York City on a beautiful April morning, arriving at the Port Authority Bus Terminal in mid-town Manhattan at a little bit after noon.

> Thousands of people were in the bus terminal when I arrived, and right away I took the subway to my mother's house in the Bronx.

> People were looking at me funny as the train made its way through Manhattan and into the Bronx, but I don't think anyone knew who I was.

Wah-Zi-Nak said she hoped Salvador would call her when he got to New York. She had planned on being there for his furlough, but since she wasn't sure of how close they were anymore, she'd decided not to come. Besides, she said, she didn't have any money.

> Right away my moms wanted me to go to church with her.
> "I had this in my thoughts," I told her, "but first I've gotta do other things."
> "My church is out there," I said philosophically.

During all my conversations with Salvador, Wah-Zi-Nak's name rarely came up. When he wasn't talking about the oppressive conditions at Fishkill, he was talking about Gail, and what a help she'd been in helping get the furlough.

> When I left my moms house, I went with her and my cousin Anita to visit with some of my other family relatives at a house a few blocks away. The first cousin I met was Papo, whom I had not seen since I was a little child in Puerto Rico. Everyone kept telling me that he was now retarded, from something that had happened to him from drugs. "He won't remember you," everyone said. But he surprised everyone when he came right over and said, "Hello, Sal, how you doin'?"

Other then what Salvador had already said about Gail, I didn't know too much about her. Only that she was a tireless worker for the rights of the oppressed, and that she belonged to many different organizations with similar kinds of agendas in New York City.

> Back at my moms house, I told her I had to make a telephone call to Gail. She was very energetic, and we were

> involved in many of the same struggles, I must talk to her, I thought to myself. She had already done a lot for me.
> After I dialed the number, a soft voice answered.
> "Hello," the voice said, "who's this?"
> "It's Sal," I said, recognizing Gail's voice.
> "Sal! Where are you calling from?"
> "Guess!"
> "The college?"
> "No, I'm right here, at my moms house in the Bronx.!"
> "Wonderful," she said, cutting me off, "stay where you are. I have a car and I'll drive right over."

Meeting Gail in front of Aurea's house, they went upstairs. Salvador introduced her to Esmeralda, and then they left for a drive in Gail's car. As they drove, they talked, then stopped and visited with some of her friends, before returning to Aurea's house later on that evening.

Aurea had already met Gail at one of the festivals, and they spent the rest of the evening, talking, drinking coffee, and listening to Aurea tell them stories about when Salvador had been a little boy in Puerto Rico.

> Sitting in the car with Gail, I noticed for the first time that she was a beautiful woman. I had not really seen her in this way before because our meetings had always been very casual. But now I was seeing that she was also a woman—a lovely woman. I tried not to show any feelings that create any illusions of romantic love. This was easy to do, however, because I had disciplined myself while in prison and now my discipline came in handy.
> She took me everywhere and we visited different parts of the city. We talked to different people who had supported my clemency drive. It felt so good to function like a worthwhile human being again. I had spoken with people who had wanted to meet me in person and now they knew that I was real, made of flesh and blood.
> When it was time for Gail to leave Aurea's house, I walked her downstairs. Saying good-bye, we agreed on a time when

she would come the next evening so we could go and see Genoveva.

As she drove off, I stood there wondering, thinking thoughts which are wordless. Then I went back upstairs.

"Sal," Aurea said, "she's nice, I like her alot."

"Yes," I agreed, "she is very nice. But now I'm afraid that I'm getting to like her a little too much, sis, it troubles me."

"Brother," she reminded me, "How about the Indian girl?"

"That's what's bothering me...I may be in love with the two of them."

"Damn, bro, you fall in love too much," Aurea said with a broad smile across her face.

"This evening I looked at Gail and she was like...lovely, sis. I mean something happened to me inside.. I'll just be cool and let things take their natural course."

"She's a nice person," Aurea said, "that's all I know."

Later Salvador would write that the next three days passed so quickly that when he got back to Fishkill, it had taken him a few days just to sort out all his emotions.

Gail had introduced him to scores of people before taking him out to Brooklyn to see Genoveva.

The next day when Gail came over, we stayed at my moms house. My moms made tea, and we sat around looking through family albums. Mother and Gail tried to converse, and somehow they seemed to understand each other. When Gail and I left, I kissed moms as I stepped out the door, and said in Spanish, "Don't worry, Moms, I'm in good hands." Mother smiled and Gail looked on as though knowing I had said something good to moms.

While I was in the bathroom, I called Wah-Zi-Nak in Canada. It was a strained conversation. Something had died in us and what had died was the romance. But at least we parted as friends.

Gail and I went to Brooklyn to see Genoveva. We drove first to Manhattan and took the subway to Brooklyn. Things began to get more familiar as the train got to Brooklyn. We got off at a stop and when I cam out into the open I knew where I was, and the familiar surroundings made me relax.

Genoveva lived on Adelphi street, not that far from my old stomping grounds near the Brooklyn Paramount, just a few blocks from the Brooklyn House of Detention on Atlantic Avenue.

As soon as she opened the door, we hugged one another, and then we danced around the house a little bit before sitting down to a meal she'd made of green bananas, rice, and beans.

After leaving her house, I took Gail by the hand and I showed her all my old haunts in Brooklyn. I took her to all my old hang-out. I showed her where the Mau Maus had the gang wars. They were the meanest gang in Brooklyn back in the 1950's.

Driving back to the Bronx with Gail, I was at a loss to tell her my feelings. What should I say? How did one really talk to a woman, face to face. I really did not know. But I did realize that I was in love with Gail, but could not find the right words to tell her so. Already she was an important part of my life, and I was sharing experiences with her that I had not shared with any other woman.

But I was afraid to show my true feelings. After being away from the opposite sex for over eighteen years, one does not really know if he is saying or doing the right or wrong thing. While at the college, I socialized with the opposite sex, and yet I still remained a virgin of eighteen years.

After Gail dropped him off at Aurea's house, he'd tried to rest, but something kept whispering to him that there was one thing left for him to do before leaving the next morning for Fishkill.

It was the last day of my furlough before returning to Fishkill the next morning, and there was one thing left for me to do.

I walked the streets of the Bronx, and across the Triboro Bridge into Manhattan. Then I was in El Barrio, and the ghosts started calling out my name, but I kept going until I reached Black Harlem. Then another ghost called out my

> name, "Sali, yo Sali," and turning around I saw it wasn't a ghost but a flesh and blood man that I'd know for many years when I was in Attica.
>
> Walking and walking until I was at Central Park West and 77th Street, and the ghosts of my old neighborhood started whispering to me as I passed the places where I used to hang out with the Vampires long ago in 1959. I felt strange, like I was from another place, and another time. Then another ghost called out, and again it wasn't a ghost but a guy I'd known when we were boys together in the death house. His name was Carlo, and he was no longer a boy, but a man. We hugged each other, and said gracias dios to one another because neither of us had died in the electric chair.
>
> Walking and walking until I came to the forties on Eight Avenue. I kept my eyes open and I was alert. I passed by the playground on 46th street, and I went inside. I saw kids playing basketball and I sat down on the same bench where I had sat like an invading soldier on that hot August night in 1959.
>
> I sat there and tried to remember. But I could not remember stabbing those two boys. Suddenly I felt my body tremble and tears started rolling down my face.
>
> A little boy came close to where I was sitting.
>
> "Mister," he said, "why are you crying."
>
> "It's a long story, kid"
>
> Then I got up and walked out of the park.

Back at Fishkill, several people commented on how distraught Salvador appeared whenever they talked with him. To one man, an activist in prison affairs, he had said, "I think they're gonna try to drive me crazy," and he alluded to a pending keep-lock in his cell that he was facing the next weekend for what he felt was only a minor infraction of prison rules.

Other friends noted that his hands frequently moved very rapidly, and his face would redden before lashing into a tirade about the oppression of his rights at Fishkill.

Like a mournful blues song waiting to be sung, his was a sadness that would not die. Perhaps it had been the conditions at Fishkill, the emotional impact of the furlough, or simply the prospect of spending the next weekend keeplocked in a cell that reminded him of the box at Attica; but whatever it was, no one was prepared for what happened next, on the morning of April 15th, 1977.

> On the morning of April 15th, I got out of bed at my usual time of 4:00 AM, took a shower, and went into the search room where I stripped, changed into civilian clothes, and then took the bus to New Paltz. I bought some coffee in the cafeteria, and then went to class.
> Later that day, I got a ride to New York City with a guy named Joe, and when he asked me my name, I said it was Melendez. The guy drove me to Grand Central, and from there I walked over to Times Square. There I got a room in a cheap flophouse kind of hotel, the same kind of place I used to stay in when I was roaming the streets back with the Vampires in the 1950's.
> The next day I went to the Port Authority Bus Terminal and bought a ticket for Tucson, Arizona, and I bought it for Arizona because I figured it would be a warm climate like Puerto Rico, and there would be lots of Spanish-speaking people there.
> After paying for my ticket, I had about fifty dollars left, and before getting on the bus, I went into the men's room. From a bag I was carrying, I put on fresh clothes, and then I mailed all my other identification papers to someone in New York who I knew would watch over them for me. All I kept with me were some papers identifying me as Miguel Melendez, a man I'd known from Brooklyn, who had been shot down by the police unjustly. And by using his name, it felt like I was bringing him back to life, at least in name anyway.
> Through the afternoon, and into the night, the bus made its way across the country until finally arriving in Tucson, and when I looked out the window of the bus, I knew that I was in a whole new place unlike anything I had ever known before.

The first call came at a little after two in the morning.

The voice was muffled, as if the person was tying to disguise his voice with a handkerchief wrapped around the mouthpiece. But no matter how hard he tried to shield his identity, there was no mistaking the guttural sound of Salvador Agron.

"Where are you, man? You sound weird," I said, still half-asleep.

"I can't tell you that but I'm not in Fishkill no more, that much I can say."

"You escaped? Are you fucking crazy or what?"

There were reasons he said for his having gone on the run but he couldn't go into this right now, and besides, my phone might be tapped.

"I'll keep in touch, " he said, and before I could answer the phone was dead.

> Leaving the bus terminal in Tucson, I asked a guy where there was a good place for me to rent a room for the night. He pointed across the street at a run-down looking place, and said that even though it was not that clean inside, the rooms were comfortable, and it was cheap.

Not being able to sleep after Salvador's call, I made some coffee, and then sat at my little school desk, looking out at the palm trees, as I tried to figure out why he'd escaped with so little time left to serve. On the surface, it seemed simple enough. Oppressive conditions at Fishkill had slowly driven him to a near desperate state, and the only way he thought he could save himself was by going on what the convicts called "a run," as a form of protest.

Most convicts who went on a run were long-termers who had somehow managed to climb a wall, go over a fence, or walk out of the visiting room dressed as women. Facing an eternity of time with few options for parole, they saw nothing wrong with making a run for it whenever the opportunity presented itself. But the risks were great, and the rewards were few. Most convicts who went on a run were either caught, or gave themselves up, within thirty days of their initial escape. Once caught, they not only faced charges of escape, but additional time as well for any other offenses they might have committed while free. Criminologists called these runs "a flight into custody."

Salvador's situation was dramatically different. Had he not escaped, the most time he was facing was another seven months, and unless his behavior record was totally outrageous in terms of infractions, then surely the Parole Board would have cut him loose.

> Crossing the street, I entered the Conventions Hotel, and registering under the name, Miguel Melendez, I was shown to a room on the fifth floor. It was very small, and it had a bathroom, with a toilet and a sink. It looked like any of the prison cells that I'd lived in over the years.
> The only difference was that there weren't any bars on the window.

Obviously upset when I called her the next morning, Aurea said the police had already called her as well as people from the prison. No one knew where her brother was, but it was all over the news that he had escaped.

Figuring that her telephone might be tapped, I didn't say anything about the call I'd gotten from Salvador last night, but I made a note to drop her a letter later on that morning, In the meantime, I rode my bike to a local newsstand that specialized in out of state newspapers.

Buying the New York *Daily News,* along with several newspapers from upstate New York, I sat and read them while sipping coffee at a local cafe on the boardwalk near the beach.

New York *Daily News*
New York, Monday, April 18, 1977

By Mark Liff

3-State Alarm Issued for Capeman of Hell's Kitchen

A three-state alarm was issued yesterday for the "Capeman" murderer of two teenagers in a Hell's kitchen playground 18 years ago, who failed to return Friday to the Fishkill Correctional Facility.

New York City police are combing Hell's Kitchen for Salvador Agron, now 33, who failed to return to the minimum-security prison after leaving earlier that day to attend classes at New Paltz State University.

State police are also searching college bars in that Ulster County town where Agron was known to have stopped to flirt with college girls. State police said that Agron "had a few female associates in that area."

Prison officials said that the 5'10" Agron took a bus from the prison to the school, where he has been studying philosophy. He was enrolled as a full-time student, and went without a prison escort, officials said.

When he failed to show up by late Friday, prison official issued a felony warrant for his return. By yesterday, the alarm had been flashed throughout the state, and to New Jersey and Connecticut.

He would have been eligible for parole next year.

Early the next morning, I left the hotel, and walked to the corner grocery. There was a small hot plate in the hotel room, and I bought a can of tomato soup, and a container of coffee.

When I got back to the hotel, I borrowed a can opener from the guy at the front desk, but when I tried to open the can I didn't know how to do it. I knocked on the door next to mine, and when this old guy opened the door, I asked him if he would help me get the can open. He looked at the can, and then at my face.

"When did you get out?" he said.

Looking at the picture of a very young Salvador that accompanied the article from the New York *Daily News,* I saw that it was the same one taken on the night of his arrest in 1959 for the killings. Curly haired, with world-weary eyes that were soft and hard at the same time, it was a photograph that would probably follow him right to his grave.

New York *Daily News*
New York, Wednesday, April 20, 1977

By William Hefferman

State Prisoners in Escapist Mood

Salvador Agron, the "Cape Man" killer who escaped while participating in a prison education program is one of hundreds of inmates who are walking away from the state prison system.

Agron made his getaway Friday while on an educational release from the Fishkill Correctional Facility that allowed him to attend classes at nearby New Paltz State College without supervision.

Agron was convicted of the 1959 murders of two rival gang members in a Hell's Kitchen playground. He wore a cape during the attack. At the time of his conviction he told the court: "I don't care if I burn, my mother can watch."

Agron, who has now spent more than half his life behind bars, became a basis for the Broadway musical "West Side Story." Eight days before Agron was to die in the electric chair, his sentence was commuted by Governor Nelson Rockefeller.

Agron now faces possible criminal charges for escaping from the prison, which could add four years to his prison time, nullify his chances for parole and make him personally ineligible for future release programs, prison officials said.

Agron's escape created a furor among officials of the

New York State Parole Officers Association, who say that prison escapes throughout the system have been skyrocketing in recent years.

> When I left the hotel, it was still very early in the morning, and the sun was barely in the sky. I had no idea what time it was, so I stopped at a pawnshop and bought a cheap watch for twenty dollars.
>
> Outside the pawnshop, I struck up a conversation with an old Black man, He said he lived nearby and he invited me to his house to get something to eat. When we got there, he made me some bacon and eggs, and looking around at his house, I could see that he didn't have much money and he was very poor.

The next call came early one evening just as I was about to leave for work at the restaurant. It was from the police in New York City, and the caller identified himself as a New York City detective. A warrant had been issued, he said, for the arrest of Salvador Agron, and did I have any knowledge of his whereabouts?

"Why should I know something like that."

"Because you're one of his friends, Mr. Jacoby, and we have good reason to believe that he might be headed your way."

"Yeah, well, I wish I could help you..."

"Could you tell me, Mr. Jacoby, when's the last time that you saw Mr. Agron?"

"Uh...well, it was quite a while ago..."

"Could you please be more precise?"

"It was just before I left to come out here..."

"And when was that?

"About a year and a half ago."

"And you haven't heard from him since?"

"Not a word."

Beacon Evening News
Monday, April 18, 1977

Fishkill, New York

"The Capeman" killer remains free, according to state police at Fishkill.

In an interview with the Evening News last January, Agron acknowledged he's gotten the reputation as a militant inmate because he agitated for school programs and prison reforms.

But, he contended, it was only through fighting for these programs that he became rehabilitated

"I hate the guts of prison," he said. "They just store human flesh away without helping people. Prisons don't rehabilitate. What's released back into the community are desperate men."

Agron was also critical of the clemency petition, Governor Carey granted him last Christmas. Other inmates given clemency were eligible for immediate release, which in had to wait until 1978, he complained.

Agron said he had several job offers and might go to work in a bookstore when he got out of prison. He also wanted to continue writing and possibly go back to school.

When I asked him if he would like to change clothes with me, and I would take his old ones, and he could have my new ones, he looked closely at me, but then said okay. After we changed clothes, I offered him my black leather bag, and when he took it he offered to drive me wherever I wanted to go.

The next time I talked with Genoveva she said she had the feeling there was someone following her every time she left her apartment building in Brooklyn. She assumed that it was someone from the police, but couldn't really say for sure. And, no, she hadn't heard anything from Salvador. He hadn't called, there had been no notes, and she was just as baffled as everyone else as to why he'd run away. She just hoped that wherever he was, he was okay.

> *I asked the Black man to drop me off in the ghettos because I had the feeling that this was where I'd be the safest.*
> *He dropped me off at the house of a friend of his, someone he said I could trust, and then he wished me luck and said good-bye.*
> *When I saw that the people I was with were just as poor as he was, I went out and bought them some food. We talked for awhile, and then I left. Outside where they lived was a big tree, and just before I started walking, I sat down by the fire. Then I took all my personal papers, and threw them in.*
> *Now I was Miguel Melendez through and through.*

There was a new man in Wah-Zi-Nak's life, and when I called to find out about Salvador, I could sense that something was different. Where in the past, whenever she spoke of Salvador, there was always a noticeable hint of excitement in her voice, now it seemed like she wished to talk about anyone else but him. Normally quiet and soft-spoken whenever we talked on the telephone, she was even more so, and I wondered if maybe her new man wasn't standing several feet away, listening to every word.

She had no idea where Salvador might be, she said, or if she did know, she wasn't saying.

> *I walked all over Tucson, talking and walking.*
> *I lived with bums and winos, exchanging clothes and food, and then slept side by side with them at night in hobo jungles all over Tucson. I even looked for work but the identification I had wasn't enough, but I did help other people at the unemployment and welfare offices when they needed help filling out the forms because they didn't speak too much English.*
> *I met a little boy on a bicycle who stopped when he saw me walking. He wanted to know if I would buy his bike and when I asked what he needed the money for, he said it was to help bail his brother out of jail, and that he needed all the money he could get.*

> "Do you want to trade your bike for this twenty dollar watch?" I asked.
> When he said, yes, I took off the watch and handed it to him."
> "Here," I said, "it's yours, but you can keep your bike."
> He looked at me funny before thanking me, and then he turned around and rode away.
> On April 24th, I celebrated my thirty-fourth birthday in freedom with a poor white, an Indian, a Black, and a Chicano—all bums. Hobos, all of them, and without a house to live in, under the trees, drinking Thunderbird wine and eating tortillas while sitting around a campfire, like spoiled boyscouts! But it was the best birthday I ever had in my whole miserable life and it happened amidst misery and poverty. Life is funny this way.

Even with an unlisted telephone number, people calling about Salvador still found their way to my house in Santa Monica. Most were from women, a few were from newspaper reporters, and one that I received in the middle of the night was from someone who refused to give his identity except to say that he was an "old friend" from the days when Sal had run with the gangs in New York City. If I did talk with Sal, he said, wouldn't I please convince him to give himself up?

> I walked all over Tucson, sleeping and eating wherever I could, until finally I walked into the Peoria Police Station on April 28th, and after I told the guy behind the desk that I had no money, I asked for a telephone book so I could call my mother and have her send me some money. But they didn't have a telephone book from the Bronx, so the guy said for me to wait because the sheriff would give me bus fare to Phoenix where there was a crisis intervention center, and that they would give me money to get back to New York City.
> I waited awhile and then he gave me a dollar and a half for the fare to Phoenix, and said he'd drive me to the bus station. Before leaving, he wrote down my name and date of birth.

> When I got off the bus in Phoenix, two policemen were waiting for me. One of them told me to get up against the wall, and then the other one searched me. Handcuffs were put on my wrists. When he asked me my name, and I said, "Salvador Agron," he put in a call on his radio.
> "We got him," he said.

It was nearly midnight when I picked up the telephone and the operator asked if I would accept a collect call from Salvador Agron.

He was in the Maricopa County Jail in Phoenix, Arizona, and when I asked him if he was okay, or if he needed anything, all he said he wanted was a thousand dollars and a key to the front door.

The New York Times
April 30, 1977

"Capeman" Recaptured in Phoenix; Motive for His Escape Is a Puzzle

By M.A. Farber

Salvador Agron, who came to be know as the "Capeman" after he murdered two youths in a West Side playground in 1959, has been arrested in Phoenix two weeks after he absconded from a work release program.

Why, when he was so near release after serving more than half his life in prison, had he fled? It was a question that bothered not only Mr. Agron's friends and family, but also prison and college officials.

Interviews with many people who were close to Mr. Agron said that he despaired at having to carry on "two existences."

In a letter to several newspapers after he disappeared, Mr. Agron accused the corrections officials of "conspiring" to bring about his "destruction" and the destruction of the "moral spirit and independence and freedom of other inmates." While he briefly mentioned a few specific incidents, his theme was that the authorities were trying to modify the behavior of rehabilitated inmates to "propagate the idea" that criminals could not be reformed.

Guards at Fishkill described Mr. Agron as an "average" prisoner who came back each night, ate, and generally went to bed early.

But Mr. Reid, the superintendent, said that "the facts they have accumulated indicate that perhaps we weren't as cautious with Mr. Agron as we might have been."

"You have to treat a person with acute appendicitis differently than a person who has measles," he added.

Salvador had already called Aurea when I reached her the next morning. He'd seemed okay, she said, and she wanted to know if I was close to where they were holding him. I said it was one state over, maybe an hour or so by air, but I wasn't sure if I'd be able to visit him or not.

"What you think's gonna happen to my brother now?" She wanted to know.

"They'll probably send him back to New York unless there's something they're charging him with there in Arizona."

"So he could get more time for this right?"

"Yeah...I guess so."

"So why you think he ran away like that?"

"I don't know."

A long time ago, in a faraway police station, people had whispered, "Did you do it, Sal? Did you do it, or what?" And now, years later, in a police station, several thousand miles from New York City, "Did you do it" became "What made you run, Sal? What made you run?"

Phoenix Police Department
Phoenix, Arizona

4/29/77
Interview with Salvador Agron

On 4/29/77, Detective Rudy Santa Cruz interviewed Salvador Agron in the Maricopa County Jail in an attempt to ascertain why he escaped from the Fishkill institution, and how he ultimately arrived in Arizona. Agron told Santa Cruz that when he was seventeen years old, he was a member of a New York street gang, and during a gang war he killed two members of a rival gang, and was sent to prison for life. He said that he became involved in an educational program at Fishkill that allowed him to go to school during the day and return to the institution at night.

He said he was admitted to the program through efforts of his friends and the New York Governor's office. This outside pressure caused people at the institution to apply undue pressure on him, The pressures got so great that while he was on a four day furlough, he decided to run rather that to contact the news media and expose them.

He stated that he left New York on foot, with no money, and headed for Arizona, thinking that he might go on to Mexico.

Investigation showed that Salvador had no money, no papers, or identification, when he was arrested. His physical appearance indicated that he had been traveling by foot for a great distance.

Salvador told Santa Cruz that he believed the educational program was a very good one, but that the people running the institution had it in for him and applied undue pressure. It was this pressure that forced him to run, even though he knew he was due for parole in January. Salvador would not elaborate on what the pressure was, or name any individuals who allegedly were applying the pressure

A contact with Lt. Roy Folds, of the Peoria Police Department, disclosed that Salvador walked into the Peoria Police Station on 4/28/77, asking for directions to Phoenix and some help. Peoria Police Department furnished him with some money and transported him to Sun City, Arizona, where he was able to obtain a bus ride, via Greyhound Lines, to Phoenix. He had given Salvador a detailed map with directions for an assistance center in Phoenix. Folds further stated that after Salvador was placed on the bus, and they fed his name into a computer, a reply came back indicating that Salvador was wanted as an escapee from New York. After his arrest and incarceration, Mr. John J. McCarthy, New York Department of Corrections, was notified by phone with the details of this investigation and Salvador'statement.

Salvador stated that he would waive extradition and voluntarily return to the institution.

May 19th, 1977
Dutchess County Jail
Dear Richard:

O, lion hearted one, how you be? I hope you're well and doing okay. I am presently in this shithouse awaiting charges to be lodged against me. I will be charged with absconding, but I will prove that I was being targeted for harassment and a subject of experimental behavior modification!

Your letter to me at the Maricopa County Jail was warm and really made me feel good. I also got the money order. Thank you!

Sometime soon, I will issue a statement of fact as to why ran away, and I will send you a copy.

Please give Gail a call, and she will fill you in with more details. And also give Aurea a call when you get the chance, and say hello to my moms for me.

Your brother, forever
Salvador Agron

When I called Gail a few weeks later, her voice was just like Salvador had said it would be. Soft, with just a touch of a New York accent, she was glad I'd called, and said efforts were under way to make sure Salvador received a fair trial.

Salvador was fine, but he was frustrated with how long it was going to take before he'd actually go to trial.

The issues surrounding his escape were complicated, she said, and what was important now was to find a good lawyer.

Promising to keep me posted on events, she said she looked forward to meeting me the next time I was in New York.

6/1/77
To: Commissioner Benjamin Ward
    Department of Correctional Services
    State of New York

Dear Commissioner Benjamin Ward:
   I am presently in the Dutchess County Jail awaiting my trial on the "absconding" indictment for leaving the Fishkill Correctional Facility's so-called "temporary release program" in order to publicly protest (not escape) the adverse conditions that existed at Fishkill.
   I turned myself in by going to the sheriff's office in Arizona and giving my real name and not Miguel Melendez, which was the name I had been using all along during my flight.
   Mr. Ward, I have many good ideas about programs and how to make the temporary release programs of work and education really work. However, the present conditions are counter productive and your programs will be lost if they are not corrected, and violence will increase in prisons due to this backward move.
   My case will begin in several months, and I have asked the judge, through my attorney, to remain here at the Dutchess County Jail, and this was granted until this case is settled because Auburn Prison is too far away from my relatives and supporters, and also because Auburn is counter-productive to my progress and rehabilitation.

   Respectfully,
   Salvador Agron
   Dutchess County Jail

When I called one of my professors in New York to talk about Salvador's case, he had already read the many accounts in the newspapers. What concerned him wasn't so much Salvador's situation, but more what would happen to the existing programs. Nothing, he said, would please certain elements of the prison community more than to be given an open mandate to close down anything they felt was even remotely progressive. If what Salvador and his supporters were saying about Fishkill was true, then what would be the justification in continuing to allowing anymore inmates into the program?

7/23/77
Dutchess County Jail
Dear Lion-Hearted:

    Richie, I want you to do the following: make photocopies of all my poems and prose, and photocopies of the autobiography. Then send all this to Gail. She is the chairwoman of my defense committee and a very close person to my soul. She has lots of other material and will hold it until I get out and you and I can finally finish the work together.
    As for Joyce—well, we have taken different paths, and I am now with Gail.
    Gail works hard on my defense and has shown me great love and concern. I want you to meet her when I get out. As for Joyce, I wrote and told her, and I am hoping we can still be friends.

    With a warm embrace from your brother,
    Salvador Agron #16486

Early in August, Aurea called and said her father had died. She didn't know the circumstances, but from what she was told by a woman who knew him in Puerto Rico, he had died peacefully, and he was buried somewhere in Mayaguez.

When she went to the jail to tell her brother, he didn't say anything right away, he just got up and walked out of the room. She figured that maybe he was so upset that he just couldn't sit there anymore. and that was why he'd walked away, but when he came back, he handed her a piece of paper. It was a poem called "Honor thy Father." When he'd left the visiting room, he'd gone into the bathroom and wrote it just like that, real quick, she said, like he didn't even have to think about it or nothing. It was so beautiful, she said, that she'd started crying right there in the visiting room.

She'd made a few copies, and when she got off the phone, she'd send me one.

"I think you and my moms were like the last people to see my dad when you was all together there in Puerto Rico that time."

"I'll light a candle for him..."

"Really? You'd do that for him?" Aurea said.

"I'd like to...is it okay with you?"

"I'd really like that...and I think my father would've like it too."

9/3/77
Dutchess County Jail

Dear Gail:

I enjoyed your last letter very much, but I must tell you that I have certain problems relative to radical politics.

I have no moral fiber...it seems. I do not understand the term 'faithfulness' in marriage and cannot quite see myself as being disciplined enough to take such a vow. This of course contradicts the Marxist morality. This concept is strict, and promiscuity or sexual freedom seems to contradict its structural outlook. But I also find another force within me which *tells me that I should settle down with a woman and be a married man and put aside my loose values. How should I deal with sex, marriage, faithfulness or other problems in this area?*

My other problem is religion. At times I believe in God and at other times, I do not. I can be both a Christian and an atheist. Thus I live as if I cannot prove this or that. I've read the pros and cons of the God problem extensively but cannot work out a solution one way or the other. Even the term God has a million interpretations. I've also studied evolution but cannot quite believe in it. These two contradictions tug at my brain day and night. I know how they got there and I'm trying my best to deal with them as a communist should for his development into a complete human being.

I will need your help.

Love,

Salvador Agron

The church was St. Monica's, on the other side of the city, about three miles from where I was living by the beach.

Except for the homeless man, who stood like a silent sentinel, staring up at the church with blazing eyes, the church, with its massive oak doors, and elaborate stone work, could have passed for a cathedral in Florence.

The homeless man went by the name of Joe, or at least this was the name he gave whenever anyone would ask. Rumor had it that a long time ago he'd killed a priest, gone to prison, and now lived under freeway exits at night. Food and water came from a local shelter, and when he wasn't at the shelter, or under a freeway bridge, he was standing in front of the church, staring at who only knew what with his blazing eyes. Dressed in rags, and with long, matted hair, he looked like a fallen Jesus Christ, who'd long ago lost all his disciples.

Nodding to him as I passed him on my way inside, I thought to myself that he was probably not much older than

Salvador, and I wondered if the prison authorities had simply dumped him outside the gate when his time had been up. In New York, they gave a man a box lunch, forty dollars, and a bus ticket to wherever it was they had come from at the time of their arrest. You could spend thirty years in Attica, and in the meantime all your family could have died, gone away, or just didn't care about you anymore, and still, this was where the bus would take you. Salvador said it was like the prison people wanted you to confront your ghosts, and what better way, I thought, than to send you back to wherever it was you came form.

Lighting the candle, I thought of Sindo Agron, and my mind went back to how the unrelenting sun of Puerto Rico had burned his face to a color close to copper, when I'd seen him last by the old folk's home in Mayaguez. Where was he right now, I wondered? Sindo Agron, father of Salvador and Aurea, husband of Esmeralda. Was he finally at peace in the earth somewhere, and did Aurea even know where he was buried? And what had she felt, Esmeralda, when Aurea had told her Sindo was dead, had she cried?

Watching the flame as it flickered from a soft spring wind drifting through the door, I wondered what would happen to Salvador when he finally got out of prison, free of work-release, strip searches, and a never-ending volume of rules? Would he end up like Joe, standing in front of a church, or on skid-row somewhere? The implosion of prison was so overwhelming with its power to kill the spirit, and rob the guts of all but the strongest, that if Salvador succumbed, he would neither be the first, nor certainly the last. The line of broken-hearted ex-convicts who had fallen by the wayside could easily stretch around the earth several hundred times, and for a second I had a vision of a million Salvador Agrons, each one holding the other's hand as they lined up side by side, and they made their way around the earth.

Leaving the church, I locked eyes with Joe for the briefest of moments, and as I passed him by, I put a ten dollar bill into his hand.

"This is from Salvador Agron," I said, before turning around and walking away.

> 10/4/77
> Dutchess County Jail
>
> Dear Comrade Jacoby:
>
> You must really look like a semite from all that California sun you've been getting! It's good for your soul, brother, so enjoy it. Your letter was warm and a reflection of what a good person you are. We have traveled a long road together, and I never forget this.
> I received the articles you sent, and the one I enjoyed the most was the one about Wiltwyck. At last this resort of evil and childhood perversion will close. Bravo!
> When you finally get back here, we will have lots of work to do on the book. Or Gail and I can come out and stay with you while we work on this together. If you decide to go to Puerto Rico, you can always stay with my mother. She considers you to be her son.
> William Kunstler will probably be handling my case. He said he would do anything to help, and he is one of my heroes! Buses of students will be coming up sometime during the trial to show their support. I know you can't be here, so I've asked friends to call you as the trial is going on to fill you in with details.
> Mrs. Davis has been giving me a hard time! She wants $25,000 dollars from me! She's really crazy, man! I don't even have enough money to buy toilet paper! My supporters will protect my rights. She came to visit recently, and really gave me a headache!
> I told the warden to never let her in again!
>
> All my love to you,
> Salvador Agron

If Salvador's life could be defined by a search for keys, then what he desperately needed now was a lawyer with a symphony of words capable of unlocking all but the coldest of hearts. And had he tried to conjure up the ideal lawyer to represent him on the charge of absconding, he could not have done better than William Kunstler.

Known as a movement lawyer with a touch of the poet, Kunstler was a graduate of Yale who had served as a major in World War II. Graduating from Columbia University Law School, he had worked for several years in his brother's law office writing wills and creating contracts before beginning his radicalization by traveling south to help with voter registration in the early 1960's.

Sensing something rotten in the system of American justice, he'd begun taking on clients no one else wanted: everyone from the Black Panthers to people who thought nothing of dealing drugs and then shooting it out with the police in order to avoid being captured.

What changed his life forever had been the trial of the Chicago Seven. With his face spread across America on the evening news, he looked like a poster boy for revolution with his long hair and thick sideburns, and he became an instant celebrity. A darling of the Left, he took on all comers, including many of the people Salvador had broken bread with from Attica to Greenhaven, and back again.

What Salvador admired most about Kunstler had been his ardent defense of William Morales, the Puerto Rican militant who'd lost his hands in an explosion at a Queens "bomb factory," and later made a sensational escape from the prison ward at Bellevue Hospital. Salvador had never met Morales, had never written to him, or even heard him speak. Yet when he spoke of Morales, he spoke of him as a brother, a mentor, and a fellow revolutionary.

11/5/77
Dutchess County Jail

Dear Brother Richie:

   I just received your letter and I'm sitting in my cell reading it. I love hearing from you.
   This is what I have in mind for our book: When I finally get out next year, I will put all the materials together, and then sit down in a room with a good I.B.M. electric typewriter and finish the book. When it's finished, you and Gail can go over it and add and correct. Then maybe we'll ask William Kunstler to do the introduction, or one of the other writers you suggested. Then we will call different publishers, such as Viking Press or Doubleday, and whoever offers the best contract, we'll welcome as our publisher.
   Seriously, brother, I want you to know that as soon as I get out I will complete the book.
   My trial will be starting shortly, and rest assured that I will make sure you are provided with all the relevant details as the trial progresses.
   Write soon!

   Love, forever
   Salvador Agron

The trial started in mid-November, and true to his word, Salvador arranged with several of his supporters to keep me up to date with all the specifics as the trial progressed.

Each step of the way, someone called with all the details, including the strategy that the defense had agreed would be the best way of defending Salvador on the charges of absconding.

   I absconded from the Fishkill Work Release Program because the College program is undermined by the prison facility, which used to hold criminally insane female prisoners before they moved them out and moved the work release prisoners in. Everything is done to make the person become a criminal again

I found that I could not study or pursue my education without suffering irreparble damage, both mentally and physically.

In the beginning, the legal strategy was thought to be a simple one: the circumstances that Salvador had endured while in the work-release program had been so overwhelmingly oppressive that he'd had no other recourse other than to run for his very life.

Kunstler argued, however, that while this line of thinking might very well be true, it still would not win an acquittal for Salvador. The laws in New York State were very specific, he said, when it came to what would, or would not, justify why a person might go on a run. If Salvador had absconded because of some immediate danger, such as a fire, or the threat of physical harm, such as sexual violence from other inmates, then it was possible that an argument could be made in his defense. Even then, the convict would first have to exhaust all acceptable avenues of help before he could escape with some kind of justifiable excuse if and when he was ever caught.

Acceptable avenues of help meant becoming a snitch, a rat, or a stoolie. In other words, as Salvador put it, a piece of shit not even worth talking about.

If prisoners were not on the bus at 6:00 AM, or they overslept, they got a disciplinary report and must report to the Adjustment Committee. This committee consists of a lieutenant, a sergeant, and a civilian (either a nurse or someone else who works for the department).

New York State law was very specific in that it did not sanction a convict's fleeing as "justified" if they should flee because of psychological problems, so that for Salvador, the only defense could be that he fled because of "temporary insanity," or in the language of the law, "by reason of mental defect or disease."

Kunstler suggested that perhaps this could be avoided by simply claiming that Salvador was "insane," through and through, for good, and not just at the time of the absconding, but Salvador would not consider this, even for a moment. What he had done was a rational act, and if nothing else, his trial would allow his defense to show the contradictory nature of the work-release program in such a way as to convince a jury that he had no other recourse but to run when the pressures became too great.

> *If they give you a keep-lock for your violation of the rules, it means that you are locked up in a room alone, usually for the week-end. This means that you don't get your furlough for that week-end. They bring you cold food, and give you the bare minimum just to make sure that you won't starve.*

The defense would be to show that the contradictory nature of the program was so severe that Salvador had been driven into a pre-psychotic state and consequently the state of mind that had led to his absconding. The program itself, then, would not come under attack, but rather the way it was administered.

> *Other things besides oversleeping, or missing the bus in the morning, will also get you keep-locked:*
> 1. *Riding in an unauthorized vehicle*
> 2. *Returning late from a furlough*
> 3. *Refusing to let a guard give you a full strip search whenever they feel like it (this means a probing with a finger in your rectum in search of contraband).*
> 4. *Bringing in food from the messhall to your room*
> 5. *Not making your bed.*

What Salvador would have to understand, however, and what Kunstler told him more than once so that there would be no misunderstandings later on, was that in the event of a verdict of "not guilty by reason of mental defect or disease" Salvador would no longer be under the jurisdiction of the Department of Correctional Services. Instead, he would be under the supervision of the Department of Mental Hygiene, under whose auspices he would receive psychiatric "care" until he was deemed to be sane enough to qualify for an appearance before the Parole Board

> *If you should get caught masturbating in your room, you also would go before the Adjustment Committee, and will suffer the same consequences as you would for sleeping late, or not making your bed.*

Lasting a little less then two weeks, the trial was held in a dimly lit Dutchess County courtroom on Market Street in Poughkeepsie, New York. Representing the State of New York, the case against Salvador was argued by Assistant District Attorney Paul Sullivan. Salvador's fate would be decided by a jury consisting of 6 white women, 2 black women, and 4 white men.

When the two sides finally came together in the courtroom, the issue to be decided was a simple one. The prosecution attempted to prove beyond a reasonable doubt that Salvador did abscond from the program and that his mental state at the time was such that he could fully understand the consequences of his actions. The defense, while not denying that Salvador had absconded from the program, attempted to prove that the stress of the situation had forced him to flee in order to preserve his sanity.

> *I am a very outspoken person and because of this fact, the Fishkill administration has been constantly trying to frame me or put me in a mental state that a psychiatrist would define as schizophrenic.*

Expert psychiatric testimony was presented by both sides in order to testify as to Salvador's state of mind at the time of the escape.

Arguing for the defense, a psychiatrist testified that when Salvador absconded, he was in a state of "pre-psychosis" brought about from all the pressures of being forced to live two separate lives, and that this in turn resulted in a "substantial degree of confusion between fact and fantasy." This "borderline" state of uneven thinking left Salvador unable to fully comprehend the consequences of running away, the psychiatrist testified.

Psychiatrists for the prosecution countered that Salvador's was an "anti-social personality," and that when he'd absconded, he knew full well the consequences of his actions, and was never, as the defense was contending, in a state anywhere approaching psychosis.

> My sanity was in question for awhile, and I had three alternatives: 1) I could summit to the dehumanization of my spirit, 2) accept negative behavior modification of my character or 3), abscond as a protest against the vendetta being carried on by the administration or Fishkill Correctional Facility.
>
> In other words, go insane or run and maintain my dignity by using such an act as a symbol of protest.

During a lunch break on the second day of the trial, a busload of students who had driven up from New York City to show their support for Salvador, lined up across the street from the courthouse where they waved banners and changed slogans such as, "Dismiss the charges and set Sal free. We want him back in the community."

At one point, Salvador, who was in a holding cell during the lunch recess, came to the window of the four-story courthouse. Thrusting his arm through the bars, he made a raised a clenched fist to the crowd.

As the days wore on, and the trial continued, both sides presented witnesses. The defense presented witnesses who corroborated their basic premise that Salvador was far from emotionally stable the day he absconded, and the prosecution countered that he always knew what he was doing at all times. One witness for the prosecution, a Fishkill prison official, testified that shortly before Salvador had absconded, he had been found guilty by the prison adjustment committee of having returned from the college in an unauthorized vehicle. He was supposed to have returned in a prison vehicle but instead had been driven back by Gail in her Toyota. This infraction, he said, had cost Salvador two weekends of keep-lock, or confinement to his room.

Under questioning by Kunstler, the witness testified that even though Salvador had stated to the Adjustment Committee that he was not responsible for having missed the bus, as it had left without him before his usual meeting time, the Committee had not investigated any further, and instead had taken the side of the officer who had originally filed the charge.

> *I did not harm anyone or commit a criminal or anti-social acts in my flight. I have committed no crime. I just broke a promise that I return to Fishkill each night after school.*
>
> *Believe me, when I say that I am a different person than I used to be. At one time I used to get angry, but it was an anger that came from ignorance. I would react to conditions. Now I study conditions and try to control the environment around me.*

Witness followed witness, with the Reverend Ed Muller at one point testifying that in all his years of prison work he had never seen such a remarkable transformation as he had seen in Salvador during the course of their friendship which, he said, dated back to Salvador's arrival at Greenhaven Correctional Facility in 1971. On the stand, he spoke of his concern when Salvador had entered the work release program, which in his opinion was the hardest way for anyone to do time, and he said that he'd always felt that Salvador should have been set free in December of 1976, when his clemency had gone through.

> *I once questioned a Fishkill Facility about not being able to take my civilian clothes and my cash money inside the housing unit. This developed into an argument in which I was trying to show him that there was nothing illegal about money or civilian clothes. It was my property, and I should be allowed to keep it. For this, I was accused of being drunk, and ordered to take a urine test. When it came out negative, and I asked for an apology, he just walked away.*

Finally it was Salvador's turn to testify, and while his defense team had been tempted to coach him in the "art" of addressing a predominantly middle-class jury, they resisted the temptation. "Let him speak from the heart," Kunstler said, "it's exactly the thing he does the best."

Salvador was on the stand for more than four hours, and in his deep and guttural voice, he gave the jury a living tour through the sideshow that he called his life. From the poorhouse in Puerto Rico to the Brooklyn streets where he ran with the gangs, he gave the jury a powerful rendition of his early life, followed by a tour through several of New York State's many maximum-security institutions. Along the way, he told the jury, he had learned to read, and then with help from people like the Reverend Ed Muller, and his South Forty Corporation, he had completed course work for an Associate of Arts degree. Speaking of his months in the Fishkill educational release program, he said, "I loved that college, but I could not stand to return to prison at night. I left in order to preserve my humanity and sanity."

Kunstler summed up the case to the jury when he said, "I believe you saw here more than a simple absconding case.

Salvador Agron is the combination of a very intelligent, compassionate, sensitive person with a tough working class kid. He's a real fighter. He hates injustice, and he simply wants to see the prisons made more humane. He's far more unusual than I am. He never began at the starting line like most of us. He's a rehabilitated human being. In being saved, he saves us all. That human beings can start in the gutter, can reform themselves, is a miracle. And so I ask you to deliberate in the spirit of love, and charity, which gives our world any meaning at all. Consider the legal issue, but come back in and save his life. It's too precious to let die. I give him to you now, and I ask you to give him back to us."

Then it was the prosecution's turn, and Sullivan addressed the jury. "What is the issue here?" he asked the jury. "The issue is, solely, did the defendant intentionally fail to return to the prison on April 15th? You have been subject to a clever defense tactic which has diverted your attention from the real issue in the courtroom today. Society has been put on trial here, but you should not consider things that evoke sympathy or emotion except where they relate to the defendant's state of mind. Leave leniency and compassion to others, that is not your job. Rule out collateral issues, and stick to the facts of the case."

After giving instructions as to three possible verdicts: guilty, not guilty, and not guilty by reason of mental disease or defect, the judge surrendered the case to the jury.

The New York Times
Sunday, November 20, 1977
'Capeman' Murderer Is Acquitted Of Fleeing
Jail-Release Program
By Ronald Smothers

Poughkeepsie, New York, November 19. Salvador Agron, the murderer known in the 1950's as the "Capeman," was found not guilty here today by reason of mental defect at his trial on a charge of "absconding" from a prison educational-release program.

Mr. Agron's trial was considered important not only because of his reputation but also because his absence from the educational-release program had figured in the legislative criticism and reassessment of all state programs that provide word and educational opportunities for inmates.

Mr. Agron's lawyer, William Kunstler, did not deny that his client had failed to return to the prison. But he contended that Mr. Agron was temporarily insane because of confusion between the different kinds of treatment he received while in classes and while in the prison.

On the witness stand, Mr.Agron recounted much of his early life, and he termed himself the "scapegoat for the whole 1950's"

11//77
Mid-Hudson Psychiatric Center

Dear Brother Richard:

There seems to be no win with these people, even when you do win!

I am in the bughouse again: Mid-Hudson Psychiatric Center due to the verdict of "not guilty by reason of mental defect or disease." It was the only defense that the fucking judge permitted. My stay here is doubtful, and it looks like the Department of Corrections lost jurisdiction over me and now I must contend with the Department of Mental Hygiene.

Most of the patients here have not gone to trial yet because they are "crazy," and so far I am the only "ex-state prisoner" in the whole hospital. But Kunstler said he'll try to get me out soon!

Well, brother, let's hope for the best. Please call Gail and Aurea whenever you have the chance.

Happy Thanksgiving!

Love, hope, and understanding,
Salvador Agron   Ward # 4

Chapter Ten

PRISON

Auburn Correctional Facility
Salvador Agron
60 ASI
Auburn Correctional Facility

Dear Mr. Jacoby:

    We are writing in the interest of the above-named person, who is presently under our care, and who has requested authorization to visit and correspond with you.

    Because Departmental objectives include the re-socialization of offenders and assistance in resolving their problems, it is felt that correspondence and visits could contribute to their morale and rehabilitation, both in the facility and in the community.

    The policies governing the correspondence and visiting programs, require that you submit answers to the following questions for review as basis for authorizing correspondence and visiting. Any false statements will be cause for rejection.

    This form must be completed and returned by mail and approved before correspondence and visits are granted.

Office of the Superintendent

Auburn Correctional Facility
11/79

Dear Brother Richard:

    Thank you for your letter and the stamps. It was good hearing from you, and I also got the letter you wrote to the Parole Board on my behalf. It was a work of art!
    I'll send the pictures you sent to Aurea. You look good! Stay in good health, brother, it's important.
    Enclosed is a visiting and correspondence form.

Love always,
Salvador Agron   # 60 ASI

Where Greenhaven was literally in the middle of nowhere, Auburn Correctional Facility was in the center of town, and as I drove my long-neglected jeep into the parking lot in late November of 1979, I couldn't imagine a prison looking any worse.

    Greenhaven at least gave the illusion of order and cleanliness, with its nearby farms and rolling fields of wheat, but here at Auburn, there was nothing green, or even remotely comforting. Nothing but a dirt-streaked gray wall that stretched around an entire city block, and which in the sunlight looked all washed up and very old.

Auburn Correctional Facility
11/79

My Dear Brother Richard:

    I've already seen the Parole Board twice since I've been here, and they said they're waiting to see the results from the independent panel of psychiatrists who were appointed by the New York City Regional Office of the Department of Mental

Hygiene to evaluate my sanity! After that, I'll probably have to see the psychiatrist here at Auburn, and if that works out, I can finally appear before the board and maybe get the fuck away from these places for good!
I'm looking forward to your visit.

Tu Amigo y Tu Hermano,
Salvador Agron   #60ASI

Within hours of the verdict, responsibility for Salvador had been transferred from the people who ran the prisons to the people who ran the loony bins, the New York State Department of Mental Hygiene.

A year at the Mid-Hudson Psychiatric Center, was followed by three more months at the Bronx Psychiatric Center. Examined over and over by dozens of psychiatrists, psychiatric nurses, and social workers, everyone came to the same conclusion: Salvador was sane enough to be sent back to prison until yet another psychiatrist at Auburn could examine him, and maybe then the state would set him free.

Nassau County Medical Center

This independent psychiatric review panel was appointed by the New York City Regional Office of the Department of Mental Hygiene to evaluate Salvador Agron, a patient in the Bronx Psychiatric Center pursuant to Section 330.20 of the Criminal Procedure Law, having been acquitted by reason of mental disease or defect of the crime of absconding from temporary release in the first degree.

We were given the opportunity to examine all records relation to Mr. Agron's present hospitalization, as well as those of his prior confinement at the Mid-Hudson Psychiatric Center.

All agreed that, while at Bronx Psychiatric Center, Mr. Agron showed has shown no signs or symptoms of mental illness.

Mr. Agron was pleasant and cooperative. Appearing his stated age, he was appropriately dressed in causal clothing, including a headband.

We examined Mr. Agron collectively. He began by noting that it would be, in his estimation, "one hell of a throwback," and "counterproductive" for him to return to prison from the psychiatric center. He would like to be seen by the parole board while here at Bronx Psychiatric Center, since he says that it's "more progressive" than the prison facilities.

It should be noted that the patient denies the original offense of murder in a gang fight of which he was convicted some eighteen years ago. He felt that his story would not be believed, so he says he "took the rap." Describing himself as "ignorant" and "semi-illiterate" at the time, he has no recall of using a knife to harm anyone else. He admits to being involved in gang fighting and other juvenile offenses at age 16 and before, but considers his mind to have been that of a three year old at the time of the homicides. His confession to the police, which reportedly ran to some 49 pages, he now rejects. His explanation for the confession is that at the time, at the age of 16, he enjoyed the notoriety and extensive media coverage which was of a sensational nature. The newspapers dubbed him the "Capeman."

While in prison, he was known as something of a troublemaker, and was often transferred from one prison to the next. He considers himself to have been a leader, perhaps an agitator, and rather militant in the cause of prison reform. However, he can recall being involved in only three fights in the past 18 years, the most recent having taken place approximately ten years ago. He now can "control my emotions" and walks away from physical confrontations.

It is our opinion that Salvador Agron can be released without danger to himself or other. In fact, he will be returning to the custody of the Department of Corrections. Looking at the situation from a longer range perspective, it is also our opinion that he can ultimately be released to the community without danger to himself or to other individuals.

It is not unlikely that there may be future antisocial conduct by Mr. Agron should he be released into the community but it is extremely unlikely that this conduct would take the form of physically violent behavior to others.

Had Salvador been a nameless hoodlum convicted in 1961 of killing a clerk during a failed robbery in Queens, or if he'd hacked a man to death for insulting his girlfriend, he would have been sent to a reformatory designed specifically for young men eighteen to twenty-five, instead of to Auburn Prison where the average age in 1961 was forty-three.

But Salvador was not a nameless hoodlum, he was the Capeman.

> On February 7th, 1962, my death sentence was commuted to life in prison. I was seventeen years old, and I was handed a piece of paper which said, "Eligible for parole in September of 1989."
>
> I was taken out of the death house, and placed in solitary confinement for about two weeks before being sent to Auburn Prison in February of 1962.

Lining the walls of the corridor on my way to the visiting room were dozens of faded photographs. Looking closely, I saw the beginnings of Auburn Prison rising from the earth in the early eighteen hundreds. Gazing at the long-gone faces of convicts hauling stone, carrying water, or pails of mortar, I wondered at the reception Salvador must have had when he walked through the doors of Auburn for the first time. With all the publicity, and his youthful good looks, his arrival had no doubt been something of a prison event. Aging convicts, sexless for years, with nothing in front of them but more of the same, must have welcomed Salvador as if he were an exotic delicacy to be smelled, touched, and enjoyed.

Dressed in stripes of black and white, the men in the faded photographs looked like a herd of zebras, or at least they did until you got up close and saw the sad and dirty faces, like the living dead, I thought, and I wondered if what Salvador had written about the dungeons had been true.

Deep in one of the basements, he said, was a dungeon filled with screaming men locked in tiny cells.

> When I got to Auburn Prison in 1962, everyone already knew who I was. As soon as I got there, they put me into a reception cell and kept me under lock and key for about a week until I was processed.
> Then I was put out in the yard.

The visiting room was just like the one at Greenhaven. Long and rectangular, the convicts sat on one side, visitors on the other, and up front, on a raised platform, sat the visiting room officer. Over in one corner were some vending machines, and in another corner a camera was set up to take Polaroids of convicts and their visitors. They could pose in front of a blank white canvas, or in front of a cluster of palm trees that was painted in bright colors on an adjacent wall.

Ancient lighting filled the visiting room, but unlike at Greenhaven, there was nothing to see through the windows but stone walls and a tiny sliver of the large prison yard. Buying some coffee at one of the vending machines, I could barely make out some passing figures through the window. Off in the distance, one man was shooting baskets, while two others, holding hands, walked so close to where I was standing behind the window, that except for the bars, I could have reached out and touched them.

With a population of two thousand men at any one time, Auburn was considered overcrowded, and I wondered if all of them were ever in the yard at the same time.

Despite the coming holidays, the only other person in the visiting room was a brightly dressed Latina. Assigned a seat just a few seats from where I was sitting, I could see that she looked to be no more than eighteen at the very most.

> I walked the Auburn prison yard in 1962 with a Bible under my arm, ready to preach the word of God to all the lost

> souls at Auburn. I considered myself a saved and born again Christian.
>
> My gospel preaching began to take a twist. I was blending revolutionary ideas with the gospel and testifying to the fact that Jesus was a socialist revolutionary who was put to death for his crimes of "insurrection" against the Roman empire.
>
> I was so thoroughly brainwashed that I thought anyone who was not a Christian was thoroughly wrong and living in sin. This kind of preaching was considered dangerous by the prison administrators and I was considered a religious fanatic and a prison agitator from my very first day at Auburn.

When Salvador finally came through the door, I could see right away that he had gained some weight. It had been two years since my last visit, and aside from the extra weight, I could see that he'd aged considerably. His face seemed to have more lines, and there were dark circles beneath his eyes.

"It was all that sitting around when I was down there in the bughouse is what did it," he said, as if reading my mind.

Like longlost friends we talked for hours, sharing notes, and exchanging the stories in our lives since we'd seen each other last. We talked about Jennifer, and how I still missed not having her in my life, and he wanted to know if I'd heard from Wah-Zi-Nak, and he hoped that she was doing okay. We talked about his coming parole, and I told him how I'd decided to go back to school for my teaching credentials.

> I was put in the spin shop even though I demanded the school. When I refused the school program, I also quit working. When I was called in front of the Principal Keeper, I told him that I would not work for ten cents a day because I was no slave and would not sell my golden sweat so cheap. I was accused of being a fanatic because I used to carry the Bible wherever I went and was told that I had to begin to face the fact that I was a "subject of the state" and a prisoner with a number.

As the Latina woman locked in tight with a dark-skinned man of uncertain age, Salvador talked through the morning and into the afternoon.

"I saw her," he said.

"Who'd you see?"

"Mrs. Kresinski, I saw her when I was on my furlough."

"You fucking saw who!?"

"Mrs. Kresinski, I saw her in Manhattan."

"You went to her apartment!?"

"No, no," he said, with a sweeping gesture, as if what I'd said was ridiculous,

"It was like she was walking down this street in Manhattan and our eyes locked, but she was gone before I could say I was sorry...but it was her, I know it was."

"So like you didn't actually go to her apartment or nothing... you just saw her in the street...but how did you know it was really her?"

Looking at me like I was just not getting it, and talking to me like I was a small child, he reassured me again that it was absolutely Mrs. Kresinski and no one else that he saw walking down the street during his furlough. After all, he explained at length, it had to be her because when he'd set out from his moms house that night he'd said a silent prayer that Mrs. Kresinski would pass him on the street so that he could say how sorry he was.

"No question about it," he said, "it was her."

Listening to Salvador talk on and on about Mrs. Kresinski was like listening to a small child talking about a visit from Santa Claus or the tooth fairy.

He believed so much in the simplicity of what he was saying that it would have been unthinkable for him to have ever seriously considered the alternative.

Listening to him speak about Mrs. Kresinski, I thought to myself what her reaction might've been had she actually seen him on the street, near her door, or for that matter anywhere else on earth. Her reaction, I thought, would not have faltered for a second. Reaching into whatever reservoir of strength she still had left, she would have done whatever it took to rip out his eyes, and tear him limb from limb.

> *When I finally went to school at Auburn in 1962, I was in trouble almost from the beginning.*
> *One day while the teacher was telling the students about Franklin D. Roosevelt and the Depression, he said that if it wasn't for Roosevelt's programs, capitalism would have died. I got up and told him, "You mean that if it wasn't for the programs Eleanor gave Franklin which she extracted from the People's Socialist platforms, this country would have been destroyed?" The teacher started arguing with me, and the teacher called the guards, and I was keep-locked in my cell for thirty days for causing a disturbance.*

One of Salvador's many women correspondents had written to me recently that what had originally attracted her to Salvador had been a certain sweetness, and looking at Salvador as he talked about his future plans, I thought that what she meant was more like an innocence born and nurtured by a lack of tenure in the outside world.

Prison had been his home for a long time, and had taught him much in the way of survival skills, but more than anything else it had been like a felon who'd robbed him blind. Instead of allowing his youth to mature, ripen, make mistakes, and blossom, it had crippled him in so many ways that now, sitting across from me, he seemed forever young, with the emotions intact, of a boy not long from puberty.

"You think my book's gonna be a best-seller?" he asked.

"I don't know...I never thought about it."

"Yeah, well..you should...because as soon as I'm outta here, and I get myself situated some wheres, that's what I'll be doing, finishing my book."

"Won't you be working when you get out?"

"Yeah...so? What's that got to do with anything?"

"Well... if you're working all day, it might be hard for you to work on your book at night because you'll be too tired... so maybe now's the best time."

"Listen, don't worry so much about the book...just get me another sandwich, OK?"

> Another time I was keep locked in Auburn in 1962, it was because I was snitched on by a rat. A note was sent to the warden by someone in the kitchen that said I was having a love affair with another boy who also worked with me in the kitchen.
>
> While in my cell, I thought about Dannemora State Hospital for the Criminally Insane. Maybe I could pretend that I was crazy and go there and study psychosis until I could escape.
>
> I really wanted to escape, go to Mexico and forget all that I had been through.
>
> I took some of my clothes, and putting them into a corner, I poured some lighter fluid on it and lit it up. Within seconds, flames and smoke was all over the cell. Guards came running, and once they got to the cell, I stuck my hand through the bars. I was holding a home-made shiv and I tried to stab one of the guards in his eyes. Jumping back, he said, "The fucking spic tried to stab me, we've gotta take him to Segregation." More guards came, and eventually they stormed the cell, handcuffed me behind my back, and then took me to the box.

As I waited for Salvador's sandwich to drop down the chute of the vending machine, I wondered if he would ever finish his book. Legions of convicts had begun scores of books, only to push them aside once they were back on the streets. Finding a job, and reuniting with whatever family remained, was usually more than enough to deal with, let alone trying to write a book.

> Once in the box, or segregation, at Auburn in 1962, I broke the glass on the light, and I was taken to the hospital, and then brought back to the box, but then I was placed in a strip cell. I waited until the next day and took toilet paper and the towel

and stopped up the toilet and began to flush until the whole of segregation was flooded with water.

The guards could not handle my craziness anymore so they took me to the hospital and put me in a room where they could watch me. I had a bed and I felt more comfortable. The doctor put me on Thorazine which helped settle my nerves. When the civilian doctors came to see me I told them that I was hearing voices telling me to kill myself.

The next day I was put in handcuffs and taken to the Dannemora Hospital for the Criminally Insane. This was in December of 1962.

"So you're really goin' up to Dannemora after this?" Salvador asked when I joined him back at the counter with another sandwich.

"Yeah...it's justa couple of hours away, so why not, right? It'll be good for the book...and I got someone I can visit."

"Just don't hang out there too much..."

"How come?"

"You'll see what I mean once you get up there."

As we talked there was a squishing noise coming from somewhere. At first I figured the sound was coming from the Latina woman and the dark-haired guy, and feeling too embarrassed to turn in their direction, I'd ignored it, but when it got louder, and closer, I had no choice. I turned around, but there was no one there. Visiting time was almost over, so I figured they'd left a little early.

"It's El Nino," Sal said in a loud whisper.

"What the fuck are you talking about?" I answered back, in a similar whisper.

"Take a look in the other direction, but just don't make it too obvious."

Turning slowly around, I saw where the noise was coming from. El Nino was an elderly convict, with white hair and a tired face with many lines, who was swinging a mop back and forth across the visiting room floor. With few people in the visiting room, the sound was like a kiss, magnified a thousand times.

"He's been here more than forty years..."

"What'd he do?"

"I dunno...but he probably killed someone to be in here that long...and people in here are always giving him stuff..."

"Why do people give him stuff? I don't understand."

"For luck...'cause if you take care of him then it'll come back to you in some other way, you know what I'm sayin'?"

Looking around again, as he came almost within arm's length, I saw that he had the passive look of someone heavily medicated. No expression, just a kind of blind motor humming inside, keeping him moving, with no complaints, no rage, nothing. But his medication wasn't found in a bottle.

No one really knew why some criminals suddenly stopped being criminals, stopped robbing banks, holding up liquor stores, or killing people. All the criminologists knew for sure was that whenever all the schools of the world had failed to stop the criminal, and prisons everywhere had thrown up their collective hands in despair, what would always work no matter what, was the simple avalanche of time.

State of New York-Department of Correction
Proceedings for Commitment of Insane Persons to
Dannemora State Hospital
In the Matter
of
The Commitment to Dannemora State Hospital
of
Salvador Agron

December 8th, 1962
Psychiatric Report
Name: Salvador Agron   # 56824

The diagnosis is Psychosis with Psychopathic Personality, Episode of Depression. This inmate is emotionally unstable, psychopathic personality of borderline intelligence or, at best, dull normal intelligence who is unable to adjust to the prison environment and who has vacillated between episodes of excitement and episodes of depression.

Transfer to Dannemora State Hospital is recommended so that he may receive further care and treatment and also for the safety of himself and others.

By the time I left the visiting room at Auburn and started driving north on the Adirondack freeway, it was nearly three-thirty. Within an hour it would be dark, and if it didn't snow, and the roads stayed clear, I would arrive at Dannemora by six.

When I'd telephoned ahead to reserve a room near the prison, there was only one motel, a place called Johnson's on Cook Street, in the heart of town, the owner said, and yes, he'd be glad to hold a room for me. As the night deepened, and the night got darker, the temperature dropped. Fewer and fewer cars were on the road, and by the time I took a right off the highway, I was the only one left.

Twenty miles of winding roads, with Willie Nelson crying the blues on a local radio station, as a light snow swept across my windshield. The road widened, and I was driving down Cook Street, in the heart of Dannemora.

On my left was the town, breathing with people, stores, schools, and houses. On my right was a tall iron fence with brick buildings set far back behind sweeping lawns.

> *I was taken to Dannemora State Hospital by two guards by train. I can remember the exact time I arrived because I was taken into the hospital director's office, and he pointed to the clock on the wall and said, "This is a hospital. You are a criminal convicted of murder. A dangerous man. The clock on the wall says 9 p.m. and there's a calendar. Remember the date. You must always remember that time and date if you are ever to be discharged."*
>
> *Looking at the guard next to me, he continued, "Fifty milligrams of Mellaril. Take him away."*

I was taken to Ward 3. I was stripped and given a hospital gown to wear. I was put into a cell with a mattress, a piss pot, and a blanket. Being about 18 years old, I was afraid. The place looked like the places I had seen in some psycho movies. During the night I got a pain in my lower back. After tossing and turning for a while, I got up and knocked on the door. The guard came over with, "What the fuck do you want?" I responded by complaining about the pain and the guard said, "You spic bastard. How do you think those two white boys you killed felt? Go to sleep before we go in there and give your spic ass a good whipping." I backed up from the door when the guard kicked it and went to bed trying to figure out where I had come to.

I was afraid at first because of the filthy way the guard called me. I was still in pain so after a while I went over to the radiator and put my back on a hot pipe. and bit into the sheet. The pipe burned my back and after a little touch I went back to bed. To my surprise my pain left me. I went to sleep and woke up in the morning when breakfast was brought to my room. I stayed in the room until I saw the psychiatrist and had a physical which was procedural.

When the fence ended, there was an open space of several feet before the prison wall began. Stretching down Cook Street as far as the eye could see, and rising thirty feet in the air, the prison wall was like a dark shroud flooding the town.

When I got out of my jeep in front of the motel, the stone wall of the prison was less than fifty feet from where I was standing, and as the snow swirled and blew in the dark night, I remembered Salvador saying once that sometimes he would wake up in the morning feeling as if the Wall was right in bed with him.

Even though the front door was open, there was no one in the lobby, and after I rang the little bell on the desk, I took a look around.

Except for the framed photographs on the walls, the

motel lobby could have been any one of ten thousand just like it stretched all across America, the cheap motels, with their plastic chairs, potted plants, and registration books.

Providing a history of the prison, the photographs were spread across the walls like a dark mosaic of human suffering. And like those at Auburn, the photographs on the walls depicted scores of men in zebra stripes, building, hauling, and constructing.

> *Dannemora State Hospital in 1962 was divided into fifteen wards. The inmate population was about 1500. The place was run by the guards (who were called attendants) and by a supervisor. The Department of Corrections really ran the place even though the staff of doctors claimed they had more power. The doctors often followed the dictates of the guards. The blue towels that the guards carried in their back pockets were not only for drying their hands, but they were also used for when an insane person could not be controlled to put around their necks and "choke them out." The guards did this more out of abuse than out of protection. Speaking of bedlam, I guess the Bastille was paradise on earth compared to the horrors and brutalities of Dannemora. The whole place was run on fear and clear brute force. I had reached the last stop. I was told very clearly, "Here they kill you or you escape, or you go crazier, or you submit to their system." Well, I was resolute that no matter what they did, I would remain strong 'til this citadel of madness was normalized.*
>
> *After a month I was transferred to Ward 6. Things were real slow there. It was an idle ward and the patients were really sick. I used to sit next to a "swinging bug" He would suddenly get up and go over and hit someone on the ward, knock them out, and return to his seat. I would look at him and told him, "If you swing on me, I'll kill you right here." I guess he understood me. At times we would talk and he made it clear that he was my friend.*

"You can take them down for a closer look if you'd like." Turning around, I was face to face with the speaker, a middle-aged man with bright blue eyes, who wore a hunter's cap, and who introduced himself as John Holmes, the owner of the motel.

"Uh...I'm Jacoby, the guy who called you about a room."

"I kinda figured that," he said, with a broad smile, "because we don't get too many visitors up this time of year."

"Yeah, I'll bet...it's really cold out there!"

"Cold? You think this is cold? This ain't nothing! It's still in the twenties out there...when the real winter starts it's mostly below zero."

"You lived here long?" I asked him.

"All my life. Born and raised. My father was a guard, and so was his father, so that's where all the photographs come from...you wanna look at any of them?"

"Nah, but thanks. Uh, where's the hospital from here?"

"Which one you looking for?"

"The one for the inmates..."

"Oh, you mean the bughouse!"

"I guess so..."

"It was in those buildings across the street, you probably saw the fence on your right when you drove in, but it's been shut down since 1972."

"How many patients did it have?"

"A thousand, maybe more...it's one of those pictures up there on the wall."

Looking at the pictures again, I could vaguely make out some buildings behind the fence, but like the other photographs, they were old, and hard to make out.

"You sure you wouldn't want me to take those down for you?" He asked.

"No, maybe tomorrow, I think right now I'd just like to check into my room."

"No problem, just sign the register, and I'll give you a key."

My room was down a long corridor, and as I walked I noticed a sign on the wall with the prison visiting hours.

Small and clean, the room has a television, and a large double bed with plenty of blankets. As soon as I was settled in, I went back to the lobby to call Aurea.

> *I felt nervous on the ward. I didn't like it. The nervousness was probably due to the Mellaril I was being given which sometimes makes the nerves worse. I told the doctor and he said, "Don't worry Mr. Agron. I have a nice place for you." He ordered me transferred. I thought I was going to a working ward rather than an idle ward and I was in for a surprise. The guards took me to segregation. I was put in a room which had two doors and a window which one could not hardly reach or look out from, for it was too high to do so. I had a mat on the floor and a piss pot. There was nothing else in the isolation room save the four walls, the ceiling and the floor.*

No one was in the lobby, but looking around I found the pay phone mounted on a wall by the entrance. As I dialed Aurea's number, I looked through the window, At first I thought I was looking at a giant fog bank, but then I remembered where I was.

The fog was the Wall, and when I looked closer, I saw the snow had picked up considerably.

"Hello," Aurea said, when she answered the phone with her usual cheerfulness.

"It's me, your brother, Jacobo."

"Hi! How you doin'? Did you see my brother?"

"Yeah...he's great, and he sends love and everything...hey, guess where I am."

"I dunno...the Bronx?" She said.

"Dannemora!"

"What you doin' way up there?"

Just as I was about to answer, I heard a noise behind me, and when I turned around it was John Holmes. He was looking through some papers at his desk. Feeling instantly self-conscious, I told Aurea I'd call her later, or when I got back to New York.

"Get through okay?" he wanted to know, when I hung up the phone.

"Yeah, no problem."

"The lines get real bad up here sometimes because of the weather..."

"You think it'd be safe for me to walk around the town a little bit?"

"Safe? Oh, absolutely, we don't even lock our doors around here, but I haveta tell you that there's not that much to see..."

"Yeah, well, I just wanna get a little fresh air, that's all."

"Then you just go on ahead, the front door'll be open when you get back."

> *I walked back and forth in the room cursing the doctor for deceiving me. He spoke so nice to me and now I felt betrayed. That day I was given a tray of food but no spoon. I asked for a spoon and was informed that I could not get a spoon to eat with until approved by the doctor. I got so angry that I took the tray and threw it in the guard's face. I was pushed back in the room and I started kicking the door. They called the doctor to report my behavior and he ordered me put in the restraining sheet. I was taken out. A straightjacket was put on me and a towel wrapped around my neck and I was taken to the craziest ward in the hospital—Ward 2. The guard would kick me from behind and then one would smack me in the face every time I objected. I would just say, "You guys, do what you want to do but I'm going to write everyone I know and expose this place to the public."*

Walking down one street, and up another, with my jacket pulled tight against the cold and the blowing snow, the Wall was everywhere. Rising up in front of me on one street, peeking at me from another, or suddenly appearing as if from nowhere until I felt like I was buried in the belly of a giant whale.

When I got to the building that John Holmes had said

was the local school, I decided to go inside and look around. The door was locked, but with a full moon rising there was more than enough light to see from one end of the building to the other. During the day, little children roamed the halls. They sat at desks, flirted with one another, and raised their hands to answer questions.

> They laughed it off as though my threats did not matter. And they did not matter because Dannemora State Hospital was run by the guards similar to the way Nazis ran concentration camps. They were big and powerful guards and they acted just like Gestapo. When they pushed me to Ward 2 the guards there already knew me. "Hey, looka here! We got the Capeman here," one of the guards said, adding, "Is he giving us a hard time already?" One grabbed some loose straps and came over as I was being put in the jacket and in the restraining sheet. While the others held me, I was hit on my bare ass with the straps. Then I was tied to a chair in the restraining sheet. I was told by the patient-inmate working there that I was lucky that they didn't put the thick paddle on my ass which hurts more.
>
> I looked at him in disgust and said, "Don't worry. I will never forget this humiliation. This shit is going to stop even if we have to burn the place down." He smiled as though saying "I wish you luck" and said, "Well, you better be cool or these bastards might kill you." I looked at him and said, "I'm not afraid of death, my friend. If they kill me, then my misery will end." I was resolute to come out alive. I was kept tied down for forty days and nights, as I grew weak.
>
> While tied down, one guard saw my feet trembling. He came over with an alcoholic smell on his breath and said, "Stop shaking those feet!" I looked up, knowing he was drunk and up to no good and said, "Sir, but that's an involuntary muscle. I can't help it!" He again ordered that I stop my feet from trembling. When I could not, he hit me on my chest with his feet so I spit on him. Again he did the same and I spit on him again. Now, he was calling me all kinds of "spics" and brought over a heavy-set guard who weighed about 300 pounds.

> "Listen," he said. "I'm going to hit you again and if your spic ass spits on me again, this guy is going to sit on you" I got scared because this fat guard had already killed a couple of patients from sitting on them. It was common knowledge among those in that ward.

Looking at the Wall, as I stood by the school, I could barely make out a gun tower and a little slice of window from a building right behind the Wall. Could the convicts see the children in the classroom, I wondered, when the light was right? Given that the Wall was no more than several thousand yards away, it was conceivable, and I wondered if Salvador had ever looked through that very window.

> The drunk guard told me that he was going to hit me again and if I spit at him, then the fat guard would sit on me and squash me to death. He hit me about four times and obediently but with supreme hate in my heart I did not spit again. However, by some miracle my feet stopped trembling. I looked at the other guys in the restraining sheets and this black guy said, "Listen, nigger. Be cool. These motherfuckers will kill you and think nothing about it. Lay cool. You'll get out." The restraining sheet was being used to punish inmates and not for psychiatric reasons.

With the snow coming down harder and harder, I made my way back to the motel. Everywhere I looked was the Wall, and I thought to myself that if the people of Dannemora shared nothing else in common with the convicts, one thing was certain: all of them were living together in the very belly of the beast.

> After being in the restraining sheet (where we had to even do our basic toilet necessities in a bed pan), I realized I had reached the last stop. I knew I was in hell. I decided that the best thing now was to lay low. Inevitably I was taken out of restraint and put in a room where I was kept in a hospital gown for months and I slept on a mattress on the floor, with my piss

> pot and bowl of water in the corner. I was given Thorazine every day, and it kept me numb and weak all the time. When food came around I would have to crawl on the floor, from being so weak.
>
> Then I went to Ward 2 where I was hit by the swinging bug. I ducked but he got me good. I wanted to hurt him, but the guards came over and pulled him away. I looked in amazement and really saw insanity for the first time in the core of a man's eyes. I felt sorry, but I had to be strong. So I chucked it off and decided to learn more about the hospital.

At the door of the motel, still restless, and wanting to get away from the Wall, even for a few minutes, I kept walking. Down another street, up another, at least a mile or so, until I came to a cemetery. A little metal sign said, "State Prison Cemetary," and walking down the rows of graves, I noticed that some had nothing on them except a number. No name, no date of birth, or death. Nothing but a number. Was this what Salvador and others had meant when they'd said that the biggest fear convicts had was that of dying in prison? Friendless, and without families, were they afraid of being dumped like garbage into a backfield cemetery with just their prison numbers?

The wind whistled, the snow flew, but still no answers came.

> After this, I knew one thing. It was me against them. I went to Clinton Prison.
>
> This was still in 1962. There I continued my studies and then back to Dannemora State Hospital after playing crazy. I kept going from prison to prison, meeting the brutal system face to face and creating disturbances. I was in hell and like my friend, Juan told me, "Sal, forget about the Bible. This is a prison, not a church." I knew it. I was in hell and had to get out someday.

"There's a good place up the street for coffee in the morning," John Holmes said when I got back to the motel.

Thanking him, and borrowing an alarm clock, I went to my room.

> *The fact that Mrs. Davis wrote the director and would come visit me and the fact that my family wrote and visited me kept the guards from murdering me, as they did with others who refused to conform. But I was threatened many times, beaten, and brutalized.*

The good place that John Holmes had mentioned was called the "Front Gate," and was right across the street from the main entrance to the prison. Through the windows, I could see the Wall. The snow had stopped, but it was still a dismal gray outside, and probably not much more than twenty degrees.

Almost as soon as I was through the door, and had ordered a breakfast of coffee and toast, a female guard had taken a seat right next to me.

"You hear to visit someone across the street?"

"Yeah, how'd you know?"

"The colder it gets, the less visitors we get, and I ain't seen you around here before, so either you're a visitor, or you're just passing through to somewhere else."

Looking at her closely as she continued to talk, I figured she was no more than thirty, give or take a year or two, and from what I could see of her face beneath the Corrections hat she was wearing, she appeared to be attractive, with light eyes and a nice smile.

> *From Ward 3 (reception) I was sent to idle ward 6, which kept extreme violent cases. I could not conform to Ward 6 and so I asked the doctor for another ward (a working ward). He questioned me about my crime and I told him that I did not do it but took the blame for it. This infuriated him as it did other doctors and he banged on the desk and in a foreign accent said, "You don vant to faze your guilt. You are a murderer, boy, a killar" I could hardly understand his English. He ordered*

> that I be put in a strip room.
>
> I was whisked away and put naked in a room with a mat on the floor which had two doors to it and a high window with screen and bars, no toilet or sink, dirty walls and floor, with shit and urine smell. It was called "double doors." I was kept there in those conditions under heavy doses of Mellaril and rationed food. But isolation was driving me mad (insane) and so I did what any human being would do under such conditions.
>
> The food was always given to me without a spoon—doctor's order. I had to eat with my bare hands on a plastic tray. I took the tray and smacked the two guards across the face with it. About twenty guards were summoned and they entered the room, beat me almost unconscious, threw a towel around my neck and squeezed until my face was ashen.

Her name was Connie, and from the way she was talking, I knew right away that there was nothing she liked more than to talk about the ways and whys of prison.

People who worked in prisons, either as guards, social workers, or whatever, could be divided into two distinct categories. There were those who avoided talking about the prison no matter what, never giving out an opinion, how they felt about convicts, nothing but silence whenever you asked. Then there were those, like Connie, who took a kind of perverse pride in their work. Gentle probing yielded all kinds of philosophical interpretations of convict behavior. Convicts weren't like you and I, Connie hinted, as she bit into a piece of sausage. Void of light and reason, convicts were slightly less than human. More like dogs in need of beatings if and when they strayed too far. Listening to her talk, I wondered what she'd say after a beer and a few shots of whiskey.

> I was dragged to Ward 2 (restraining ward), bent over a bed and beat with leather straps till I was black and blue. Then I was put into a straightjacket and then was put into a restraining sheet made of canvas. I was tied to a wooden chair in a room known as the "restraining room" with some other

inmates who were in the same condition. When I fully became conscious, this black inmate was rubbing a wet towel across my face, cleaning the blood on my nose and face.

The guard came in with his blue towel in his back pocket and said, "Next time we'll kill you, you fucking spic. You will not get away with those two murders." Another inmate who had been kept in restraint for almost seven years started spitting at the racist guard. The guard quickly threw a towel on his face which could have suffocated him and smacked Camacho three times across the face. I could not believe the brutality. I was shocked. I thought it was a nightmare, but it was real—very real. I started praying to God and Jesus! I was in the midst of madness.

I was kept tied down for 40 days and 40 nights. My bones ached. If I wanted to defecate, a bed pan was placed under me and the sheet on the chair was my toilet paper. To piss I had to urinate in a bottle. The only time I was let out of the restraining sheet was once a week for a five minute shower and a change of the canvas. Behind the chair in which I sat tied down all day was a bed which I saw only at night. I was tied down to the bed. I was fed by inmates from a tray with a spoon.

"What was it like growing up so close to the Wall?" I asked Connie.

"That wall over there?" she said, pointing across the street, as she got ready to leave the cafe. "I never gave it a second thought."

It was one day, while in restraining that a new doctor came around, spoke to me and ordered that I be immediately untied and put in a room.

"There is nothing wrong with this patient. He should not be tied down like this!"

I was taken out of restraint. When the regular ward doctor discovered this, he put me on 200 milligrams of Thorazine three times a day. That was a total of 600 milligrams. I could not move in the room and had to crawl to my food while wearing only a gown open in the back. I was weak, slept day and night. My medicine was increased to 1200 milligrams when I *asked to be taken off it. I fell unconscious for days. This is the time that my inner self or what is known as the "astral body" left my physical body.*

I was free, out on the streets. The institution had given me a "furlough" which up to this day remains real to me. I was released to New York. Whether this actually happened or not, I still cannot tell. I only believe it to be a psychic experience. I spent time with my family and then was hit over the head after seven days, brought back to the hospital and awoke in the same strip cell. I had been out for days. A doctor was shining a small light into my eyes when I woke up. I could not believe what happened. I could no longer distinguish reality from dream existence.

The doctor was in my room. The guards were standing around and staring at me on the floor.

"He'll be all right, man," the doctor said. But after my medicine was reduced to 50 milligrams a day, I had a dream in which I looked upon my own body on the mat on the floor while standing in the room. Everything was so real that I really did not know which "me" was really me. Up to this day I still suspect that LSD or some other drug was mixed with my Thorazine because afterwards it started tasting different. I was sure I was used in an LSD experiment.

I followed her across the street and into the prison. Inside was a very small vestibule, with two corrections officers seated behind a big mahogany desk.

"These guys'll take care of you," Connie said, before going thorough the metal detector, and out another door.

After showing my ID, and giving them the name of the person I wanted to visit, I walked through the metal detector.

"Just go out the door there, and follow the path to the first building." One of the corrections officers said, pointing to the door that Connie had just gone through.

Outside the door, I found myself in a small courtyard. With the Wall to my right, I walked several yards down a pathway to a building marked "Administration." Clinton had three visiting rooms, and all of them were in this building. One was for non-contact visits, not even hand-holding, in a small room with a sheet of Plexiglas separating you and the convict, and was reserved for convicts who'd been busted for smuggling in the main visiting room, The other two, designated, "North" and "South" were for all the rest of the population, but were rarely ever in operation at the same time.

Handing my pass to the officer inside, he sent me down a long corridor until I came to a locked door. Someone inside buzzed me in, and I was assigned a seat directly in the middle of the horseshoe-shaped room. Like the visiting room at Greenhaven, or at Auburn, the table was about thirty inches wide, and convicts sat on one side, and visitors on the other.

At Greenhaven, there had always been at least several people visiting at the same time, and even at Auburn there had been the Latina woman with the dark-haired man, but here at Clinton, there was no one but me.

> After being in the room for what felt like months, I was called before the new doctor and some men in civilian clothes who looked more like detectives than doctors. I was extensively interviewed about my stay at the hospital. How much could I tell them about my experiences while at the hospital and whether I was "innocent" or "guilty" of the crime for which I was convicted. I suspected something strange going on and said that I was "guilty" but that I could not remember anything about the time I'd spent at the hospital because I'd been psychotic.
>
> They whispered to each other and told me that I would be let out of the room and then after a month I would be sent to Ward 14, the hospital ward for the physically sick mental patients so I could work. I was put in the dormitory of Ward 2 and assigned a chair. I got visits and observed the abuse and brutality that went on, but I minded my own business. I was all alone. My visitors (sister, mother, and Mrs. Davis) did not believe my stories so I decided not to tell them any more. I had to survive. I did not tell anybody about the LSD because at that

time I did not know what it was.

One day when the officers were not around I noticed that the medicine cabinet had been left open. I told an inmate who was not so crazy and a "friend" to watch the guards for me. I went inside the office and looked at my record. One page said, "This man needs more treatment. He is not yet cured." The word "cured" was in capital letters and underlined by red pencil or pen. I then looked into the cabinet and began to write down some of the names of the medicines. This list was later confiscated from me by guards on orders of a doctor.

On my small notepad on the next page, I jotted down "Prolixin" (orange and purple in color) and "Lysergic Acid Diethylamide" This was not confiscated but was stolen together with a book manuscript which was fiction and my poems and the minutes of my appeal and other things. There was also another bottle without a label—sealed—which was crystal clear, but I did not know what it was. I put the notes in my pocket. The inmate I had watching told me the guard was coming. I picked up the garbage basket and as I walked out, I said, "Joe Johnson told me to dump the garbage for him." Joe Johnson was the inmate who cleaned the office. The guard cautioned me about going into the office while no guards were there.

"Okay, sir," I said respectfully.

When Joe came from picking up the towels, I said to him, "Listen, Billy. The police almost caught me in the office. I told him you had told me to dump the garbage basket for you."

"I got you covered, Sal," he said.

The guard did ask him and he responded in the affirmative, but he also told him to tell me not to go in the office any more. Reading my notes that night, I traced practically all the medicines except Lysergic Acid. It was about two years later that I discovered what it meant while in Clinton Prison where a fellow had accused the Auburn and Clinton authorities of putting LSD in his food or drink while in the box and then in the bug cell. I asked him what "LSD" meant and he told me the name. It was then I realized what had been given to me and others at Dannemora State Hospital.

Then something happened that later on I would see as a

new beginning for me.

One day, a guard took me and another patient down to the basement to help him clean out some old boxes that were stored down there. There were hundreds of boxes down there, and in one of them I found some old condemned books, and when the guard wasn't looking, I hid some in my pants. There was a book on Spinoza, a small one on constitutional law, and a copy of the Communist Manifesto by Karl Marx. That's when I really started to read. The guard would walk by to see what I was reading and would only see the false cover and title I had on them. On the Spinoza book, I had written "Catholic Mass" and on the Communist Manifesto I had written "Ten Commandments." This I did on the advice of another inmate, who had been in the bughouse for a long time and knew how to fool the guards.

With little light coming through the windows from the dark morning, the visiting room felt spare and bleak. A small Christmas tree, without any ornaments, stood alone in a corner, and looking around, I noticed there weren't any vending machines. When I asked one of the guards he said there were some in the other visiting room next door, and if I liked I could walk over there if I wanted to buy something.

Dark and unused, the adjacent visiting room had several vending machines lined up, side by side, between two windows. Outside was the Wall, Cook Street, the motel, and the town. Several guards were standing by the machines, drinking coffee, when I walked in, and as soon as they saw me, there was sudden silence. As the quarters dropped to the bottom of the vending machine in the now quiet adjacent visiting room, I thought for a moment about the man I had come to visit. His name was Rocco Santini, and he was a boyhood friend from Brooklyn. We hadn't seen one another for over twenty years, and then it was just before he'd been sent to prison on a charge of armed robbery. Rumored to be connected to a Brooklyn crime family, he seemed to be caught in a revolving door, with Clinton his home for the last five years. Had it not been for a mutual friend who'd seen me at one of Reverend Ed's cadre meetings at Greenhaven, we would've remained at a distance. But then we had exchanged some letters, and I'd promised to visit whenever the timing was right.

As I left the adjacent visiting room with my coffee, I could hear the guards start talking again.

> After about a year or so, I was pronounced as being "cured," and sent next door to Clinton Prison, or "over the wall," as the convicts called it.
>
> When I entered Clinton Prison from the bughouse, I was put in reception. I was taken in front of a deputy warden and I was put in the weave shop, but after being accused of some sabotage, I was transferred to the school.
>
> All the books I'd found in the hospital basement were taken away as soon as I got to Clinton, but I did manage to hang on to Karl Marx. Very slowly, I started to read and study.
>
> This was in 1964, and I was beginning to detect something new happening in the prisons. Inmates were beginning to speak out and sort of rebel. It wasn't an active thing, but the beginnings were there. Militancy was still dead, and only the Muslims were around, and even they were in small numbers. The guards would still call people "spics," and "niggers," and among the guards (who were all white) these seemed to be their favorite words. The Black Muslims fared the worst. Thrown in the box, beaten, and abused.
>
> I was taken before the Disciplinary Board and when the Warden called me "spic" I reacted by calling him a "cripple cracker" and said that his mother was a "jew bastard." The guard were about to beat me up, but instead I was sent back to the hospital.

**State of New York-Department of Correction
Proceedings For Commitment of Insane Persons to
Dannemora State Hospital
In the Matter
of
The Commitment to Dannemora State Hospital
of
Salvador Agron**

Salvador Agron   # 39650   June 3, 1965

Inmate referred for psychiatric evaluation following an acute disturbance in his cell when he threw glass jars out of his cell, creating a disturbance, and yelling that someone was after him. Claimed a vision kept coming in front of his cell.

There is a history of an admission to the Dannemora State Hospital from 12/19/62 to 3/13/64 with recovery from Psychosis with Psychopathic Personality Schizoid Traits.

He was found to be sullen, uncooperative, angry, and vague. He said that his lawyer sent him the pictures of the corpse he had in his possession but he refused to elaborate. When he was asked specifically if this was the person he killed, he denied that he had ever killed anyone and also said that juries find everyone guilty. He said that God talks spiritual talk to everyone and that he heard it last night as the wind blowing in the window.

He said everyone hates him and he reciprocates by hating them back. He said he was depressed but didn't know if he wanted to kill himself.

It is my opinion that this inmate is psychotic and it is advised that he be transferred immediately to the Dannemora State Hospital for psychiatric treatment.

Connie the guard was waiting for me when I got back to the still empty visiting room. Sipping coffee, I listened as she explained that the guy I was planning to visit had an infection in one of his eyes and wouldn't be able to see me today.

"What happened?" I asked.

"Other than what I already told you, I can't say anything else, just that he can't have any visitors right now."

"Yeah, but I came all the way here from California, so can't there be an exception made just this once?"

"I'm sorry, but that's the rules."

"Well, while I'm here, you think maybe I could get a little tour of the prison?"

Giving me a quizzical look, she wanted to know why I wanted a tour, and seemed to feel better about the idea when I explained my background. That I'd been a student of criminology for years, had been working on a dissertation, and was very interested in the way things worked in prison. Saying she'd try to find someone to see if something could be arranged, she said for me to wait for her in the visiting room.

"While you're waiting, why don't you look at the photographs on the walls," she said, pointing to a series of black and white photographs lining the walls, "All of them were taken inside the prison here."

> After I got back to the bughouse, I was taken to court in Plattsburg to determine my sanity, and I was declared incompetent and found criminally insane because I claimed I was "a law unto myself and did not recognize their sanity hearing" and that "I was God." Mrs. Davis was present at the hearing and a lawyer was appointed for me. I was asked if I had committed murder and answered that I was innocent.
>
> I was going to be given shock treatments, but since my mother did not sign anything, I was given large doses of Thorazine.
>
> While I was in Dannemora this time, I was called to New York City for a hearing to determine the admissibility of my original confession for the playground killings.

Like the photographs in the motel lobby, all of them were black and white, and all of them were of convicts. But where the ones at the motel lobby depicted scores of convicts constructing prisons, here the convicts were playing football, catching baseballs, and running around a track. One picture stood out from all the rest. Clear as day, and with the Wall in the background, it showed what looked like some kind of ski jump, with men on what appeared to be makeshift sleds, halfway down the jump. Just as I was about to examine the photograph a little closer, I heard Connie's voice coming from behind me.

"We're on! Someone upstairs gave the okay, but we just can't go into the cellblocks."

Walking back with her through the door she'd just come through, we were in a long corridor.

"First I'll show you the yard!" she said, with a broad smile that spoke volumes about her enthusiasm.

Whether or not someone upstairs had actually given her the okay, or whether she was simply acting on her own volition, was hard to say; but nothing, I thought, could have pleased her more than to give me a guided tour of her locked-in world. And as I gazed at her now flushed face and overly bright eyes, I realized my request must have arrived like an answered prayer,

> I was first sent to the mental ward of Riker's Island, and then after a short time to the "Tombs," or the Manhattan House of Detention. This was in 1966, and by the time I got to the Tombs, my name was once again in the news. Reaction and old hates were once again stirred up. It was the same old atmosphere as in 1959.
>
> But things were slowly changing out in the world. The voice of Malcom X was starting to be heard, militancy was on the rise. Along with this, the long-haired people and the drug culture started entering the Tombs, and they were mostly called "hippies." I was taking all this in stride and felt good because people of my wild spirit were on the rise.
>
> I was put on the eight floor of the Tombs, on the A-side, where mental observation and bizarre murder cases were kept

isolated. The crazies were on one tier, and the homosexuals on another. There was a white line drawn down the tier, and when the homosexuals and the crazies were let out at the same time, they would sit on opposite sides of the line. A guard was specifically assigned to the gallery to maintain order.

"The gym's over there," Connie said, as we kept walking, and as we passed by "F" Block, and then "H" Block, with their hundreds of cells, I wondered whether or not what she'd said about my friend's eye had been true. Although canceled visits were not unusual because of sickness or keeplocks, this was prison, and paranoid visions were known to have a peculiar way of becoming reality.

"Here's the yard," she said, opening a door.

Although Salvador had told me a little about what was in the yard at Clinton, his descriptions had been so outlandish, that I had more or less said, sure, sure, that's nice, but had never really taken him too seriously.

Spread out in front of me like a painting of Dante's inferno, was a prison yard unlike any other that I'd ever seen before.

"This is where we play football and baseball," Connie said, with a wide sweep of her arm.

"Yeah, but what are those up there," I said, pointing to a gigantic hill rising in the air like a volcano.

"Those are the courts," she said, laughing. "You wanna take a closer look?"

> I began to meet lots of old friends from the 1950's in the Tombs. I was twenty-one years old and began teaching things to the new inmates. I spoke to the homosexuals and told them it was discriminatory to be kept behind a white line. They applauded my speeches. By this time I was a radical, not a socialist or a communist, but a radical who had revolutionary ideas. I met up with men I had known when I was in the death house, and one day I met the man who'd shot Malcom X. His name was Butler, and while I did not hate him, I did question

him because Malcom X was a good brother.

I also met many strange people, hippies, crazies, killers, mafia, militants, and Young Lords.

After a few days in the Tombs, I began to feel depressed with all the madness around me. When I went back to court, I told the judge that I did not feel good. He ordered me back to Bellevue for further psychiatric evaluation.

Salvador had said Clinton was built on the side of a mountain, but until that moment I hadn't really understood what he'd meant. The "volcano" turned out to be a a series of terraces with what looked like hundreds of tiny spaces reserved for groups of four or more inmates. The spaces were tiny "courts," tiered on the hill, and as I walked with Connie higher and higher, through the courts, to nearly the top of the hill, I saw that most had cooking stoves made from giant oil drums.

Convicts wrapped in layered clothing, with everything hidden save their eyes from the cold, cooked gigantic pieces of meat using huge forks to keep them in place over the converted oil drums. Other convicts gave us hard-eyed looks as me and Connie the guard slowly made our way from court to court.

"Keeps them busy," Connie said, when I asked about the courts.

"How many are there?"

"About three hundred, more or less," she said.

Looking at the courts, some vague memory stirred of a book I'd read about the Mafia, and how when Lucky Luciano had been here years ago, in the 1930's, he'd had a court somewhere on this very hill.

Between the huge pillows of smoke, the all-pervasive smell of burning meat, and the wandering convicts bundled up like homeless hobos, I felt like I'd suddenly landed in the bottom most layer of hell.

"And the prison lets all this go on?" I asked.

"Why shouldn't they? It don't cost them nothing... besides, don't they look right at home?" she said, gesturing to several of the bundled up convicts, who looked as though they wished to be anywhere else but here.

I was about to answer, when suddenly, from over my head, I heard a swishing sound, and when I looked up I realized we were walking beneath some kind of slide.

"What's that," I said, pointing upward,

"That's our ski jump!" Connie said, with the same pride in her voice that I'd heard just a few minutes ago when she'd pointed out the Segregation Building, or the box, where the more violent prisoners were locked up, alone, sometimes for years.

Built on pylons, and running above one section of the courts, the ski jump was a home-made affair built by the convicts years ago.

When I said to Connie that it seemed like the men sliding down the hill were having a good time, she got a look on her face that told me I had just made a mistake,

"Fun? They don't deserve to have no fun," she said, her frozen smile looking more than ever like a Halloween Jack'o-Lantern.

"I just thought..."

"Are you one of those people who believes criminals ain't gettin' a fair shake?" she said.

"Well..." I started to say, but then, thinking better of it, stayed silent.

Standing side by side with Connie as the snow got heavier, we watched as the convicts stomped their feet to ward off the ferocious cold, and tried in vain to shelter their burning meat from the wind-blown snow. And as I watched, I wondered what kind of person would damn them forever to a place like this.

At Bellevue Hospital, I was put in a cage. Across from me was Richard Robles. He looked at me and said, "I know you,

I saw your picture in Detective Magazine about six years ago when I was in Elmira. You're the Capeman, isn't that right?" I found out who he was. At Bellevue, Robles and I got together to see if we could escape. He told me he was innocent.

Robles and I were caught up in the inside hollow of the ceiling looking for a way out—we were taken into a room, and beaten by the guards. Then I was placed in a room by myself and put in a straightjacket. But still I tried to escape, and after awhile I was tied to the bed so that I couldn't move anymore.

By this time the newspapers and television had gotten hold of the story, and right away I was put in a section with the five-percenters, across the hall from where I was. When the newspapers reported that I had been beaten, the Department of Corrections wrote a report claiming that my bruises were self-inflicted, and when the judge who had sent for me from Dannemora found out, he believed the report, and made me stay at Bellevue a little longer.

I was used as an interpreter for the mental cases, and all the five-percenters claimed that I had been blessed with some kind of knowledge! So I had respect throughout the Tombs. I heard later on that whenever two prison groups were antagonistic to one another, or something was unclear, the saying was, "the Capeman knows."

I was finally sent back to the Tombs from the Bellevue bughouse because the doctors said I was now competent to have the hearing to decide whether or not my confession had been coerced.

At the Tombs again, I went to court, and my writ was denied. El Diario, the Spanish newspaper in New York, came out with the headline: "Agron Pierde Ultima," or "Agron Loses Last Battle."

I was kept at the Tombs at the request of my lawyer and Mrs. Davis, who now relished the publicity and sought more by falsely claiming that he would handle my appeal. Mrs. Davis tried to help by creating a "positive" image of me in the press and pushing her bi-linqual program while using the "rehabilitation scheme to get funding for her program. I was beginning to feel trapped between the two of them, and I was starting to feel powerless all over again, just like I'd felt when

I was on death row.

I began to organize inmates under a vague socialist banner because so many people were coming to me with their problems about being abused as prisoners. I put a writ against the Tombs for physical and psychological harassment.

My radicalization and revolutionary outlook began to take shape during my time in the Tombs in the 1960's. But I was also almost killed in the Tombs when I was brutalized by the riot squad and accused of trying to take over the 8th floor. I was beaten so bad that I was taken to Bellevue Hospital with a concussion and a broken hand. Right before this happened I had testified in favor of another inmate who had been beaten, so now I was on the revenge list.

The City of New York
Department of Correction
Manhattan House of Detention For Men
125 White Street New York, NY 10013

January 26th, 1967

R,E, Herold, M.D. Director
Dannemora State Hospital
Dannemora, New York

Re: Salvador Agron #7622

Dear Dr, Herold:

With reference to the communication of January 24, 1967 concerning the above mentioned inmate, please find enclosed Report of Infraction and Medical Consultation Request.

In brief, the investigation conducted into this entire incident revealed, at that time, that Salvador Agron was the aggressor in the incident wherein he had to be forcibly restrained by the Officers on duty to prevent him from furthering his attack upon one of them. During this brief struggle a group of inmates in the housing area became unruly and openly defied the tour commander of the institution who had responded to the emergency call for help. However, order was quickly restored and the general disturbance was quieted when all inmates finally locked in their cells. The seriousness of this situation was precipitated and aggravated by Agron's actions. He has been known to be an aggressive recalcitrant and agitating type of inmate and has always been housed in Administrative Segregation status while in this institution. Two Corrections Officers were injured during the restraining action against Agron. One of these officers has not returned to duty to this date due to such injuries.

Salvador Agron was given immediate medical attention at this institution and at Bellevue Hospital and would have continued to receive the necessary medical attention while under our jurisdiction but was returned to your institution upon receiving an order from the Supreme Court requesting his return to your institution.

> Sincerely yours,
> A. Neena
> Warden

Our tour ended abruptly a short time later when Connie got a call on her walkie-talkie that she was needed upstairs. Whether or not this was a ploy to cut our tour short, or it was just in the nature of things, was hard to say.

Shaking hands, and wishing one another the best, we parted company by the Administration Building, and a few minutes later I found myself walking on Cook Street, past the tall iron fence, with the former bughouse off in the distance.

> *Back at Dannemora in the bughouse, the doctors said I looked like I'd just got back from Vietnam, which was funny at the time because just before I'd left for New York City for the hearing, I'd been under some very heavy medication, and I'd written a legal brief to President Johnson, asking to join the army so I could fight in Vietnam.*

To: Lyndon Baines Johnson, President of the United States

Excellency, sir:
Having determined that it is my solemn duty to serve my country in all cases whatsoever, and having determined that I am physically and mentally capable of discharging this duty, I therefore ask you that I be allowed to fight against the revolutionary forces, also known as the Communist Viet Cong, in South Vietnam.

I am petitioning your Excellency, the President of the United States, for an Executive Order that would permit me to enter into the United States Army, and be fitted for active duty service in one of the front line units now serving in South Vietnam.

Respectfully submitted,
Salvador Agron   #39640
Box B
Dannemora Hospital for the Criminally Insane

State of New York
Department of Correction
Dannemora State Hospital

Februrary 20th, 1967

Salvador Agron   #7622
   In accordance with the provisions of Section 386, Chapter 243 of the Laws of 1929, I hereby certify that in my opinion the hereinafter described convict has recovered his right mind and reason.
   Received at Sing Sing Prison on October 6, 1960, Auburn Prison on February 21, 1962; Dannemora State Hospital on December 19th, 1962; Clinton Prison on March 13, 1964; and the Dannemora State Hospital on June 8, 1965.

Director, Dannemora State Hospital

Salvador had written that the poorhouse in Mayaguez reminded him of Dracula's castle from the comic books. It had a look of foreboding, he'd written, and when I stopped to look between the bars at the bughouse, I had the same feeling.

> *After the doctors declared me sane once again, I was again sent "over the wall" to the prison next door.*
>
> *This was in 1967, and I was now twenty-four years old, hard, and ready for prison life, experienced, and ready for school. I was already an intellectual but I was in need of a woman because my sex drive was so strong.*

State of New York Department of Correction

**Proceedings For Commitment of Insane Persons to Dannemora State Hospital
In the Matter
of
The Commitment to Dannemora State Hospital
of
Salvador Agron
March 21, 1969**

Salvador Agron   # 39650

He was depressed, sat with head bowed. Spoke in a low tone, and questions had to be repeated. He stated, "I feel depressed," and everything depresses me."

He sleeps poorly. States he's been depressed for several months now. Says he hears God talking to him at night, and then states "I don't want to die but I'm afraid I'll kill myself."

The clinical picture is of an inmate depression with psychomotor retardation, continuous weeping, and suicidal ruminations. He further manifests auditory hallucinations and mixed religious grandiose and persecutory delusions.

It is advised that he be transferred to the Dannemora State Hospital for care and treatment. He is a danger to himself.

In may of 1967, Raphael came to Clinton Prison. He was a sweet boy but not totally homosexual. I was working in the messhall when I saw him walk in. I asked someone I knew from the streets what his name was, and he said Raphael Rivera.

I went over to the guy who was giving out slices of bread. I told him to give me his gloves, and that I would give out the bread. When Raphael came by the line, I said, "Hello, Raphael, you can have all the bread you want." He stared at me, and we both looked deeply into one another's eyes. "Okay, brother," he said, and gave me a smile which said, "Come and get me!" I did just that. Raphael and I carried on a sexual relationship, and the whole prison was aware of it. We even held hands out in the yard. I got myself a home-made knife, and made Raphael my lover. Our romance was common knowledge. But in the end, we were caught. The prison administrators wanted to keep us separate, but we managed to be sent together to the bughouse.

**Dannemora State Hospital
Interdepartmental Communication**

January 20th, 1970
From: Paul Agnew, Acting Director
To: Charles Davies, Security Advisor

Today I received a call from Warden LaVallee to convey the following information. He said that at Clinton Prison, the authorities had received a tip that two different inmates intended to fake being psychotic so as to get over to the state Hospital to join up with Salvador Agron to carry out a plan to escape from Dannemora State Hospital.

Warden LaValle assures us that if either of these inmates is transferred to the Dannemora State Hospital, he will give us advance notice and full details of any information they have about this alleged plan to join up with Salvador Agron.

In the meantime, I would like to ask you to make a special check of Agron and possibly keep him under general surveillance in that this tip has been forwarded to us about alleged plans on his part to perpetuate an escape.

Thank you very much.

This was my third time in the bughouse, and this time things were a little better than before. Things were changing, prisoners were asking questions, and the administration seemed to be listening a little bit.

I went from ward to ward, agitating whenever I could for convict rights.

Then I was accused of trying to escape, and I was put in isolation as punishment for several months.

Raphael and I were still together in the bughouse, but we were not on speaking terms. We were no longer in a relationship. I had embraced another love: the struggle for human dignity, for change, for the independence of Puerto Rico and for socialism.

I wanted to move on. I wanted to go to Attica because I knew what was coming but the administration said it was no go for me.

Dannemora State Hospital
Interdepartmental Communication

July 7th, 1970
From: Charles Davies
To: Dr. Paul Agnew, Director
Subject: Incident Report

On July 4th, 1979, patient Salvador Agron # 8272, attempted to escape by trying to saw bars in washroom of day-room.

Investigation revealed the following: the washroom of Ward 12 has been divided in two by a wall constructed by the contractors of the new recreation yard. An opening was left in the wall where the shower controls are located. Steel bars were imbedded in the cement, yet a hole remained, approximately four inches by six inches between the two rooms. A board was braced against the hole from the outside.

Agron forced the board to one side and used a grapple hook made from several four inch hooks which are ordinarily used to hold curtain rods on the ward. He fashioned a fish pole from a window slat and shoe laces. He was then able to fish through the hole and bring up a workmen's hacksaw that was being stored on the other side.

The time for obtaining the hacksaw was approximately nine o'clock during the shower and medication period after outdoor night recreation. The time of using the hacksaw was after the majority of patients were in the dormitory and the remainder of the patients were left on the day hall to watch late television.

Each ward had its own dayroom, and Salvador said most of his days had been the same. Up early, go to the dayroom, wash up, have breakfast in the mess hall, and then back to the dayroom. Some patients curled up on the floor and went to sleep, some spent the day watching television on the wards, while others went to occupational therapy, patient and staff meetings or, weather permitting, time in the yard. Afternoons and evening were the same, he said, but sometimes he'd be assigned to the kitchen, washing dishes, or to a cleaning crew. Once he was assigned to help clean out old boxes in the basement, and that was when he'd found his stash of books. The routine rarely varied, he said, except for two evenings a week when they were allowed to stay in a downstairs room and watch late movies.

Salvador said his fellow patients had been a varied lot. Some had assaulted guards, thrown feces in their faces, stopped up sinks, or pissed in someone's mouth. Whatever and however, the bughouse, like the poorhouse, took them all.

Some had been sent directly from the courts, while all the rest had come from New York's many prisons and jails. Some were really sick, he said, real "bugs," while others had been sent there as a secret form of punishment.

Then something Salvador said came back to me. It was from a conversation we'd had several years ago about how he'd been able to keep his sanity when things really started coming down on him. Rage was one way, he said, because on a very simple level he just wanted to live long enough so that he'd be able to testify about what he'd gone through while he was here. But he had another way of feeling better that was even simpler.

The wards and dayrooms all had windows, he said, and behind each window was a single set of bars. With most wards facing the back of the hospital, there was neither fence nor Wall separating them from the woods beyond. Opening the window just a bit, Salvador said he'd slide his arm through the bars, just to have a part of him that was "free."

> As soon as I was declared sane again, I was sent back once again to Clinton Prison next door, but right away they sent me to Auburn. This was in 1971.
>
> I was received at Auburn very reluctantly. I had been here when they had sent me from the death house, so at least I knew my way around. But I was a changed person. I went before the adjustment committee and I was told by the guard in charge that they didn't want me in Auburn, but I would be transferred or put in the box if I even attempted to organize inmates.
>
> I had cut my hair, wore a baldy, and the administration knew I was a militant and a Puerto Rican nationalist.
>
> Auburn had just come out of a riot and things were a bit disorganized. I gave the Young Lords the written lessons, and told them to start getting things together.
>
> After six days at Auburn, I was put on a special transfer to Greenhaven.

As I walked back to the motel to get my car, I thought about Karl Marx, buried somewhere in faraway Europe. Was there snow falling on his grave, I wondered? And if he was walking in Heaven now with the angels at his side, did he know that a long-ago convict had embraced his soul in the basement of a loony bin?

I arrived at Greenhaven in 1971, and right away met up with the Reverend Ed Muller.

When I was assigned to the school as a porter, I started organizing things right away. I took the rest of my regents examinations in History and Spanish, and was finally given my regents diploma.

After the Attica rebellion broke out. I wanted the inmates at Greenhaven to follow suit, but this was voted down. I gave a speech in the yard on top of a table. On September 14th, 1971, there was a demonstration in which everyone at Greenhaven participated. No one ate, and complete silence fell over the messhall.

After that, the prison was more or less in the hands of the convicts. After Attica, we began to organize the peoples' party and the Puerto Rican Cadre met everyday in the yard, studying and organizing. A general meeting of all Hispanic groups was called and the Latino Revolutionary Party was born. On August 9th, 1972, we celebrated a Puerto Rican holiday in one of the yards. We invited the heads of the administration and Rev. Muller spoke, and the warden also attended. During the celebration, a guard tried to put up an American flag. I got up, and grabbed the microphone, I gave a speech on how the flag should not fly on this day because it stood as a symbol of oppression against Blacks, and Puerto Ricans. I gave an order for the flag to be pulled down, and when the warden saw this, he walked away from the party.

We kept organizing, but in 1973, I was transferred out of Greenhaven because the warden and the prison authorities accused me of being a "communist," and of having more power in the facility than the warden. I was accused of agitating three takeovers of Greenhaven, chasing the doctor out of the facility, and numerous other charges.

When I got to Attica, I was put into reception, and almost immediately was accused of trying to agitate a takeover by the inmates. Books were found in my cell, and I was accused of trying to start a riot by preaching in the yard. I was handcuffed and taken to the Special Housing Unit (HBZ) or the box, where I spent the next eighteen months under intensive harassment, gassings, death threats by the warden because it was claimed that I was ordering movements from the box to the inmate population.

My first letter from Richard Jacoby came to me while I was in the box at Attica. He was writing to ask me about the time I'd spent on death row, and eventually we agreed to write a book together about my life. Mrs. Davis wrote to the Commissioner asking that I be transferred, but she was turned down. Genoveva Clemente also wrote, and eventually I was sent back to Greenhaven in the early part of 1974.

As waves of snow fell across my windshield later on that evening, I thought to myself that if anyone had come full circle with Salvador Agron, it had been me.

From Esmeralda's soft singing in the Bronx, to Greenhaven, to Dannemora, to Auburn, and back again, I had walked the walk, and talked the talk. I had sat in the playground on a rainy night to see what he had seen, and feel what he had felt. I had visited the death house, and listened for ghosts in the cell where he had slept. I had walked with the nuns in Puerto Rico at the poorhouse, and sat on the bed where he'd been born. I had listened to prayers in faraway churches, and I had searched for his roots in a long-ago reform school

We had broken bread together in prison visiting rooms, and we had shared our secrets, passions, and lies. I had written letters, signed petitions, and honored his name a thousand times, so that the Governor would set him free.

I had shaken his father's hand, and watched him cry for something he could not even name. I had embraced his son as a brother, and listened for hours as Aurea and Esmeralda had walked me through the private hell that was their brother, their son, my friend, Salvador Agron.

The New York Times
State to Free the "Capeman," Street Gang Leader Who Killed 2 in 1959

By Robert D. McFadden
September 20, 1979

Salvador Agron, the "Capeman" murderer who was sentenced to die in the electric chair for the knife-slaying of two teen-agers on a West Side playground during the height of street-gang violence in New York 20 years ago, will be paroled, state parole officials announced today.

Mr. Agron, now 36 years old, will be released from the Auburn State Correctional Facility after submitting "an acceptable residence and employment package to the parole board," said Edward Edwin, executive director of the state's Board of Parole.

A three-member panel from the parole board interviewed Mr. Agron at Auburn this week, Mr. Elwin said, and agreed to his release on or after November 1st, following 20 years and two months in custody, including 18 months as the youngest person ever to sit on New York's death row. No reason for the release was given; the board customarily only cites reasons for denying parole applications.

Chapter Eleven

HOME

**State of New York
Division of Parole**

**Parole Board Hearing
Auburn Correctional Facility
Salvador Agron   NYSID   #738735**

Q. Are you Salvador Agron?
A. *Yes.*

Q. How do you feel?
A. *I feel okay.*

Q. Mr. Agron, as you well know, you are serving a sentence of twenty years to life, is that correct?
A. *Yes.*

Q. It's been reduced a couple of times, I guess.
A. *Yes*

Q. Two counts of murder one?
A. *Yes*

Q. You were a youngster then, what are you now, thirty-five?
A. *Yes*

The first thing Esmeralda did at Salvador's homecoming party in the Bronx was to show everyone his white suit. Bought for him to wear to his junior high school prom, it had hung in her closet for the past twenty years like an errant tenant with nowhere to go.

With its broad lapels and pegged pants, it was terribly outdated, but from the blissful expression on Salvador's face when she held it proudly across her outstretched arms as if it were a newborn baby, you would have thought the jacket had been straight off the rack at Brooks Brothers instead of from Alexander's discount department store on Fordham Road.

Smiling as he looked at the white suit he kissed Esmeralda. Then someone gave him a plate of rice and beans, and he went to look out the window. They were in Aurea's apartment, not far from Mosholu Parkway, and touching the window, he sensed how cold it was outside. The party had been Aurea's idea, and they'd even sent out invitations. With Christmas a little more than a week away, she figured they could combine Salvador's homecoming party with one for the season.

> Q. Mr. Agron, we are here today to consider you for parole, and one of our main functions is to decide whether a person is rehabilitated enough to go back into society without being a threat. In order for us to do this, we review your file and use whatever information we can get, in addition to the information from your other parole hearings. So I would basically like for you to explain to us why you feel you're ready for parole.
>
> A. *I have been here nineteen years. I've participated in practically every program you could imagine. I utilized my time constructively. I've had a couple of setbacks in nineteen years. I came in here illiterate and I didn't even know how to read and write, and I have developed my growth. I think this is obvious from looking at my past history and my present, I'm altogether a different person. I got an edu-*

cation while I was in here, and I would say that despite everything, there's still a little flame left inside of me. I've always built on that.

His last night in prison had been a restless one. Sleep had not come easy. Back and forth, he'd walked through the night, and whenever he'd closed his eyes, the past had invaded his cell like an uninvited guest on a snowy night.

Over the years he'd probably said good-bye to at least a dozen friends who'd served long terms and were going home. Some had walked straight ahead, gone through the door, and never once looked back. Others had lingered, shook hands with friends, real and imagined, saying good-bye, again and again. Still others had walked away with tears in their eyes, while others had openly wept.

An hour before dawn he'd carried to the Administration Office the few possessions that he hadn't already sent home. He filled some forms out, and waited on a wooden bench, as he read over his parole papers. He would be living with Gail, and at least for the foreseeable future would be under "Intense Parole Supervision"

Under the heading, "Maximum Expiration Date of Sentence," it said, "Until the *1st day of death.*"

> Q. The reports indicate that you have matured in your educational areas and other areas people that made judgments of you. But it says here that you also remain quite immature in some areas even today.
>
> A. *Professionally speaking, I don't think anybody matures completely. Otherwise, we hit the graveyard. It's a correct statement. We all have imperfections. I am not an angel.*

Over and over again he told his friends and family that no matter what he would not cry when he got out. Little children cried, not men, boys perhaps, but not Salvador Agron.

When it was time for him to leave, he walked down several corridors, looking neither to the right nor the left, and when he'd been near the final gate, he started to cry. First a little, then more, until the guard said, hey, take a minute, man, there's no hurry, take your time.

When he pressed his head against the cool wall of the jailhouse corridor, Salvador Agron was a little boy all over again, the one with the wide-brimmed hat in Puerto Rico, and the one later on in the playground, the death house, and Dannemora.

The manchild who cried in the jailhouse corridor like there was no tomorrow because Salvador Agron, the Capeman, was finally getting out.

Q. Are you going to live in a half-way house if you're released on parole?
A. No, I plan to live with my girlfriend, and her name is Gail.

Q. And she's a girlfriend of yours?
A. My woman, common-law.

Q. How long you know her?
A. We call them friends now. Before they used to be common-law.

Q. Is she someone you knew when you were out on the street?
A. I didn't know her out on the street. I met her in college.

Q. What college?
A. I met her before that. She used to come to college and visit me sometimes. She came to the prison. She used to visit with me, and she helped me quite a bit with my case.

Q. What's her profession?
A. She studied to be a teacher. She used to teach little children. Sort of social work. But now she works in the city somewhere.

Q. Where?
A. *Manhattan*

Q. Does she have any children?
A. *No.*

He stayed with his family in the Bronx for a few days, before he settled in with Gail on the Upper West Side of Manhattan, not far from Broadway, and just a few blocks over from Riverside Park and the Hudson River.

Gail's apartment was huge, or at least it was for a person who'd lived for years in a walled-off space no bigger than six by nine. Walls of books were everywhere, and he and Gail had a bedroom all their own. There was also a kitchen, a bath, and a living room.

Blessing one another with friendship and intimacy, they tried to forge a life together. Sharing coffee and toast in the morning, they'd go to work, cook for one another in the evenings, and read the *New York Times* together on quiet Sunday mornings.

But the immensity that he craved, yearned for, and dreamed about, was far more complicated than he could ever have imagined. Twenty years of having other people make all his decisions had left him nearly incapable of making any for himself. When he was in prison, time was controlled, regulated, and observed. But here in the streets, time had a way of beating him, whereas in prison it had been the other way around.

His first job, though menial, was at least dependable. Sponsored with funds provided by CETA, it put food on the table, made him feel good, and sometimes helped to pay the rent.

On weekends they visited with Aurea and Esmeralda in the Bronx, took in movies, and once they'd marched with hundreds of others down Fifth Avenue in a demonstration for the rights of labor.

Sometimes they'd go their separate ways. Gail would attend a political meeting, or visit with friends, while Salvador took long walks, visited Esmeralda and Aurea, or sat by himself in the playground on Forty-fifth Street.

The New York Times
Refurbishing of Park at 45th Street Is Snagged
By Mary Breasted

The old narrow playground that runs from West 45th Street to West 46th Street between Ninth and Tenth Avenues is a sorry little poor man's haven, with bathrooms that do not work and benches that smell strongly of wine.

The playground has been that way ever since the local children can remember, and bureaucratic snags and the city's fiscal crisis now threaten to keep it that way in the indefinite future.

For about a decade the people of the surrounding area have been seeking improvement in the park, which had achieved a brief notoriety in 1959 when Salvador Agron, the "Cape Man," stabbed two teen-agers to death there one summer night.

With unlimited access to telephones, his letters had been few and far between. Brief, and to the point, they contained little of substance, except to promise that he'd start writing the book again as soon as he'd gotten himself better situated.

Maybe the three thousand miles separating us made it easier for him to bare his soul whenever we talked on the telephone, or it was just that there were few other people around that he felt close enough to talk with; but whatever it was, as the months passed, the calls became as frequent as they were unpredictable in terms of what we'd discuss.

Sometimes we talked about his relationship with Gail, and he wanted to know if I'd been in touch with Wah-Zi-Nak, and then every once in awhile he'd say that he was sorry that he'd never really had the chance to say how sorry he was to Mrs. Kresinksi for how her son had died in the playground. Sometimes he said good-bye, and sometimes he hung up right in the middle of our conversation. Suddenly the line was dead, and he was gone until the next call.

Either unconscious, oblivious, or both, to the difference in time, his calls often arrived in California at midnight, or three in the morning, New York time.

> Q. In talking in terms of rehabilitation, it means different things to different people. Are you saying due to the face that you are confined it may have contributed to the fact that you were able to observe what was going on within the prison and that may have contributed to your motivation to improve yourself and that you did not appreciate what was going on? If that is the case, then didn't the penal system have a part to play in motivating you?
>
> A. *I can't say in spite of the system. The system has changed a bit since the time I started. The adverse conditions around me and the negative conditions around me were actually what prompted me to help myself*

Whether it had been the size of her apartment, or simply that he'd lived with men in dark places for too long, in less than a year, he broke up with Gail, and moved back to his mother's place in the Bronx. No longer living on Davidson Avenue, Esmeralda had moved into a ground floor apartment, just steps away from Aurea, and directly across the street from Mosholu Parkway.

A dark apartment with blue stucco walls to give it some light, it had two bedrooms, and when Salvador moved back in, she'd given him a choice of either one. Plain and simple, his was the lighter of the two, with a full-sized bed, a chest of drawers , and a radio that was always tuned to an oldies station.

He remained friends with Gail, and when he lost his job

because of funding cutbacks, she'd soon found him another where he worked as a porter for a downtown psychotherapy institute. Every morning he took the subway to 14th Street in Manhattan, and then walked a few blocks over to the institute. He spent the day cleaning out garbage cans, helping around the office, and doing whatever janitorial work needed to be done.

After leaving prison, he'd been surrounded by people. Embraced by the Left as a hero, a man of substance, and a potential leader, he'd been courted by many to help with a wide variety of movement causes. But as the years passed, and he was thought to be of little use, all his friends had come and gone, until there was no one left but his family and his cousin Papo.

The story went that Papo had overdosed on LSD in the late 1960's, had been hospitalized somewhere in New York City, and was never the same again. His memory was shot, and even the simplest of tasks had to be learned all over again. Back in Puerto Rico, we'd met him when we'd stayed at his father's house, and I remembered him as a nice-looking man who smiled alot, but who hadn't said very much.

Returning to the Bronx a few years later, he moved in with a cousin, not far away from Esmeralda and Aurea on Mosholu Parkway. He worked at odd jobs, shopped for Esmeralda, or ran errands for people in the neighborhood. He didn't say much, was always smiling, and whenever you asked him a question, even just, "How are you, Papo?" he'd always answer by saying, "Sure, why not?"

When Papo wasn't running errands, or busy shopping, he'd sit on one of the huge boulders in the park across the street from Esmeralda's apartment building, smoking marijuana, and talking to himself.

> Q. So the system did force you to change, is that right? That is what caused you to motivate yourself. And that's a point that I would like to bring out once in a while.

A. *In helping to change those conditions, I helped change myself. I became involved in something that has social value. If in these places the only thing a person does is sit around and vegetate because there is nothing of social value to get involved in those negative changes, then that's no good. So in that sense, those conditions helped to change me.*

Everyone said that Papo was retarded, and he won't even know who you are, they told Salvador, so don't be surprised when you see him again. But right away Papo knew him, and later Aurea told me it was because when Papo had been a little boy in a foster home on Staten Island, Salvador had been the only one who'd gone to visit, month after month, for many years.

When Salvador was released from prison, Papo's life had undergone a radical transformation. Instead of being all alone, he'd suddenly found a friend. Someone to share his thoughts with, and even more so when Salvador moved back in with Esmeralda.

In the early evenings he'd wait at the subway station for Salvador to come home from work. Sometimes they'd go for walks, or eat the meals Esmeralda had prepared, but mostly they sat on the boulders in the park, smoking and talking.

Q. If you had stayed out in the world you may never have gone to school, am I right?

A. *We can't judge on that possibility. It's possible I would have turned out a drug addict or something like that in the 1950's. Back then it was basically gang fighting and things like that. Then the whole culture turned to drugs.*

When Esmeralda decided to move back to Puerto Rico, Aurea's eldest daughter had taken her place in the apartment. Her name was Rosie, and with her dark hair and soft brown eyes, she resembled her mother. She moved in with several children, and not long after that she'd given birth to another child. His name was Daryl, and he was born in the Bronx at North Central Hospital in 1983.

Until Esmeralda left for Puerto Rico, Rosie stayed in the living room, where she slept on the couch, and her children made do on a makeshift bed between two chairs that she'd put together. Esmeralda and Salvador stayed in their own rooms, but for meals everyone ate together in the kitchen at a large oval table. There was always lots of food in the house, and whenever they ran out, Papo would smile and do the shopping.

Rosie's kids sat on the floor, eating heaping plates of rice and beans, and whenever any of them had gotten sick, Esmeralda had always known the perfect cures, like chicken soup, with fennel seeds, to cleanse the system, or water with ginger to help the digestion. Whenever Salvador's dreams kept him awake at night, she made him tea by boiling lettuce leaves, to keep the demons away.

Q. Would it be fair to say that when you came to prison you lived a slowed-down life?

A. *The system itself allows your life to slow down. It's not the same speed as it is outside. It's different and I found that out when I went out there a couple of times. It's much faster than the process in here. It was like standing by and watching everything move in front of you. I was able to accomplish lots of things in here. I obtained the certificate from the Church of Christ, I have obtained my high school equivalency diploma, my regents diploma, I obtained a certificate in legal research. I have also obtained a liberal arts degree and I was still interested in pursuing my development and basically I learned a whole lot. I have worked in different shops. I worked in the mess hall. I didn't do that much work. I did more studying. I liked to improve myself. I constructed a couple of programs down in Greenhaven. I taught Puerto Rican history and taught*

> pre-columbian history. I was involved with the black studies program in the thing down there and I was also involved with the prison newspaper. As a matter of fact we started the newspaper way before the official sanction came down. We used to make copies with our own hands and then spread them around. Albany finally gave permission for the newspaper to be printed.
>
> I have never attacked an officer, but I have had antagonisms with the administration because of their policy of doing things in Clinton and Dannemora and here in Auburn and different places. I expressed myself and by expressing myself I was labeled militant, and at one time I was even suspected of being a nazi. I've been labeled so many things I wonder if people really know my real humanity, and how I relate to my environment. I went to Fishkill. I went to the college. I contributed to the college. I gave lectures over there on Juvenile delinquency, on the prison system, things like that. I over participated in the college program and created antagonisms again.

Rosie had always felt close to Salvador. He was her mother's brother, her uncle, and her friend. Someone she'd met years ago in a prison visiting room, and someone she'd started writing to not long afterwards as a way of expressing her feelings whenever there'd been trouble in her life. She'd been in a foster home when she'd written to him the first time, and he'd written back that if he got out first, he'd come and rescue her.

Over the years, she always remembered what he'd said, and if nothing else, this had drawn them very close.

Q. You could have been on a slab.

A. *I could have been running around somewhere. I could have been shot. Something could have happened.*

When Esmeralda left for Puerto Rico, what little stability remained in Salvador's life quickly disappeared. Later Rosie would say that it had been impossible for anyone to have taken her place. No one, she said, could've been happier than Esmeralda when Salvador had come home, and no one could have ever been more attentive. Esmeralda cooked for him, bought him clothes, and took care of him whenever he'd been sick.

> Q. Let me ask you this question. Have you found your middle ground yet? What I mean by that is that usually when a minority member understands who he is he goes to one extreme. What one considers a radical and stays there for a period of time. Okay? Then he finds a middle ground where he can live and exist at. Have you found this yet?
>
> A. *Politically, I would say that I favor social democracy but..I used to be involved in the extreme movements of the black panthers and such in the 1960's.*

Rosie took Esmeralda's room, and although her children gave Salvador whatever he needed in the way of attention, it never seemed to be enough, and more and more he was gone from the apartment for several days at a time.

> Q. I want to say this to you. I have a lot of letters here and petitions of people in support of you. They're in support of you because you're a celebrity of sorts, which is also a responsibility. Can you, due to your position as a celebrity, as one who's been projected as an articulate leader, and even a militant leader by a number of people, can you work successfully under supervision with the parole officer?
>
> A. *I understand very well what you're saying. I will be truthful. I won't go out to a lecture, I won't go out unless I can get approval. I don't want a parole officer that is either so limited that he doesn't understand how I relate to the world, and my development to the world. And I want to make some contribution without going out there and picking up a gun and maybe start shooting some cops. That's*

not my thing. That's not the so-called revolutionary that probably people have in mind. It's not in my mind to go and be a member of the Weathermen or something.

Most of his calls had come at odd hours, had been collect, and for a long time had been filled with hope, passion, and plans for the future. But as the months had passed, the tone of the calls had changed, and except for some vague plans about joining Esmeralda in Puerto Rico so that he'd have the needed time and space, he talked less and less about his book, and after awhile I no longer asked.

Q. I'm going to make this as clear as I possibly can. You get out of prison if you're paroled. You can go out and call yourself a leader if you want to. I have no problem with that. I also have no problem with your having an ego. That's good at times, and I really believe that. Just don't let it get the best of you. Don't let it make a fool of you. Make sure whatever you do it's something you believe in, because in the final analysis you're going to be the one that suffers. Those people who signed your petitions, they're not on parole. You have a life sentence facing you. Anything less then that is a bargain. Parole is not a given for you, It's something that one struggles for. And this is regardless of how you feel about it. I've heard all kinds of feelings. It's the quickest way you can get out. The fact that you have improved yourself is commendable and I will say that we have no problems with that. But I also say to you that you must be careful. Make sure you do what you want to do and do it under certain kinds of restrictions that parole is going to command. Don't violate parole, Remember the people who signed all those petitions.

A. *I thought of that situation which you're speaking about. I've decided that I'm not going out there and then try to buck the parole system. I think the parole officer should sit down with me and we could reason out things because I'm reasonable. I'm not a hardhead. If a person sits down and says, Sal, this is wrong because of this and that and if I could see it I have to admit it even though it may hurt my ego. It may hurt my ego but I have to admit it and go along with it.*

Salvador had been out of prison a little over a year, and a month away from Gail, when someone he met in front of his parole office, had offered him a hit of crack cocaine. They were in midtown Manhattan, not far from the playground, and when he told the guy with the crack that he knew a good place for them to smoke, and that it was somewhere quiet where no one would see them, the guy said, okay, just as long as it isn't very far away.

It was the middle of January, and by the time they arrived at the playground it was nearly five o'clock, almost dark, and very cold. But when they tried to use the restroom in the little brick house that was in the middle of the playground, the door was locked, and instead they'd hid in back, out of the wind, and away from what they thought would be the prying eyes of strangers.

From his coat, the guy had taken out a small glass pipe, and from his pocket a small aluminum package filled with tiny, white rocks. He placed one in the pipe, lit it up, breathed in deep, and than handed it to Salvador. The effect had been instantaneous, and later Salvador would say that he knew exactly what people meant when they said the first hit of crack would sweep him off his feet. All of a sudden it wasn't cold anymore, and for just a second or two, there'd been a warm feeling in his crotch as if he were about to explode. Then it was over, just like that, one, two, three, and it was cold outside all over again, and when he asked the guy with the crack, why the rush hadn't lasted longer, the guy had roared with laughter, when he told Salvador, "This kind of high doesn't last too long, bro, and if you want more, you're gonna have to chase after it."

Chasing after it meant "chasing the dragon," by smoking, injecting, or snorting until you got high all over again, and when he'd heard this expression, he'd laughed because it reminded him of the nuns at the poorhouse. Years ago they'd told him children's stories about St. John, the slayer of dragons. The dragon, they said, was really Satan in disguise.

Cocaine became his drug of choice. But instead of using a pipe, and smoking it, he found the rush to be smoother, more potent, and longer lasting, if he shot it intravenously.

> Q. This panel would like to see you stay out there and not come back to prison, that is, if we decide to release you. We want you to make it because we think you have a lot of good ideas. But things won't be easy for you. I think you've worked hard on yourself, and I think you can make it. Just don't let yourself get exploited. Don't confuse what others want with your obligations to the state. And don't let yourself go where your ego tells you not to, okay?
>
> A. *I have been dealing with my ego.*

Rosie said the cocaine made him very hyper, even paranoid, and one time she'd heard him late at night in the kitchen. He was talking to himself, something about a hospital room, Dannemora, she thought, but couldn't be sure. She told her mother, and Salvador had seemed okay for a few days, but then it looked like he was using again because of all the people who were coming and going from the apartment, many of whom she knew for sure were junkies.

He'd be gone for days at a time. Sometimes with Papo, and sometimes all alone. No one knew where he'd gone, who he stayed with, or even how he'd somehow managed to get back home. Sometimes it looked like he'd been in a fight. His face was puffy, and his clothes were dirty, like he'd slept in them, and just didn't care anymore.

Sometimes, late at night, she'd hear him come in, and when she stood by his bedroom door, she could hear him talking to Papo about faraway things, and faraway places.

> Q. We all have an ego, how is this any different for you?
>
> A. *I have a Puerto Rican background. I was taught since I was very small to stand tall with my ego. It is hard. You just don't get over it easy. This is something that my father taught me. Somebody smacked you in the face and you hit them back, or don't come home crying.*

That Salvador was obsessed with the playground, and that he would go there as often as he could, from wherever he was, and at anytime of day or night, was something which no longer surprised me. For Salvador, the playground was a sacred shrine, not unlike a place of birth. And had he been able at a moment's notice to stand, to weep, or to mourn in front of the death house at Sing Sing, the poorhouse in Puerto Rico, or the hospital at Dannemora, no force on earth would have prevented him from going there.

So much had happened in the playground that his going there was a kind of emotional pilgrimage to find some measure of peace from whatever demons had been chasing him. From the playground he'd been threatened with death in the electric chair, had been nearly torn apart at Dannemora, and then had woven his way through too many prisons, and too many hospitals until, here he was, right back where he'd started from.

> Q. While on parole, you are walking on eggs. You may have to take a slap to keep your ass out of prison. You may have to miss some parties. You are going to be around some people who are smoking marijuana. You may have to leave. If the police come and bust everybody, you're the most vulnerable. Don't think that you're alone. A lot of us have to do the same things. I can't go to places I used to

go to , understand the point I'm trying to make?

A. *Yes, I do.*

Whenever Aurea or Rosie had talked to Salvador about the way he was running around, staying out all night, and taking drugs, things would get better for a few days, but then it would start all over again.

Nothing seemed to matter, and Aurea said it was like he just didn't care anymore. First he lost his porter's job in September of 1985 because of funding cutbacks, and then about two weeks later he told his parole officer that he'd been using cocaine intravenously for several years, and needed help. Having no choice, they'd taken him into custody and he was sent to the Queensboro Correctional Facility on Van Dam Street in Long Island City until a determination would be made as to whether or not he'd be sent back to prison for a parole violation.

When Aurea visited him a few days later, and she'd seen how pale and thin he was, she realized that everything people had been telling her about her brother's drug-taking had been true. A rash had covered his chest and arms, but when she asked him about it, he told her not to worry. "It's just a kind of chicken pox, and it should go away in a few days."

Q. You need to broaden your views. Let me say this to you. It's not inmates that fought for these rights. People outside the walls and people who stayed out of prison. And they came from the same circumstances you did, and they fought just as hard as you. Remember that.

A. *That opportunity arose from the struggle that the prisoners were able to carry out within the prison the opportunity for college programs. I know how the college program came about. How it developed. How it broadened to the prison. No, because Albany wanted it, or the prison,*

> *or the guards, but it was because the inmates were able to organize themselves and they fought for those gains. That's how all that stuff started.*

They kept him at the jail in Queens until the early part of February when the parole people held a hearing and decided that since he'd openly admitted his drug problem, and had never been a bother to the parole people, there was little reason for them to send him back upstate.

They thought he was still a good candidate for rehabilitation, and when he promised to obey all the rules of his parole, and to enter an out-patient drug program, he was given a baloney sandwich on white bread, and a subway token to take him back to Rosie's house.

> Q. You seem to be intellectually prepared and parole calls for rules and compliance. If you are found guilty of one of those rules, it means you've violated, and you'll be coming back to prison. I don't think this should be difficult for you. I think you are intellectually prepared. If you are prepared not to commit crimes, then it should be easy for you to follow the rules and regulations of parole. You are no longer a guy that should be told what to do. You should know what has to be done in order to be in compliance with the contract of your parole. You should know what's wrong from right. There is no reason why at this point you should be lectured what to do and what not to do. You know right from wrong.
>
> A. *I don't have any idea of going out there and committing a crime.*

Even though he'd gained a little weight from the five months of starchy jailhouse food, he was still at least twenty pounds too thin, and when he looked at his reflection in the subway window on the way to Rosie's house, he quickly turned away.

Instead of the boy with the curly hair and the innocent eyes from the New York *Daily News* of twenty years ago, what he saw in the glass was a heavily lined man of uncertain age, with the pale skin of a convict, a junkie, or someone very sick.

The rash came, went, dried up, and returned, again and again, like a hungry animal in search of food. But what worried him more was that he was always tired, could hardly walk without having to stop and catch his breath, coughed alot, and got sudden chills all over his body.

> Q. We want you to know that if we release you that we will be taking a more intensive look at you for a period of time and more so then probably other people we release. Not that this means there's something in the reports which would warrant this. But it's because of the crimes you committed, and also the period of time you have been in prison. For awhile you will be under intensive supervision where the parole office will be working more closely with you then he would with other people. Anything else you would like to say?
>
> A. *Nothing but thank you for whatever it is you might consider*

His room at Rosie's had been untouched, and as soon as he walked through the door, and put his things away, he slept from one side of the night to the next.

Weeks passed, he collected unemployment insurance, and attended drug counseling until he saw that if he didn't go, no one would miss him. There were too many felons, and not enough watching eyes. They couldn't test everyone, and soon he was shooting up whatever he could buy, or whatever Papo was able to hustle up.

He was gone for days, and when he came back he looked exhausted, like he'd been through a war, Rosie said, or like he'd gone to hell and brought the devil home for dinner.

Sometimes he'd stay home for a while, sleeping mostly, and once when Rosie'd gone to cover him up because it was getting cold outside, she'd seen an ocean of sweat rolling down his back.

The dope stopped when he caught pneumonia and was taken to North Central Hospital in the Bronx. It was the middle of April, Rosie said, and she remembered because it was right near his birthday on the twenty-fourth, and they'd been thinking of having a little party to celebrate him turning forty-two.

When Aurea found out he was in the hospital with pneumonia she'd gone over right away. When she arrived, it was very late, and when she walked into his room there'd been something strange, she said, around her brother's head, like a light or something, and when she looked at his face she'd known right away that Salvador was dying because of the way his skin had looked so white, and she wondered if maybe the light was from another world or something, because when Salvador had gotten out of prison he'd been saying all the time that he was really from another planet, here on a mission, and she used to laugh whenever he said that, but when she looked at her brother as he lay in the hospital bed, with that light around his head, she thought that maybe what he meant when he'd said that stuff about him being on a mission was that everyone on earth was here for a purpose, lived a life, and then they died.

His hand was warm when she squeezed it tight, and when he opened his eyes for just a second or two, he smiled, before he pulled her close, and then he whispered that first she'd know sadness in her life and then she'd know happiness, but when she tried to ask him what he meant, he talked instead of the sea and how he used to swim naked in Puerto Rico when he'd been a little boy with the sun moving on the waves as they slid down his back, but then he pissed in his bed and the nuns had sent him to prison, and that's when he missed the sea the most, he whispered, when he'd been in prison, and why had they robbed him of his youth for something dead and gone so long ago, and did she know if someone was still waiting for him at the playground? She listened, but the words had been too much, too quick, and then her tears had come because she knew that her brother was traveling, moving fast, through time and space to heaven, perhaps, and then he'd fallen back to sleep.

Early the next morning as the sun streamed through the hospital window like a gospel song with nowhere to go, Aurea held her brother's hand, kissed his forehead, and stroked his face, until the nurse shook her head, covered him up, and he was gone.

Chapter Twelve

THE SOUND OF SILENCE

After Salvador died, we all drifted apart. Aurea changed her telephone number, Esmeralda was in Puerto Rico, and it wasn't until two years and several months after his death in 1986, that an old friend had called from New York with the news about Paul Simon.

Her name was Mary, and she was married to a convict named Larry who'd known Salvador for many years. Was I aware, she wanted to know, that Paul Simon had been up to Fishkill recently to interview him about his friendship with Salvador?

He was conducting research for a musical he was writing based on Salvador's life and times. She had no idea how much he'd already written, who he'd interviewed, or what parts of Salvador's life he was planning to write about. Only that he'd started with Ed Muller, had interviewed Larry, and was slowly working his way back to me in California.

Several days later, Paul's assistant called and left a message on my answering machine. Her name was Linda, and the message was that she and Paul were planning to be in California the following week. Paul would like to get together to discuss his work, and would I please call her back at my earliest convenience?

A meeting was set for the following Tuesday morning at my house in Santa Monica, and a few minutes before they'd been due to arrive, the telephone rang. It was Linda. She was calling from a telephone booth in the parking lot of a local take-out place, just off the freeway. They were lost, and would I please give her the directions again or, better yet, would I mind driving over to where they were parked, and then they'd follow me to my house?

They were sitting in a shiny Mercedes Benz when I pulled up next to them in the parking lot. Linda was in the driver's seat, and when I got out of my car and approached her window, she rolled it down, stuck out her hand, and introduced herself.

With her thick New York accent, dark hair, and dark eyes, she could've been any number of women I'd grown up with back in Brooklyn.

"Pleased ta meet ya," she said, "and this is Paul Simon."

With the sun on my face, I reached past her, stuck out my hand, and took his hand in mine. Dressed in a T-shirt, sport coat, and khaki pants, he looked much as he had on a score of early album covers. But paler, with more lines in his face, and older. He smiled, wearily, I thought, and then shook my hand with a weakness that spoke either of caution, or from having touched the hands of too many adoring strangers over the years.

As he and Linda followed me to my house, I wondered what he'd think about where I lived. Had I cleaned enough for his visit? Would he wonder where I'd bought my furniture. And would he drink the Perrier that I'd bought especially for his visit?

Like the majority of people in Santa Monica, I'd been living in a rent-controlled apartment for many years. Mine was a sun-drenched townhouse, with a bedroom downstairs, and a large living room and kitchen upstairs. Although spacious and light, I wondered what he'd think when he was sitting in my living room? Would he compare it to what I'd heard were his many homes in New York? His penthouse on Fifth Avenue? Or his estate on the tip of Long Island, near

Montauk, and not far from the estate of Edward Albee?

With his clothes draped on his body like a tender kiss, Paul sat in my living room and came right to the point. Did I have any letters from Salvador, and would I be willing to share them for a musical he was writing about Salvador's life?

"What kinds of things you think you'll be dealing with?" I asked.

"Well...it's a fantasy...because I can't really deal with everything in his life...just the big events."

As I looked at him across my dinning room table, I thought how tense he looked, and how similar he seemed to many celebrated artists and entertainers who were used to getting their way. Serious to a fault, and rarely engaging in small talk, their focus was unusually myopic.

Paul was not an exception. He had come to talk about Salvador Agron, and as far as my house was concerned, what it looked like, or how clean it was, I could've been living out of a greasy paper bag on the nearby beach for all the difference it would've made to him. As the afternoon passed, and I listened to him speak about his plans for the musical, what would be in it, and what would not, I tried to juxtapose in my mind the images I'd always had of Paul Simon, the celebrity, with the man who was sitting across from me in my living room.

From years of listening to his songs, and watching him in concert, my sense had been that in addition to being an accomplished song writer, there was a certain frailty about him which most people, including myself, found endearing. Bathed in bright colors and pictures, his songs had delivered sadness and sorrow, minus the blood and the stains, to hordes of adoring fans.

But the man who sat across from me at my kitchen table was another matter entirely. Although he'd never met Salvador face to face, his words carried the authority of someone who'd broken bread with him in a thousand different situations, and had anyone else been listening to our conversation, they would've thought for sure that he and Salvador had been brothers and friends, instead of virtual strangers.

"Did you know that we'd been writing a book together?" I asked.

"Uh...yeah...Aurea showed me some of it...and also lots of his other writing..."

"What'd you think of it?"

"What I saw was okay...but it wasn't very grounded...and I think that even if he'd lived, he never would've finished it."

If there was any truth to the old wive's tale that people rolled in their graves whenever they were disturbed or distraught about something that was happening in the world of the living and breathing, then surely Salvador had rolled several times, and then some, as Paul had sat in my living room and talked of the potential for his musical to "redefine" in his words, Salvador's life in a way that had never been done before.

It wasn't that Salvador had disliked Paul, or that he hadn't particularly cared for his music, it was simply that he'd had a hard time reconciling what he said was Paul's sentimentality with his own hard vision of reality. Paul Simon spoke to someone who believed in a clean America, free of violence, tears, and poverty. An America filled to overflowing with flowers, corn, and light, or at the very least, he spoke to a place that was the very opposite of the dark and despairing landscape where Salvador had spent the majority of his childhood.

The exception was "The Sounds of Silence." He liked it so much, and had attributed so much meaning to it, that he'd written about it for a college English class.

The Sounds of Silence

By Salvador Agron

> The song "The Sounds of Silence" by Paul Simon is more mystical than religious. In the song, expressed in symbolic language, we find the aesthetic quality of silence and the possibility for social consciousness which the most alienated can aspire to reach.

Aside from a myopic focus, Paul shared another trait particular to celebrated artists and entertainers. All seemed to have an uncanny ability to duck and dodge whenever someone disagreed with whatever it was they were saying. Theirs was an ability to don emotional blinders, and then to rely on the enormous impact of their celebrity to intimidate their adversaries into either shutting up, or changing their minds.

> "Darkness" in the song, "The Sounds of Silence," is merely representative of wisdom which, after all, is the oldest "friend" of mankind. Wisdom is the same identified in the Song of Solomon, a play written by Solomon, as the Shulamite, who says: "I am Black, but comely, O ye daughters of Jerusalem, as the tents of Kedar, as the curtains of Solomon. Look not upon me because I am Black, because the sun has looked upon me: my mother's children were angry with me; they made me the keeper of the vineyards; but my own vineyard I have not kept." (Song of Solomon 1:5:6)

As Paul talked and talked, I'd known right away that I wasn't an exception to the rule about stardom, and how otherwise emotionally together people often acted in the presence of celebrities. Something seemed to fall to the wayside, was forgotten, and in its place was a naked person asking silly questions, or simply agreeing with whatever the celebrity said or did. There were many variations of this behavior, but basically it all came down to being totally enveloped by the celebrity, and the more famous, the more consistent it seemed was this kind of behavior.

When I brought up something even remotely contradictory, his celebrity had been intimidating enough that I found myself incapable of pursuing it for very long. Why bother, I thought, to bring up Salvador's obsession with Mrs. Kresinski, or his need to wander at all hours, and in all seasons, in the playground, if Paul would simply dismiss it with a casual wave of his hand?

"Uh...would you like to see Salvador's letters?" I asked.
"Oh...of course...I'd really like that."

> *Solomon as well as Shakespeare have identified wisdom as a "dark lady," and as an "old friend." Wisdom is the experience from which the past that has been left, so the saying is mystical in this respect. There is a difference between the mystical and the religious—for only our "old friend" (wisdom) can creep softly and softly at night and in visionary (or symbolic language) sleep or dream state plant the seed of knowledge and socialize our other self.*

Like a long sermon waiting to be read, the stack of letters Salvador had written was Bible thick, and when I handed them to Paul, I saw from the new light in his eyes that this was precisely the focus he'd been looking for.

"You think maybe I could take these back to the hotel?" he asked.

> *"Night" in the song "Sounds of Silence" has also been identified with "silence," for it is when people sleep. This is why the song is on two levels: 1. The Social Being and 2. The Social Consciousness.*

Whatever reservations I had about his sincerity, or whether he was really the man to tell Salvador's story, all of this was quickly cast aside as the intimidation factor had kicked in all the way. Here was Paul Simon, one of America's favorite sons, asking for my help, and had he asked for every piece of furniture in my house, no force on earth could have stopped me from giving it to him.

> *The second stanza in "The Sounds of Silence" describes the emergence into awareness ("Flash of Beam") from the "night" (wisdom, experience) of a person with positive sensory perception. When social consciousness stabs the "eyes" (to "see is to know") there occurs a leap in the mind and new knowledge of one's surroundings is registered.*

As I handed him the letters, along with some of Salvador's other writings, I thought of the advice friends had given me when they heard Paul was coming to look through my materials. Some had said to ask for money, but most had spoken of scratching one another's back. That I should show him some of my writing and ask for a tangible show of support, like help in finding a publisher someday. Others said that perhaps after reading the letters he would sense the closeness I'd had with Salvador, and would ask for my help when it came to writing his musical.

> *The third stanza of Paul Simon's song describes the social consciousness that emerges over time.*

As he and Linda had been about to leave, I asked if he would be visiting any other prisons aside from Fishkill. He said he'd been to Sing Sing, but didn't see any need to visit more than one, and from the surprised look on his face I could sense that he was wondering why I'd even asked in the first place.

"Will you be going to Puerto Rico at all?" I asked.

"Not right away...but maybe later on."

"I've got pictures of when I was down there with Esmeralda...you want me to send them to you?"

"How many do you have?"

"I don't know...maybe a hundred...I'm not sure."

"Yeah," he said, "I'd love to see them."

When it turned out that all I had were the negatives, and that the originals had been sent to Salvador years ago after I'd returned from Puerto Rico with Genoveva and Esmeralda, we agreed that I would make copies from the negatives and send these to his office in New York, along with some of Salvador's other writings.

> *The third stanza in "The Sounds of Silence" is talking about "people" who are not yet socially conscious of the multiple "selves" that exist within different institutional conditions and which one must take as a social role in order to survive within a capitalist society.*

Although all the letters I'd given Paul were original documents, I hadn't hesitated for a moment when Linda had called later on that evening from their hotel in Beverly Hills, wanting to know if it would be okay if she and Paul took the letters with them to New York. The Xerox machine at the hotel wasn't working very well, and Paul needed better copies. She would take care to make sure nothing happened to them, and as soon as possible she'd send them back.

> *The third stanza in "The Sounds of Silence" also describes the conservative attitude that a socially conscious person can fall into if he is not willing to use his five senses through practice and struggle. Inactivity, theory without practice, grows like a cancer inevitably destroying the socially weak.*

A few weeks after their visit, a long letter arrived from Aurea, followed by many telephone calls, and more letters.

9/30/88

Dear Richie:

Well, how are you?
My moms and all the family are fine. Thank you for the precious letter you sent after Paul came to visit with you.
There is so much happening that I don't even know where to begin. I hope you come for Christmas, and if not this year, then next time. Please keep in touch.
My moms is always praying for you. She thinks of you as if you were her son, and she loves you very much, and is always asking for you. Right in the middle of a conversation, she will say, "Whatever happened to Jacobo? God bless him wherever he may be.
When I told her that you were still alive, and living in Santa Monica, she was overjoyed. She wants you to write to her, and she said that when you come to Puerto Rico that you should stay with her at the house she has down there in Mayaguez. She loves Puerto Rico, and feels better there than in the Bronx. She's still a very strong lady, and I love her more and more.
Did you know that I've been working at "Jacoby Hospital" for the last four years? Yes, the name is the same, and everytime someone mentions the name of the hospital, I always think of you!
As you must know, we all love you very much in this family. I have never forgotten all the thoughtful things you did for Salvador. You meant much to him, and he always talked about you and remembered.
Paul Simon came to visit with us a few days ago. And then afterwards, he and his assistant, Linda, went to church with us, and they stayed for one of the English services. When he told us he had spoken with you, I was surprised and very happy. It has been so long since we've seen or talked with you.
Salvador gave me a tape of when you were with my moms and Genoveva in Puerto Rico years ago. It was funny hearing your voice.

With all my love, always, your sister,
Aurea Agron

Another year passed before I finally made it back to New York shortly before Christmas in 1989.

Still living on Knox Place in the Bronx, Aurea had welcomed me back as though I'd been the prodigal son who'd returned from a long journey, and in many ways this was closer to the truth than anything else. Salvador was dead, Paul Simon was writing a musical about his life, and I'd stayed in California. I'd worked in restaurants, gone back to the university, and had been working in a public school for the past several years with profoundly handicapped children.

> *In stanza four of "The Sounds of Silence," we find that practice can also fall "like silent raindrops" and only those who listen to the beautiful sound of rain can hear. Otherwise, they merely echo within wisdom (night).*

Just before I left for New York, I called Linda at Paul Simon's office. Paul, she said, would like to see me, and would the third week in December be okay?

Paul's production company was on the fifth floor of the Brill Building on Broadway. Directly in his office, and a few feet from the entrance, was a large glass cabinet filled to overflowing with memorabilia from Paul's career, including a pair of slippers with tiny fake diamonds embedded in their soles. A gift from an adoring fan, Paul said, when I asked.

The receptionist who took my name had introduced herself as Arlene. Paul wasn't here yet, but I was welcome to wait in his office. He was at his recording studio, but should be back pretty soon. Did I want some coffee, or maybe some fruit while I waited?

With a plate of apples and a piece of cantaloupe, I made myself comfortable in an easy chair in Paul's office, but no sooner had she closed the door behind her, then I put down the fruit and started to explore.

His was a vast corner office with windows east onto Broadway, and south down its length to the Battery and beyond. Banks of pictures lined the walls, including one of Paul as a roaming teenager, when he'd sung with Garfunkel, in clubs all over Brooklyn and Queens. Several couches, a table, and a few comfortable looking chairs gave the illusion of someone's living room. A grand piano stood in a corner like a monument to its owner, and when I went over for a closer look, I was astonished to find Xeroxed copies of the letters Salvador had written to me over the years spread across the top of Paul's piano like a peacock in full bloom. Looking closer, I saw that he'd marked them up. Underlining a passage here, a passage there, even circling whole paragraphs. Was he writing lyrics as he read the letters? Or was he simply trying to climb within the soul of Salvador Agron, this Puerto Rican, lean and mean, who'd committed mayhem and madness no more than several thousand yards away from this, his splendid office filled with warmth and light, nearly thirty years ago?

> *Stanza Five has described a religious belief that the prophets have already returned (through reincarnation) and that this is reflected through the "neon god" (or the god of light), and also from people's higher social consciousness.*

Out the window was Broadway, and several blocks away was the playground, and I wondered, as I glanced through the letters, where Paul had been that warm and humid August night. Had he been singing with Garfunkel? Had he been eating dinner with his mom and dad in Queens? Or had he been seeking his fame and fortune in a recording studio?

Suddenly the door opened, and as Paul entered the office, the first thing I noticed was the baseball cap. Aurea had mentioned that when she and Paul had gone to Puerto Rico earlier in the year, he was never without his baseball cap. It was like his security blanket, she said, and looking at him, I could see why it was probably one of his prized possessions. With its full front beak, it could easily hide his face, allowing him to blend in with the crowds of Broadway, without too many adoring fans getting in his way.

"Nice to see you, Richard," he said, as he took off his hat and removed his heavy winter overcoat.

"Yeah, Paul, good to see you, too." I said, as we moved closer to one another and then exchanged brief hugs before sitting down.

Looking briefly annoyed, he said that he wanted me to hear a song he'd done for the musical, but had left the demo tape at his studio.

"So like you've written lots of songs for the musical?"

"Not really...but they're coming," he said.

> Stanza five in "The Sounds of Silence" also shows where the proletarian class have, through graffiti, written their wisdom and how intelligent people speak about the socially existing conditions.

"Did you get that record I sent you?"

"What record was that?"

The record was an obscure song by a doo-wop group who were popular in the late fifties. One of Salvador's favorites, I'd sent a vinyl copy to Paul several months ago, along with a note explaining how partial Salvador had been to the song, and how it was undoubtedly one of many he'd been listening to in 1959 when the killings in the playground had taken place. I'd even suggested that maybe it would make good background music for his show.

"So you never got it, right?" I asked.

"Well, we get lotsa stuff in here, people are always sending things...so maybe it came and I didn't see it."

I started to say something, but stopped myself. Sticking out from one stack of letters like a plastic bookmark, the record was in plain view, along with everything else on the piano. Either Paul had forgotten about it, or for some reason, perhaps as obscure as the record itself, he hadn't wanted me to know that he'd been listening to its lyrics.

> *Stanza five in "The Sounds of Silence" also shows how poor people know about "the prophets" (those who teach of better tomorrow) for those who are socially active (even when they "whisper") bring hope and change for those in need.*

Several weeks later a package arrived early in the morning at my house in California. From Paul's office, it contained all of Salvador's letters, along with a letter from Paul.

Apologizing for not keeping in touch, he mentioned being inducted into the Rock and Roll Hall of Fame. He wrote that he hadn't heard from Aurea lately, but was still very committed to writing about Salvador's life for a Broadway musical.

Wishing me a belated Happy New Year, he wrote that he would keep in touch.

> *"The Sounds of Silence" by Paul Simon reinforces conventional sociology with a slight touch of Marxian ideology.*

Chapter Thirteen

PUERTO RICO (1991)

Honor thy father
By Salvador Agron

He was poor
My father
At the very bottom of poverty,
He cut sugar cane
and ran numbers during the depression

Salvador was buried in a cemetery in Puerto Rico, not far from Esmeralda's house in Mayaguez, and when Aurea called to say that Paul had bought a stone for his grave, I said that now would be the perfect time for us to get together.

Several days later she called me back. The plan was simple. She and her family would meet me in Puerto Rico, and all of us would stay at Esmeralda's house. After everyone agreed that the third week in June would work out best, I made arrangements for a flight from Los Angeles to the airport at Dallas-Forth Worth. From there I'd take another plane to San Juan, followed by yet another plane, across the island to Mayaguez, and then a publico, or taxi, to Esmeralda's house.

my father
Sindo Agron
swept the streets of Mayaguez,
Honor thy father

As rivers of sweat rolled down my back, I knocked on the door to Esmeralda's house at a little past two on a blazing Monday afternoon. Aurea had wanted my coming to be a surprise, but when Esmeralda opened the door, and saw me standing there, she welcomed me in like a long expected guest.

"My moms really something...all afternoon before you came she was saying your name like she does...Jacobo, Jacobo, and it was just like she knew you were coming."

Her house was plain and simple. A large living room, a few bedrooms, a bath, and a kitchen. On one of the walls was a picture of Jesus, and next to it a hanging wooden crucifix. Adjoining her kitchen was a small patio with a hammock, and across the street was an empty field, where children walked, played ball, or rode their bikes.

Compared to the house of her brother Israel, where I'd stayed years before, her house was filled with luxury, including a six-cup coffee maker that Aurea had brought with her from New York as a gift for her kitchen.

Seeing that I wasn't used to the heat, Aurea suggested that I take a shower, and then maybe rest awhile before I went with her to see if we could find out where her father was buried. No, she didn't drive, she said, but her mother's pastor had volunteered to drive us into Mayaguez later on that day.

"It'd be good if we could do it today because it'll be hard when the family gets here and then we'll be going over to see Salvador and everything."

Sindo Agron
Who watched a revolution
And voted for Munoz Marin
from the Democratic Party
of Puerto Rico
honor thy father

Tall and handsome, Jorge was Esmeralda's pastor, and he reminded me a little bit of Uncle Israel. He had the same fire in his voice whenever he spoke of the almighty, and his belief was strong enough to be both endearing and touching at the same time.

"The pastor says he'd like to have us attend one of his services later on this evening," Aurea said.

"Tell him that'd be great," I said, as we made our way from Esmeralda's house to the first place on Aurea's list of places of where she thought her father might be buried. We were in the pastor's van, a many-seated affair that Aurea said he used to transport his parishioners. Many were like Esmeralda, elderly and alone, without transportation, and the pastor not only helped them get to church but also took them shopping or to what Aurea said was an endless series of medical appointments.

The first cemetery we stopped at was on the outskirts of Mayaguez, and the most likely place, she said, for her father to have been buried.

"He's got to either be here or at this cemetery near a funeral parlor that's in the center of town, there," she said.

Sindo Agron
On May 25th, 1977
he died
In poverty
In an old man's home;
My father
Died
An unknown

> *In the squalid conditions*
> *Of neo-colonialism in*
> *Mayaguez, Puerto Rico*
> *honor thy father*

The man in charge was sympathetic. People came to him all the time looking for people they'd loved and lost, but when he looked for Sindo's name in a ledger filled with handwritten names, his was nowhere among them.

"That doesn't always mean that they're not buried out there," he said, as he made a sweeping gesture to the sun-drenched cemetery beyond the windows of his office, "just that someone might've forgotten to write it in the book here."

"Could we look around?" Aurea said.

"Be my guest, but just let me know before you leave if you found him or not."

Without shade of any kind, the sun was like a burning curse as we made our way from stone to stone, looking for Sindo's name. Down a line of graves, and up another, until we'd both said that we couldn't do this anymore, and drove with the pastor to our last stop, the funeral parlor with the cemetery in the back.

> *Unemployed*
> *And broken in spirit*
> *my father*
> *died*
> *But the battle has just begun*
> *And we will be victorious.*
> *honor thy father*

This time the man in charge remembered Sindo, or at least he remembered the circumstances surrounding his death and burial. Sindo had made an arrangement with the woman he'd been living with. He wasn't sure of the exact specifics, only that he and the woman had put money into a savings plan, which in the event of their death would guarantee them a coffin and a burial site. Somewhere he thought he had some correspondence about the plan, and would I mind if he and Aurea took a few minutes together to look through the files in his office?

As soon as they were gone, I closed my eyes for a few minutes to better enjoy the cool air from the air conditioner that was mounted on a ledge, just a few inches from the ceiling. Except for several chairs, and a raised platform in the middle of the room, there was no other furniture.

> *because*
> *He sleeps forever now*
> *in a grave*
> *I know not where*
> *unknown*
> *Which I cannot even try to*
> *visit*
> *because I am also poor*
> *honor thy father*

This was the room where the bodies were bought after they'd been treated with embalming fluids in another room, and then dressed for burial in yet another room, before finally coming here for the family to sit and mourn before they were taken to the cemetery.

When I opened my eyes, the first thing I saw through the window was a wall. Something about it looked familiar, and when I pointed it out to Aurea after she returned from the office, she had to look only once to know exactly what it was.

"That's the poorhouse over there, I'd know it anywhere," she said.

"Are you sure?"

"Yeah, because it's right down the street over there," she said, as she pointed at the wall beyond the window. I was about to suggest that maybe we could walk over there, even make a quick visit, when Aurea said the man she'd just been talking to might know where her father was buried.

"He says he might be in a cemetery a little ways from here."

> *You, Puerto Rico,*
> *have killed my father.*
> *He died of a broken heart,*
> *Of malnutrition; and now*
> *He lies*
> *in a poor man's grave*
> *as a silent witness*

Like the other cemetery, this one was crowded with stones, and like the other, the man in charge had a ledger filled with names. Unable to find Sindo's name, he and the man from the funeral parlor had spoken in Spanish for several minutes before Aurea turned to me and said they thought they might've found him. Aurea said the man seemed to remember that the woman who was supposed to have kept up the payments for Sindo had suddenly stopped coming around.

> *Honor thy father*
> *who took my hand*
> *when I was a little*
> *boy*
> *and*
> *who tried*
> *to comfort me whenever I cried*

We followed the man from his office, down a corridor, out a door, and to the cemetery. We followed him until there was nowhere else to go except for a patch of dark brown earth. Shaded by palm trees, and surrounded by a tiny white fence, there were no visible markers of any kind. No flowers, no crosses, no names, nothing.

"This is where we bury the people who've got no money," he said.

honor thy father

Dressed in her Sunday best, Esmeralda was waiting for us when we got back, and no sooner had we walked through the door, then she said she was ready for church.

All wood and open windows, the church was stuck in a hollow high above her house. From the sea beyond, gentle breezes crossed the mountains, and drifted in through the open windows.

Seated between Aurea and her daughter, Madelyn, I watched as different church members rose to give testimony, and I thought back to the first time we'd done this, years ago, in the church of Uncle Israel. Esmeralda had given testimony about Salvador, our friendship, and his someday leaving prison. She had thanked me for helping him to write a book about his life, and then had given thanks to Genoveva.

As if she'd read my thoughts, Esmeralda suddenly rose from where she'd been sitting behind us, and quickly walked to the front of the room. With her flowing white hair, she looked like a risen angel as she spoke in a slow and measured Spanish.

Years ago, Genoveva had been my translator, and now Aurea did the same.

She talked about Salvador, how he lived, and how he died, and she thanked Aurea for always taking care of her, and for being such a good daughter to come all this way to say good-bye again to her brother, who had always loved her, and she thanked God for letting us all come together again as a family.

"All praise to God," she said, "to Jacobo for being here with my daughter and her family so that we can gather at the cemetery to honor my son, Salvador Agron, and all praise to Jacobo for being his friend for so many years."

"And all praise to my daughter Aurea and her family for being here in Puerto Rico once again, and I am, *"muy contento,"* she said, before leaving the makeshift stage and sitting down with the rest of us.

> *because*
> *he always did*
> *the best he could*
> *honor thy father*

When we returned to the house, Richie and Joey, Aurea's sons, had already arrived with Madelyn and her daughter, Jeanette. Madelyn I'd known for many years, and I'd met her daughter years ago on Christmas Eve in New York. Like her mother, she had dark hair and eyes, but slightly lighter skin. Her father lived not far away, and Madelyn said they would visit him tomorrow if time allowed.

Richie, a tall young man, with dark hair, who spoke no Spanish, had been just a baby when I'd met him for the first time at Aurea's house in 1974. Joey, a lifer in the army, had the dark hair of his mother, and spoke Spanish like a native.

Alone in the kitchen, I was making a pot of fresh coffee when I heard someone talking softly in the patio beyond the window.

Stretched out in her hammock, Esmeralda was swinging back and forth, and as she swung, she was talking either to herself, or to someone only she could see. I thought she'd been calling out my name, "Jacobo," but then I heard her say, "Salvador," and I knew that she was doing what Aurea said she sometimes did whenever she was all alone. She would pray for me, for Salvador, for Aurea, and then sometimes have long conversations in her head with the three of us, wishing us well, and god speed.

*place flowers on his grave
and
remember him.*
> Dutchess County Jail
> June, 1977

"Jacobo," Esmerada said, several hours later when everyone had begun to settle in for night, as she took me by the hand and led me to a small bedroom in the back. Opening the door, she pointed to the bed, and with a wave of her hand, she made it clear that this was where I would sleep.

Aurea said this was the room where Salvador would've lived had he ever made it home again from New York City. It was the same room where in his mind he might've written his book, walked to the sea, and maybe found some peace with his beloved Esmeralda.

The bed was large, probably a double, I thought, as I unpacked my bag, and looked around. Across from the bed was a wooden chest of drawers, and neatly stacked inside were several pairs of men's underwear, along with shirts of every color, size, and description.

On top of the bureau was a small plate filled with what looked like burnt chicken bones, and next to it a framed picture of Aurea and Paul Simon. Their arms were around one another, and both of them were smiling. Later Aurea would say it had been taken right outside, in front of the house, and she remembered this, she said, because of how hot it had been that day, and how her moms had made some kind of cool drink for Paul.

Next to that was a picture of Salvador as a little boy, and when I looked closer, I saw that it was the same one he'd asked me for in a letter years ago.

> *There is one piece of information that I will need for the piece I am working on. Find out when I got that photo with the hat taken. I think it was right before I came to New York that first time, maybe like a few months before. How old am I in the photo?*

Filled with angels carved from stone, the cemetery seemed to stretch on endlessly, and it took us more than an hour before we finally found where Salvador had been laid to rest.

Unlike graves that I'd seen before, his was aboveground, and after we found his grave, and were all gathered around, Richie and Joey slid the stone cover just a bit so that all of us could take a peek inside. Down at the bottom was a small box, and Aurea said that this was the second cemetery Salvador had been in, and that the box was filled with his remains. Aurea had bought some flowers, and after Richie and Joey had opened up the grave, Esmeralda had stepped forward. Then she held my hand, and threw the flowers into the grave.

As we stood together, I said aloud that all of us were gathered here to honor the memory of Salvador Agron.

"Who wants to be the first to speak?" I said.

With Aurea and Madelyn at her side, and each one translating, Esmeralda spoke:

> *First, I give thanks to all the family that's gathered here and to Richard Jacoby, who is a professor of education in California. And I give thanks to this blessed day because we are here reunited in front of Salvador Agron's grave, my son, and he is my son because he lives with Christ.*
>
> *I am also grateful to Paul Simon for telling the story of my son's life.*
>
> *I am also grateful to my pastor, who is present here with his family. My grandchildren, Madelyn, my daughter Aurea, and to all who are gathered here today.*
>
> *I want to salute all of you and give thanks to Puerto Rico, New York City, and anybody else who will ever read these words.*
>
> *Salvador once told me in a dream to bring white ribbons to his grave. At the time of the dream, it was unclear, but now I know that the white ribbon that he was talking about in the dream was the tape we are making of these words, and God gave me the knowledge that we should all be here today.*
>
> *God bless and thank you.*

When Esmeralda finished, Madelyn stepped forward:

> We're gathered here with loved ones and friends, and people who really loved you, and we just want to tell you that even though you're distant from us in the arms of the Lord, we still love you and we care, and we miss you, and although we've lost you, we've gained alot of things that you're not aware of.
> Our hearts break because you're not here to see them, and we wish you were here with us.
> We love you very much.

Aurea spoke next:

> Thank you, Sal, for being my brother, and because I love you.

When everyone had spoken, I stepped forward, and read what I had written on the plane from California:

> *Salvador Agron*
> *God bless*
> *April 24th, 1943*
> *Mayaguez,*
> *Puerto Rico*
> *God bless*
> *the poorhouse*
> *God bless*
> *New York City*
> *Bellevue Hospital*
> *Children's Court*
> *Wiltwyck School for Boys*
> *God bless*
> *Rock and roll*
> *God bless*
> *La Escuela de Correctional*
> *God bless*
> *Fort Greene, Brooklyn*
> *The Mau-Mau Chaplains*

God bless
The Vampires
God bless
The Capeman
God bless
Robert Young
and
Anthony Kresinski
God bless
The Brooklyn House of Detention
and a sentence of death
God bless
Auburn Prison
Dannemora Prison
Dannemora Hospital for the Criminally Insane
God bless
Attica Prison
Greenhaven Prison
God bless
Freedom
and
God bless
Salvador Agron
Our brother
Our son
Our uncle
and
Our friend
God bless
Salvador Agron
God bless.

Mayaguez, Puerto Rico
June 25th, 1991

Epilogue

Shortly after we returned from the cemetery, Esmeralda told us of a long-ago dream she'd had, just before Salvador had been sent to the death house at Sing Sing Prison.

Esmeralda's dream:

Before Salvador went to Sing Sing prison, she had a dream about the Lord.
Many angels surrounded her, and all of them were smiling. She kneeled down with them, and on the ground were many thorns. Many people watched them. Some of the people had sad looks on their faces, but most of them were laughing at her, the angels, and the Lord. Esmeralda and the angels started walking to Sing Sing, while the Lord looked on.
When they reached the prison, the angels disappeared. There were many people in front of the prison. Some people were standing and others were sitting. All were silent. As Esmeralda waited in front of the high stone walls of the prison, two white hands reached over and handed her a baby. It was Salvador. Sitting down in front of the prison, she placed him on her lap. When the hands gave Salvador over to Esmeralda, some people stood up from the chairs, and went instead to sit on the electric chair, one by one. Salvador was there, but Christ had already saved Salvador. In the dream, this brought back many memories of Salvador when they lived together in Puerto Rico.

The dream changed and in the dream, someone talked about her sister's illness. She was in a room in New York City, and she is staring straight out the door when suddenly she felt someone taking her from the room and straight to Heaven. When she got to Heaven, there was a building that looked just like a courthouse, and all around the buildings were the angels who'd be passing judgment on her son for what happened in the playground. In the dream, Esmeralda's sister passed away, and twenty-two days later, Salvador died. The dream shifted and Esmeralda was back in the Death House, visiting Salvador. He says that if they kill him in the electric chair, it will be okay, and for her not to worry.

Someone, someday, he says, will tell my story.

Afterword

With the blessing of Salvador's family, I have tried to write about the significant events in the life of Salvador Agron.

All official documents in this book were either obtained through the Freedom of Information Act, were in the possession of Aurea Agron, or were given to me years ago by Salvador himself. His prison file alone ran several hundred pages, and contained not only his movements within the system, but also copies of his legal briefs against various prison officials throughout the State of New York. With few exceptions, all official documents between various wardens and prison officials were copied exactly as they were received from his prison file. Where changes were made, they were more of omission than anything else, and were done in order to avoid repetition of facts that had been stated elsewhere.

As a trained researcher, I often took voluminous notes, and this was particularly true when I was conducting research for my death row dissertation. Careful notes were made and kept of my initial meetings with Salvador at Greenhaven, as well as with Genoveva, Esmeralda, and Aurea. I also kept careful notes for each of the trips I took to Puerto Rico. All of this was used to re-create dialogue, and specific incidents, as accurately as possible.

Except where there was obvious repetition, or his meaning wasn't clear, all of Salvador's writings, including his personal correspondence, are reproduced in this manuscript exactly as he had written them.

I took the liberty in several instances of combining his letters, or other writings, into a single document, either to avoid repetition, or to give clearer meaning to a particular piece of writing.

Where Salvador's writings and the official documents were not used verbatim, they were used, along with my own personal observations, and interviews with friends and family, to construct the narrative that runs throughout this book.

Although the events depicted in this work are accurate, some names, dates, and specific locations, have been changed to protect people's privacy. All of the men and women depicted in this work are real, but some are composites, including the character *Rachel*, as she appears in chapter 3 (*San Juan Bautista*). *Jennifer,* the name of my girlfriend in New York and California was a pseudonym designed to respect her privacy.

I would like to thank the following people for helping to make this book possible:

> *The Agron family, for their endless and unconditional love in making this book a reality. Thank you, Aurea, Emilio, Rosie, Madelyn, and Stacy.*
>
> *Esmeralda Rodriguez Agron. May you rest in peace for all of eternity.*
>
> *Salvador Agron, for allowing me to honor my commitment to tell your story.*
>
> *Genoveva Clemente, for coming back into my life.*
>
> *Wah-Zi-Nak, for the journey.*
>
> *Joe and Gail Sullivan, for your support and friendship.*

Richard Traunstein, a dear and noble friend, for allowing me to open my heart.

Steve Gilbert, for listening and encouraging, during the long nights of writing.

Dwayne Harvey, for reading every word of this manuscript, and for listening to my ruminations during our many walks at night through the streets of Santa Monica.

The Reverend Ed Muller, for reading this work as it progressed, and for providing valuable insights along the way.

Hubert Selby Jr., for his great soul and depth of vision.

Jo Sgammato, my agent and friend, who encouraged me to write this great work, and without whose encouragement, it would not have been possible.

John Whitesell, for helping to keep me whole.

Judi Wilde, for her love and unflinching support.

Trinidad Rios, for her unwavering suppport of Salvador at the time of his original arrest and trial in 1959, a grateful thank you and God bless from all of the Agron family.

Ira Fraitag (of Entertainment Management Group), a new friend and brother, for his faith and encouragement

Larry Klein, for his unconditional friendship.

Jo-Ellen Fox, for her generosity of spirit.

Steve Feinberg, for Brooklyn Heart street.

Randi Hall, for her love and warmth, everlasting.

Claudia (Coville) Suszka, for having faith in me.

Bill Sullivan, of Painted Leaf Press, for his belief in this story, and for publishing this work.

Brian K. Brunius, for using his great craftmanship to make this book a work of art.

And to Marguerite wherever you may be.

And finally, acknowledgment must also be made to the scores of men and women who actively took part in securing Salvador's freedom and to the more than three thousand people who wrote letters of support on his behalf to the various clemency boards, offices of the Governor, and the New York State Parole Board.

>Richard Jacoby
>October 4, 1997
>Santa Monica, CA.

The author, Richard Jacoby, in 1972, shortly after meeting Salvador Agron for the first time.

ABOUT THE AUTHOR

RICHARD JACOBY is a native New Yorker who was brought up in the Bronx and Brooklyn. He became acquainted with Salvador Agron in 1972 while working on a doctoral dissertation detailing the effects of long-term confinement on death row. As Mr. Agron contributed extensively to this study, he and Mr. Jacoby because close working associates. This led to a trip to Puerto Rico in 1974 by Mr. Jacoby and Mr. Agron's mother, Esmeralda Rodriguez, in order for Mr. Jacoby to gather information about Mr. Agron's early life. As part of the research on death row, Mr. Jacoby corresponded with other prisoners as well. He is presently working on a novel, *Slow Dancing*, that deals with a young woman's journey from the streets of Brooklyn through the New York State correctional system. He lives in Santa Monica, California where he is employed as a special education teacher in a public school; he works with profoundly handicapped children.